T0305345

Security Analysis and Business Valuation on Wall Street

Founded in 1807, John Wiley & Sons is the oldest independent publishing company in the United States. With offices in North America, Europe, Australia, and Asia, Wiley is globally committed to developing and marketing print and electronic products and services for our customers' professional and personal knowledge and understanding.

The Wiley Finance series contains books written specifically for finance and investment professionals as well as sophisticated individual investors and their financial advisors. Book topics range from portfolio management to e-commerce, risk management, financial engineering, valuation, and financial instrument analysis, as well as much more.

For a list of available titles, visit our Web site at www.WileyFinance.com.

Security Analysis and Business Valuation on Wall Street

A Comprehensive Guide to Today's Valuation Methods

Second Edition

JEFFREY C. HOOKE

John Wiley & Sons, Inc.

Published by John Wiley & Sons, Inc., Hoboken, New Jersey.
Published simultaneously in Canada.

For general information on our other products and services or for technical support, please contact our Customer Care Department within the United States at (800) 762-2974, outside the United States at (317) 572-3993 or fax (317) 572-4002.

Wiley also publishes its books in a variety of electronic formats. Some content that appears in print may not be available in electronic books. For more information about Wiley products, visit our web site at www.wiley.com.

Library of Congress Cataloging-in-Publication Data:

Hooke, Jeffrey C.
    Security analysis and business valuation on Wall Street : a comprehensive guide to today's valuation methods / Jeffrey C. Hooke. — 2nd ed.
        p. cm. — (Wiley finance series)
    Includes bibliographical references and index.
    ISBN 978-0-470-27734-8 (cloth)
        1. Investment analysis. 2. Securities—Research. I. Title.
    HG4529.H66 2010
    332.63′2—dc22

                                                                    2009042888

Printed in the United States of America.

10 9 8 7 6 5 4 3 2 1

Contents

Preface

When one hears the term *security analyst*, the impression that comes to mind is a green-eye-shaded number cruncher, hunched over a desk piled high with financial reports and computer screens. Sifting through reams of data, the analyst looks endlessly for undervalued stocks trading on the public exchanges. In a narrow sense that stereotype holds true, but the security analysis profession has spawned a deliberate business valuation process that is copied by many disciplines, including private equity, mergers and acquisitions, corporate appraisals, and government regulators. As a result, the users of the principles of security analysis represent a broad cross section of individuals, such as:

- Equity analysts at mutual funds, pension funds, commercial banks, endowments, insurance companies, hedge funds, and sovereign wealth funds.
- Private equity professionals at buyout funds, venture capital funds, and hedge funds.
- Corporate financial executives.
- Investment bankers involved with mergers and acquisitions (M&A).
- Institutional loan officers working with M&A and buyout transactions.
- Business students at college and MBA schools.
- Investor relations professionals at corporations and public relations firms.
- Business appraisers, including those at appraisal firms, accounting firms, and consultancies.
- Lawyers who work with corporate clients on financial and tax matters.
- Independent public accounting firms that must review securities pricing estimates, business appraisals, and corporate valuation reports.
- Government regulators at the IRS, SEC, FDIC, PCAOB, Comptroller of the Currency, and Federal Reserve (and their international counterparts).
- Bank trust and private wealth advisers.
- Sophisticated individual investors.

Fortunes are made and lost on Wall Street based on advice from security analysts and business valuation experts. They evaluate the prospects of companies issuing common stock, borrowing money, or selling out in M&A transactions. For the serious investor, financial executive, or corporate manager, knowing how professionals price companies is important. After all, an ownership in a business is only worth what someone will pay for it. Since that someone is typically a full-time portfolio manager, private equity firm, hedge fund, or corporate acquirer, understanding the evaluative framework of such practitioners is a prerequisite for optimizing investment results.

The need for this book is more critical now than at any time since the depression-ridden 1930s. Over the past 10 years, we have witnessed two global stock market collapses and a financial crisis that required massive government intervention. A major contributing factor was the failure of investors, lenders, and regulators to ad-here to the basic principles of security analysis. The tactics of in-house due diligence, contrary thinking, cross-checking, and recession-tested forecasting were sacrificed at the altars of expediency, cost-cutting, and short-term profit. Hopefully, one re-sult of this trillion-dollar calamity is a renewed emphasis on the fundamentals that withstand the test of time and are outlined in this book.

WHAT IS SECURITY ANALYSIS?

Security analysis is the body of knowledge directed toward the valuation of a com-pany (or its securities) in a rational, systematic way. It has a key principle: Over a long period, such as two to three years, the price of a common stock reflects the busi-ness prospects of the issuing firm and its economic environment. Over the short term, however, powerful trading and emotional forces impact share values, so the pricing of an equity (or the overlying business) is often a tug-of-war between the "long-term" and "short-term" groups. Full-time practitioners are well versed in the principles and methods of assessing equity interests in public and private companies. The results of their research are aimed at providing superior investment performance.

Equity Values Reflect Uncertainty

The value of a security (or a company) depends upon so many highly variable factors—and hence, is subject to such rapid changes—that pinpointing the validity of one analyst's reasoning *a priori* is difficult. Furthermore, predictions are confounded by, among other matters, unexpected changes in macroeconomic indicators such as interest rates, unforeseen developments in company-specific matters such as new competitors, and unusual shocks to an industry such as technology advances. All three factors can sharply alter corporate pricing. At other times, an equity value changes for reasons totally unrelated to the general economy, a company's industry, or its underlying business. For example, distinctive patterns in a public stock's trading activity prompt people to buy and sell, strictly on the notion that past trading trends are predictive of future values.

The market price of any business thus represents a jumble of contradictory expec-tations and hypotheses, influenced constantly by investors processing new data and evaluating changing circumstances. If this analytical process isn't difficult enough, the careful public investor, private equity fund, or corporate acquirer must also consider the human factors that affect financial asset values and react accordingly. From time to time, the emotional sentiments of investors envelop either an individ-ual firm, a specific industry, or the broad market. A herd psychology takes over the pricing, defying rational explanation. Investors seeking an economic justification for the resultant values are best advised to step out of the way of the ensuing stampede.

Since disparate investment styles and unpredictable future events both exercise a major influence on equity prices, it is not surprising that many public and private eq-uity managers cannot consistently select securities that outperform the general market indexes. Indeed, according to a large body of academic theory, beating the market on a regular basis is impossible. Public share prices reflect all available information, and private deals are widely shopped. As a result, no amount of study can achieve above-average investment results, and those managers with superior investment records are simply beneficiaries of the laws of chance. Sooner or later, the odds catch up with them, and their performance returns to norm. The growth of equity index funds and exchange-traded funds is evidence of the acceptance of this theory.

The Rationality Concept

As a field of study, security analysis rejects the idea that public equity investors are doomed to earn the market return over time and nothing more. Rather, it dictates that the selection of specific stocks for purchase or sale should be based upon a rational analysis of investment values. Applying this philosophy in a disciplined manner over the long term produces superior results. Advanced in a comprehensive way by Benjamin Graham and David Dodd in their seminal work, *Security Analysis*, this "rationality concept" has gained a wide following since the book's publication in 1934, and their step-by-step process of corporate valuation has been copied by other disciplines, such as private equity, mergers and acquisitions, and business appraisals.

RECENT TRENDS

When published in 1996, the first edition of *Security Analysis and Business Valuation on Wall Street* was warmly received. *Barron's*, the prestigious financial magazine, called it a "welcome successor to Graham & Dodd," and the CFA Institute, which awards the chartered financial analyst designation, adopted a portion of the book as required reading for the global CFA exam. At the suggestion of several business professors, the first edition was modified into a textbook for MBA students, a rare occurrence for a finance book written by a practitioner. And the book's real-world approach drew international interest: The Chinese translation, for example, had a print run nearing the English version. Nevertheless, since 1996, the landscape for evaluating investments has changed dramatically. These shifts include:

> *Expansion of the Internet.* The expanded use of the Internet and the heightened availability of broadband connections means that new public information is transported instantaneously to market participants. With major investors tied electronically to stock exchanges, trading in the affected securities takes place milliseconds after the information is provided.
>
> *Increase in computing power, coupled with a decline in its cost.* Immediately upon its arrival, the new information is sliced and diced in innumerable ways by sizable players with massive computing power. Employing sophisticated software that incorporates the principles of security analysis, the computers sift for pricing discrepancies in real time and execute trades accordingly, essentially replacing, for short periods anyway, the humans who programmed them. Once an investor's initial responses are processed, the computers help practitioners consider long-term decisions by processing vast amounts of numerical and related data.

Impact of two market crashes. The market crashes of 2000–2001 and 2008–2009 showed that investors face a more hazardous environment than was apparent at the time of the first edition. The failure of regulators, accounting firms, and credit rating agencies—the market's most important referees—to stem the abuses leading to booms and busts brings new concerns to the practitioner.

Extreme growth in derivatives. Derivative products, such as forwards, futures, options, and swaps, have grown extremely quickly, quintupling in volume over the past 10 years. This is due to improved technology in the structuring and trading of such instruments and the fact that the size of the derivatives market is not limited by the physical supply of the underlying securities. The notional value of U.S. corporate bond swaps, for example, is several times greater than all corporate bonds outstanding, and the notional value of equity derivatives roughly equals the total value of publicly traded U.S. common shares. Derivatives are used for both hedging and speculation.

Heightened use of independent experts. At the time of the first edition, the study of a publicly traded business was heavily dependent on information provided by management. Access to independent sources was limited due to the practical considerations involving the time and cost of developing such contacts. The Internet has reduced much of that dependence. Furthermore, multiple companies now offer investors the opportunity to consult with thousands of experts who offer insights on hundreds of companies and industries, usually at modest fees of a few hundred dollars per hour. Analysts thus gain alternate views regarding corporate tactics and industry trends.

Globalization of security analysis. As the world's major economies become increasingly interdependent, the proper analysis of equity securities requires an international bent that was unnecessary in the late 1990s. Trends in Western Europe, Japan, Australia, and other developed areas become important to the pricing of domestic equities. The popularity of emerging market stocks, a moribund asset class just eight years ago, provides additional challenges.

Boost in private equity and M&A transactions. The assets controlled by private equity have multiplied exponentially, and these funds have closed huge volumes of transactions worldwide. Their analytical approach is closely allied to security analysis. At the same time, public (and private) corporate M&A deals grew many times over, as firms sought growth through buying, rather than building.

Rise of hedge funds and short-selling. At the time of the first edition's publication, hedge funds were bit players in the financial markets, but not for long. The Internet-stock-driven collapse in equity prices from 2000 to 2001 convinced institutional investors that long-only funds had limitations and that market-neutral returns were desirable. With the supposed ability to profit in down markets by selling short and to make money in up markets by going long, hedge funds offered such possibilities, although the 2008 market crash showed these claims to be illusory. Now accounting for up to 50 percent of trading on the New York Stock Exchange, these funds put a spotlight on the practice of short-selling.

Valuation scandals at brokerage firms, accountants, and business appraisers. The great bull market of the late 1990s was fueled in part by equity analysts at the Wall Street brokerages, who issued overly optimistic reports on speculative Internet firms and shaky technology companies. The analysts compromised their research in order to curry favor with their supervisors and to win advisory business for their banking colleagues. In 2003, the brokerages paid $1.4 billion to settle charges that such research misled investors. In accordance with the legal settlement, they instituted a number of reforms. The sell-side analyst community was shaken by these events, and its credibility, which was never pristine, will require years of rehabilitation. At the same time, accountants and business appraisers were signing off on lowball option prices for executives at private firms, and thus distorting accounting results and income tax obligations.

Increased requirement for business valuation reports. These abuses prompted the federal government to institute regulations mandating that public companies (and soon-to-be-public companies) obtain third-party valuations (independent of their outside auditors) for executive options, M&A-related intangible assets, and other items. This requirement spilled over to many private firms using outside auditors.

Growth of index funds, exchange-traded funds, and shadow indexing. Index funds and exchange-traded funds (ETFs) offer low fees and, on behalf of investors, buy a preset basket of stocks corresponding to a broad market index, like the S&P 500, or a specific subindex, like the Russell Mid-Cap. Now representing 30 percent of mutual funds' assets, their growth shows investors' lack of faith in the ability of active managers to select stock portfolios with premium returns. At the same time, many of these managers have little confidence in their own skills; they buy stocks that mimic a given index, cutting their risk of underperformance, but also reducing their likelihood of overperformance. The practice is called *shadow indexing* or *hugging an index*. The dual trends of index funds and shadow indexing provide opportunities for analysts who do their homework, go against passive selection, and take the long view.

WHY STUDY SECURITY ANALYSIS AND BUSINESS VALUATION?

The stock market has a strong impact on economic policy, corporate decision making, retirement planning, and employment, and yet many investors, businesspeople, government officials, and students fail to understand business valuation, which is the conceptual underpinning for stock prices. Indeed, a sizable number consider the exchanges to be floating crap games. Speculative elements play a large role in the equity markets, but the discipline of security analysis warrants the sustained interest of many people.

On the international side, as more large developing countries, like China and India, increasingly rely on equity markets to allocate capital to local businesses, they must build a domestic capacity for business valuation.

OVERVIEW OF THE CONTENTS

To facilitate the reader's understanding of the subject material, *Security Analysis and Business Valuation on Wall Street* is divided into five parts.

> *Part One: The Investing Environment.* Part One provides an overview of the environment in which common stocks are issued, researched, bought, and sold. In addition to examining why investors analyze companies in the first place, we look at the roles of the players, rules and regulations of the equity markets, activities surrounding an initial public offering, and sources of investment information. The prices of publicly traded common stocks are highly influential in setting values for private corporations, which are critical for nonpublic investments, tax and accounting calculations, and a host of other purposes.

> *Part Two: Performing the Analysis and Writing the Research Report.* The investment merits of a particular business are evaluated through a methodical approach. Both the *history* and the *prospects* of the company are considered. The sequence of this study and the format of the evaluation report are discussed in Part Two.

> *Part Three: Valuation and the Investment Decision.* At the conclusion of the report, the equity analyst must answer two questions: (1) Is this company fairly valued? and (2) Based on the previous answer, should I recommend investing in the business? M&A, private equity, and other users have somewhat different actions to consider from their reports. Part Three provides the necessary framework to deliver the answers.

> *Part Four: Special Cases.* The model company for security analysis training is a U.S.-based manufacturer with a history of improving sales and earnings. Most firms don't fit this model. Part Four reviews specific industries, private equity tactics, and international markets.

> *Part Five: In Conclusion.* Part Five looks at how investors are reacting to two major market declines in 10 years. The book closes with some observations and a few maxims.

WHAT'S NEW IN THE SECOND EDITION

The step-by-step methodical process needed to produce a reliable security analysis (or business valuation) has not changed since the first edition, and has remained fundamentally the same over the past 75 years. However, investing environments, valuation techniques, and industry definitions evolve over time, requiring continued modifications to the basic approach.

The second edition contains revisions to add insights and updates on such practical applications. Among them:

- *The investing environment.* Chapters 1 through 4 provide updates on the new environment, such as the dominance of commercial banks on Wall Street, the inability of security analysts to foresee pricing bubbles, the effect of the 2008 crash on the industry, the reliance of institutions on computerized models rather than human analysts, and the continual reluctance of regulators to show initiative in regulating. Chapter 4, "Other Sources of Information," has been revised to capture the use of the Internet and independent data services.

■ *Starting the analysis, industry analysis, and company-specific analysis.* Chapters 5, 6, and 7 have been revised and updated. The principal themes remain the same, and the chapters are more concise.

■ *Financial statement analysis.* Chapter 8 highlights, once again, the primary elements of this part of the company evaluation process and introduces an entirely new case study from 2008. The chapter reminds practitioners to assume a recession in their forecasts, a necessity ignored by competing books and avoided by many investors in their quest to close transactions. It also points out the use of software to conduct financial statement analysis.

■ *The limitations of accounting data.* Chapter 9 includes a discussion on the recent accounting scandals that made the security analyst's job more difficult. The lack of enforcement and punishment ensure that such scandals will repeat themselves in the future.

■ *Financial analysis and company classifications.* Chapter 10 explicitly defines pioneer, growth, mature, and declining companies and provides a methodology for placing a subject firm in its category. Despite the wide use of this terminology on Wall Street, many practitioners lack a firm foundation for making such classifications.

■ *Valuation methodologies.* These chapters have been updated with new examples and cases. The application of each methodology (discounted cash flow, comparable public companies, comparable M&A transactions, and leveraged buyout) builds the foundation for making a decision, rather than just focusing on the process. Chapter 17 acknowledges changes in leveraged buyout dynamics. Chapter 18 adds commentary on the income tax ramifications of breaking up a conglomerate.

■ *The investment recommendation.* Chapter 19 showcases how a proper evaluation report reaches a buy or sell decision by applying the Wall Street approaches explained in the book. The material is updated to 2009.

■ *Special industries.* Most companies do not fit the textbook model of a profitable, domestic manufacturer. Chapters 21 to 25 provide new case studies in this regard.

■ *International.* Commerce is increasingly global in nature, and the book reviews changes that affect the investment decision process.

In addition, the second edition has four new chapters:

"Intrinsic Value and Discounted Cash Flow" (Chapter 13). Included previously as a part of an earlier chapter, this topic now merits a separate treatment, with added emphasis on the practitioner including a recession scenario in any forecast.

"Discounted Cash Flow: Choosing the Right Discount Rate" (Chapter 14). The popular capital asset pricing model (CAPM) has flaws in its application. Chapter 14 reviews the flaws and provides a case study of using both the

CAPM and an alternate approach to figure an appropriate discount rate for a business. Rather than providing complex theories and formulas for what is essentially a straightforward task, the book explains it in only 10 pages.

"Private Equity." Chapter 20 shows how private equity firms and hedge funds consider investments in private corporations, and how their approach differs from an investor buying a security that is traded publicly on the New York Stock Exchange. As a former private equity investor, I provide the inside scoop.

"Asset Booms and Busts." Having witnessed two market crashes within the past decade, public stock investors, private equity firms, corporate acquirers, and government regulators should work within a framework that anticipates a downturn every 7 to 10 years. I discuss this topic in Chapter 28.

To download a valuation spreadsheet for DCF valuation and comparable companies, visit the companion web site at www.wiley.com/go/hooke. Instructors may also visit the Wiley Higher Ed site (www.wiley.com/college) for additional classroom tools.

For convenience, the pronoun *he* has been used throughout this book to refer nonspecifically to capital markets participants. The material herein will be equally useful to both men and women who evaluate security issuers.

This book does not promise to help you obtain superior stock market results, close better private equity deals, make optimal M&A transactions, or write the best corporate appraisal reports. No book can honestly claim such results. *Security Analysis and Business Valuation on Wall Street* provides a practical, well-rounded view of business valuation and investment decision processes. After completing this book, you are better prepared to make sound judgments and to confront the financial markets' numerous intrigues.

JEFFREY C. HOOKE

Chevy Chase, Maryland
March 2010

One

The Investing Environment

CHAPTER 1

Why Analyze a Security?

This chapter covers the origin and evolution of security analysis, which focused initially on publicly traded stocks and bonds. The herd psychology and gamesmanship that are endemic to the capital markets are discussed, along with modern valuation approaches.

Some investors analyze securities to reduce the risk and the gambling aspects of investing. They need the confidence supplied by their own work. Other investors seek value where others haven't looked. They're on a treasure hunt. Still others have fiduciary reasons. Without documentation to justify an investment decision, clients can sue them for malpractice should investment performance waver. Many investors analyze shares for the thrill of the game. They enjoy pitting their investment acumen against other professionals.

Security analysis is a field of study that attempts to evaluate businesses and their securities in a rational way. By performing a rigorous analysis of the factors affecting a company's worth, security analysts seek to find equities that present a good value relative to other investments. In doing such work, professional analysts refute the efficient market theory, which suggests that a monkey throwing darts at the *Wall Street Journal* will, over time, have a performance record equal to the most experienced money manager. In fact, the proliferation of business valuation techniques as well as advances in regulation and information flow contributes to the market's transparency. Nevertheless, on a regular basis, pricing inefficiencies occur. An astute observer takes advantage of the discrepancies.

THE ORIGINS OF SECURITY ANALYSIS

Benjamin Graham and David Dodd made the business of analyzing investments into a profession. With the publication of their book, *Security Analysis*, in 1934, they offered investors a logical and systematic way in which to evaluate the many securities competing for their investment dollars and their process was eventually copied by M&A, private equity, and other business valuation professionals. Before then, methodical and reasoned analysis was in short supply on Wall Street. The public markets were dominated by speculation. Stocks were frequently purchased on the basis of hype and rumor, with little business justification. Even when the company in question was a solid operation with a consistent track record, participants failed to apply quantitative measures to their purchases. Procter & Gamble was a *good company* whether its stock was trading at 10 times or 30 times earnings, but was it a *good investment* at 30 times earnings, relative to other equities? Investors lacked the skills to answer this question. *Security Analysis* endeavored to provide these skills.

The systematic analysis in place at the time tended to be centered in bond rating agencies and legal appraisals. Moody's Investors Service and Standard & Poor's started assigning credit ratings to bonds in the early 1900s. The two agencies based their ratings almost entirely on the bond's collateral protection and the issuer's historical track record; they gave short shrift to qualitative indicators such as the issuer's future prospects and management depth. In a bond market dominated by railroad and utility bonds, the rating agencies' methodology lacked transferability to other industries and the equity markets. On the equity side, in-depth evaluations of corporate shares were found primarily in legal appraisals, typically required for estate tax calculations, complicated reorganization plans, and contested takeover bids. Like credit ratings, the equity appraisals suffered from an overdependence on historical data at the expense of a careful consideration of future prospects.

Graham and Dodd suggested that certain common stocks were prudent investments, if investors took the time to analyze them properly (see Exhibit 1.1). Many finance professors and businesspeople were surprised at this notion, thinking the two academics were brave to make such a recommendation. Only five years earlier, the stock market had suffered a terrible crash, signaling the beginning of a wrenching economic depression causing massive business failures and huge job losses.

The market drop of 1929–1933 outpaced the 2007–2009 crash. On October 28, 1929, the Dow Jones Industrial Average fell 13 percent and an additional 12 percent the next day. The two-day drop of 23 percent followed a decline that began on September 3, when the Industrial Average peaked at 381, and then declined 22 percent in the weeks preceding October 28. The market staged modest recoveries in 1930 and 1931, but the 1929 drop presaged a gut-wrenching descent in stock prices, which wasn't complete until February 1933. Over the three-year period, the Dow dropped by 87 percent. The index didn't return to its 1929 high until 1954, 25 years later. In contrast, the Dow's sizeable decline from 2007 to 2009 was 54 percent, and the 1999–2002 bear market represented a 34 percent drop.

At the time of the publication of *Security Analysis*, equity prices had doubled from 1933's terrible bottom, but they were only one-quarter of the 1929 high. Shaken

EXHIBIT 1.1   Graham and Dodd Approach to Stock Selection

1. Study the available facts.
2. Prepare an organized report.
3. Project earnings and related data.
4. Draw valuation conclusions based on established principles and sound logic.
5. Make a decision.

by the volatile performance of equities, the public considered equity investment quite speculative. Not only was there a dearth of conservative analysis, but the market was still afflicted with unregulated insider trading, unethical sales pitches, and unscrupulous brokers. For two professionals to step into this area with a scholarly approach was radical indeed.

The publication of *Security Analysis* coincided with the formation of the Securities and Exchange Commission (SEC). Designed to prevent a repeat of the 1920s abuses, the SEC was given broad regulatory powers over a wide range of market activities. It required security issuers to disclose all material information and to provide regular public earnings reports. This new information provided a major impetus to the security analysis profession. Previously, issuers were cavalier about what information they provided to the public. Analysts, as a result, operated from half-truths and incomplete data. With the regulators' charge of full disclosure for publicly traded corporations, practitioners had access to more raw material than ever before. Added to this company-specific data was the usual storehouse of economic, market, and industry material available for study. It soon became clear that a successful analyst needed to allocate his time and resources efficiently among sources of information to produce the best results.

NO PROFIT GUARANTEE

It is important to remember that security analysis doesn't presume an absolute value for a given security, nor does it guarantee the investor a profit. After undertaking the effort to study a stock, an analyst derives a range of value, since the many variables involved reduce the element of certainty. After an investigation, assume the analyst concludes that Random Corp. shares are worth $8 to $10 per share. This conclusion isn't worth much if the stock is trading at $9, but it is certainly valuable if the stock is trading at $4, far below the range, or at $20, which is far above. In such cases, the difference between the conclusion and the market prompts an investment decision, either *buy* or *sell* (see Exhibit 1.2).

If the analyst acts on his conclusion and buys Random Corp. stock at $4 per share, he has no assurance that the price will reach the $8 to $10 range. The broad market might decline without warning or Random Corp. might suffer an unexpected business setback. These variables can restrict the stock from reaching appraised value. Over time, however, the analyst believes that betting on such large differences provides superior investment results.

	$0	$8	$10	$20	
Buy	Buy the stock when its price is way below your appraisal.	Your valuation conclusion is $8 to $10 per share.	Sell the stock when its price substantially exceeds your appraisal.		**Sell**

EXHIBIT 1.2   Random Corp. Stock

DAY-TO-DAY TRADING AND SECURITY ANALYSIS

For the most part, participants in the stock market behave rationally. Day-to-day trading in most stocks causes few major price changes, and those large interday differentials can usually be explained by the introduction of new information. A lot of small price discrepancies are attributable to a few professionals having a somewhat different interpretation of the same set of facts available to others. This results in one investor believing a stock's price will change due either to (1) the market conforming to his opinion of the stock's value over time, or (2) the future of the underlying business unfolding as he anticipates.

In the first instance, perhaps the investor's research uncovered a hidden real estate value on the company's balance sheet. The general public is unaware of this fact. As soon as others acknowledge the extra value, the stock price should increase. In the second situation, the investor has more optimistic growth assumptions than the market. Should the investor's predictions come true, the stock price should increase accordingly. Perhaps 300,000 individuals follow the markets full-time, so there are plenty of differing views. Even a small segment of investors with conflicting opinions can cause significant trading activity in a stock.

It is not unusual that investors using similar methods of analysis come up with valuations that differ by 10 to 15 percent. This small percentage is sufficiently large to cause active trading. As we discuss later, the popular valuation techniques require a certain amount of judgment with respect to sifting information and applying quantitative analysis, so reasonable people can easily derive slightly dissimilar values for the same stock. As these differences become more profound, the price of a given stock becomes more volatile, and divergent valuations do battle in the marketplace. Today, this price volatility is evident in many high-tech stocks. The prospects of the underlying businesses are hard to appraise, even for experienced professionals.

HERD PSYCHOLOGY AND SECURITY ANALYSIS

Ideally, a security analyst studies the known facts of a business, considers its prospects, and prepares a careful evaluation. From this effort a buy or sell recommendation is derived for the company's shares. This valuation model, while intrinsically sensible, understates the need to temper a rational study with due regard for the vagaries of the stock market.

At any given time, the price behavior of certain individual stocks and selected market sectors is governed by forces that defy a studied analysis. Key elements influencing equity values in these instances may be the emotions of the investors themselves. Market participants are human beings, after all, and are subject to the same impulses as anyone. Various emotions affect the investor's decision-making process, but two sentiments have the most lasting impact: *fear* and *greed*. Investors in general are scared of losing money, and all are anxious to make more profits. These feelings become accentuated in the professional investor community, whose members are caught up in the treadmill of maintaining good short-term performance.

Of the two emotions, fear is by far the stronger, as evidenced by the fact that stock prices fall faster than they go up. Afraid of losing money, people demonstrate a classic herd psychology upon hearing bad news, and often rush to sell a stock before the next investor. Many stocks drop 20 to 30 percent in price on a single day, even when the fresh information is less than striking. In the crash of 1987, the Dow Jones Index fell 23 percent in one day on no real news. Buying frenzies, in contrast, take place over longer stretches of time, such as weeks or months. Exceptions include the shares of takeover candidates and initial public offerings.

True takeover stocks are identified by a definitive offer from a respectable bidder. Because the offers typically involve a substantial price premium for control, investors rush in to acquire the takeover candidate's shares at a price slightly below the offer. The size of the discount reflects uncertainties regarding the timing and ultimate completion of the bid, but a seasoned practitioner can make a reasoned decision. Occurring as frequently as real bids are rumored bids. Here, speculators acting on takeover rumors inflate a stock's price in anticipation of a premium-priced control offer. Frequently, the rumors are from questionable sources, such as a promoter trying to sell his own position in the stock, so the price run-up is driven primarily by emotion, game theory, and momentum investing.

All of these factors play a role in the next hard-to-analyze business—the initial public offering (IPO). Many IPOs rise sharply in price during their first few days of trading, such as Chipotle Mexican Grill. It went public in January 2006 at $22 per share, and jumped 100 percent to $44 per share on the first day of trading. Within three months the stock was selling for $63. Unlike existing issues, an IPO has no trading history, so the underwriters setting the offering price make an educated guess on what its value is. At times this guess is conservative and the price rises accordingly. More frequently, the lead underwriters lowball the IPO price in order to ensure that the offering is fully sold, protecting themselves from their moral obligation to buy back shares from unsatisfied investors if the price were to fall steeply.

When underwriters get their publicity machines working and an IPO becomes hot, a herd psychology can infect investors, who then scramble over one another to buy in anticipation of a large price jump. At this point, a dedicated evaluation of the IPO has little merit. For a hot deal, many equity buyers operate by game theory—what's the other guy thinking and what's he going to pay for this issue? Others use momentum investing logic: I must buy the stock because others are buying it.

MOMENTUM INVESTORS

Extremely influential in short-term pricing moves, momentum investors predict individual stock values based on trading patterns that have happened repeatedly, either in the relevant stock or in similar situations. Thus, if they notice the beginning of a downward price trend, they may sell the stock in anticipation of the pattern reaching completion. Naturally, the selling pattern may be a self-fulfilling prophecy as other momentum investors are motivated by the increased selling activity and follow suit.

Often lumped together with emotional investors by the media, momentum players attempt to take advantage of the common belief that stocks move in discernible patterns. Two of Wall Street's oldest expressions, "You can't fight the tape" and "You can't buck the trend," are evidence of the futility of injecting a security analysis bias into any price move driven by emotional and momentum factors. The herd instinct that is set off by such behavior has contributed to several market crashes in the past, and stock exchanges reserve the right to stop computerized program trading, which activates upon the observance of such trends, if market indexes drop too much in a given day.

GAME THEORY AND SECURITY ANALYSIS

The average portfolio manager does not have a controlling position in his shareholdings. Public corporations are owned by numerous other equity investors, perhaps numbering in the thousands. With this diversity of ownership, the portfolio manager's return in a given stock, or in the general market, is dependent on the behavior of his rival investors. If he holds on to a stock because he thinks it's a good investment, while others are selling because they think the opposite, he loses in the short run. Future results of the company may bear out his original analysis, but in the present he looks bad. This is a dangerous position in the investment industry, which tends to measure results quarter by quarter rather than year by year. For this reason, knowing how others think and react to events is critical to success.

Some investors bring this dynamic into the realm of game theory and attempt to influence the market's thought processes. Several examples are instructive:

- *False takeover*. An investor with a reputation for hostile takeovers acquires a position in a company's shares. He files a public notice or leaks his interest to the rumor mill. As other investors react to a potential takeover, they buy the stock and its price increases. In this case, the takeover artist has no intention of bidding for the company. He sells his shares into the buying activity sparked by his original interest, thus realizing a quick profit from speculative expectations. Equity analyst Clinton Morrison remarked, "It's called a self-fulfilling prophecy. You advertise your position and then you sell into it."
- *Phony promotion*. A key market player, such as a large fund manager, indicates publicly his strong interest in a certain industry sector, such as cable television. As other investors follow the fund manager's direction by purchasing cable TV stocks, the manager busily unloads his own holdings into the trading strength. As an example, one large fund manager was criticized in 2007 for advocating a software stock in public, when his fund was selling it in private.
- *Story stocks*. A professional investor establishes a significant position in a little-known company. Using financial publicists, stock newsletters, and aggressive brokers, he weaves a story behind the scenes about the company's unrecognized earnings potential. Although the analysis is sketchy, the growth story is entertaining. Carlton Lutts, editor of the *Cabot Market Letter*, summarized such game theory dynamics well: "A stock, like love, thrives on romance and dies on statistics." As the drum beating becomes louder and louder, a cross section of investors takes notice. They buy in and the price climbs. When the professional's profit objective is reached, he bails out of his position and winds down the publicity machine. Shortly thereafter the stock price collapses. This strategy is most effective with early stage companies and technology firms. Their

business prospects are difficult to analyze, making fanciful forecasts hard to dispute. Sometimes, just the rumor of an important investor is enough. In 2007, Macy's stock jumped eight points on rumors that Edward Lampert, the hedge fund guru, was building a position. When these rumors proved untrue, the stock fell 20 percent in days.

In each of the preceding situations, the outcome of a competitive move by one investor depends on the reactions of his rivals, much like a good chess game. A seemingly irrational reaction by competitors may make a fine strategic move unsuccessful. What happens if a professional feeds the takeover rumor mill and no one buys? The risk of the game is that his competitors don't act as expected. This risk decreases if he commands a visible leadership role in the market and has a strong public relations operation. Carl Icahn, for example, is a top game player, running a fund with billions under management and having a history of shaking things up. Of course, the selection of the target stock must be made carefully. Competitors may see through a promoter's strategy or simply ignore the new information presented to them.

THE PREMISE OF SECURITY ANALYSIS

Practicing security analysts acknowledge the impact of human emotions, herd behavior and game theory on stock prices, and they factor these elements into their investment conclusions. Generally, such influences are short-term in nature and, sooner or later, most share prices reflect a rational view of underlying economic values. This rational view is far from absolute. Investment evaluation is not an exact science, and reasonable people examining the same facts are bound to have differences. Over the long haul, an analytical approach toward stock selection offers superior results, as occasional instances of price irrationality provide obvious opportunities. Maintaining a discipline in emotional markets is one of the analyst's hardest challenges. Few people want to face the ridicule of going against the crowd by sticking to accepted standards, despite the fact that equity investors invariably return to normal measures of determining value after periodic infatuations with untested themes. These notions of rationality and consistency form the bedrock of the security analysis profession.

A large part of a stock's price is set by expectations of its future growth in earnings. While a competent study of the past frequently provides the basis for an earnings projection, even the most talented practitioner has a limited ability to predict the growth rate of a given company for years ahead. This implies that a major portion of any analyst's valuation is the product of educated guessing. As with similar vocations, many conclusions look terribly wrong with 20/20 hindsight. Sometimes the actual earnings of a company come in substantially lower than forecast data, and the stock price drops accordingly. An analyst who recommended the stock has made a mistake. But level-headed investors, realizing the field's limitations, don't demand perfection. Rather, excellence can be achieved by partial success. In baseball, a .300 hitter fails 7 out of 10 times at bat, yet he is among the best. For security analysts, the grading process is more complicated than baseball, but a professional who is right 60 to 70 percent of the time is considered exceptional. Luck plays a role in compiling this kind of track record, but over time the importance of chance diminishes in favor of skill.

Graham and Dodd summarized the analyst's requirements many years ago in *Security Analysis*:

> To do these jobs credibly the analyst needs a wide equipment. He must understand security forms, corporate accounting, the basic elements that make for the success or failure of various kinds of businesses, the general workings not only of our total economy but also of its major segments, and finally the characteristic fluctuations of our security markets. He must be able to dig for facts, to evaluate them critically, and to apply his conclusions with good judgment and a fair amount of imagination. He must be able to resist human nature itself sufficiently to mistrust his own feelings when they are part of mass psychology. He must have courage commensurate with his competence.[1]

SCIENTIFIC METHOD

According to serious practitioners, security analysis is a quasi-science, like medicine or economics. Its systematized knowledge is derived from the observance of decades of stock market data and the application of common sense. The field's basic tenets have thus been tested by the use of the scientific method, which calls for carrying out three basic steps to reach a conclusion. Exhibit 1.3 summarizes the scientific method alongside its application in the securities market.

Two supermarket stocks can serve as an example. Suppose the respective shares of Safeway and Kroger, two national chains, have the key financial characteristics shown in Exhibit 1.4. Safeway's stock is trading at 15 times earnings. Given the similarity, what should be the price/earnings (P/E) multiple of Kroger's stock? All things being equal, Kroger shares should have a 15 P/E multiple, meaning a $30 price (i.e., 15 P/E times $2 EPS equals $30). Thus, if the Kroger shares are trading at $25, the stock is a buy. In practice, analysts take the $30 theoretical value as a starting

EXHIBIT 1.3 Scientific Method Applied to the Securities Market

Scientific Method	Securities Market Example
Step 1: Formulate a hypothesis.	Two similar stocks should have similar prices.
Step 2: Collect data, make observations, and test hypothesis.	Observe historical price performance of the two stocks. Determine if their prices converge over time.
Step 3: Conclude the validity or predictive ability of the hypothesis.	Sooner or later, two similar stocks will have similar prices. By following this conclusion, an investor looks for two similar stocks with *different* prices. He predicts that the cheaper of the two stocks will rise in price. He acts upon his prediction by buying the cheaper stock.

EXHIBIT 1.4 Similar Stock Hypothesis—Two Supermarket Stocks

	Safeway	Kroger
Financial Data		
Five-year compound annual growth in earnings per share	12%	12%
Expected annual growth rate in earnings per share	11%	11%
Debt-to-equity ratio	20%	20%
Earnings per share (EPS)	$1	$2
Share Data		
Price-to-EPS ratio (P/E)	15×	?
Share price	$15	?

Note: The earnings growth rates and debt-to-equity ratios are identical. The P/E ratios should be similar, all things being equal.

point. They then study the future prospects of each company. Certain factors may justify the $25 value, despite the apparent similarities.

The "similar stock/similar price" supposition is easy to describe and it makes sense. Unfortunately, proving this theory and other basic tenets of security analysis in a scientific manner is difficult. In a true science like physics, observations are repeated in a laboratory environment to verify their accuracy (e.g., a ball is dropped in a vacuum 100 times to confirm the pull of gravity). Security analysis theories, in contrast, are subject to the vagaries of the stock market, which has far too many uncontrolled variables to provide the appropriate conditions for a truly scientific test.

Even the "similar supermarket" example is hard to prove scientifically. Finding two publicly traded supermarket chains with identical financial results is impossible, and most chains have significant differences in market conditions, business operations, and managerial styles. Even with two firms that resemble each other in financial and business attributes, the scientific method is problematic. Much of a company's value is represented by its future potential to generate earnings, as opposed to its present condition and past history. Determining the consensus view of a company's future is accurately described as educated guesswork, rather than scientific deduction.

Despite the drawbacks of injecting scientific methods into the stock market, investors and finance professors keep trying. Certain of their theories are proven academically, while others have a commonsense appeal that heightens their acceptance. For example, most professionals consider the next two hypotheses to be valid:

True   Companies with low interest coverage ratios go bankrupt more frequently than those with high interest coverage ratios.

True   Companies with high P/E ratios have better growth records than those with low P/E ratios.

A combination of academic proofs, commonsense ideas, and intuitive beliefs supports these and other notions of security analysis. The systematic application of these concepts has evolved into a rational discipline, which one studies like other quasi-scientific fields such as medicine, economics, or sociology.

EXHIBIT 1.5   Common Business Valuation Approaches

1. *Intrinsic value.* The worth of a business equals the net present value of its future dividends.
2. *Relative value.* Determine a company's value by comparing it to similar companies' values.
3. *Acquisition value.* Calculate a company's share price by determining its worth to a third-party acquirer, such as another operating business.
4. *Leveraged buyout value.* One prospective price for a business is its value in a leveraged buyout.
5. *Technical analysis value.* A share price can be predicted by examining its historical trading pattern and applying it to the future.

SECURITY ANALYSIS TECHNIQUES

As we have discussed earlier, emotions and trend followers influence the values of companies, but an underlying discipline governs share prices. Over time, this discipline, which is founded in security analysis, tends to correct stock market excesses. Thus, if a hot stock such as sensor maker MEMSIC goes public at a valuation of $300 million despite the fact that the company has little revenue and no earnings, inevitably the stock price goes back to earth, as investors lose their fervor and evaluate the business in terms of its risk-adjusted potential. VISICU Software was a *good* company but a *speculative* stock in April 2006, when its initial public offering sold at $16 per share and soon rose to $24 per share. One year later, it was a good firm but a better equity value at $8 per share, which was in line with the company's future prospects.

Frequently, the life cycle of pricing excesses begins with a security being bid up to an irrational price level by anticipation investors and momentum players, who are then battled by more scientifically inclined investors. The latter argue for a realistic valuation based on time-honored value anchors, which are derived from the five valuation approaches set forth in Exhibit 1.5.

BASIC VALUATION APPROACHES

Of the five principal approaches to business valuation, the first four lend themselves to the scientific method—the intrinsic value, relative value, acquisition value, and leveraged buyout approaches. All four approaches forecast stock prices on the basis of historical economic, capital market, industry, and corporate statistics, which are then used to establish predictive trends for firm operating results and share prices. The principal decision variables are earnings projections and comparable company values.

Under the *intrinsic value* method, future dividends are derived from earnings forecasts and then discounted to the present, thereby establishing a *present value* for the stock. If the stock is trading at a price lower than this calculation, it is a *buy*; if the market price is higher then the intrinsic value, the stock is a *sell*. For most businesspeople, the intrinsic value approach (i.e., discounted cash flow) is their first introduction to security analysis since it is the approach emphasized by business schools and most valuation books. The intrinsic value concept makes economic sense and is theoretically sound, but in the real world its applicability is limited. No professional investor places much weight on projections extending past two or three years, and dividend discount rates are hard to pinpoint. Furthermore, even devoted advocates of this technique are hesitant to promote its use for analyses involving (1) growth companies that don't pay dividends, (2) established companies that are consistent money-losers, or (3) complex companies that are liquidation or restructuring candidates.

The *relative value* approach considers intrinsic values too difficult to determine, owing to the arguments over hard-to-make projections and controversial discount rates. Instead, various valuation parameters of a given publicly traded stock, such as its P/E, price/book, and price/sales ratios, are compared to the stocks of companies in the same industry. If the value ratio of the stock being evaluated is substantially lower than its peer group, and if there is no justifiable reason for the discrepancy, the relative value approach views the stock as a buy. Stock valuations are therefore made in a manner similar to many other asset appraisals. In real estate, for example, the value of a house is established by comparing the target house to nearby houses that have sold recently.

The relative value approach is attractive to analysts because it takes most of the guesswork out of relying on future projections and discount rates. Its weaknesses stem from three factors. First, few publicly traded companies have exact comparables, leaving a lot of room for subjectivity in the appraisal. Second, investors are in the market to make money in absolute terms, while the relative value method focuses on *relative* performance. Suppose an entire industry is the subject of speculative interest, and its share prices crash when expected operating results fail to materialize. The relative value picks fall 20 percent, but the industry's decline is 30 percent. The successful relative value investor is losing less money than other investors committed to the industry, but he's still losing money. Third, relative value places a heavy emphasis on contrasting the historical operating results of similar businesses, when future prospects are critical. Driving by looking in the rearview mirror is a perilous investment tactic.

The *acquisition value* approach suggests that a publicly traded stock should never trade at less than 70 to 75 percent of its worth to a sophisticated and well-financed third party. The analyst evaluates industry acquisition prices in comparison to the relevant company, and he tests it for feasibility as a leveraged buyout or liquidation candidate. If the stock trades at less than 70 percent of its acquisition value, it is probably a buy. By relying on data about so-called comparable companies, the acquisition value approach suffers from the same weaknesses as the relative value method, with the further proviso that comparable public M&A deals are rare in many situations.

The *leveraged buyout* (LBO) approach is a subset of the larger M&A methodologies. However, many businesses lack the attributes of an LBO candidate, often rendering this approach unworkable. Also, strategic buyers tend to pay more than LBO funds, so this approach is seen as a low-end acquisition value.

The fifth approach, *technical analysis*, has a wide following but it lacks the broad institutional acceptance of the first four approaches. Often referred to as Wall Street's version of "voodoo economics," technical analysis is concerned solely with

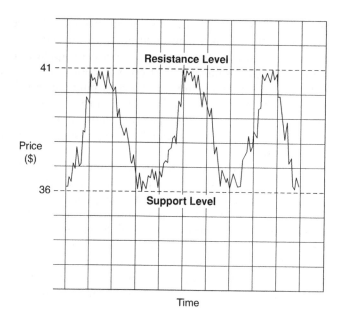

EXHIBIT 1.6   Technical Analysis—Consolidation Pattern

the price and volume trading patterns of a stock. This technique does not consider a company's operating history, its earning potential, or other microeconomic factors as relevant to the valuation process. Rather, the technician believes that trading patterns reflect all logical and emotional forces affecting a stock price. An analysis of these patterns, usually in conjunction with industry and market trading indicators, provides predictive trends that enable the technician to forecast stock prices.

Suppose a stock price fluctuates in a small range over a period of months, after it has made a big upward move. This behavior is called a *consolidation* pattern because the stock is consolidating its previous gain. Once the stock price breaks through the top end of this consolidation range, this is a buy signal because technical theory says it is poised for another run-up (see Exhibit 1.6). Numerous investors and academics have tested this and other technical theories and concluded that there is no evidence to support these claims. Nevertheless, Wall Street is one place where perception easily becomes reality. Since thousands of investors believe in technical analysis, market participants are sensitive to technical opinions in evaluating stock prices. Equity research reports usually include charts outlining the trading activity of the stock in question, and most professional money managers use such charts as one ingredient in buy/sell decisions.

OTHER VALUATION APPROACHES

Technical analysis represents a systemized body of knowledge and numerous books review its procedures. Nevertheless, it straddles the line between rational inquiry and educated speculation. Three other common stock-picking approaches that fall into

EXHIBIT 1.7 Stock-Picking Alternatives to Security Analysis and Technical Analysis

1. *Momentum investing.* Momentum investors attempt to follow buying or selling binges for individual stocks, regardless of the economic rationale behind the price move.
2. *Paired trading.* Paired trading investors track the traditional pricing relationship between two securities that may or may not have business similarities. If the relationship changes for no discernable reason, a transaction is triggered.
3. *Market anticipation.* Valuation parameters change precipitously among industries and companies. Anticipation investors try to predict dramatic changes before the market consensus.

a similar category are *momentum investing, paired trading,* and *market anticipation* (see Exhibit 1.7).

All three approaches require a sophisticated knowledge of the market's inner workings and an experienced hand in equity trading. They are best employed by professional traders, who participate in the securities markets on a full-time basis and are thus in a position to react quickly to the sharp price movements endemic to these investment strategies.

Momentum Investing

Conventional security analysis is sometimes characterized as the art of buying low and selling high. Momentum investing, in contrast, is frequently referred to as *buying high and selling higher,* because its adherents look to buy shares that are rising quickly in price. Because momentum investors pay close attention to trading trends and give short shrift to the underlying company's sales or earnings, they represent a subset of the technical community. Having played a major role in many share price run-ups, they are a key source of market volatility, often through automated program trading. Such trading is typically initiated by a series of signals such as an upward 90-day moving price average, a large positive net cash flow into the stock, or a big jump in trading volume.

Paired Trading

With the huge advances in computing power, investors can now examine the historical pricing relationships among thousands of securities and track the consistency of these relationships on a real-time basis. Should a traditional pricing relationship distort for no discernible reason, the investor may buy or sell one of the affected securities in the expectation that the relationship will revert to the norm. In some cases, the securities might be similar, such as Ford and General Motors common stock, while in other cases the securities could be dissimilar.

Market Anticipation

The market anticipation approach acknowledges that most stocks are fairly priced by the many security analysts using the intrinsic value, relative value, and acquisition value methods. At some future point, however, the consensus view on any given stock's earnings power or business risk changes, providing impetus to a higher (or lower) stock price. A typical pronouncement from a market anticipation analyst might be, "The Starbucks shares will increase in value as the market realizes the reduced volatility of the company's earning stream." Such conclusions carry little analytical weight and are most effective when repeated loudly and continually, thus echoing the "squeaky wheel gets the grease" tactic used by promoters in any business.

Despite the speculative nature of this approach, even the most rigorous disciples of security analysis are cognizant of the sometimes relentless drum beating of market anticipation investors, who are trying desperately to influence the consensus decision on a stock's value. Their influence has been strong in certain cases and has been observed in the rise and fall of numerous high-flyer stocks, the peak prices of which defy rational explanation for periods of time. Consider USEC, the uranium processor, which had a rocket-like rise from $7 to $25 in 2007, only to plummet to $9 that same year. Alibaba.com, a Chinese Internet company, had a market value of $26 billion in 2008, indicating valuation ratios (e.g., a 320 P/E) far higher than those of more established firms such as Yahoo! and eBay.

SUMMARY

Security analysis is a field of study that maintains that stocks can be valued in a methodical and sensible way. While acknowledging the stock market's periodic spasms of emotion and irrationality, it suggests that, sooner or later, the price of a security (or a business) approaches its economic value, as determined by a reasonable person with the requisite background in business operations, economics, finance, and accounting. This value cannot be pinpointed definitively because security analysis is not a science. Its results are dependent on its surrounding environment, which constantly changes with new information regarding developments of the business in question. As a quasi-science, security analysis has its limitations, yet it provides a reasonable framework for comparing and contrasting investment opportunities. As a result, security analysis is widely accepted in the institutional community and it is the primary means for justifying investment decisions.

Despite its lack of exactitude, security analysis provides careful investors with sufficient tools to recognize pricing anomalies in the market, and then to benefit from them by making the appropriate buy/sell decision. These evaluation tools provide the pricing anchors from which a rational decision can be reached, and they include the intrinsic value, relative value, and acquisition value methods. Technical analysis, a popular stock-picking technique based on trading patterns, is often used as a complement to these approaches.

Because so much of a typical share's value is based on hard-to-predict future results, the stock market is fertile ground for unscrupulous promoters who exaggerate the prospects of investments in which they have a financial interest. The rumor mongering and tub thumping of these players sometimes has the desired effect of inflating the price of a stock. The impact is transitory in nature and share prices generally return to a modest valuation range in which reasonable people achieve a consensus. Within this band, however, investors still face uncertainty so investment selection remains a challenging activity.

CHAPTER 2

Who's Practicing Security Analysis and Business Valuation?

In this chapter we discuss the individuals and firms that employ security analysis techniques. The role of the analyst differs, depending on the institutional context.

Hundreds of thousands of individuals make their living from working in the capital markets, but only a small percentage are full-time security analysts. About 40,000 can be classified as practitioners. Perhaps 65 percent of them work for institutional money managers such as mutual funds, hedge funds, pension funds, and insurance companies. These institutions invest their cash flows through the purchase of securities, so the trade refers to them as the *buy side*. Approximately 20 percent of analysts work for securities firms, publishing research reports which are provided free of charge to institutional and individual clients. These reports purport to sell an analyst's investment ideas to an investor in exchange for fee-generating brokerage business. Securities firms are called the *sell side*. If an analyst issues a recommendation on a stock and the investor chooses to follow this advice, the analyst hopes the investor executes the order through the trading department of the analyst's firm.

A smaller group of analysts, about 15 percent, labor for credit rating agencies, market letters, and independent research firms. These enterprises market security analysis opinions either for flat fees or for shared commissions. Regulators such as the Securities and Exchange Commission (SEC) and the Financial Industry Regulatory Authority (FINRA) also employ hundreds of analysts.

The commitment of a firm to employing analysts is a function of its size, style, and activity. Fidelity, the mutual fund giant with $1.5 trillion under management, is an active stock picker and has over 500 analysts on staff. In contrast, Berkshire Hathaway, Warren Buffett's investment vehicle, manages $150 billion with only two analysts, Mr. Buffett and Charles Munger, a close associate. Vanguard Index 500, a $125 billion index fund, uses no analysts. Its portfolio deliberately mirrors the composition of the S&P 500, so stock pickers need not apply. Employing a full-time analyst is uneconomical if a fund's size is less than $75 million. With this relatively small portfolio, the portfolio manager generates his own research or uses the sell-side reports provided to him in exchange for brokerage commissions.

Like buy-side institutions, securities firms show a broad range in their commitment to security analysis. Bank of America/Merrill Lynch, the largest brokerage house, employs over 200 analysts. Its principal competitors show staffs of a similar magnitude. Small regional firms and specialized brokerages employ only a few analysts. Sometimes, their securities salesmen double as analysts in order to develop investment ideas.

The stock market includes thousands of participants, but the vast majority of analysts work for four employer categories:

1. Securities firms.
2. Major institutional investors with $2 billion-plus under management, such as mutual funds, hedge funds, pension funds, and university endowments.
3. Small money management firms.
4. Rating agencies.

SECURITIES FIRMS AND THEIR ANALYSTS

Often referred to as *investment banks* or *brokerage houses*, securities firms are in the business of creating, marketing, and trading stocks, bonds, derivatives, and other securities. Most realize substantial revenue from ancillary businesses such as investment banking, merchant banking, and asset management. For the 10 firms that own the lion's share of the equity marketing business, a research department full of security analysts is critical to maintaining the firm's credibility with buy-side institutions and investment banking clients.

A security analyst's job requirements include:

- Writing research reports on specific companies.
- Reviewing companies and investment ideas with institutional clients.
- Indirectly working with the investment banking department.

Most of their research analysts specialize in one industry—for example, mining, electric utilities, or health care—and monitor 20 to 30 companies in that industry. A narrow focus enables the analyst to become a so-called *expert* in his industry. This specialization is important to preparing quality reports and impressing institutional clients. Studying the industry, visiting its companies, and reading corporate financial statements support these endeavors.

The sell-side analyst is a storehouse of industry information for the securities firm and its clients, but his primary responsibility is the publication of regular written reports covering the investment attributes of specific companies. These reports, called *research reports*, have several functions. First, they review new corporate information such as earnings announcements and management changes. Second, they suggest investment ideas for stocks in the analyst's industry, based in part on the new information. Third, they provide written earnings projections to the reader and present formal buy/sell recommendations to the firm's clients. Fourth, such reports assist the investment banking department of the securities firm in the solicitation of new advisory assignments by demonstrating knowledge of the relevant industry. About 50 percent of the analyst's time involves talking with institutional investors, and the other 50 percent is spent writing the research reports that are distributed to institutional and individual investors. Most reports are quite short—only 2 to 3 pages—but others, particularly those describing new investment ideas, are 30 to 40 pages long.

Making accurate earnings projections and good stock recommendations is important, yet many investors place an equal emphasis on the analyst conveying industry information and identifying related trends. Until recently, few institutional investors kept track of analyst predictions. Due to this lack of accountability, the sell-side profession was referred to as a *page business*, meaning the analyst's productivity was measured in terms of writing volume, rather than results. The advent of data services that catalog forecasts and recommendations directs more attention to analysts' accuracy.

Equity research departments help investment bankers obtain financial advisory assignments. Many times, when a corporation plans a public offering, it examines closely a securities firm's ability to generate quality research reports on its shares. If a brokerage firm employs an analyst who covers the company's industry well, the firm is apt to be rewarded with the transaction's implementation. Following the placement of the offering, favorable research reports support the share price, publicize the issuer's business, and foster trading interest in its stock. Although analysts are barred from participating in the investment banking function, their research is critical to advisory assignments. One senior banker at Stifel, Nicolaus & Co., a St. Louis-based securities firm, stated, "We could never get a company's underwriting business unless we covered its stock."

Generating Trading Revenues with Security Analysis

While corporate advisory fees are important for the big investment banks, trading activity is the larger source of revenue for the average securities firm. When buy-side institutions purchase or sell securities, they do so through a broker, who realizes a commission for executing the trade, collects a small spread on the order, or receives revenue from another broker that actually fills the institution's request. Since most trades usually have an institutional buyer indirectly connected to an institutional seller, one order eventually results in two commissions. Sizable trading volumes thus lead to significant commissions and spread revenues for brokerage firms. Institutions reward quality research by placing buy and sell orders with the analyst's employer. A reputable security analyst who captures this institutional order flow for his firm is therefore a valuable employee.

In addition, the trading department takes short-term positions in a given security, either to fulfill its commitment as a market maker or to speculate on an expected price movement. Referred to as *principal* trading, because the firm's own capital is at risk, this activity sometimes involves a consultation with the relevant security analyst, who serves as an information source for the traders. The security analyst's responsibility is thus enhanced beyond his research responsibilities.

The Chinese Wall

According to industry regulations, the research department of a brokerage firm operates independently of the investment banking and trading departments—in other words, it is surrounded by an imaginary Chinese wall. Only in this manner can institutional clients be assured that the analyst's conclusions are free of conflicts of interest. In practice, this ideal is unworkable and an analyst's opinions are compromised frequently. Many are reluctant to annoy corporate banking clients by issuing sell reports on their respective shares. Furthermore, analysts who write sell reports on companies are often denied access to corporate informational meetings and question-and-answer sessions, thus depriving them of data crucial to their jobs. As a result, most analyst recommendations are buys, which make investment bankers and potential corporate clients happy. Recent studies have proven the obvious: Over 80 percent of analysts' recommendations at brokerage firms are buys. Institutions recognize this problem and place more emphasis on the analyst providing timely corporate and industry information.

In the end, the securities firm practitioner is a good source of information and new ideas, but he cannot be considered a totally objective observer. Brokerage firms are first of all in the business of generating banking fees, commissions, and trading profits. Providing unbiased research to investors ranks low on their priority list. This fact was made all too clear in August 2007, when it became obvious that sell-side experts had been completely wrong in recommending the purchase of financial company stocks. Following a collapse in the subprime mortgage market and subsequent battering of these stocks, not one Wall Street analyst was fired for giving bad advice, despite the fact that investors lost tens of billions. Indeed, William Tanona, a Goldman Sachs analyst, was considered brave for recommending a sell on Citibank in November 2007, even as the company had already written off $11 billion in bad loans and the stock had dropped 40 percent.

MAJOR INSTITUTIONAL INVESTORS

A major institutional equity investor has $2 billion or more under management. Sizable mutual funds, hedge funds, money management firms, in-house corporate and government pension funds, bank trust departments, and large insurance companies fall into this category. For the most part, these institutions invest someone else's money on a fee-for-service basis. Representative clients are individuals, endowments, corporate retirement plans, and government pension funds lacking the expertise and resources to make their own investment decisions.

Professional money managers typically charge annual fees that are a fixed percentage of the market value of the assets under management, usually in the range of 0.5 percent to 1.5 percent annually. For the most part, clients pay these fees whether their investment funds realize profits, make losses, or break even, although consistently poor performance sometimes results in a client withdrawing its funds from a given manager. Under the standard management arrangement, conventional money managers have no direct participation in the profits (or losses) realized by their investment decisions. Rather, the rewards of above-average performance are indirect. A good track record results in an expanding client base, which means more management fee income. Likewise, the individuals actually selecting investments—the portfolio managers—have no direct participation in portfolio gains or losses. They receive salaries and bonuses. Consistently superior performance on their part results in better pay and improved job prospects. Hedge fund compensation is an exception to this rule in that managers receive fixed fees *plus* 15 percent to

20 percent of portfolio profits that exceed a preset rate of return, usually 8 percent per year.

By virtue of their substantial revenue bases, major institutions can afford to hire a full-time staff of practicing analysts. The size and sophistication of this staff depends on the institutional commitment to in-house evaluation, as opposed to the use of Wall Street or independent research. Portfolio managers work with the in-house analysts to evaluate ideas, investigate companies, and compile research reports on specific stocks. In most institutions, the stock selection process is channeled through a formal investment committee comprised of senior executives. The committee considers research reports that provide a valuation range and a buy or sell suggestion for a particular stock. After the review of a report, the committee decides what to do with the analyst's advice.

In most firms, the committee rubber-stamps the portfolio manager's opinion. The portfolio manager is an influential executive and frequently instigates the research report in the first place. If the committee agrees to buy (or sell) a stock, the portfolio managers may be required to take action. In many institutions, however, the portfolio manager has considerable latitude in whether to follow the committee's decision. In fact, some progressive funds and many hedge funds have eliminated such committees, believing they encourage mediocrity and hamstring the portfolio manager.

Besides assisting in the stock selection process, the analytical staff is a storehouse of knowledge for the portfolio manager. Large money managers own hundreds of different stocks, and their respective portfolio managers are preoccupied with strategy, allocation, and buy/sell decisions. As a result, the managers don't have the time to be familiar with the detailed developments of specific companies in their portfolios. Questions such as "What do you hear about Time Warner? What's new with Verizon? What do you think of Google?" are directed to in-house analysts, who are constantly monitoring individual companies and industries. The portfolio manager supplements this in-house feedback with Wall Street opinions and fee-for-service research.

A DYING ART?

In many large institutions, individual stock picking is a dying art because the classic buy-and-hold style is out of touch with the times. The traditional analyst's forte is finding an undervalued situation, investing in the stock, and then waiting for others to realize the stock's unrecognized potential. This process requires a medium- to long-term horizon, but portfolio managers today are under pressure to produce superior results every three months. Moreover, the increasing sophistication of the money management industry means that finding bargains is more difficult than it was 20 years ago.

The two quasi-scientific approaches to investment—intrinsic and relative value—are well known and widely accepted. The intrinsic value method pioneered by Graham and Dodd tells the analyst to find a stock so intrinsically cheap that it has little chance of declining. Sooner or later, its price must go up. The relative value approach says to find stocks with (1) solid growth prospects and (2) reasonable prices *relative* to competing stocks in the same industry. Over time, these stocks outperform the others. The disadvantage of the intrinsic value approach is that everyone

EXHIBIT 2.1   Institutional Reasons for Deemphasizing Security Analysis

- Security analysis doesn't provide immediate results.
- Bargain investments are hard to find.
- Analytical process is expensive and time consuming.
- Huge asset bases of institutions reduce individual stock importance.
- Shadow indexing, sector rotation, market timing, macro finance, and quantitative investment styles are in fashion.

believes it; virtually all shares meeting the criteria have been bid up in price. The problem of relative value is its reliance on questionable comparisons and uncertain future earnings. Either approach requires a thoughtful, time-consuming analysis of a company, along with constant monitoring of the investment. Exhibit 2.1 lists the reasons most of today's portfolio managers can't afford to follow this classic style.

As the principal institutional investors grow larger and larger, they diversify their stock selections accordingly, and any one share investment represents a correspondingly smaller impact on overall investment results. Substantial holdings are concentrated in the widely followed Fortune 100, where valuation discrepancies are hard to find. Not surprisingly, many institutions deemphasize the search for bargain stocks, with the exception of a few special situations, and focus instead on alternative investment styles such as shadow indexing, sector rotation, market timing, macro finance, and quantitative analysis.

Shadow Indexing

Most asset managers describe themselves as fitting into a particular investment style, such as *large capitalization stocks*, *growth stocks*, or *value stocks*. Each style corresponds to a given stock index, and the manager measures himself against the relevant index. If the large-cap manager produces a 10 percent return, when the large-cap index increased 9 percent, the manager beat the index. Rather than risk a sizable divergence from the index, the typical manager now dedicates perhaps 70 percent of his portfolio to stocks comprising (or resembling) the index. Only 30 percent of equities under management are selected on the basis of careful study, and the resultant need for security analysts declines.

Sector Rotation

Rather than looking for individual stock bargains by meeting corporate management teams and scrutinizing financial statements, the *sector rotator* portfolio manager looks for a specific industry which he perceives as inexpensive relative to other industries. Once the search is complete, the manager divests his share holdings in the overvalued industry and rotates the proceeds into the shares of companies participating in the undervalued industry. The security analyst plays a secondary role by setting up an approved list of stock selections within the industry groupings. The key decision points are sector shifts; corporate shares are purchased from the approved list with little follow-up study. In a way, this style is reminiscent of the relative value approach, and the sector rotator can be found saying things such as "Pharmaceutical

Step 1: Invest in Sector 1.
Step 2: Sector 2 offers better value. Sell Sector 1 and buy Sector 2.
Step 3: Dump Sector 2 stocks when Sector 3 looks better.
Step 4: Sector 1 prices fall. Portfolio manager sells Sector 3 shares and enters Sector 1 again.

EXHIBIT 2.2   Sector Rotation

stocks are cheap relative to hi-tech stocks" or "Cyclical industries look like a good play compared to growth industries." Jeff Vinik, formerly of Fidelity's Magellan Fund, was a good sector rotator. Exhibit 2.2 illustrates the pattern followed in sector rotation.

Market Timing

Share prices of companies tend to move in tandem with the broad market. Thus, if the market indexes are going down, most stocks follow the trend, as macroeconomic factors such as interest rates, currency volatility, or oil prices overwhelm positive company-specific indicators like higher earnings. Many portfolio managers combine stock-picking and sector rotation techniques with a forecast of major market movements. If they think that stock prices will rise, they become 100 percent invested in equities. Anticipating a downward movement, they reduce their equity exposure and place a portion of the portfolio in cash. If managers think market timing is more important than stock selection, they lessen the security analyst's role in the decision process.

Macro Finance

Macro finance investors select individual stocks and industry groups on the basis of global themes. If U.S. interest rates are supposed to fall, they buy utility stocks, which tend to rise in price during periods of lower interest rates. Political problems in the Middle East might prompt the acquisition of domestic oil company shares. Frequently, the purchase or sale of company-specific securities is done with little detailed knowledge of the underlying business. The in-house analyst's role is thus diminished, and the approved stock list is derived primarily from Wall Street research. George Soros of the Quantum Fund is the best-known macro finance manager.

Quantitative Analysis

Quantitative investors rely heavily on powerful computers and sophisticated software to make money by conducting convertible arbitrage, paired trading risk arbitrage, foreign exchange carry trading, and a host of other tactics that rely less on a security's underlying value than its historical trading relationship to other securities.

The past 10 years have seen an explosion in the use of *derivatives*. Derivatives are investments that draw their value from an underlying security (a stock, bond, or index). Popular derivatives include convertible bonds, put/call options, futures contracts, and index notes. Many Wall Street firms custom-tailor derivatives contracts at a client's request. Quantitative managers use derivatives to exploit brief discrepancies in value between the derivative and the underlying security, as well as discrepancies in the values of competing derivatives. The profits on a given trade are typically a fraction of a percentage point, but the trading position only lasts a day or two, giving the manager the opportunity to turn his capital over quickly. As an example, if you make only 0.1 percent per day on your trading, your annual return on investment is over 40 percent.

Many determinants of the sector rotation, market timing, macro finance, and quantitative styles have short lives. Institutions using these styles have a high turnover, easily trading the value of their portfolios five or six times per year, so the average stock is held for less than 90 days. This frenzied activity leaves little time for the security analyst to monitor companies effectively and write research summaries.

All of the preceding approaches are called *active management* strategies because the portfolio manager is making definite investment decisions based on his philosophy of investment. Despite the immense amounts of time and money that institutions dedicate to this exercise, few portfolio managers are able to outperform the broad market indexes, such as the S&P 500 Index, on a consistent basis. Even the best managers of mutual funds exceed market results by only 1 or 2 percentage points annually. While there are sensible explanations for this situation, it remains problematic for the customers who place funds with these managers. With most institutions offering returns that are less than the market indexes, clients turn to the passively managed index funds.

INDEX FUNDS AND EXCHANGE-TRADED FUNDS

Index funds and exchange-traded funds (ETFs) mirror the performance of a stock index by owning a representative sample of the stocks comprising the index. Once the sample is established, there is no need to actively manage the portfolio since it tracks the index's movements. Existing funds and ETFs copy dozens of indexes ranging from a broad index such as the S&P 500, a high-tech index like the NASDAQ computer index, or a foreign index such as the Morgan Stanley Emerging Markets index. About 25 to 30 percent of U.S. equity funds under management are placed in index funds and ETFs. The nation's largest index fund, Vanguard Index 500, had $125 billion in assets as of 2008 and it ranked as the third-largest fund in the country, trailing only the Fidelity Magellan Fund and the Investment Co. of America Fund.

Index funds and ETFs represent a victory for the efficient market theory, which contends that stock prices reflect all available information. The analyst's search for an undervalued security is therefore futile, since its attributes have been fully appraised by others. The growth of index funds and ETFs also signals the investor's frustration with security analysts and portfolio managers. Indeed, the S&P 500 beat 72 percent of actively managed large-cap funds over the past 10 years.[1] Index funds are now major institutional players.

SMALL MONEY MANAGEMENT FIRMS

Because of their size, management limitations, and diversification requirements, large institutional investors that are fully invested in equities tend to have performance results that closely track the broad market indexes. Smaller firms have less than $2 billion under management and retain considerably more flexibility in designing a strategy that beats the market. They can search out value among the many companies too small for large institutional investment. Small-cap stocks far outnumber big-name equities like Coca-Cola and Ford Motor, and pricing inefficiencies are more prevalent. Simply defining a small-cap universe as stocks with a value between $50 million and $1 billion creates over 5,000 potential names for study. Exhibit 2.3 provides a list of advantages for small investment funds.

With his limited asset base, the portfolio manager of a $1 billion fund can make meaningful commitments to individual stocks without unduly influencing their prices. Large institutions can't do this. To gain a significant position in a small-cap stock, their own buying efforts upset the normal price behavior. Accordingly, second-tier institutions can afford to be research intensive, scouting the market for cheap stocks and spending substantial time analyzing special situations. A stronger orientation toward security analysis is also found among the smaller funds that focus on just one industry. A biotech fund, for example, needs only one or two security analysts to cover the principal public companies in the industry. Thus, it provides fund-wide analysis in a cost-effective manner. Other small institutional investors emphasize just one theme, such as buying growth stocks or value stocks. The firm's analysts do not cling to a specific industry focus, believing that growth companies exhibit certain characteristics which are common among all fast-growing businesses. Likewise, a value analyst sees repeated patterns in the evaluation of shares trading below their intrinsic worth.

In a small fund, both portfolio managers and security analysts generate investment ideas which are forwarded to an investment committee. Like the committees of larger institutions, small fund committees rely heavily on the portfolio manager's guidance. In certain small institutions, such as hedge funds, the governance structure is looser, and portfolio managers operate without formal investment committees.

Most of the smaller mutual funds, asset managers, and bank trust departments charge clients a fixed annual service fee based on a percentage of the market value of assets under management. Like the larger institutions, these money managers charge fees whether or not the client makes money. They typically pay their portfolio managers and security analysts a salary plus a variable bonus. An increasing number are set up as investment partnerships or hedge funds, whereby the manager receives a

EXHIBIT 2.3 Security Analysis for Small Investment Funds

- Specific stock selections can make a difference in overall portfolio returns.
- A small fund can make a major commitment to an attractive small-cap stock.
- Small funds have the ability to focus on analysis of complex situations such as distressed securities.
- A small fund can focus on one industry group and take advantage of specialized analytical knowledge of that industry.

---

percentage of the profits. The portfolio manager and his key analysts are the general partners and the clients contributing most of the money are the limited partners. A common arrangement is for the general partners to put up 1 percent of the capital in exchange for 20 percent of the profits. A minimum return, such as 8 percent annually, is required before the general partner's profit participation, or *carried interest*, applies.

The term *hedge fund* originated many years ago with groups of investors who pooled large sums for buying stocks they thought would rise in price, at the same time selling shares they thought would decline. In this way they profited from either a general rise or fall in share prices. The potential for losses was lessened by the counterbalancing bets (i.e., the hedge), a tactic that is nowadays referred to as being *market neutral*. In the old-time hedge funds, the general partner received 20 percent of the profits, and the nickname stuck to subsequent equity partnerships involving a large management carry. Today's hedge funds, in contrast, trade stocks in a wide-open fashion, and sometimes very little is hedged. In fact, hedge fund managers pride themselves on making large bets on narrow investment themes. Because a hedge fund manager multiplies his 1 percent capital investment by a factor of 20:1, security analysts relish the opportunity to join hedge funds and actually *pick* stocks, rather than just recommending them. Many successful analysts make the transition to lucrative hedge fund positions.

RATING AGENCIES

The rating agency business is dominated by Standard & Poor's, Moody's, and Fitch. These three companies together employ about 5,000 analysts whose principal job is to assign credit ratings to fixed-income securities issued by corporations and governments. Unlike the equity business, where investors pay for outside research, the rating agencies charge the issuer for a credit rating, which is then disseminated to the public. Because of the various scandals involving irresponsible banks and insurance companies in the past 20 years, regulators now require participants in these industries to buy principally fixed-income securities (or loans) with credit ratings assigned by one of these top agencies. Since government agencies essentially backstop bank and insurance company obligations, the idea was to have an independent and objective organization to determine loan values, rather than a financial firm eager to close a deal or boost short-term earnings. The system works reasonably well, but the subprime mortgage collapse of 2007 and 2008 stemmed, in part, from rating agencies assigning collateral debt obligations (CDOs) with higher ratings than were deserved. The tens of billions of subsequent debt downgrades called into question the rating agencies' ability to evaluate risk, the quality of the institutional investors' in-house evaluations, and their own overreliance on the rating agencies.

INDIVIDUAL INVESTORS: A SPECIAL CATEGORY

The vast majority of individual investors lack the time, training, and experience to analyze intensively their equity investments. Most avoid the pain of specific stock selection by purchasing mutual funds or index funds. Others indulge in the occasional equity speculation based on a broker's suggestion, a friend's advice, or a news item. A small minority apply the tools reviewed in this book to evaluate share prices.

As noted earlier, information is the lifeblood of the stock market. In this regard the individual investor operates at a significant disadvantage relative to securities firms and prominent institutions. The majority of new corporate information is distributed in an even-handed fashion, but frequently word of a significant event leaks out to key market players, who are then in position for a short time to make a profit. Indeed, one study showed that 40 percent of takeover stocks rose significantly in price before any public announcement of the deed. Besides access to leaks, institutions and securities firms have better access to corporate management in getting questions answered. On Wall Street, the individual hears information last. For example, a number of sell-side analysts move stock prices when issuing recommendations to buy or sell, as investors quickly follow their advice.

Professional traders and computerized institutions have advantages over individuals in profiting on such new information. Few individuals spend their days tracking research reports, stock prices, and news items on a minute-to-minute basis, yet any data coming over the Internet from the news services is read immediately by at least 100,000 such professionals and instantaneously processed by institutional computers. Printed information in the *Wall Street Journal* and the *New York Times*, while only 12 to 24 hours old, is already discounted by practitioners. Thus, the individual player works off stale information that is days old. Only superior analytical effort overcomes this disadvantage.

Despite these obstacles, some individuals apply security analysis techniques to their equity investment activities and realize superior performance. In my experience, the most successful individual investors fall into two groups: (1) those with prior financial experience, which enables them to perform their own analysis; and (2) those with a strong industry expertise, which allows them to foresee developments impacting stock prices in that one industry.

Although the odds are stacked against individual investors, the situation is far from hopeless. There are thousands of publicly traded stocks, and the vast institutional and brokerage communities can't monitor every company on a continual basis. Valuation anomalies occur on a regular basis because the thousands of tape watchers can't maintain complete coverage and the computers are only as skillful as their programmers. As individuals search for discrepancies, they can also practice common sense in the selection of widely followed stocks. Full-time players inevitably get caught up in Wall Street's herd mentality, which frequently produces outlandish valuations for the stock of the month. Inevitably, prices of these businesses return to earth after practitioners face their excesses, so an occasional short sale by a knowledgeable individual is appropriate. Likewise, common sense sometimes triggers a contrarian approach on the buy side, as an individual purchases selected stocks that have fallen from grace.

The 2004 run-up in biotech stocks was a good example of institutional investors going overboard in betting on the financial prospects of a specific industry. Over a 12-month period, the NASDAQ Biotech index nearly doubled, only to fall 40 percent in three months.

BUSINESS VALUATION

In addition to capital market participants, a vast army of individuals use security analysis techniques in a profession loosely termed "business valuation." Practitioners produce reports attesting to the value of a firm or its securities, and the reports are utilized in a variety of tax, accounting, and legal functions. Because of abuses in the Internet boom era, the federal government mandated an increased use of such reports by audited companies and private equity firms. To save money, such users have watered down the mandates and the resultant reports often resemble "file stuffers" rather than thoughtful analysis.

Another large segment of the profession is the corporate development community. Every large corporation has a department examining opportunities, such as acquisitions and new business lines. The relevant employees are well versed in security analysis.

SUMMARY

Hundreds of thousands of individuals participate in the equity markets on a regular basis, but there are only 40,000 full-time security analysts. Most of these professionals work in four settings: security firms, major institutions, small institutions, and rating agencies. Securities firms have the greatest concentration of analysts, with the larger firms employing dozens of professionals specializing in distinct industries. They follow specific companies, publish research reports, and work with institutional clients to figure investment choices. On the institutional buy side, the analyst's role is close to that of a pure stock picker. As the in-house industry expert and resident numbers guru, he works closely with portfolio managers in establishing a rational basis for investment selection.

The analyst's status is magnified in smaller institutions, which can make meaningful commitments to his investment recommendations, but his impact is less in the large institutional context. A big mutual fund company has multiple funds covering hundreds of stocks, and few shares are individually important to overall results. By virtue of their size, large institutions rely frequently on sector rotation, market timing, macro finance, and quantitative investment techniques. These methods deemphasize security analysis in favor of broader investment themes.

CHAPTER 3

Seeking a Level Playing Field

How level is the playing field? The stock market provides participants with a reasonably fair chance of matching the other guy's success. Nevertheless, certain players either have inherent advantages in playing the market or exploit weaknesses in the regulatory system. In this chapter we examine the system's safeguards and look at their impact on an initial public offering.

The stock selection process employed by brokerage firms, institutions, and individual investors relies heavily on informed trading. The convergence of a security's market value to its rational value doesn't depend merely on the coincidental meeting of supply and demand. Rather, the more important consideration is the quality of information on which investors' decisions are based. Thus, before issuing a buy or sell recommendation, the analyst knows (1) the present and future earnings prospects of different investment opportunities, and (2) the fair prices of securities competing for the investment dollar. This emphasizes the importance of correct and reliable information on corporate activities and on open and honest trading in the various markets.

Besides enhancing the process of business valuation, good information and orderly markets facilitate the rational allocation of investment funds. In an ideal situation, the share prices arrived at through supply and demand reflect the collective opinion of technically trained investors, who use such data to intently study the long-term investment prospects of industries (and companies within a given industry) before making a decision. The long-term expectations of each investment are considered relative to others, and the decision is finalized after an exhaustive comparison of each investment's relative price and risk. While intelligent speculation plays a role in this ideal setup, the exacting nature of the average decision process ensures that capital flows to those companies demonstrating the best potential for economic success. Correspondingly, the rigorous analysis diminishes the money-raising ability of those firms with less justification for development.

The foregoing is a perfect system. It is referred to as an *efficient market* in academic parlance. The real-world market, as noted earlier, deviates substantially from this ideal, but it comes closer with better corporate information and improved order execution. In fact, government recognizes an efficient stock market as a legitimate social goal. After all, the economic well-being of the United States requires that capital moves into the most deserving industries and that investors receive fair value. For this reason, from time to time, the federal government pushes regulatory initiatives that steer the securities market closer to the efficient model. For example, it encouraged the stock exchanges to pursue a stronger self-regulatory regime by merging their separate efforts into the Financial Industry Regulatory Authority (FINRA), and it pushed through a number of accounting changes to make financial statements more accurate.

As demonstrated by the market crashes of 2000 and 2008, the securities market still exhibits many weaknesses and has an inclination to over- and undercorrect. That being said, the corporate disclosure and trading standards imposed by the government and the exchanges are largely successful, and most widely followed shares trade at prices that are justifiable based on a studied review of their earnings prospects. Despite these successes, ill practices continue to hamper the market's ability to price shares properly. A listing of the dubious exercises includes:

- The release of misleading information by companies that issue securities, make quarterly filings, or participate in merger and acquisition activity.
- The manipulation of a stock by the issuer or by investment bankers, fund managers, syndicates, or individuals interested in the stock.
- The covert interest in a company's equity through off-exchange equity derivatives or credit default swaps, both of which are largely unregulated.
- The purchase or sale of a stock based on inside information.
- The use of high-pressure sales tactics and false rumors to attract the investing public.
- The utilization of excessive leverage either to acquire shares as a principal or to broker stocks as an agent.

Regulators have been enormously influential in reducing the frequency of such abuses, but it is essential to appreciate the limitations under which they operate. The markets represent hundreds of thousands of brokers, institutions, and individuals executing millions of transactions in thousands of securities each day. Even with multimillion-dollar budgets, high-speed computers, and dedicated employees, the regulators are outmanned and outgunned many times over by the major corporations, investment funds, large securities firms, and professional investors who dominate the stock market.

Even when a crooked participant is caught red-handed, the regulators face difficulties. The most egregious violations of securities laws often require years of litigation before restitution is reached, and large participants are politically influential and have enormous legal budgets. It is clear that unscrupulous participants have a motivation to bend the rules. For these reasons, professionals realize that the regulators are the investor's friends, but *caveat emptor* reigns supreme. There is no substitute for a comprehensive analysis before an investment decision is made.

BRIEF HISTORY OF SECURITIES REGULATION

Abuses have occurred throughout the stock market's history, but they became highly visible in the 1920s. This was the first decade when the general public played a large role in buying and selling stocks. During this time, stock prices advanced rapidly.

Many unsophisticated investors, seeing the profits being made, decided to place a portion of their savings into the equity markets. By the late 1920s, over 10 million individual investors held the majority of publicly issued shares, a sharp contrast to earlier times. For many years, the stock markets had been the province of professional traders and speculators. Most established institutions, such as insurance companies and bank trust departments, avoided common stocks, which they thought to be too risky, and they displayed a marked preference for conservative government and corporate bonds. The entry of the individual investor on a broad scale was positive, since it broadened the number of participants and introduced more capital, but it also provided unscrupulous practitioners with additional opportunities to take advantage of unknowing players.

While important to American finance, the stock markets of the 1920s were primarily speculative. A key contributor to this situation was the lack of information supplied to investors by the issuing companies. Even on the New York Stock Exchange, where many of the larger firms traded, companies provided public stockholders with little more than an abbreviated income statement and balance sheet on an annual basis. Information requirements at the exchanges and for over-the-counter issues often failed to meet this bare minimum. For example, in 1929 a Sloan and Standard study showed that 257 of the 323 leading public companies refused to report annual sales to the public. Quarterly income statements were frequently absent and executives often withheld information about corporate activities, while positioning themselves to take advantage of changing stock prices when the news became public. Also, accounting standards varied widely among companies, and such disparities made a comparative analysis of corporate income statements and balance sheets very difficult. Investors decried their inability to obtain relevant data, but the companies tended to resist for, among other reasons, fear of alerting competitors to their progress. The exchanges backed up the issuers, although many investment bankers had begun to realize the unsustainability of minimal disclosure. In sum, serious analysts lacked the requisite information on which to make a rational investment decision, although they were pressed to make commitments as equity prices boomed.

As stock prices spiraled upward, the quality of new issues declined. Investment banks and commercial banks rushed to fill the distribution pipeline with product, without paying sufficient attention to the issuers' long-term earnings prospects. This phenomenon, which is played out in every bull market, saw underwriters making marketing decisions without the careful analysis that prudence required. Prices of these low-quality and overvalued securities gyrated widely and thus contributed to the market's shaky underpinnings.

Compounding the problem of scant information and speculative issues were other complications. Unsavory investment practices such as outright fraud, price manipulation, insider trading, secret investment pools, and bear raids were a constant presence behind the scenes. At the same time, high-pressure sales tactics were used by many dishonest securities firms, referred to as *bucket shops* or *boiler rooms*, in order to separate the inexperienced investor from his money. And finally, commercial banks and brokerage firms greased the trading wheels by supplying customers with liberal credit. Loan-to-value ratios for stocks went as high as 90 percent in the 1920s, versus 50 percent for individuals today. The provision of easy money only accentuated the casino atmosphere of the markets and further distorted the realistic values for equities.

In the absence of meaningful oversight of these activities at the federal level, many states passed laws designed to regulate the in-state sale of securities by out-of-state issuers. Set up to protect local investors, the laws were called *blue-sky* regulations since the selling of highly speculative securities was like selling a piece of the blue sky. Because few states coordinated their efforts, the blue-sky restrictions were different from state to state, representing a patchwork of regulations that were vague and ill-defined. Furthermore, state securities departments were poorly trained, undermanned, and underfunded. They were not a formidable obstacle to the shenanigans crafted by Wall Street operators.

Self-supervision by the exchanges over their members was tantamount to inmates running the asylum. Few regulations existed at the exchanges, and those on the books were only enforced if the violator blatantly repeated his abuses in the face of warnings. Over-the-counter trading was wide open.

Federal regulation of the 1930s grew out of the notion that dishonest behavior and speculative excesses played a key role in the disastrous crash of 1929, when stock prices dropped 23 percent in two days. Besides dramatically reducing investors' wealth on paper overnight, the crash paralyzed the nation's financial system and contributed with other economic events to the ensuing Great Depression. As the Hoover administration and the exchanges dragged their feet on implementing stronger protective measures, abuses continued making headlines in the newspapers, resulting in a Senate investigation that justified forceful oversight. Within the first six months of Roosevelt's election, the Securities Act of 1933 was passed. By 1934 the Securities Exchange Act dictated the formation of the Securities and Exchange Commission (SEC), a separate agency devoted to protecting investors and maintaining fair and orderly markets.

THE CHIEF REGULATOR: THE SECURITIES AND EXCHANGE COMMISSION

The SEC's original purpose was to supervise the flow of information between the issuing corporations and investors, and it quickly gained a reputation as a disclosure agency. Before issuing securities trading on national exchanges, companies submitted lengthy registration statements for SEC approval, describing the securities and the company's business, financial history, and likely prospects. (Later, in 1964, Congress extended the regulations to over-the-counter issues.) Regular filings with the agency continued thereafter and all such documentation was made available for public dissemination. Companies were required to disclose many other matters of relevance to shareholders, such as details on takeover inquiries, significant business changes, and management compensation. A public company also needed to have its annual financial statements audited by an independent accounting firm, thereby transforming the accounting business into one of the growth industries of the 1930s. The availability of this level of corporate information is taken for granted today, but its appearance following the SEC legislation spawned the growth of new corporate information gathering and security analysis businesses. No more would investors be operating primarily from spotty data, half-truths, and misinformation.

Prior to the SEC, security offering documents were designed as marketing devices rather than disclosure documents. The offering prospectus contained bits and pieces of information that hardly provided the raw material for an independent assessment. The guiding principle of the document was inducing the potential investor to buy, so many prospectuses provided inadequate disclosure, extravagant promises, and outright misstatements. Consider the claims of Texas Eagle Oil Company in a 1919 offering announcement. With only a six-month operating history and no record of sales or earnings, the firm announced:

> ... *With the claws of an eagle we have gripped the oil fields of Mid-Texas. Only 10,000 shares open to public subscription.*
>
> *This company is as sound as a bank. Insured profits, verified accounts, open books. No secrets.*
>
> *Deposit your money with us [i.e., buy shares] with the same confidence that you have in your bank.*

The SEC regulates by information. For new issues, companies are supposed to furnish a sufficient amount of information so that a "reasonable person" can make an informed investment decision. At the same time, the sponsoring investment banks are required to make an investigation of each issue before it is brought to market. The issuers and other responsible parties are liable in court for any important misstatement or omission of fact that contributed to investors buying an issue and subsequently losing money. In effect, the SEC tries to reverse *caveat emptor* by making the *seller* beware, although proving such omissions and collecting lost monies is a daunting legal process for the investors.

The SEC has a staff of accountants, attorneys, and financial analysts for new issue evaluation, but it relies primarily on the information supplied in the filing process. It has neither the staff nor the resources to conduct its own inspection of the companies behind the issues. As a result, the disclosure system is based primarily on the combined self-regulatory actions of the issuers, investment bankers, attorneys, and accountants involved with a transaction, some of whom have obvious conflicts with the public's right to know. Such is the investors' primary line of defense against outright fraud or unintentional misrepresentation in the written materials provided for their consumption.

The disclosure system works pretty well, but it has several important flaws. Perhaps the most prominent of these is the manner in which corporate disclosure documents are written. In order to reduce the chances of their issuer client being sued by an investor, lawyers have taken over the entire descriptive process. The end result of their efforts is that the required review of the issuer's business and prospects is set forth in a dry and stilted fashion that is comprehensible only to professionals. The average investor is turned off by this documentation, fails to study it, and is therefore easy pickings for unscrupulous promoters, particularly for new offerings that haven't been tested in the market.

The disclosure system fails in ferreting out the major risks of an issue. As I have seen repeatedly, companies, lawyers, and bankers do their best to obfuscate important business risks by burying them in legal mumbo jumbo, such as the following sentence from TDK Solar's 2007 initial public offering prospectus:

> *Reduction or elimination of government subsidies and economic incentives for the solar power industry could cause demand for our products to decline, thus adversely affecting our business prospects and results of operations.*

Why not just simply say the truth:

> *Solar power is uneconomical without massive government subsidies. If oil prices fall below $70 per barrel and governments pull the plug on subsidies, the solar power industry and this company are in deep trouble.*

The splitting of legal hairs in IPO prospectuses and other documents also extends to a variety of accounting conventions which allow the issuer to report sales and earnings in ways that may not reflect economic reality. Repeated financial scandals, such as the Internet stock meltdown, management stock option wrongdoing, Enron blow-up, and the Structured Investment Vehicle (SIV) crisis, forced the SEC into a position where it takes strong stands on how financial results are reported, a task traditionally delegated to the Financial Accounting Standards Board (FASB).

Finally, a corporate security derives its value primarily from the company's prospective performance—not its past history. Why can't a prospective issuer disclose management's projections for the business? The corporation can provide this information—and the SEC encourages the practice—but the issuer's lawyers almost always advise against distributing projections to the public. Our legal system is to blame. Even with cautionary warnings included in a prospectus, the issuer faces a good chance of being successfully sued by investors should they lose money on the deal. Similarly, prospectuses contain neither comparable public company value ratios nor the pricing of recent industry takeover deals. As we will see, such material is an integral part of a security analysis, yet it never appears in a prospectus.

The SEC admits that its "truth in securities" laws don't prohibit either the sale of speculative securities or overpriced stocks, nor do they ensure that investors receive a fair return on their investments. This is an odd position, considering the government insists on restricting many less apparent financial abuses, such as hidden interest charges in leases and misleading insurance marketing practices. By mandating disclosure, the SEC regulations try to provide investors—and security analysts—with sufficient information on which to make an intelligent decision. Thus the market, not the government, makes the ultimate judgment on what a security is worth. Exhibit 3.1 lists aspects of the SEC's regulatory role.

SALES AND TRADING PRACTICES

Besides requiring adequate and accurate information from public corporations, the SEC administers laws that seek to maintain fair and orderly markets. These laws give the SEC broad authority to supervise the activities of the principal players in the stock market—the stock exchanges, securities firms, and money managers (and, of course, their various employees)—and to regulate unfair trading practices such

EXHIBIT 3.1   The Regulatory Role of the Securities and Exchange Commission

- Information for new issues.
- Oversight of accounting conventions for public companies.
- Maintenance of information flow for existing public companies.
- Fair trading and sales practices by securities firms.
- Registration of exchanges with SEC oversight on self-supervision activities.
- Registration of securities firms and supervision of honest business practices.
- Regulations governing investment companies and investment advisers such as mutual funds, bank trust departments, and insurance companies.

as insider trading, undisclosed investment pools, and price manipulation. Like the disclosure rules, sales and trading regulations are essentially carried out by self-regulatory mechanisms. The New York Stock Exchange, American Stock Exchange, NASDAQ, and regional exchanges have rules, as do individual brokerage firms, that are supposed to protect investors, and FINRA operates monitoring and enforcement departments to find and punish violators (Exhibit 3.2). Thus, a securities firm with an inadequate capital base or a renegade stockbroker should be caught first by the industry's own regulatory efforts and by FINRA, rather than by the SEC.

If the exchanges discover a dishonest action by someone *outside* of the internal regulatory scheme, the violation is referred to the government. Brokerage firms are on guard to look for customer insider trading; to deny their facilities for stock price manipulation; and to restrict speculative excesses by in-house traders, brokers, and

Investment Players	SEC Is the Referee and Rulemaker	Issuers and Agent Players
Individual Investors	The SEC tries to act as a referee to promote honest markets.	Issuers
Want full disclosure ========> and fair markets	The backup referees are the self-regulatory systems of the exchanges, but they are dominated by the agent players.	Tend to resist full disclosure <========= and dislike regulation of marketing, sales, and trading practices
Institutional Investors		Securities Firms Stock Exchanges

EXHIBIT 3.2   The Investment Game and SEC Regulatory Framework

account holders, but the system is far from perfect. Many securities firms look the other way when they see improper behavior, and the SEC fosters this complacency by regulating in a reactive way, waiting for someone to complain before investigating problems. FINRA is relatively new and it has yet to establish a track record.

The slack is frequently picked up by the *class action* bar, which is constantly on the lookout for corporate and securities firm abuses. Class action law firms search the financial markets for violations that can be turned into lawsuits from which they can derive fees. In the vast majority of such lawsuits, aggrieved investors receive little, if any, compensation, but the law firms' aggressive posture costs time and money for the offenders. Thus, it is a second line of defense for stockholders. Finally, state attorney generals have the power to go after listed companies that break laws, and proactive state attorney generals have sparked investigations that led to major financial scandals.

Based on my own experiences in the investment banking business, I conclude that the regulatory system is effective in halting most egregious abuses, but it falters consistently around the margins. Instances abound of shoddy marketing practices directed at unsophisticated investors, poor brokerage firm execution practices that cheat customers, mutual funds that overcharge clients, banks that fail to mark securities to market, and insider trades that go undetected. These abuses hurt investors, but they do little to affect analysts' estimates of specific share values, which, as I have noted earlier, can deviate several dollars from a midpoint estimate.

Insider trading is another activity that hurts the market's credibility from time to time. The illegal insider trading of Amergy Bancorp, just before the $2 billion Zion's Bancorp takeover bid was announced in 2007, upset the Amergy share price for 48 hours. Afterward the news was widely available, so the manipulation was of short duration. Nevertheless, the integrity of the stock price was damaged for several days. Perhaps one-half of takeover stocks go up before the official transaction announcement, yet the authorities rarely go after the perpetrators.

Furthermore, the SEC does nothing to eliminate the conflict of interest inherent in the respective jobs of individual stockbroker and institutional securities salesman. Inevitably, the compensation of these individuals is directly related to the amount of fees they generate from their customers rather than the investment results achieved. As a result, they are under constant pressure to do more fee business, even if the related activity is not in the customer's interest. Likewise, permitting mutual funds to direct order flow to friendly brokers, to put customers' spare cash in expensive money market funds, and to facilitate other sweetheart arrangements is a conflict of interest that should be addressed. Furthermore, even as custom-made derivatives play a sizable role in the markets, the SEC has little ability to monitor them, just as it has minimal control over hedge funds, which represent a large portion of trading activity.

With the financial crisis of 2008 causing major economic damage on a global basis, U.S. and foreign regulators are examining ways to minimize the likelihood of another occurrence. Despite the massive subsidies provided to financial institutions, the industry is trying to moderate changes. The crisis began with real estate loans and fixed-income securities, and then spread to equity instruments.

The problem of regulation of the stock markets is thus a difficult one. The problem involves not only the oversight of the thousands of corporations whose securities are publicly traded and the markets and dealers in these securities, but also the control and suppression of an endless variety of stock promotion and trading schemes.

Furthermore, the SEC now plays an important role in setting accounting policies. An increase in the regulatory budget, an expansion of the Justice Department's efforts against securities fraud, a federal takeover of FINRA, and a combining of regulators covering equities and equity derivatives would improve the environment.

MARGIN REGULATION

For the most part, such abuses don't amount to large amounts of money in comparison to a typical day's trading volume, and, with few exceptions, they tend not to affect a security's economic value for a long period of time. If left unchecked, these actions have a cumulative negative impact by undermining investor confidence. Unless investors and issuers sense that they are being treated fairly, the markets don't function properly and can't ensure an adequate supply of capital for economic growth.

The control of speculation is assisted by the government's control of margin buying. *Margin* is the use of credit to buy securities. Liberal credit contributes to unrestrained bull markets. In an effort to reduce speculation on borrowed funds, the government, through the Federal Reserve, sets the maximum loan-to-value ratio for common stocks. This has been set at 50 percent for many years. Institutions like hedge funds, however, employ tactics that effectively increase this leverage ratio, and the government does little to restrain this activity.

THE LIFE CYCLE OF A NEW SECURITY ISSUE

As set forth in Exhibit 3.3, the regulatory machinery follows a publicly issued security through its creation; sees that relevant information flows continually to the investment community; oversees the buying, selling, and marketing of the issue as it becomes seasoned in the aftermarket; and requires proper disclosure when the security is delisted, either by repurchase, takeover, merger, or bankruptcy.

The SEC review is at its most intense during a security's initial public offering (IPO), although most equity trading volume is accounted for by seasoned issues that are beyond the IPO stage. This daily trading, buying, selling, and marketing of aftermarket issues is dominated by FINRA and the self-regulatory system, with the SEC intervening when obvious violations occur or when illicit activity is reported to it. Signifying the end of one security and perhaps the expansion of another, mergers and acquisitions are reviewed by the SEC to ensure adequate disclosure of the insider deals, executive golden parachutes, and nontransparent processes endemic to such transactions. M&A transactions represent tens of billions of investor dollars and tend to be complicated, so the potential for unscrupulous behavior is enhanced. Similarly, the SEC evaluates many Chapter 11 reorganizations, which involve a level of analysis far above that possessed by many professionals.

Case Study: Springdale Publishing Company

A case study is helpful in tracing the regulatory scheme. Springdale Publishing Company ("Springdale" or the "Company"), a privately owned business, reviews its capital budget for 2009 and decides it needs $250 million in additional equity

EXHIBIT 3.3   Regulation through the Security Life Cycle

Life Cycle Phase	Regulatory Framework
1. Initial public offering.	▪ Ensure proper disclosure. ▪ Meet exchange listing requirements. ▪ Due diligence investigation by underwriters.
2. The IPO becomes a seasoned issue, bought and sold in the aftermarket.	▪ Company (issuer) supplies financial reports and other relevant data regularly. ▪ SEC reviews reports for adequacy of disclosure and accounting methods. ▪ SEC supervises stock exchanges and securities firms in their self-regulatory efforts to prevent abuses in trading, buying, selling, and marketing of the stock. ▪ SEC looks for price manipulation, insider trading, and other illegal actions outside of the exchange system. ▪ FINRA performs regulation on behalf of the exchanges. ▪ Class action bar monitors public companies for violations. ▪ State attorney generals look for problems.
3. Delisting of an issue.	▪ SEC requires full disclosure on takeovers and mergers of public companies. ▪ To protect public investor interests, the SEC can participate in the bankruptcy proceedings of public companies. ▪ Exchanges remove companies that fail to meet listing requirements.

capital. After evaluating financing options, the management concludes that an initial public offering of common stock represents the optimal financing strategy. This decision sets in motion a five-step process culminating in the firm's shares trading in the aftermarket, as shown in Exhibit 3.4.

Step 1: Selecting an Investment Bank   Based on previous banking relationships or associates' recommendations, a typical prospective issuer invites two or three

EXHIBIT 3.4   Springdale Publishing Company—Initial Public Offering Process

1. Springdale selects an investment bank.
2. Springdale, its banker, and other advisers prepare a prospectus for the SEC.
3. The marketing process for Springdale's IPO begins.
4. Springdale's shares are priced and sold into the market. The Company receives its needed capital.
5. Springdale's shares trade in the aftermarket.

investment banks to study its business, estimate an equity valuation, and promote their respective abilities to carry out a transaction. Depending on the complexity of the issuer's business, the state of its financial and operating records, and the reputation of its management, this preliminary evaluation activity lasts from a few weeks to several months.

In Springdale's case, the evaluation process goes quickly because the Company presents no difficult valuation issues. As a publisher of specialty trade magazines, Springdale is in a low-tech business with a low fashion content. It has audited financial statements, which is important, and they indicate steady growth in sales and earnings. The information technology and record-keeping systems are up-to-date and allow the potential underwriters to access operating data readily. Finally, the management team is experienced and well respected, eliminating the need for lengthy background checks. Preliminary information about the firm is shown in Exhibit 3.5. Financial data appear in Exhibit 3.6.

Three investment banks study the Company's business for several weeks, preparing financial projections, and compare these results with existing publicly held magazine publishers. Afterward, each bank meets separately with Springdale's owners

EXHIBIT 3.5 Springdale Publishing Company

Objective	To raise $250 million via an initial public offering of common stock.
Use of proceeds	The net proceeds are intended to be used in the Company's capital expenditure program.
Business	Springdale publishes a group of specialty trade magazines targeted at niche industries.
Financial summary	Selected financial results are set forth in Exhibit 3.6.

EXHIBIT 3.6 Springdale Publishing Company Summary—Financial Data (in millions)

	Year Ended December 31		
	2006	2007	2008
Income Statement Data			
Sales	$1,150	$1,300	$1,500
Gross profit	400	460	530
Earnings before interest, taxes, depreciation, and amortization (EBITDA)	100	120	150
Net earnings	40	53	70
Balance Sheet Data			
Working capital	$ 210	$ 240	$ 220
Total assets	990	1,080	1,160
Total debt	200	250	300
Stockholders' equity	360	400	450
Per Share Data (10 Million Shares)			
Earnings per share	$ 4.00	$ 5.30	$ 7.00
Book value per share	36	40	45

Note: Springdale's track record is good and its balance sheet is solid.

EXHIBIT 3.7 Springdale Publishing Company—Proposed Initial Public Offering

	Castle Stone & Co.	Branch Day, Inc.	Levy Brothers
Gross proceeds	$250 million	$250 million	$250 million
Commissions and expenses (as a percentage)	7.0%	7.0%	7.0%
Net proceeds	$233 million	$230 million	$233 million
Number of shares	2.0 million	1.9 million	2.1 million
Expected price per share	$125	$133	$118
P/E ratio	18×	19×	17×
Percentage ownership represented by IPO	17%	16%	17%

Note: Branch Day offers the highest proposed IPO price.

and managers to discuss expected prices for the Company's shares and to review their respective marketing plans for the offering. As is typical in these situations, the three investment banks—Castle Stone & Company, Branch Day, Inc., and Levy Brothers—have well-honed presentations and show price estimates for Springdale's shares that are reasonably similar. Describing the process of having his company valued by New York investment bankers, Drew Peslar, co-owner of Automotive Moulding Co., once remarked, "I felt like a kid in wonderland." The Springdale information is shown in Exhibit 3.7.

Although Branch Day's pricing of $133 per share is higher than the others, management selects Castle Stone & Co. as the investment banker. The firm's selling point is its experience with publishing concerns. In concert with its new financial adviser, Springdale commences the preparation of an offering prospectus for its shares.

Step 2: Preparing the Prospectus The prospectus is the principal disclosure statement for Springdale's financing. Like most such documents, this prospectus is going to be lengthy—probably 90 to 100 pages including audited financial data. Ensuring that the prospectus contains accurate and adequate information requires the joint efforts of a large team of professionals. (See Exhibit 3.8.)

EXHIBIT 3.8 Springdale Publishing Company—Initial Public Offering Prospectus Preparation Team

From Springdale

- Various Springdale executives, including finance, legal, accounting, and operations personnel.
- Springdale's outside legal counsel.
- Springdale's independent accounting firm.

From Castle Stone

- Three to five investment bankers, with some experience in publishing companies.
- Castle Stone's outside counsel.
- An outside publishing expert.

EXHIBIT 3.9   Springdale Publishing Company—Initial Public Offering Prospectus

Table of Contents

Prospectus Summary
Certain Risk Factors
Use of Proceeds
Capitalization
Selected Consolidated Financial Data
Management's Discussion and Analysis of Financial Condition and Results of Operation
Business Description
   Overview
   Product Line
   Research and Development
   Distribution and Significant Customers
   Marketing and Customer Support
   Manufacturing and Suppliers
   Competition
   Trademarks
   Litigation
   Personnel
   Properties
Management
Principal Stockholders
Underwriting of the Common Stock
Legal Opinions
Consolidated Financial Statements

Working off prospectus models from previous publishing deals, the team puts in long hours constructing a document that describes fully the Company and the securities being offered. Most of the descriptive drafting is done by Springdale's chief financial officer, two or three junior bankers, and senior associates from the law firms. Financial data is provided by the Company and its independent accountants. The accountants also check the veracity of Springdale's operating statistics, such as magazine titles, numbers of subscribers, and volumes of ad pages. All the prospectus language corresponds to the dry legal style that is *de rigueur* for SEC documents; as a result, the team has a tough time putting a good marketing spin in the document. Springdale's prospectus outline is representative of an initial public offering and contains the sections required by the SEC and outlined in Exhibit 3.9.

As Exhibit 3.9 indicates, the majority of the prospectus is descriptive, relaying facts to the investor, who then forms an opinion from this data and related information, such as industry conditions, comparable stock prices, and general economic expectations. A full description of a large business runs into hundreds of pages but Springdale, like most companies, doesn't provide too much data for competitive reasons, so the prospectus authors judge what's important from an investor's standpoint and what's not, provided that the SEC's requirements are addressed.

Springdale's executives, bankers, and attorneys quickly form a consensus on which facts should be included to inform investors, but certain disclosure items become a topic of debate. Subscriber cancellation statistics and advertiser renewal rates head the list. Are they necessary? Do they make a meaningful difference in the investor's decision process? Due diligence reveals substantial volatility in subscriber cancellations and Castle Stone's lawyers insist on disclosure. Despite management protests, the lawyers win the argument through their usual tactic of casting the specter of future litigation over the deal.

As the drafting continues in stops and starts, the investment banker continues the investigation of Springdale's business. The bankers collect and analyze financial and operating data, question Springdale's management, interview its lawyers and accountants, and visit selected operating sites. Supplementing this due diligence is a wealth of outside data developed by Castle Stone regarding the magazine publishing industry and related businesses. As the due diligence process unfolds, the bankers obtain a thorough understanding of Springdale's business from a financial point of view and they develop a mental list of the Company's strengths and weaknesses. Two of the bankers worked on previous publishing company financings and they bring industry comparisons into their evaluation efforts. After several weeks, Castle Stone concludes that its first impressions of Springdale's business were accurate. The bank's underwriting committee authorizes the firm to continue with the transaction.

Most of the legal team participates in the prospectus drafting, but two lawyers concentrate on legal due diligence. This task begins with a review of Springdale's legal status as a corporation. It then proceeds to a review of the Company's bylaws and all minutes of meetings of shareholders and directors to determine if they were conducted appropriately. Books and records relating to share ownership and voting control are studied. Other legal due diligence for Springdale consists of a review of its trademarks, significant contracts, litigation, leases, and other relevant corporate issues. The SEC mandates disclosure on many such items, and the attorneys make special note to publicize the details of an important lease and a significant lawsuit.

With the drafting nearly complete, the Company's chief financial officer and the investment bankers renew their request to eliminate the "Certain Risk Factors" section from the prospectus. The section attaches a speculative element to the offering, lowering the price and making the marketing effort more difficult. Undue risk isn't the case, in their opinion, since Springdale is a strong company with a good track record. A "Certain Risk Factors" section, therefore, is inappropriate. Springdale is more established than most first-time issuers, but the lawyers resist the notion of dropping the section, maintaining that Springdale is untested as a public company and lacks the resources of larger publishers. The description of risks stays in the document, but the lawyers water down the section's warnings.

In my experience, the "Certain Risk Factors" section of a prospectus hides the real truth while covering the issuer's backside from legal liability. These sections are chock-full of generalities, yet they largely ignore the specific risks of an issuer's individual business. Explicit concerns are papered over with incomprehensible financial and legal jargon. Exhibit 3.10 provides examples of risks described in IPO prospectuses, against my translation in plain English. As the exhibit indicates, SEC risk disclosure is "disclosure" in name only. Security analysts must diligently make their own evaluations.

Springdale's IPO prospectus outlines 20 risks, which is slightly below average for an IPO. Most contain 25 to 30 risks, of which three-quarters are boilerplate items found in every IPO prospectus. The first-place award for most risk factors in my experience goes to the Blackstone Group deal, which had 35 pages describing

EXHIBIT 3.10 Initial Public Offerings—Selected "Risk Factors" Language

Risk Factors from Actual IPOs	Author's Translation
Limited Operating History The Company commenced operations in March 2007 and has a limited operating history upon which investors may evaluate the Company's performance.	This boilerplate means the issuer is a start-up operation which is highly speculative. The deal rightfully should be sold only to sophisticated venture capital firms.
Recent Losses The Company has incurred significant operating losses to date and there can be no assurance that the Company will be profitable in the future.	Boilerplate. The Company is a speculative operation; it's selling stock without a decent operating history.
Competition: Ease of Entry The Company's industry is intensely competitive. There are many well-established competitors with greater resources than this issuer.	This generality is contained in 95 percent of prospectuses. Most documents fail to specify those factors that insure the issuer's survival. Few outline the select competitors that can destroy the issuer's business. For example, in June 2006 Verizon, the major phone company, announced it was contesting an important patent of Vonage Holdings, the upstart Internet phone operator. Within two weeks, Vonage's stock fell 60 percent.
Rapid Expansion The Company intends to expand rapidly. There can be no assurance that the Company will be able to achieve its goals.	There are no guarantees, so the boilerplate states the obvious. Incredibly, this passes for disclosure in today's marketplace.
Reliance on Major Clients A significant portion of the Company revenues will be derived from relatively few clients.	If the Company loses a major customer, it will go broke. How does an investor gauge the strength of these relationships? The prospectus remains silent on this matter.
Risks Associated with Acquisitions The Company intends to pursue strategic acquisitions to pursue growth. Acquisitions involve a number of special risks, including . . .	The Company may roll the dice on a large acquisition. You've been given fair warning.
Reliance of Key Personnel The Company is dependent to a large extent upon the efforts of a few senior management personnel, including . . .	The Company has no management depth. Investors are betting on one or two individuals.
Reliability of Technology The Company may not be successful in anticipating technological change or in developing new technology on a timely basis.	The Company is successful in high-tech now, but it's not sure how long the success can last. Time for the owners to cash out!

(Continued)

EXHIBIT 3.10   (*Continued*)

Risk Factors from Actual IPOs	Author's Translation
Pro Forma Deficit to Fixed Charges The Company had a deficit of earnings to fixed charges last year.	The Company is having trouble servicing its debts. Equity is needed to strengthen the balance sheet.
Concentration of Product Line The Company's revenues are almost entirely dependent upon sales of one product.	If the market changes in this product, the Company will fail.
Patent May Not Protect Our Technology We rely on trade secrets rather than publicly filed patents.	Management is unsure of the proprietary nature of its technology, or is worried that competitors can copy it without penalty.
Government Regulation The regulatory environment is subject to change, which could adversely affect the Company.	This is a popular boilerplate warning. Few specifics are offered to investors.
Amortization of Intangible Assets Approximately 70 percent of the Company's assets consist of goodwill arising from acquisitions.	The issuer is alerting you to the fact that you're paying for thin air, rather than hard assets like inventory, plant, and equipment.
Dilution After giving effect to this offering, the new investors will experience substantial dilution in the net tangible book value of their shares.	The insiders and venture firms which founded the company paid $3 per share two years ago. You, the public investor, are paying $20 for shares that will have a tangible book value of $4. You must hope that earnings growth continues for a long time, because there's a lot of room between $4 and $20.
Anti-Takeover Provisions The Company's bylaws make it difficult for a third party to acquire the Company (i.e., without management permission).	Even though the IPO is a hot issue, management disenfranchises stockholders by limiting their voice in takeover matters. This arrangement is universal in new IPOs.
Other Common Provisions Absence of prior market for common stock. Shares eligible for future sale. Potential conflicts of interest (i.e., between management and investors). Possible volatility of stock price. Possible need for additional financing. Absence of dividends.	Typical boilerplate that states the obvious for new and untested issues.

63 separate risks. This surplus of caution obscured Blackstone's key survival issues, making the investor's analysis more difficult. Blackstone's stock dropped 50 percent within six months of the IPO.

Along with numerous exhibits that the public never sees, the completed Springdale prospectus is sent to the SEC's Washington-based corporate finance department for review. At the same time, the offering is forwarded to the NASDAQ, which must approve Springdale's share listing on its electronic stock market. The deal is placed in the queue at SEC headquarters and Springdale's attorneys are told to expect an SEC response within four weeks. During the first week, an SEC corporate finance analyst is assigned to the proposed transaction. Trained to look for possible omissions or misstatements in the prospectus, he has available to assist him a variety of in-house experts and databanks.

Because of the experience of the Springdale team and the solid operating history of the Company, the analyst finds only a few items requiring further clarification. Consulting with his colleagues, he sends the SEC's comments in a letter, which is forwarded to the Company's attorneys. Although the letter covers a number of disclosure items, the attorneys review only a few comments in an actual conversation with the SEC analyst. Specifically, these areas cover additional information on annual subscriber cancellation rates, year-to-year ad page growth, and long-term distribution contracts. The SEC also objects to several exaggerations of the Company's future prospects in the document.

For a first offering, the SEC's suggestions on the Springdale document were less than average. After a discussion of the SEC's exact requirements, Springdale's team redrafts accordingly and sends the prospectus to the SEC for its final approval. The cover page of this document appears as Exhibit 3.11.

Step 3: The Marketing Process   Confident that the prospectus (or registration statement) will receive the SEC's green light, the investment bankers commence their marketing effort in earnest. Castle Stone orders copies of the preliminary prospectus to be e-mailed to hundreds of clients who have an interest in the transaction and prints thousands of hard copies to be mailed to clients. The bankers write a two-page crib sheet for retail brokers and institutional salesmen, outlining the principal attractions of Springdale and justifying the proposed asking price of the shares. For large institutions' clients, the bankers schedule a series of meetings in key investment centers—New York, Boston, Chicago, Minneapolis, San Francisco, and London—where management gives slide show presentations, takes investors' questions, and provides the information to the public on the Internet and over dial-in calls. Institutions with a keen interest and a deep pocket receive individual one-on-one discussions with Springdale management before and after the road show presentations.

A key part of the marketing effort is generating enthusiasm among Castle Stone's sales force. Springdale's management visits the New York offices of Castle Stone twice to charge up the sales force, and the firm's sales manager reminds salesmen of two key facts: In-house allotments are large and IPO commissions are 20 times the size of normal order commissions. As the road show meetings go on, the sales force is pumped up and sings the praises of Springdale Publishing.

During these marketing sessions, analysts and investors focus on the Company's growth prospects. Few look at the balance sheet or object to paying 3.5 times book value. With many questions directed at projections (which are unavailable in the

PRELIMINARY PROSPECTUS DATED APRIL 10, 2009
1,900,000 Shares

Springdale Publishing Company
Common Stock

All the shares offered hereby are being issued and sold by Springdale Publishing Company (the "Company"). Prior to the Offering, there has been no public market for the Common Stock. See "Underwriting" for information relating to the factors considered in determining the initial public offering price. The shares of Common Stock have been approved for quotation on the Nasdaq National Market under the symbol "SDPC." The expected offering price is $130 to $140 per share.

See "Risk Factors" beginning on page 10 of this Prospectus for a discussion of risk factors that should be considered by prospective purchasers of the shares of Common Stock offered hereby.

THESE SECURITIES HAVE NOT BEEN APPROVED OR DISAPPROVED
BY THE SECURITIES AND EXCHANGE COMMISSION OR
ANY STATE SECURITIES COMMISSION NOR HAS THE SECURITIES
AND EXCHANGE COMMISSION OR ANY STATE SECURITIES
COMMISSION PASSED UPON THE ACCURACY OR ADEQUACY
OF THIS PROSPECTUS. ANY REPRESENTATION TO THE
CONTRARY IS A CRIMINAL OFFENSE.

	Price to Public	Underwriting Discounts and Commissions (1)	Proceeds to Company (2)
Per Share			
Total (3)			

(1) The Company has agreed to indemnify the U.S. Underwriters and the Managers against certain liabilities, including liabilities under the Securities Act of 1933, as amended. See "Underwriting."

(2) Before deducting estimated expenses of $1,300,000, all of which will be paid by the Company.

(3) The Company has granted the U.S. Underwriters and the Managers a 30-day option to purchase up to an additional 250,000 shares of Common Stock on the same terms as set forth above solely to cover over-allotments, if any. See "Underwriting." If all such shares are purchased, the total Price to Public, Underwriting Discounts and Commissions, and Proceeds to Company will be $ _____, $ _____, and $ _____, respectively. See "Underwriting."

The shares of Common Stock are being offered by the several U.S. Underwriters and the several Managers named herein, subject to prior sale, when, as and if received and accepted by them and subject to certain conditions. It is expected that certificates for shares of Common Stock will be available for delivery on or about April _____, 2009 at the offices of Castle Stone & Co., 700 Wall Street, New York, New York 10001.

Castle Stone & Co.

EXHIBIT 3.11   Springdale Publishing Company Prospectus

EXHIBIT 3.12 Springdale Publishing Company
Initial Public Offering of 2 Million
Shares—Investment Banker's Order Book

Volume of Buy Orders in Shares	Maximum Price Tolerance per Share
1,800,000	$135
2,500,000	133
4,000,000	130
5,000,000	128
6,000,000	125
5,500,000	123
7,000,000	120

widely distributed prospectus), Springdale managers respond to questions like "Will you earn $8.50 this year?" with vague answers like "Maybe," or "There's a good chance of this." Behind closed doors, bankers and managers can nod and wink to institutions, but truly substantive information must be publicly released.

Fortunately, the stock market climbs steadily during the road show, and investors are inclined to buy. The Company has a good story to tell and the preliminary price talk is in line with similar publishing stocks. As a result, Castle Stone receives numerous orders for Springdale shares over the two-week marketing period. By the end of the road show, Castle Stone's order book appears solid, as shown in Exhibit 3.12.

Like any seller of merchandise, Castle Stone receives more orders as the offering price decreases. The book stands at 7 million shares @ $120, versus 1.8 million shares @ $135.

Step 4: Pricing the Deal   With clearances from the SEC and the NASDAQ on the registration statement, Castle Stone is ready to underwrite and sell Springdale's shares.

As the firm's syndicate manager examines the order book, he indicates a preference for a $128 offering price. At this level, demand is 5 million shares, even though Springdale is selling only 2 million shares. This smaller amount appears to be fully saleable a $133 per share. Like most investment banks, however, Castle Stone prefers to sell a deal at the lower price where the shares are heavily oversubscribed. Although this practice tends to shortchange corporate issuers, it protects the bank in several ways. First, sensing a popular offering, many of Castle Stone's clients goose up their orders in anticipation of Castle Stone allotting them 50 percent or less of their original request. If the firm filled all orders completely, thousands of shares would be dumped into the market, leaving the underwriters with the moral obligation to support the share price by purchasing the excess supply. With clients playing games, the syndicate manager is unsure of the deal's true demand and he uses an IPO rule of thumb which dictates that his order book should be 2 to 2.5 times the size of the offering. Two and one-half times 2 million is 5 million shares.

Second, the bank has substantial flexibility in setting the IPO price, so it can almost guarantee a short-term capital gain to the first investors. Accordingly, Castle Stone has an incentive to price the shares slightly below the market value. By allocating shares carefully, the firm rewards favored institutional clients that do a lot of commission business with the firm. Rubicon Technology's 2007 IPO, for example, was priced at $14. After the first day of trading, the stock price was $17.50. Investors who bought the offering before the first trade were 25 percent ahead of the game.

As Castle Stone's syndicate managers and bankers reveal their $128 pricing suggestion to Springdale, they concurrently recruit a group of securities firms to participate in underwriting the deal. The 5 to 10 firms that choose to act as co-underwriters receive small allotments of Springdale shares to sell (along with a small underwriting fee) in exchange for bearing the risk that the deal falls apart shortly after its pricing. The underwriting group (or syndicate) has a life of one month and assumes the moral responsibility for maintaining the market for Springdale shares by repurchasing shares that are offered in the market below the public offering price. Records are kept of institutions that buy Springdale shares only to dump them on the syndicate later. Given that Castle Stone has orders for 5 million shares and only 2 million are available, the likelihood of a price collapse in Springdale's shares is remote. Even then, the syndicate may only support the price for a few days, limiting losses.

Listening to the banker say that "A deal that goes up in price is a good deal, because everyone makes money," Springdale agrees to the $128 price. After brokerage commissions, underwriting fees, and expenses, this figure nets out to $119 per share. A final prospectus, with the price now included, is e-mailed to the SEC that same day. With little new information to evaluate—and no authority to judge the fairness of the designated price—the SEC's analyst rubber-stamps the deal, and the Company releases the offering for sale the next day. As the investors remit their money to Castle Stone for distribution to Springdale, the initial public offering process ends and the aftermarket trading begins. Exhibit 3.13 illustrates the distribution of Springdale's initial public offering.

Step 5: Springdale Shares in the Aftermarket With excess demand built into the market, the bidding for Springdale's shares climbs rapidly to $142 per share—representing an 11 percent gain in two days for the lucky institutions that received allotments from Castle Stone and other underwriters. Despite telling the underwriters' salesmen that they intended to hold the shares as long-term investments, many institutions succumb to the temptation to make a quick profit by flipping the shares to others at the higher price. Over the first two days of trading, one million Springdale shares change hands, and many of the trading commissions so generated go into Castle Stone's accounts. A few weeks later, trading in Springdale stock settles down to 20,000 shares per day. Several sell-side analysts find the company to be an interesting growth story and decide to write research reports. At the same time, newsletters, stock information services, and business periodicals place Springdale in their respective databases, and the SEC and NASD establish the Company's reporting schedules. In three months, Springdale's first quarterly statement is due at SEC headquarters. The stock gradually becomes a seasoned issue.

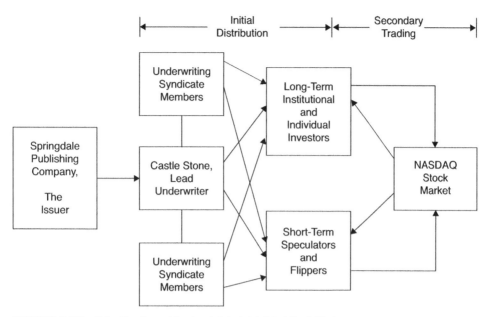

EXHIBIT 3.13 Distribution of Springdale's Initial Public Offering

With the issue becoming seasoned in the aftermarket, the SEC and NASDAQ settle down to monitoring the stock's trading rhythm and the Company's ongoing developments. Having recently finished an IPO, the stock remains susceptible to being touted by professional investors or traders, who have an interest in spreading rumors because they have either a long or short position in the shares. Regulators observe trading patterns primarily via computer. They try and guard against shrewd traders who *paint the tape* of Springdale's shares by buying and selling the stock among themselves in order to show artificial activity, which might lure momentum investors. They look for an increase in volume prior to corporate press releases, which is evidence of insider-derived activity. And they examine purchases by large buyers to see that no disclosure guidelines are violated by those accumulating large positions in the stock.

SUMMARY

The SEC, FINRA, class action law firms, and state attorney generals govern the relations between the issuers, security markets, and investors. Of critical importance to maintaining the fairness of markets is ensuring that the prospective purchaser of a security receives an accurate and adequate amount of information on which to make a sensible judgment. The Securities and Exchange Commission, an agency of the U.S. government, has the primary responsibility of ensuring that the appropriate disclosure takes place, and the United States has the most successful disclosure program in the world. The SEC also attempts to promote honest and orderly behavior in the marketing, buying, and selling of stocks among the various stock exchanges and numerous securities firms. Due to its small size relative to the vastness of the markets, the SEC delegates most of its supervision function to a self-regulatory scheme, whereby the issuers, exchanges, and securities firms try to prevent themselves and others from engaging in illegal and unethical behavior. Class action law firms and state attorney generals also place pressure on the major players to act responsibly. While the incidence of abuses is less in the United States than in other markets, the self-regulatory scheme has shown itself to be lacking in many respects and governments are looking at alternative schemes. The security analyst is thus advised of the need to redouble his investigatory efforts.

CHAPTER 4

Other Sources of Information

This chapter reviews the information sources that provide the practitioner with the raw material for his analysis. It describes the strengths and weaknesses of the sources.

The SEC mandates adequate and accurate disclosure by public corporations, but SEC reports are not the only source of information. The interpretation of corporate data is dependent on the concurrent analysis of many disparate facts and opinions. Interestingly, the sources of original information are surprisingly few. They consist, on the one hand, of official reports and press releases of the issuer, same-industry firms, and related enterprises, together with the occasional corporate meeting for investors and management to discuss matters. On the other hand are the reports of general business conditions provided by trade associations, trade journals, consulting firms, state and federal governments, and banks and securities firms. All of this data is processed by organizations and individuals who purport to be recorders and analysts of the issuer's industry, some of whom have an interest in advising on investments in such companies.

With so many experts analyzing the same data, the occasional need for hands-on investigative work by the securities analyst becomes apparent. In the case of Springdale in the previous chapter, field trips to publishing representatives, magazine distributors, printers, and retailers are a necessary part of the security analyst's job. The analyst supplements these hands-on activities by consulting with independent experts who have been recruited by the analyst himself or made available through one of the expert consultation services catering to the investment community.

THE BUSINESS MEDIA

The United States is a media-oriented society, and the media—Internet, TV, newspapers, magazines, movies, radio, and other forms of communication—has a sizable impact on business. This influence naturally extends to general stock price levels and to individual business values. Unlike official corporate reports and press releases, the material published by the media is unregulated by the SEC or the stock exchanges, so the public is exposed to whatever news, opinion, or spin that the media feels is appropriate to disseminate. The majority of institutional investors who dominate the stock market pursue a rational approach to investment decisions, but the executives devising these strategies are human beings: They surf the Internet, read the newspapers, and watch television like everyone else. Their minds respond to media interpretation of everyday events, and the executives enter this data into the mass of information used to justify a particular portfolio move.

For the general public, which still represents an important source of trading activity, the part played by the financial media is more pronounced. Only a small percentage of individual investors ever read an official SEC prospectus, because they are written in a way that discourages the average person. Nor do most individuals refer to other original sources of corporate, industry, or macroeconomic information, even though much is quickly available through the Internet. Relatively few have access to or bother to consult independent financial services such as Standard & Poor's, Moody's, or Value Line, and most avoid buying detailed research reports online because of the associated costs. On some occasions, a stockbroker directs an individual client to an in-house research report, but this action tends to be the exception rather than the rule. Even the typical stockbroker (and many an institutional equity salesman) relies heavily on the Internet and business media for corporate news updates and promising investment ideas. The Internet is full of personal finance sites that offer summary historical information on public companies, provide sell-side analyst earnings projections, and compute a number of company-specific financial ratios. Complementing these sites are investment blogs and chat rooms that offer opinions and information on specific companies. Taken as a whole, free Internet sites are the principal data source for individual investors.

Only a handful of media sources present company-specific news with the kind of depth that contributes to a serious evaluation. Television and radio, for example, generally limit their daily financial coverage to a few items on overall business conditions and whether the stock market went up or down that particular day. Several cable TV channels specialize in business and personal investment. They focus on individual companies from time to time, but in the grand tradition of television, the presentation is simplified to such an extent that its analytical value is worthless.

Business magazines with a truly wide circulation are few in number. *Fortune*, *BusinessWeek*, *Forbes*, and *Barron's* lead this media group. The latter two magazines devote a lot of space to analyzing individual companies and market trends, while *Fortune*, *BusinessWeek*, and others focus on stories of overall business interest, which often include general reviews of companies and industries. Company-specific news articles in business magazines tend to be brief, perhaps one to three pages of text, with most of the subject matter stripped of the technicalities that are necessary for an informed judgment. Written for the busy executive, these articles provide an interesting piece of information or twist of fact, thereby inviting the executive to explore the company further if he so desires.

The daily business press is dominated by the *Wall Street Journal*, which has a wide following among practitioners. Many businesspeople rely on the *Journal* for day-to-day information concerning business conditions and for a reliable interpretation of what is going on. Of the general-interest daily papers, only the *New York Times* makes a serious effort at publishing a business section. Most dailies consider business and finance to be boring and overly complex, and thus unsuitable for a general newspaper, despite the fact that the economic well-being of many Americans is tied to the securities markets. As a result, the business sections of many newspapers are filled with meaningless filler from the Dow Jones tape, AP wires, and corporate press releases, items that cost little or nothing for the newspaper to produce. Typical business reporting for a local paper includes executive promotions, corporate earnings reports, stock market performance statistics, and share price quotes.

The lack of resources dedicated to business reporting means that many news items generated by corporations, public relations firms, and stock promoters go unchallenged. A critical review of this material requires the media to provide time, money, and training to investigative reporters. Unfortunately, the low priority given to business by media sources signifies few dollars to such an effort, and the majority of business reporters lack extensive backgrounds in economics or finance. Even at the *Wall Street Journal*, the doyenne of U.S. business reporting, less than one-third of the reporters have degrees in business or economics. The situation is similar at *Forbes*, one of the better business magazines. Under pressure to produce interesting copy in a short time, business reporters are targets for the vast publicity machines surrounding the securities markets, and many hundreds of thousands of dollars are spent by interested parties in trying to garner legitimate publicity for a favored stock.

Besides the imprimatur of respectability attached to a CNBC report or a *Wall Street Journal* article, the best thing about such stories, if favorable, is that their content is unscreened by the SEC. Furthermore, corporate executives and their spin doctors are under no legal obligation to talk to the media. In order to gain access, business reporters, particularly those on television, lob softball questions at executives and essentially allow them unfettered promotional time. Exaggerations, omissions of fact, and misstatements sometimes slip through, even when an able reporter covers the story. The analyst has to balance such reporting against his own assessment of the facts.

THE FREE INTERNET

If a news article or TV show stirs an interest in a particular stock, the investor's next stop is the Internet. Many investment and personal finance sites provide descriptive and financial data on thousands of issuers at no charge, with varying levels of editorial comment included. Most offer statistical histories of the issuer's stock price and trading volume, and a number furnish financial and valuation ratios on the issuer and its industry. A few provide a summary of Wall Street projections of sales and earnings for the issuer.

For the analytically minded investor, the Internet provides immediate access at no charge to web sites operated by issuers themselves and to SEC web sites with their trove of issuer information. Most of this content is a rendition of fact with little interpretive weight behind the data. There are also blogs and chat rooms on individual stocks, where the content ranges from ridiculous rumors to sophisticated commentary. Many sites include some analysis as well as unvarnished opinions of an issuer, its strategy, or its management.

THE FEE-FOR-SERVICE INTERNET

Should an investor want to do more research on a security than the free Internet provides, there are numerous sites that offer advanced macroeconomic, capital market, industry, and individual company data, all of which is useful in preparing a business evaluation. The quality of the information varies considerably, as does the pricing. Asking other investors for recommendations on reasonable providers is a good way to begin, and a fair portion of this content is available through public libraries (via Internet connections) or in their hard-copy reference departments.

In addition to fee-for-information sites, many equity research firms offer their product over the Internet. For the most part, these providers are second-tier firms, since large sell-side organizations, such as Goldman Sachs and Bank of America, reserve their research reports for institutional clients.

The research firms offer advice on the future price of a security or the next movement in the market. Their evaluation of a stock has a wide range. It can be as thorough as the best equity analyst's report or as simple as a broker's inside scoop, with most firms falling in between. How good is the advice contained in these reports? The studies that have been done suggest that picking stocks at random is better than selecting equities based on research firms' recommendations. Many firms dispute such claims, but they offer little hard evidence to the contrary.

With most research providers having a mixed record, they are unable to charge heavily for their services. The result is that many cannot afford the staff time needed to research carefully the investment values of securities. For example, Value Line, which provides a combination corporation manual/advisory newsletter, is one of the more respectable organizations in this field, yet for cost reasons it prohibits its analysts from making field trips to see companies and managements. How insightful can research be without an occasional out-of-office visit?

TRADE ASSOCIATIONS, CONSULTING FIRMS, GOVERNMENT PUBLICATIONS, AND FINANCIAL ORGANIZATIONS

In the selection of common stocks, the analyst must combine his own specialized financial analysis with an effort to evaluate the effects of broader industry, social, political, and economic factors on a particular company's fortunes. For example, the ability of a particular clothing design firm to increase sales in an otherwise soft season for women's apparel may be an indicator of future fashion trends. A social and political drive to reduce smoking could impact the earnings prospects of a cigarette firm. An anticipated decline in interest rates could boost revenue for home builders. An appraisal of the larger factors is facilitated by the use of publications and web sites produced by trade associations, consulting firms, governments, and financial organizations. Such data is available through the Internet, subscriptions, libraries, and data services.

CREDIT RATING AGENCIES

In addition to publishing corporation manuals and stock guides, Standard & Poor's, Moody's, and other credit rating agencies each provide services that place corporate bonds into a rating system composed of various grades purporting to show an issuer's ability to repay its debts. Perhaps most notable are the two categories into which ratings are segregated—*investment-grade bonds* and *junk bonds* (i.e., below investment grade). Issuers pay a fee to these firms in order to obtain bond ratings, which are of assistance in the bond marketing process. Most public-issue ratings are distributed widely, but they attract attention only in the financial trade press or in the publications of the rating agencies.

Like most investment analysts, rating agencies are outsiders looking in. They rely heavily on management supplying them with information and they make little or no attempt to verify the raw data (including the audited numbers). One S&P spokesman, Glen Goldberg, warned investors as much by saying, "Rating agencies are not auditors, regulators, or police officers of issuer conduct." The agencies upgrade ratings on a regular basis.

Bond rating analysts are full-fledged members of the security analyst profession and their work is nearly identical to that of practitioners functioning as stock pickers. Although several firms assign grades to equities, this practice hasn't caught on with the investor community. There is no gold standard for equity ratings such as Standard & Poor's and Moody's, which together control 90 percent of the market for bond ratings. Both firms have expanded their offerings in the equity research area.

SECURITIES FIRM RESEARCH

Professional analysts read each other's reports, particularly those published by sell-side analysts. In fact, few practitioners write an investment recommendation before consulting what other analysts say about a company or an industry. Brokerage firms attempt to limit the circulation of their analysts' reports to paying clients, but inevitably such research is distributed within the financial community. It is important for both buy- and sell-side analysts to recognize the spin that others place on a given opportunity. Reading a competitor's report is of great importance to an analyst covering a large capitalization stock. Twenty or more sell-side analysts, each considering more or less the same raw information, already have opinions, so there's a substantial amount of background data available. For a small-cap stock, where the coverage is minimal or infrequent, the consensus opinion has less influence on the share price, and correspondingly, any fresh analysis of the stock places less weight on competing views.

As noted earlier, brokerage research reports are a good resource. They contain basic information and provide financial projections, along with a reasonably cogent rationale for buying or selling a specific stock. The industry knowledge displayed in these reports is generally impressive, and the authors demonstrate, in many cases, a keen understanding of the potential pitfalls awaiting a business. Nevertheless, in reading this material, the serious research consumer must necessarily be aware of the sell-side analyst's nettlesome proclivities: (1) to generate commissions for his employer; (2) to protect his employer's investment banking business by withholding sell recommendations; (3) to cover his backside with vague recommendations that cannot be definitively linked to a result; and (4) to avoid being left alone, especially when the consensus is recommending something else. Such advice, to say the least, is hardly disinterested, but the financial review can be insightful and semi-objective.

No matter, much of the sell-side research is said today and forgotten tomorrow. The part that remains a permanent record is often too hedged with reservations to pin down the analyst's record in picking winners. Thus, as a source of advice concerning equities, sell-side research reports have obvious limitations. As a source of information on how others approach an analysis and what the market is thinking, the literature is a useful tool for one's own investigation.

NEWSWIRES

Much of the daily business news originates on one of the newswires. The leading wire service, the Dow Jones, is operated by the same company that publishes the *Wall Street Journal* and *Barron's*. Other important services are Bloomberg and Reuters. Originally, such news was disseminated on rolls of narrow paper running through a clattering machine (hence the name *ticker tape*), but such services now operate over the Internet, distributing news through millions of computer terminals. Virtually every brokerage firm, institutional investor, and substantial individual investor has access, and a visit to a modern-day brokerage firm reveals a sea of computer screens flashing newsworthy items. In addition to financial professionals, viewers include every significant media outlet, public relations firm, and government or trade organization having to do with business.

Much of what the wires present as news is routine corporate press releases on earnings, financings, or similar developments, but they also cover news stories having a broader scope that influence the markets in general. All of this is accomplished in a crisp, abbreviated writing style that enables the service to alert its subscribers to dozens of fresh items on a minute-to-minute basis. In general, the editorial staffs publish news in a no-nonsense manner with little editorial spin, although they quote the opinions of selected market players on a regular basis.

In addition to covering all kinds of news relevant to business, the wires are critical sources of real-time market information, covering a huge expanse of price and volume data in any number of domestic and foreign stock, bond, currency, and commodity markets. The speed and accuracy with which they work in this regard is remarkable, and it has made them an indispensable part of the speculative trader's toolbox. For the security analyst, who must necessarily take a longer view, the ticker is of less use, since the deliberate search for value requires an extended investigation rather than a minute-to-minute historical record.

INDEPENDENT EXPERT SERVICES

In conducting research on a business and its industry, practitioners tend to develop networks of individuals who have experience within the sector and who have the ability to consult with them from time to time. As a means to complement these informal arrangements, a number of firms offer investment funds and acquisitive corporations extensive expert networks, whereby individuals with specific knowledge can be hired for an hour or two to provide fast access to expertise that is relevant and essential to their research needs.

These services categorize each individual by country, industry, company, and discipline, and they allow their clients, through the Internet, to identify experts, review qualifications, and set up consultation times. This service provides another resource to security analysts and enables them to better understand the companies they evaluate. Private equity firms, institutional lenders, and corporate acquirers are active users of independent experts.

SUMMARY

The key to any successful business evaluation is information. Information is the lifeblood of the capital markets, and the ability to gather and analyze data correctly is highly prized in the investment business. After a practitioner has made the decision to evaluate a particular company, the foundation of his study is the information contained in the issuer's filings with the SEC. Supporting this work is usually a comparative analysis of the business and operating performance of similar firms, as derived from their respective SEC documents. With this effort as a base, he consults numerous sources of information that complement the filings. Some of these sources provide original data, while others offer news, interpretations, opinions, or compilations of fact.

Sources of Information
- SEC filings.
- Corporate-sponsored information and management.
- Contacts within an industry.
- The Internet.
- Business media, such as magazines, newspapers, and television.
- Corporation manuals, stock guides, and advisory newsletters.
- Trade associations, consulting firms, government publications, and financial organizations.
- Credit rating companies.
- Securities firm research reports.
- Newswires.
- Independent expert services.

With multiple resources at hand, the analyst needs to pick and choose his sources carefully, so as to avoid being inundated with data. Zeroing in on the right information is an important skill for the novice analyst to develop.

Performing the Analysis and Writing the Research Report

Starting the Analysis

Chapter 5 describes the format that is used to perform a business evaluation. A written report is prepared by the analyst, who examines the prospects of a stock issuer in a methodical, top-down manner. The process is copied by other disciplines such as private equity, business appraisal, and corporate development.

Based on the material covered in the first few chapters, we know the pricing of businesses is basically a rational process. Most prices reflect the reasoned judgment of hundreds—perhaps thousands—of seasoned professionals who have access to substantial information regarding economic expectations, capital markets, industrial performance, firm-specific operations, and comparable company valuations. This rational process is frequently tempered by emotional and speculative excesses, which affect individual securities as well as general pricing levels. Contributing to these occasional excesses are the conscious actions of a revolving list of sharp players; they seek to profit by directing the analytical process away from the efficient market envisioned by the academic community. Instead, they want to replace studied evaluation with rumors, misstatements, and price manipulations. The resulting misperception of a stock's value can become reality. Injecting a sense of order and fairness into this dynamic marketplace are several regulatory bodies, as well as the state attorney generals and the class action bar.

With this review of the real world in hand, Chapter 5 introduces the structured format of a security analysis. It also emphasizes the discipline needed by the analyst to succeed in this charged environment. After these topics, the chapter outlines the widely accepted top-down approach. Under this method, the consideration of a corporate investment begins with a study of the principal economies in which the corporation operates. If the relevant economy (or economies) appears promising, the analyst proceeds to evaluate the prospects for the capital market in which the corporation's stock trades, the outlook for its industry, and finally, the status of the corporation's financial position and the basis for its earnings potential. A top-down study of Kraft Foods shares, for example, might proceed as shown in Exhibit 5.1.

Using the information gained from his top-down analysis, the practitioner prepares judgments regarding the likely value of Kraft Foods' stock over the intermediate to long term.

Macroeconomic prospects ↓	With most of Kraft Foods' earnings originating in the United States, the analyst inquires about the future health of the U.S. economy.
Capital markets ↓	Will the U.S. stock market increase in price over the long term? Even given strong individual corporate performance, Kraft Foods' stock price is heavily dependent on general market conditions.
Packaged food industry ↓	Demand and pricing trends in the U.S. packaged food industry affect Kraft Foods' operations. Are more competitors entering the business? Are more people opting to use restaurants, instead of cooking at home?
Kraft Foods ■ Business analysis ■ Financial analysis	A thorough analysis of Kraft Foods' business, management, and financial condition is required to predict earnings and value sensibly.

EXHIBIT 5.1 Top-Down Approach for Kraft Foods Shares

THE SECURITY ANALYSIS PROCESS

A competent business evaluation follows a tried-and-true methodology that has changed little over the past 20 years. Each step of the evaluation imposes a discipline on the practitioner, and the structured format prohibits the cutting of corners that might lead to faulty conclusions. The finished product, referred to as a *research report*, *business evaluation report*, or *investment memorandum*, is designed to be user-friendly. Thus, a properly written document is comprehensible not only to the author, but also to other professionals. Buy-side reports produced for in-house consumption are used by the analyst's colleagues (i.e., portfolio managers, private equity managers, and corporate development executives), and they must be concise and easy to read. Sell-side reports, authored by brokerage firm analysts, place even more emphasis on clear writing since these documents receive a far greater distribution than the buy-side or internal corporate product.

The practitioner's challenge, therefore, is twofold. First, he must investigate the specific investment situation in a disciplined way, covering all the requisite intellectual bases; this is the only means to reach an investment decision that is convincing to himself and others. Second, the tone and style of his report must be appealing to fellow professionals. Otherwise, no one will care to listen to his ideas. The successful evaluator is usually one with a cogent writing ability, enabling him to interest readers while getting his point across. And, since most members of his audience lack his industry expertise, the thoughtful analyst explains and simplifies the technicalities and jargon endemic to operating businesses. Complicated investment themes are boiled down to key decision points, and the analyst and his readership can then communicate effectively with each other.

The model research report for a publicly traded equity begins with a short description of the company that has issued the common stock under evaluation and it closes with a summary recommendation. Included in the introductory paragraph are the firm's product lines, its areas of operation, and its annual sales and profits.

EXHIBIT 5.2   Model Research Report

Table of Contents

Section	Topic
1.	Introduction
2.	Macroeconomic Review
3.	Relevant Stock Market Prospects
4.	Review of the Company and Its Business
	Industry and competition
	Existing business
	Future prospects
	Financial summary
5.	Financial Analysis
	Historical evaluation
	Current earnings power estimate
	Review of accounting methods
	Adjustments to historical financial data
6.	Financial Projections
	Listing of principal assumptions
	Projected data
7.	Application of Valuation Methodologies
8.	Recommendation
	Comparison of analyst's valuation to market price of the stock
	Recommended investment decision

A second paragraph might characterize the business according to the analyst's perception of its place in the industry life cycle (e.g., growth company or cash cow) and summarize its three- to five-year historical trends in sales and earnings, along with a prognosis on future prospects. The third paragraph reviews recent significant developments in the company's business (e.g., new product or acquisition), industry (e.g., more competition from imports), or country operations (e.g., recession in Mexico, which accounts for 20 percent of sales). The first section closes with the analyst's summary rationale for his recommended investment decision. For example, *sell* the stock because earnings growth will decline. This introduction encourages the reader to proceed to the body of the report.

A table of contents for a model research report for a publicly traded firm is set forth in Exhibit 5.2. The outline for a business evaluation, private equity investment, or corporate acquisition is quite similar.

MODEL RESEARCH REPORT

Following a brief introduction and the analyst's recommendation, the report closely follows the top-down model. The report begins with an economic analysis, assessing the state of the economy and its likely impact on future stock prices and relevant industry earnings growth. A healthy economy often translates into higher stock values and is usually positive for most industries. For a food company such as Kraft

Foods, a growing U.S. economy means accelerated sales growth, as more people select high-value-added convenience food. For companies operating primarily in the United States, the economic analysis tends to focus on the likely course of the business cycle and on key indicators such as interest rates. The underlying assumption is for long-term growth. For less-developed nations, such as Mexico or Thailand, the economic analysis is more involved since the economies are inherently unstable and pose more risk for the investor. Once the report concludes that the economy supports equity investment, it moves on to a study of the appropriate capital market.

As I have noted earlier, the influence of general market movements on individual stock prices is considerable. Even when the earnings per share of a given stock are advancing quickly, its share price can still decline if broad market indexes perform badly. Likewise, even companies with lousy earnings prospects may see their values rise during bull markets. A thorough research report addresses the important questions: Is the general market going up? down? How does this affect the price of the company under study? Making an accurate prediction of the short- to intermediate-term direction of an equity market is a difficult business, and few people have proven themselves to be adept market timers. Nevertheless, a complete research report presents a view on where the general market appears to be heading. There is little to be gained in absolute terms by buying a good stock in a down market. Inevitably, the stock's price will be dragged down with those of other stocks.

Most institutional managers, however, measure themselves in relative terms against a relevant index. Thus, if the Internet stock index falls 20 percent, and the manager's Internet mutual fund falls only 15 percent, the manager has beaten the index even though fund holders lose money. Analysts who select stocks that perform well on a relative basis are thus valuable commodities on Wall Street.

THE ANALYST'S RESPONSIBILITY

Few investment firms expect the security analyst to be economic forecaster, market timer, industry expert, and company analyst at the same time. The same goes for valuation professionals advising on private equity and corporate acquisition deals. The job would be impossible. Instead, the sections of the model research report are divided among three separate executives: the economist, the market strategist, and the security analyst. See Exhibit 5.3.

EXHIBIT 5.3   Dividing Responsibility for Top-Down Analysis

Economic prospects	An economist assists the analyst by providing a macroeconomic forecast.
Capital markets	The market strategist supplies an opinion on likely market movements.
Industry outlook	The security analyst is responsible for studying the industry and evaluating the company, taking into account economic forecasts.
Company-specific evaluation	A critical analyst function is predicting corporate earnings reliably.

A full-time in-house economist or an outside consulting firm supplies the macro-economic overlay for the analyst's research report. Key variables such as future GNP growth, interest rates, and foreign exchange rates are left out of the analyst's hands. Thus, if the economist predicts sharply higher interest rates, the analyst may have a hard time recommending housing stocks, which have lower earnings in times of high interest rates.

The investment firm's market strategist takes responsibility for defining the market's direction. His view is usually synthesized in a recommended portfolio allocation. If the brokerage house believes the stock market is going up, it recommends a heavy portfolio weighting to common stocks, such as 65 percent stocks, 25 percent bonds, and 10 percent cash. If the firm anticipates a bear market, the suggested stock allocation is smaller, such as 35 percent stocks, 50 percent bonds, and 15 percent cash. For reasons of being prudent and hedging bets, few strategists recommend 100 percent stock weightings (or 100 percent bonds); their record of success is too erratic to justify full commitments.

If the economic study and capital markets forecast are taken out of the analyst's hands, what's left? A lot. Even after these two top-down evaluations are provided, the analyst has considerable work ahead. First, he must present a studied outlook on the industry in which the particular company operates. Not only must the report explain the fundamental factors driving the demand for the industry's products, but it must also keep the reader abreast of significant developments. What new product lines are being introduced? Is the price/cost structure changing? Which competitors are profiting at the expense of others? A thorough grounding in a company's industry is a prerequisite to an individual company analysis, and this is the reason for professional analysts limiting their work to one or two industries. In most reports, the industry discussion is woven through the "Description of the Issuer" (see Exhibit 5.4), since the review of a company's business is best seen through an industry lens.

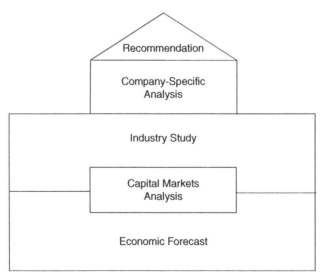

EXHIBIT 5.4 Constructing a Research Report: Important Building Blocks

Few companies are true monopolies; every action they take merits a response from competitors.

By assembling an economic review, a capital markets forecast, and an industry study, the analyst lays the foundation for his business evaluation. These three items are the building blocks for the company analysis, which provides an understanding of the subject business and looks in-depth at the issuer's financial condition and operating results. Of critical importance is determining the sustainability of the issuer's earnings stream as well as reaching a conclusion on the likelihood of future growth. Accomplishing this objective requires the analyst to synthesize his knowledge of the company and his industry into an earnings projection. In deriving this forecast, the company section covers various disciplines, including economics, marketing, business strategy, financial analysis, valuation, and management.

THE CASCADE OF PROJECTIONS

Any corporate earnings forecast is conditional on many variables. The top-down approach seeks to isolate the most important macroeconomic, capital market, and industry elements that affect a company's performance. It then establishes a meaningful predictive relationship between that variable and the company's earnings. For example, every 1 percent increase in U.S. gross national product tends to produce a 1.5 percent rise in cement sales. A cement company with a constant market share expects to see unit sales gains of 4.5 percent if GNP rises 3 percent.

The job of the analyst is to identify the most influential variables out of the hundreds available to him. Optimally, he ties in the relationships with statistical studies such as regressions. Once the connections are made, the economic forecast provides a basis for the capital markets forecast, which influences the industry forecast, and finally, one reaches the individual company level. Exhibit 5.5 illustrates the cascading of forecasts for a home builder.

Developing a chain of forecasts with real predictive ability is quite difficult. Any projection of economic or business indicators is inherently uncertain, so each forecast has a margin of error, which becomes magnified as you move from the top (economy) level to the bottom (company) section. This is particularly apparent with forecasting horizons extending past six months. The accuracy of analysts' forecasts drops dramatically as the period expands.

EXHIBIT 5.5   Cascade of Forecasts: Home Building Company

Top-Down Analysis	Sample Forecast for Home Builder
Economy	GNP will increase 3 percent.
Capital markets	Interest rates will decline.
Industry	Housing starts will increase.
Home building company	Home building company will gain market share, so its sales will rise 15 percent instead of the 10 percent industry average. Steady profit margins signify a 15 percent earnings increase.

EXHIBIT 5.6 Top-Down Analysis, Selected Factors to Study: Coca-Cola

Economy

- GNP growth in the United States.
- Timing of business cycle.
- GNP growth in principal foreign markets of Coca-Cola.
- Relationship between GNP and soft drink consumption in multiple countries.
- Demographics: Young people drink more soft drinks than older people.
- Fashion trends: Are soft drinks being replaced by fruit juices, iced teas, or bottled water?
- U.S. and foreign income tax rates.
- U.S. currency value versus foreign currencies: affects exports and accounting translation of overseas revenues into U.S. dollars.

Capital Markets

- Interest rates: Higher rates impact Coca-Cola financing costs.
- Stock market: Higher share prices could lessen financing costs and spur acquisitions.

Soft Drink Industry

- Demand trends: Is cola consumption rising?
- New products: Is the company keeping up with new products and brand names?
- Competitors: Is the competition expanding production capacity and advertising?
- Government: Will government regulation or legal liability cripple the industry?
- Raw materials: What are the anticipated prices of sugar and corn syrup, two principal raw materials?

Company-Specific

- Causes of past and present profitability.
- Growth expectations.
- Predicted profit margins.
- Product mix and new products.
- Acquisition: Will acquisitions contribute to growth?
- Management changes: Can new management carry out the plan?
- Balance sheet issues: What's leverage going to be? Are share repurchases a possibility?
- Dividend policy.

This inexactitude is understandable when one considers just a few of the top-down variables that influence the average publicly traded company. Consider a soft drink producer such as Coca-Cola, whose earnings are conditional on many factors, as set forth in Exhibit 5.6.

SELECTING STOCKS FOR STUDY: TOP-DOWN VERSUS BOTTOM-UP

In Chapter 2, we covered investment styles that portfolio managers use to select stocks for purchase or sale. Most are predicated on the top-down format. The prospective investor develops a general outlook for the economy and capital market, selects the industries that he expects to prosper within that framework, and focuses on specific companies operating within the chosen industries. As noted, portfolio managers and security analysts find themselves measured in relative terms—that is,

EXHIBIT 5.7   Top-Down versus Bottom-Up

Top-Down	Bottom-Up
Macroeconomy	Screens for relative value on financial ratios
Capital markets	Macroeconomy
Industry	Industry
Company-business analysis	Company-business analysis
Financial analysis	Financial analysis

they perform *relatively* well when their stocks decline 10 percent in price as the market drops 15 percent. Therefore they place greater emphasis on the *bottom-up* approach to identifying good investment opportunities.

With a bottom-up methodology, a portfolio manager selects shares for study by examining key financial ratios which indicate a bargain relative to similar offerings. For example, a common screening technique is investigating all industrial manufacturers that (1) are profitable, (2) record consistent sales growth, and (3) have market price/book value ratios of less than $3.0\times$ (or some equivalent benchmark). A computer search might produce 50 candidates meeting these criteria and representing many manufacturing industries. The portfolio manager then parcels out these investment possibilities to analysts covering the respective industries. Edward Lampert, the prominent hedge fund manager, is a notable bottom-up investor.

Similarly, an analyst covering a group of stocks in the same industry inevitably looks initially for those firms in the group that have a low P/E ratio (or other low valuation benchmark). This could be the sign of a potential bargain, if the consensus opinion is unduly penalizing the stock or underestimating its potential. Thus, the stock may represent a *relatively* good value compared to its peer group. The risk here is that the group's price level is already high. There are always individual issues that appear more attractive in contrast to the inflated value of similar stocks. Upon identifying a specific opportunity, the analyst prepares a top-down report justifying a recommendation.

At the extreme end of the bottom-up style are strict value investors. Although limited in number today, they follow Graham and Dodd's teachings to the letter, and screen for stocks that appear cheap on an intrinsic basis. Walter Schloss, whom Warren Buffett called a "super investor," is a money manager who has adhered to that strategy for decades, returning an average of 6 percent over the S&P 500 return. Sample screening criteria find firms whose market value is less than accounting book value. Usually, bargains in this respect have serious flaws—the company participates in a dead-end industry or has serious financial problems. A thorough top-down analysis is then required to warrant the investment. See Exhibit 5.7.

LIMITED TIME AND RESOURCES

As the partial listing for Coca-Cola in Exhibit 5.6 illustrated, the practitioner is confronted with a vast amount of information from which he can construct an analysis. To avoid being drowned in a sea of facts and statistics, he picks and chooses data that make a meaningful contribution to his report and projections. Likewise, the analyst is responsible for producing reports in real time; he can't afford to study a security forever. In most cases, he provides conclusions based on incomplete information and relies on his judgment and experience to advance opinions.

This information-sifting function varies with the industry. Different industries require different predictive factors. Economic developments expected to influence the cigarette industry do not have the same effect on the chemical business. The same can be said for industry factors at the individual company level. Certain oil industry changes may play a greater role in the performance of Exxon than Shell. Selectivity of information is instrumental to the analyst's job performance.

Obtaining certain information is time consuming and expensive. Similarly, establishing quantitative formulas linking economic indicators, industry variables, and company-specific results can be a long, laborious, and costly task. Many times, such regressions have negligible predictive value, so the time and money go for naught. Professionals recognize this situation and learn to live with imprecise valuations. To preserve the validity of this work in a world of unscientific estimates, analysts rely heavily on the notion of the *margin of safety*.

THE MARGIN OF SAFETY

The margin of safety principle is a linchpin of security analysis, for Graham and Dodd recognized early on that economic and financial forecasts of any kind were inherently uncertain. As a defensive measure, they encouraged analysts to refrain from a purchase recommendation unless the related research report provided a protective cushion between the market's price and the analyst's indicated value. A reasonable cushion in today's market is 15 percent. Thus, if your research report concludes that John Deere's shares are worth $200 each, and the market price is $160, then Deere is a buy because the estimated value is at least 15 percent higher than the market price (i.e., $200/$160 = 125 percent). The logic works similarly for sale decisions and short-sale recommendations. If your research report shows a Wells Fargo share value of $25 when the stock is trading at $30, you should recommend that the Wells Fargo shares be sold. See Exhibit 5.8.

The margin of safety principle is applicable to all valuation approaches covered in this book: intrinsic value, relative value, acquisition value, leveraged buyout value, and liquidation value. Since these methods are less than exact, a 15 percent difference provides a reasonable degree of assurance that an investment recommendation is correct. Nonetheless, applying a margin of safety is no guarantee against losses. It just reduces the probability of loss in favor of increasing the chances of profit. Consider it to be the equivalent of an insurance policy.

Going hand in hand with the margin of safety principle are sensible economic and financial projections. There's little sense in providing yourself with a protective cushion on the investment recommendation when your forecasts are unrealistic. Most people err on the side of optimism. They have trouble foreseeing economic recessions and key industry turning points. For example, few analysts anticipated the sharp rise of Internet advertising, which damaged the newspaper industry. And many professionals become captured by the companies they cover, since they are so reliant on management for information. This tendency is reinforced when analysts

**Analyst's Independent Valuation
and Related Action**

Sell	No Recommendation	Buy
$	$85 $100 $115	
	Margin of Safety Area	
	Current Share Price = $100	

$0 $85 $100 $115

Market Price of Subject Shares Is $100

EXHIBIT 5.8   The "Margin of Safety"
Principle: Subject Shares Trading at $100

accept favors from CEOs of covered companies, a common practice according to one
study. This closeness diminishes the analyst's objectivity, and management's public
relations hype can flow through to his projections. Given this possibility and the
future's uncertainty, a conservative bias in forecasting is an important complement
to the margin of safety principle.

SUMMARY

The typical research report evaluates a business in the following way: The firm is
reviewed and researched under the top-down approach. The top-down approach
utilizes what is called the *chain of projections*, first made popular by Graham and
Dodd. Analyses are completed and projections are performed at five critical levels
in the evaluation. The top of the analysis is a review of macroeconomic trends
for the country in which the subject company's operations are based. Subsequent
research is then focused on descending subject areas, beginning with an evaluation
of the capital markets and followed in succession by an industry analysis, a company
analysis (i.e., a microeconomic analysis), and a financial statement analysis. Macroeconomic, capital market, industry, company, and financial data are projected from
these analyses.

Because the dominant variables in many of these projections are macroeconomic,
the key projection assumptions lie in the macroeconomic forecast. There is then a
cascade of dependent variables that flow from the top assumptions. Consider, for
example, apparel retailing companies: The number of clothes that an average store
sells in a given year is going to be largely dependent on the strength of the overall
U.S. economy. Obvious independent variables might be new apparel fashion trends
and the store's advertising expenditure.

The model research report presents the information in an organized way.

Model Research Report

1. Introduction
2. Macroeconomic Review
3. Relevant Stock Market Prospects
4. Review of the Company and Its Business
5. Financial Analysis
6. Financial Projections
7. Application of Valuation Methodologies
8. Recommendation

The formal top-down approach is copied by other disciplines where a methodical corporate evaluation is required. These include private equity, business valuation, and corporate development.

For specific company reports, Wall Street uses the short-form approach with regard to top-down analysis. The vast majority of individual stock research reports begin with industry trends as the top theme. Macroeconomic and capital-market predictors of corporate performance are left to the brokerage firms' in-house economists and market strategists, although their macroeconomic and capital-market views are incorporated by the practitioner into his specific company report. A key objective of the short-form approach is to provide the reader with a reasonably accurate estimate of the firm's earnings for the next two or three years, along with a basic understanding of its business prospects. Long-term projections are then derived from these short-term estimates.

With financial projections in hand, the security analyst prepares his valuation. After comparing his valuation to the market price, he makes an investment recommendation.

The model research report presents the information in an organized way.

Model Research Report

1. Introduction
2. Macroeconomic Review
3. Relevant Stock Market Prospect
4. Review of the Company and its Business
5. Financial Analysis
6. Financial Projections
7. Application of Valuation-related data
8. Recommendation

CHAPTER 6

Industry Analysis

The industry analysis is an important part of the research report. The proper organization of this analysis, the five principal themes of such a study, and the common pitfalls of an industry evaluation are discussed herein.

In developing investment recommendations, the analyst begins serious research at the industry level. As noted in Chapter 5, the analyst receives top-down economic and capital market forecasts from others. His initial responsibility is tying these macro parameters into an industry outlook, thus laying the groundwork for judging the prospects of selected participants. The fortunes of an individual company are closely intertwined with those of the industry in which it operates. An in-depth study of the industry is thus a prerequisite for a proper security analysis. Achieving an understanding of the industry facilitates the evaluation process, and for this reason many practitioners limit themselves to one or two industries. This chapter reviews preparing an industry analysis, which is covered under section 4 of the model research report shown here:

Model Research Report

1. Introduction
2. Macroeconomic Review
3. Relevant Stock Market Prospects
4. Review of the Company and Its Business ✓
   - Industry Analysis ✓
5. Financial Analysis
6. Financial Projections
7. Application of Valuation Methodologies
8. Recommendation

BACKGROUND

Whatever outlook an analyst develops for a particular industry, not all companies have prospects mirroring the broader view. Some perform better than the general expectation, others worse. Consider the pharmaceutical industry in October 2007. The established chemical-based drug companies were mired in the industry's image

EXHIBIT 6.1   Snapshot of the Pharmaceutical
Industry—October 2007

Established Chemical-Based Companies	P/E Ratio
Bristol-Myers Squibb	20
Eli Lilly	16
GlaxoSmithKline	14
Newer Biotech Companies	
Abraxis Bioscience	26
Cephalon	31
Genzyme	32

of operating problems, expiring patents, and a shortage of new drugs. As a result, their P/E ratios suffered. In contrast, younger biotech-oriented enterprises carried premium P/E ratios, as the market showed interest in their strong product development programs. See Exhibit 6.1.

The dual track status of pharmaceutical firms is often duplicated in other industries. California Pizza Kitchen, for example, has enjoyed far higher valuation ratios than other restaurant chains, such as Darden Restaurants, despite the fact that many of these competitors make money. The difference has been the varying rates of growth between California Pizza Kitchen and the others.

As a general rule, institutional investors stick to industries with a positive outlook. Even the best buggy whip manufacturer was a poor bet at the turn of the prior century. Similarly, the most attractive satellite phone producer turned out to be a loser in the 1990s, as cell phones took over. The chosen industries don't have to be star performers; they just require a reasonable justification for investment.

Broad Industry Trends

The competent analyst has a broad knowledge of the industry he covers, but his research reports generally have a narrow focus, limiting reviews of the major industry trends to those that are likely to affect a specific company's performance. Contributing to the reader's understanding of the industry frequently requires comparisons. For example, analysts covering the early years of the CD player compared it to the introduction of the VCR. Original themes are important in these reports. Rehashing widely available data is of little use to the reader, unless it sets the stage for company-specific projections. Such forecasts appear toward the end of the research report, after the groundwork has been laid.

As the subject company grows larger, the industry analysis becomes increasingly complicated. Most major corporations today have multiple industry lines, many of which are not comparable. General Electric has 14 separate divisions producing products as dissimilar as gas turbines and consumer electronics. For those firms with disparate businesses, the industry analysis evolves into an *industries* analysis, as each distinct segment is valued separately as a part of a larger whole. See Chapter 18, "Sum-of-the-Parts Analysis," for a description of this technique.

Contrary Opinions

Of particular interest to investors are contrarian opinions. Most sell-side research analysts, and many buy-side colleagues, are reluctant to stick their necks out. They follow the herd and, as a result, their reports are disappointingly similar. For the most part, analysts work around the edges of the consensus view on an industry's prospects and a company's forecasts. When a practitioner has a strikingly different conclusion than everyone else, he tends to couch it in vague terms. In that way, if he ends up wrong, his error is less obvious. The depressing outcome of this environment is that most analysts, particularly those on the sell side, are reduced to arguing about a company's next quarterly earnings report. Will earnings be 46 cents per share or 45 cents? When a respected analyst goes against the grain and replies that earnings are going to be 15 cents instead of 45 cents, and then predicts a major problem in the industry, institutional investors sit up and take notice.

Few practitioners predict reversals of trends that are long accepted on Wall Street, despite the frequency of such occurrences, so a fresh look at the status quo is real news. One important industry reversal happened in 2007. After years of raising prices for brand-new homes, KB Home, Lennar, and Pulte Homes—three principal U.S. home builders—cut prices by 10 to 20 percent in response to declining demand. Some observers noticed increasing consumer resistance to high housing prices, but few analysts predicted this change, which caused home builders' share prices to decline as earnings projections fell. A similar event occurred in the retail drug business in November 2007, when Walgreen's announced that declining reimbursements and growing generics cut into profits. Every practitioner believed that retail drug revenues were invulnerable. The day of Walgreen's announcement was labeled "A Drug Shock" by *Forbes*, and the stock dropped $10 in hours.[1] Other drugstore chains' equities followed suit.

ORGANIZING AN INDUSTRY ANALYSIS

An industry analysis takes various forms, but the outline set forth in Exhibit 6.2 is customary.

INDUSTRY CLASSIFICATION

Industries are classified in two ways: (1) where they are in their life cycle, and (2) how they react to the economy's business cycle.

The industry analysis begins by positioning the specific industry into its life cycle. Defining a sector in this way is important to Wall Street. Investors place a premium on simple investment themes. Thus, the faster the analyst pigeonholes an industry into the life cycle chart, the better.

Classification by Industrial Life Cycle

In general conversation, industries are described by the product they produce or the service they provide. Hospital chains, HMOs, and physician health groups are *medical service* industries. Newspapers firms, magazine publishers, and book companies

EXHIBIT 6.2   Model of an Industry Analysis

Industry classification
  Life cycle position
  Business cycle
External factors
  Technology
  Government
  Social
  Demographic
  Foreign
Demand analysis
  End users
  Real and nominal growth
  Trends and cyclical variation around trends
Supply analysis
  Degree of concentration
  Ease of entry
  Industry capacity
Profitability
  Supply/demand analysis
  Cost factors
  Pricing
International competition and markets

Source: CFA Institute. Note how the industry analysis is broken down into key components.

fall in the *publishing* category. Sporting goods manufacturers, recorded music distributors, and toy producers are lumped into the *recreation* sector. Security analysis uses such descriptions also, but it further classifies industries by certain economic characteristics.

By far the most popular segmentation tool is the industrial life cycle, which reflects the vitality of an industry over time. A staple of business school textbooks and management consulting firms, the life cycle theory outlines four phases. These mark the beginning to the end of an industry: the *pioneer, growth, mature,* and *decline* phases.

As its name implies, the pioneer phase is the riskiest point of corporate life. At this point the industry is struggling to establish a market for its products. Cash needs for working capital and fixed assets are substantial, yet the industry is losing money or is only marginally profitable. Its potential for success has attracted equity investors, who are prepared for the possibility of taking a total loss on their investment. Indeed, 7 out of 10 start-up businesses fail to survive this stage. Many such pioneering enterprises are backed by venture capitalists or operating companies. During overheated stock markets, speculative ventures go public and become fodder for the security analyst community.

The second stage is the growth phase. Here, practitioners acknowledge the industry's product acceptance and have a brief historical framework for estimating future demand. The big questions are: How far and how fast? So-called growth industries

EXHIBIT 6.3   Industry Classification: The Industrial Life Cycle

Life Cycle Phase	Description
Pioneer	Questionable product acceptance. Unclear implementation of business strategy. High risk and many failures.
Growth	Product acceptance established. Roll-out begins. Accelerating growth in sales and earnings. Proper execution of strategy remains an issue.
Mature	Industry trend line corresponds to the general economy. Participants compete for share in a stable industry.
Decline	Shifting tastes or technologies have overtaken the industry, and demand for its products steadily decreases.

occupy a large amount of analysts' time, because they can provide excellent returns. Of particular interest to analysts is identifying a growth industry at the ground floor. After everyone jumps on the band wagon, the industry's valuation becomes inflated and investment returns decline. See Exhibit 6.3.

A classic growth industry spurs demand for a product that the consumer (or the industrial client) didn't know he needed. The best example is a new technology: Apple's iPod, for example, sparked a demand for Internet-enhanced music players, which few people realized they needed beforehand. Another growth story is the better mousetrap. Before Salesforce.com appeared, few companies realized they could rent software rather than buy it. The total market for software was stagnant, but on-demand software represented a legitimate growth industry. Growth companies prosper independently of the business cycle.

Besides experiencing rapidly increased sales, growth industries frequently enjoy fat profit margins. This happy situation continues until new competitors, attracted to the high returns, enter the business. As competition stabilizes and market penetration reaches practical limits, the industry progresses to the mature phase.

If growth industries have above-average sales and earnings increases, mature industries are those producing average results. Unit sales gains tend to follow economic growth. Thus, if the economy improves by 3 percent in one year, an analyst expects a mature industry's unit sales to rise by 3 percent. Adding a 4 percent inflation factor means the industry's sales increase by 7 percent (i.e., 3 percent plus 4 percent). Mature industries usually provide a staple product or service that is widely accepted. Examples include the food, auto, and furniture industries.

Within a mature industry may be one or more growth companies. Typically, such firms achieve above-average growth in one of two ways. First, they gain market share by offering an improved quality or service (i.e., the better mousetrap). DIRECTV, a satellite-based TV service, increased its market share from 3 percent to 11 percent over five years in the pay TV industry. Consumers preferred its channel selection and pricing to those of the hard-line cable TV competition. Alternatively, a company grows in a mature industry by gobbling up other participants. Since 1997, Washington Mutual increased its market share in the thrift business by 50 percent, principally by acquiring competitors. Gross income in its industry advanced 10 percent annually over that time, but Washington Mutual's gains averaged 18 percent.

The last stage in the life cycle is the decline phase. In this phase, demand for the industry's products decreases and the remaining participants fight over shares of a smaller market. With no need for new capacity and diminished profit margins, the industry attracts little new capital and established competitors begin to exit the sector. As demand dries up, numerous companies fail and consolidation of the remaining participants accelerates. The better-managed survivors anticipate this fate and avoid it by using excess cash to diversify into more promising industries. Vivendi's $5 billion takeover of video game maker Activision exemplified this motive. Alternatively, companies develop new products to respond to the changing client base. Facing a declining demand for conventional drug offerings, AstraZeneca entered the pharmaceutical biologics business through internal investments and acquisitions, such as the $15 billion MedImmune merger.

Classification by Business Cycle Reaction

In addition to the industry life cycle, Wall Street characterizes industries by the way in which they react to the business cycle. Market economies do not grow in a straight line. They expand, go into a recession when growth slows, and then enter a recovery, which leads into the next expansion. (See Exhibit 6.4.) The duration of a U.S. business cycle can be 5 to 10 years. Different industries prosper more than others during certain phases of the business cycle. The way in which an industry behaves places it into one of three categories:

1. *Growth*. Above-normal expansion in sales and profits occurs independently of the business cycle.
2. *Defensive*. Stable performance continues during both ups and downs of business cycle.
3. *Cyclical*. Profitability tracks the business cycle, often in an exaggerated manner.

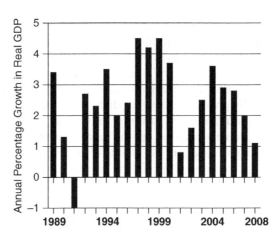

The U.S. economy has traditionally been subject to mild cycles. The 2008–2010 cycle may prove the exception.

EXHIBIT 6.4   U.S. Business Cycles, 1989 to 2008

A growth industry achieves an above-normal rate of expansion, independently of the business cycle. Even if the economy is in a recession, the growth industry's sales and earnings rise. New technology and new products are the hallmarks of a growth industry. The Internet retailing industry sailed through the 2001 recession with ever higher revenues.

Defensive industries exhibit reasonably stable performance throughout the business cycle. Sales and earnings proceed in an upward direction. Stronger growth is apparent during an economic upturn and there is sometimes a slight dip in profitability during recession years. Defensive industries usually fall into the mature category of the life cycle. Examples include (1) electric and gas utilities, since people require heat and light in their homes regardless of economic conditions; (2) food, cigarette, and beer companies, since demand for such products remain inelastic (although consumers shift to lower-priced brands); and (3) government contractors, since governments spend whether or not the economy is expanding.

Cyclical industries are those whose earnings track the economic cycle. These industries' profits are the most likely to benefit from economic upturns, but they also suffer from large earnings declines in a downturn. The earnings movement tends to be exaggerated. Boom times are followed by bust times. Thus, when economic growth moves only a few percentage points, cyclicals go from substantial losses to huge profits. Volvo's operating loss in the 2001 recession was $140 million; its 2006 operating profit topped $2 billion. Classic cyclical businesses produce discretionary products, the consumption of which is dependent on economic optimism. The auto industry is cyclical, because consumers tend to defer large purchases until they are confident of the economy's positive direction. Heavy equipment and machine tool producers represent cyclical businesses; their customers are generally capital-intensive concerns, which postpone investment during recessions and increase spending during recoveries. Exhibits 6.5 and 6.6 provide examples of three firms and how earnings changed over the previous business cycle.

Other kinds of cyclical firms experience earnings patterns that do not correlate well against the general economy, but trend against other economic variables. Brokerage firms, for example, show cyclicality based on stock prices. Mining firms exhibit earnings tied to the commodity price cycle. Such firms are usually lumped into the cyclical category.

The characterization of an industry through the life cycle or business cycle techniques tends to color the follow-up analysis. Practitioners quickly compare those industries with similar designations and try to draw inferences about future sales, earnings performance, and valuation. In this side-by-side evaluation, industry-specific nuances are ignored in favor of the broader theme.

A second problem associated with industry classification is self-deception. Once an analyst labels an industry as a growth industry, he (and his audience) is tempted to place subsequent facts which come to light into the growth framework. Thus, pigeonholing an industry is helpful in telling the investment story, but the experienced analyst doesn't let the label prejudge developments that don't fit the model.

As one illustration, consider the Internet service industry in the 1990s. Early investors compared this industry to cable TV in the 1970s. Both Internet and cable TV were hooked into the home by wire and both required monthly subscription

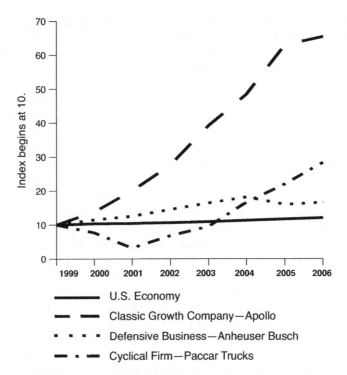

EXHIBIT 6.5 Business Cycle Comparison of GNP versus
Earnings per Share (percentage changes)

charges. As analysts monitored the Internet services industry more closely, however, they noticed a significant difference. Internet service was not a quasi-monopoly like cable TV, and customers switched suppliers more frequently than did cable TV subscribers. The Internet service industry fell into a growth classification, but practitioners needed a fresh look at its economics. Internet service stock valuations dropped accordingly.

EXHIBIT 6.6 Business Cycle Earnings Comparison: GDP Changes versus EPS Changes

		1999	2000	2001	2002	2003	2004	2005	2006
Real GDP	% Chg	4.4	3.7	0.8	1.6	2.5	3.6	3.1	2.9
Growth company—	EPS	0.46	0.58	0.84	1.16	1.65	2.04	2.68	2.79
Apollo	% Chg	32	26	45	38	42	24	31	4
Defensive business—	EPS	1.47	1.69	1.89	2.20	2.48	2.77	2.43	2.53
Anheuser Busch	% Chg	9	15	12	16	13	11	(12)	4
Cyclical firm—	EPS	1.42	1.10	0.45	0.95	1.33	2.34	3.08	3.97
Paccar Trucks	% Chg	12	(23)	(59)	111	40	76	32	29

Note: The recession officially began in 2000 and extended through 2001. The cyclical behavior of Paccar Trucks is evident.

Likewise, the bagel chain industry attracts comparisons to the formerly high-growth fast-food business. Dennis Lombardi, who heads a restaurant consulting practice, said "There's an awful lot of room for more bagel shops. All you have to do is contrast it to the hamburger chains." With 15,000 restaurants, McDonald's has several times the total number of bagel shops, but the economic differences are compelling. Hamburgers are viewed as all-American lunch and dinner foods. In contrast, bagels occupy the breakfast segment and have an ethnic tradition.

A common error associated with industry classification occurs when the analyst paints all industry participants with the same brush. Inevitably, not all companies in a *mature* industry are *mature* companies. The supermarket industry is mature, for example, yet health food chains, like Whole Foods, are considered growth companies. Property and casualty insurance is a cyclical industry, but Old Republic exhibits a stability that defies this classification. Industry analysis thus complements the company analysis described in Chapters 7 to 10.

The process of placing an industry into its life cycle or business cycle category involves performing the work outlined in Exhibit 6.2. By studying the industry's external influences, demand trends, supply factors, profitability, and competition, an analyst forms useful opinions about its prospects and suitability for investment.

EXTERNAL FACTORS

No industry operates in a vacuum. Each is subject to numerous outside influences that significantly impact sales and earnings. The first stage of the top-down analysis factors in the critical economic variables that affect industry performance, and the life cycle and business cycle techniques provide further direction in this regard. As the industry study unfolds, the practitioner examines external factors that aren't derived from economic study. See Exhibit 6.7.

EXHIBIT 6.7   Industry Analysis: Key External Factors Affecting Sales and Profitability

Technology	For established industries the question is: Does the industry face obsolescence from competing technologies? (Typewriters were replaced by word processors in the 1980s.) Infant industries introducing new technologies pose a different question: Will the market accept innovation?
Government	Government plays a large role in many industries. New regulations, or changes to old laws, can impact an industry's sales and earnings. In certain cases, government policies fuel new industries (e.g., the solar power industry).
Social	Changes in lifestyle spark many industries. The rise of two-earner families fueled the growth in the convenience food and restaurant industries. Concern for animal rights hurts the fur retailing industry.
Demographic	Demographic shifts are closely watched by analysts. The graying of America supports nursing home stocks. It is also a factor in the golf equipment industry, as baby boomers reduce strenuous activity in their later years.
Foreign	The United States is the largest economy, but its industries are subject to foreign influences. Overseas textile firms decimated the U.S. textile industry. Higher income levels in developing nations, meanwhile, contribute to huge overseas demand for U.S. software, movies, and music.

External issues fall into five broad categories: technology, government, social, demographic, and foreign. For any one of these categories, there are numerous big-picture themes that affect a particular industry, and some factors counterbalance others. The analyst's job is twofold. First, he avoids the temptation to fall into the role of futuristic visionary. Instead, he concentrates on trends that can demonstrably affect the industry over a three- to five-year period. Second, he addresses the impact of these trends in quantifiable form. It is not enough to say "advances in Internet technology and broadband capacity will fuel the mobile Internet device business"; investors want to know the prospective percentage gains in industry sales from such factors. A numerical sales forecast is better than a vague pronouncement.

In the vast majority of research reports, the basic assumption regarding the industry's external environment is that history repeats itself. Past trends continue into the future; thus, most industry sales projections are based on time series analysis. Projecting the sales of a new industry is trickier, but 99 percent of public companies are beyond the start-up stage, so analysts extrapolate brief historical results into a forecast. Unless there is a firm basis for forming a contrary opinion, this rearview mirror approach is reasonable. As noted earlier, this method encourages complacency, and the analyst relying on it can miss important reversals. Nonetheless, a historical grounding in an industry is a prerequisite for an evaluation of external influences. Exhibit 6.8 shows an evaluation for the health care industry.

Technology

The initial analysis of external technology focuses on *survival*. Will the industry's product offerings fend off perceived substitutes derived from newer technology? The eyeglass industry, for example, has competed successfully against LASIK and contact lens technologies. The CD music industry, in contrast, risks obsolescence with Internet downloading and file sharing.

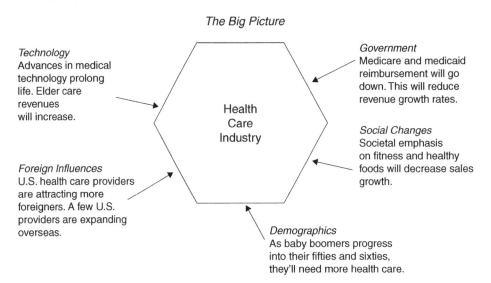

EXHIBIT 6.8   External Factors Affecting Health Care Industry Sales

In many cases, an outside technological idea enhances an industry. Gains in biotechnology transferred into agriculture, where they contributed to higher crop yields. Improvements in civil aviation technology led to a travel boom, which lifted tourist industry revenues. Flat-screen TVs represented 100 percent of appliance retailers' growth from 2003 to 2005. Pundits believe digital technology will lead to book sales growth through online activity.

Sometimes, a new technology proves to be both a blessing and a curse. Nuclear power originated in the defense industry. Eventually transferred to electric utilities, nuclear power was accepted 30 years ago because its variable costs were lower than conventional technologies, such as coal and oil generation. Unforeseen problems in safety and the environment tainted nuclear power, and the related expenses crippled several utilities.

In the case of a competing technology, the established industry usually has several years in which to prepare a defense. A common strategic response is in either of two directions:

1. Copy the competition, as Wal-Mart did in the wholesale club industry with Sam's Wholesale Club, a virtual clone of Price Club.
2. Buy the competition, as Oracle did when it acquired PeopleSoft in 2005.

Competent management teams recognize technological trends and make their companies adjust accordingly.

Government

Government taxes, laws, and regulations impact every industry in the United States. That's one reason Washington, D.C., has over 70,000 registered lobbyists.

The federal tax code serves a legitimate revenue-raising function, but it's also loaded with loopholes designed to serve special interests. For example, the oil exploration industry has depreciation allowances that are more favorable than those for the manufacturing industry. Federal tariffs on imported goods often provide an industry with extra benefits. The quota levied on Japanese auto imports, for example, protects the sales and earnings of domestic producers. A negative shift in the political fortunes of the oil exploration industry or the auto industry could result in unfavorable government actions. The analyst's projections are then adjusted accordingly.

Business organizations constantly complain about regulation, but many regulations have a role in promoting worker safety, consumer protection, and fair play. Government influence cuts both ways. Some agencies practice regulatory overkill that harms industry, but it is a fact that many businesses were either founded on new government initiatives or rely on regulation to prosper. If you're a business, what better way to avoid risk than to have the government impose a minimum price for your products, set up barriers to imports, or allow you to merge with the competition? Regulation creep continues in both Republican and Democratic administrations, and the analyst monitors government developments much more closely than his counterpart of 20 years ago.

When the State of Pennsylvania legalized casino-style gambling in 2004 for 12 locations, it had the option of auctioning the new licenses to the highest bidders, with proceeds estimated to be as high as $3 billion. Instead, the legislature authorized the sale of licenses at below-market prices totaling $600 million, essentially handing a $2.4 billion subsidy to local insiders and national gambling firms. Petrotec, based in Germany, makes biodiesel out of used cooking oil. The company went public in 2006 and it was a hot stock. When the German government cancelled a biodiesel tax credit, Petrotec's stock price fell by half.

Federal and state reimbursements account for over half the drug industry's revenues. A shift in government spending patterns influences the industry. Declines in Medicare reimbursements after 2000 prompted consolidations among nursing home and hospital chains. At the local level, the privatization of municipal garbage collection contributed to revenue gains among waste management firms. Imagine the shift in dollars if the government privatized more than just a tiny portion of the public education system!

External factors relating to government play a role in the analysis of foreign stocks. Most countries have more restrictive tariff regimes than the United States. A dramatic change in tariff policy can destroy a local industry that is uncompetitive globally. Nations set up other barriers to protect favored industries from outside threats. Japan, for example, has a maze of regulations that limit U.S. agricultural imports, thereby assisting Japanese farmers. Brazil's local content rules forestall the importation of cars and ensure the survival of inefficient local manufacturers.

Social

Social factors frequently boil down to lifestyle and fashion changes. In either case, the analyst is ready to evaluate their respective impacts on the relevant industry.

Of the two primary social influences, fashion is the more unpredictable, and this makes the job of researching fashion-oriented industries complicated. The women's fashion cycle, for example, is quite short, and one hot clothing item may have a shelf life of just six months, before it is replaced by another style. Baseline sales for the industry may trend upward, but abrupt changes impact short-term projections. Similar phenomena occur in the toy, recreation, and film industries.

Analysts sometimes mistake a short-term fashion cycle for a long-term trend. In one of my financings, an analyst projected a steady upward trend in leather outerwear sales, despite evidence that demand for such garments historically went through up and down cycles. Three years after the transaction, leather outerwear sales dropped by 20 percent.

Lifestyle changes, in contrast, take place over long periods and the affected industries react accordingly. An uptrend in health consciousness, for example, has resulted in a steady decline in hard liquor consumption. Given fair warning, several spirits producers, such as Seagram's, responded by diversifying into the production of wine, which increased in popularity over the same time span. The gradual shift of women into the workforce, from 44 percent in 1970 to 61 percent in 2005, and the suburbanization of society, acutely affected the auto business. Besides spawning a need for two cars per family, this change prompted the minivan boom, as suburban parents juggled responsibilities for ferrying children to after-school activities.

Demographic

Demography is the science that studies the vital statistics of population, such as distribution, age, and income. By observing trends, analysts develop investment themes regarding industries. In the United States, for example, the aging of the baby boomers into their fifties and sixties sparked a strong interest in retirement planning. The result was higher activity for money management firms as the boomers put savings into stocks and bonds. In Malaysia, about 50 percent of the population is under the age of 21. Analysts tout local brewing stocks, in the anticipation of an increase in the beer drinking population. In Russia, rising per capita incomes promote a demand for cell phones, making analysts optimistic about the growth of local phone companies.

Demographic trends unfold over long periods, and they are thus easier to identify and track than most other external factors. Analysts can agree on the existence of a trend, such as the rising percentage of single-parent families, but disagreement often occurs in sizing up the trend's impact on relevant industries.

Foreign

As global trade expands, industries become sensitive to foreign influences. For example, the domestic economy's health is heavily dependent on imported oil, the price of which is controlled by OPEC, a foreign cartel. Overseas disruptions in the supply/demand dynamic of this resource ripple through many industries, including the oil, chemical, and leisure sectors. Other U.S. industries are under assault from foreign competitors, particularly from competitors based in China. Electronics, basic manufactured goods, and apparel are three popular targets. At the same time, U.S. exports have never been stronger, reflecting the economic liberalization of nations that previously limited U.S. products.

In acknowledging the expansion of global trade, analysts evaluate selected industries on a global basis. Demand projections are aggregated by country and the external influences referred to herein are considered within a global perspective. This approach is most appropriate for worldwide commodity businesses such as oil, metals, and agricultural products, although I have seen it applied to other categories such as defense, semiconductors, and airlines.

Keeping Your Focus

Big-picture trends are interesting to study, but undisciplined research does little to advance an equity evaluation. Isolating the critical elements in an external analysis is difficult, and most research reports fail in this regard. They present numerous outside factors that are a jumble of competing influences, and the identifiable opportunities simply cancel out the emerging threats. The end result: Analysts extrapolate the past into the future, and fail to uncover compelling changes that move an industry's sales off historical trends. As noted earlier, this rearview mirror method is appropriate for many industries, but a more incisive effort is required to unlock a new industry's potential value or to show an old industry's incumbent weaknesses.

An external review is set forth in the following case study.

Case Study: U.S. Casino-Style Gambling Industry   The U.S. casino-style gambling industry is comprised of several hundred casinos and slot machine parlors located in 35 states. These facilities are owned and operated by publicly traded firms, as well as by private commercial operators and Indian tribes. The industry is considered to be growth-oriented for two reasons: (1) States without gambling are gradually legalizing casinos, in order to realize tax revenue captured by neighboring states; (2) states that already have casinos are authorizing more locations in order to generate money from the taxing of additional gambling activity. Like food, beer, and tobacco, gambling is a defensive industry in terms of the business cycle, since gamblers continue spending during recessionary times.

Most of the 50 states have casino gambling, but the holdouts include states with large populations, such as Texas. Furthermore, certain highly populated states, such as Illinois and New York, have casino-style gambling but the authorized locations are restricted in number, paving the way for new openings. With the majority of states limiting the number of casinos operating in their respective jurisdictions, the gambling industry is essentially a regulated oligopoly.

Research reports in 2008 emphasized a number of external factors and threats, as set forth in Exhibit 6.9.

The external factors were largely positive in 2008, and analysts concluded that the gambling industry's above-average growth rate would continue. Legalization in additional states and more casinos in existing states would enable the industry to garner a growing share of consumer dollars, while docile legislatures would restrict competition and limit tax rates. Internet gambling was unlawful at the federal level.

DEMAND ANALYSIS

The ultimate purpose of preparing an economic analysis, industry life cycle placement, and external factor review is an assessment of future demand for the industry's products. Applying such study to numerical forecasts is accomplished differently, as follows:

1. *Top-down economic analysis.* We look for specific macroeconomic variables that affect industry performance. An ideal situation is when an industry's revenues correlate strongly to one key economic statistic, thus reducing the need for multiple inputs. Cement demand growth in Mexico, for example, is historically 1.7 times GNP growth. Analysts, as a result, rely on GNP forecasts to project unit volume.
2. *Industry life cycle.* Categorizing the industry within its life cycle position (or its business cycle sensitivity) provides a framework for demand forecasts. The U.S. food industry is mature. The video game industry is growing. Such characterizations provide a guide to sales changes.
3. *External factors.* Some outside factors are stable, and their impacts on an industry are predictable. Others are highly variable and bring uncertainty into the analysis. Including these items in sales forecasts is a qualitative exercise requiring judgment.

EXHIBIT 6.9   U.S. Casino-Style Gambling Industry: External Factors and Related Threats

Technology

Opportunities

Improved player-tracking technology boosts revenues.

Better slot machines attract new gamblers and enhance revenues from existing customers.

Technology permits gambling over the Internet.

Threats

Internet technology allows offshore gambling sites to attract customers away from U.S. locations.

Technology enables new entrants to compete with established firms more easily.

Government

Opportunities

More states can legalize casino-style gambling.

Most states cling to the oligopoly model for gambling, preserving profitability.

Federal government can approve Internet gambling and reserve it for domestic companies, thus opening a vast new market.

Indian tribes are approaching capacity.

Threats

States can increase gambling taxes.

States can weaken oligopoly model by approving more casinos.

California and Florida consider stronger Indian gaming monopolies.

New laws can leave companies more susceptible to lawsuits regarding customers' gambling addictions.

Social

Opportunities

Gambling is increasingly viewed as an entertainment, rather than a dangerous vice.

Threats

In the past, American culture cycled between an acceptance of legalized gambling and a near total prohibition. Will the cycle turn?

Demographics

Opportunities

Older people gamble more than younger people. The U.S. population is aging, suggesting more demand.

Threats

No perceived threats.

Foreign

Opportunities

Rising affluence of Asian and Latin American clientele boosts revenue from gambling tourism.

Gradual growth in small, foreign-based casinos encourages gamblers to visit big-time meccas, such as Las Vegas and Atlantic City.

Threats

Internet gambling that is conducted offshore diverts U.S. customers.

Attempt by Macao casinos to duplicate Las Vegas-type environment may divert Asian customers of U.S. properties.

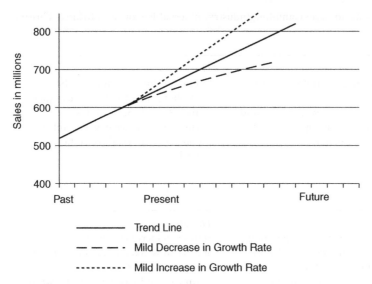

EXHIBIT 6.10   Established Industry: Common Extrapolation for Annual Sales and Earnings Results

By considering these three themes, the analyst establishes a future sales line for the industry. Most times, this forecast turns out to be an extrapolation of the past, as suggested by the trend line for the established industry in Exhibit 6.10, but not always. Sometimes, careful study reveals the likelihood of a turning point that affects the industry's fortunes dramatically. Even an extrapolation provides useful insights. For example, the water service industry historically shows a 7 percent growth rate. Suppose your analysis indicates a continuation of the upward trend, but only at 5 percent. The 2 percent difference leads you to believe the industry's prospects are overblown, and you sell your shareholdings while prices are high. In Exhibit 6.10, a mild decrease in the growth rate produces 10 percent lower sales in the future.

Once a trend has been plotted, the analyst's next step is studying the industry's customers. Who is buying and why?

Customer Study

A forecast of aggregate demand is helpful, but a full understanding of what drives an industry's revenue is only achieved through learning about the customers. Since a typical industry serves thousands of clients, evaluating them individually is impossible. Segmenting the customers into submarkets enables the analyst to study a smaller number of factors that contribute to the demand. As he sequentially studies each submarket, he builds an aggregate demand profile, submarket by submarket.

For example, the demand forecast for the Mexican cement market relied heavily on GNP trends. As a backup to this macroeconomic methodology, I subdivided the market into five segments and considered prospective demand in each segment to verify the accuracy of the GNP multiplier (i.e., annual demand growth equals 1.7 times GNP growth rate). Both methods revealed a likely demand around 42 million tons, including exports. See Exhibit 6.11.

Submarket	Estimated Demand
Residential	13.9
Commercial	11.3
Infrastructure	10.0
Transformers[a]	2.9
Export	4.0
Submarket-based demand	42.1
GNP-based demand	41.5

[a]Manufacturing of concrete block, concrete pipe, and so on.

EXHIBIT 6.11 Mexican Cement Market: Building Aggregate Demand by Submarket for 2007

In Exhibit 6.12, I categorize the submarkets by usage: home building, infrastructure projects, and commercial construction. But such demand segments can be classified differently. David Aaker, a noted business strategist, divides segments between customer characteristics and product-related approaches. Exhibit 6.12 shows samples from the United States market.

EXHIBIT 6.12 Approaches to Defining Demand Segments

Customer Characteristics	Demand Segment
Geographic	West Coast as a market for trendy clothing versus the South.
Type of business	Computer needs of restaurants versus manufacturing firms versus banks versus retailers.
Size of firm	Large hospital versus midsize versus small.
Lifestyle	Jaguar buyers more adventurous than Mercedes-Benz buyers.
Sex	Web sites for women.
Age	Cereals for children versus adults.
Occupation	The paper copier needs of lawyers versus dentists.

Product-Related Approaches	Demand Segment
User type	Appliance buyer—home builder, homeowner, small business.
Usage	The heavy potato users—the fast-food outlets.
Benefits sought	Dessert eaters—those who are calorie-conscious versus those who are concerned with convenience.
Price sensitivity	Price-sensitive Honda Civic buyer versus the luxury Cadillac buyer.
Competitor	Those computer users committed to IBM.
Application	Professional users of chain saws versus the homeowner.
Brand loyalty	Those committed to IBM versus others.

Source: David Aaker, *Developing Business Strategies* (New York: John Wiley & Sons, 1995). Reprinted with permission of John Wiley & Sons, Inc.

Geographic Market	Estimated Demand (million tons)
Central Mexico	14.9
Northern Gulf	7.8
South Mexico	7.0
Central Pacific	4.2
North Pacific	2.9
Export	4.0
Geographic market demand	40.8
Submarket-based demand	42.1
GNP-based demand	41.5

EXHIBIT 6.13   Mexican Cement Market: Building Aggregate Demand by Submarket for 2007, Geographic Basis
Sources: National Chamber for the Cement Industry of Mexico, Mexican Institute for Cement and Concrete, National Chamber for the Construction Industry of Mexico.

A careful analyst studies demand on the basis of several submarket classifications. In following Dr. Aaker's advice, I looked at Mexican cement forecasts from a geographic standpoint. I divided Mexico into five geographic markets and then looked at individual market needs. (See Exhibit 6.13.) In this instance, the *macro*, *usage*, and *geographic* methods delivered aggregate forecasts that were highly correlated. Utilizing multiple approaches is a good double check for any sales forecast.

Established Industries

For established industries, an analyst should contact long-time customers to figure what drives demand in each submarket. What guides the customer's buying decisions? How does this differ by submarket? What changes are occurring in the customer's motivation? What implication does this have on industry revenues? Discussions with customers and a study of buying habits provide an indication of whether prior trends continue.

For example, personal computers captured 62 percent of the U.S. household market in 2007. Unit growth is about 5 percent annually. MP3s or iPods represent a newer appliance. They were in 14 percent of U.S. homes but mostly in the higher income levels. The low MP3 penetration (relative to PCs) promotes a high growth rate until saturation occurs in all income segments. (See Exhibit 6.14.)

EXHIBIT 6.14   Comparable Household Penetration: Two Computer Devices

Device	1987	1992	1997	2002	2007
iPod/MP3	—	—	—	2%	14%
Personal computer	12%	24%	34%	60%	62%

Growth Industries

A growth industry has yet to penetrate all its future submarkets. In addition to researching the existing customer base, the analyst considers potential new outlets. The cell phone business, for example, was initially confined to adults. In recent years, it expanded to teenagers. India-based outsourcing firms first sold to U.S. computer software and service providers. By 2007, they expanded into the finance industry and health care sector. Identifying a new use or user group is important in confirming a growth industry's upward movement.

Untested Industries

Some publicly traded companies furnish a truly new product or service. Given a minimal level of product acceptance, these firms have little or no track record from which the analyst can build a sales forecast. Although the risk profile of these investments is higher than most, the decision process is not entirely speculative. A first step is determining whether the new industry fulfills a need that (1) exists and (2) isn't being met by another industry. The managed care business was founded in response to the needs of corporations to cut employee medical costs. After a need is verified, analysts generally forecast new industry sales based on the experience of a similar industry.

One example is the office products superstore industry typified by Office Depot and Staples. No sooner did these two companies go public than analysts settled into a comparison with the discount warehouse clubs, such as Price Club and Costco. Market share and saturation levels were calculated on models that were identical to the warehouse club experience. For every 250,000 people in a metropolitan market, analysts figured one warehouse club. After some observation, they shifted this logic to 25,000 white collar workers and 100,000 people per office products superstore.

Input/Output and Industry Demand Forecasts

Input/output analysis observes the flow of goods and services through an industry's production process, including intermediate steps as the goods proceed from raw materials to finished product. The rising consumption of the finished product boosts demand for those industries supplying the intermediate steps. For example, the Internet boom elevated the demand for data storage devices, which help fuel Internet communication.

If one industry is a major customer of another, an analyst uses input/output analysis to derive partial demand for the latter's products. Alternatively, the higher consumption of one industry's offerings sparks an increased demand for complementary products. The wide-scale introduction of the automobile in China provided a direct boost to the local tire business. Analysts calculated tire demand through algebraic formulas based on new vehicle sales, expected mileage, and tire replacement rates. One formula stated that one car purchase meant eight tire sales over five years. The demand models can be complex and contain many variables. Exhibit 6.15 shows one rendition for the tire market.

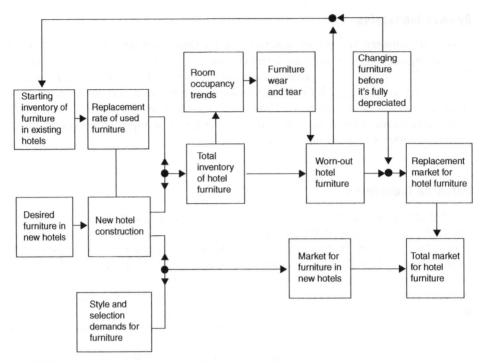

EXHIBIT 6.15   Demand Analysis Model for the Hotel Furniture Market

SUPPLY ANALYSIS IN THE INDUSTRY STUDY

In industry reviews, analysts spend most of their time studying *demand* trends. They usually assume the supply side of the equation takes care of itself. If the industry revenues are rising, more investment pours in. If revenues are declining, existing capacity services the falling demand. This model is valid in the long term, but its applicability over the short to intermediate term varies by industry.

The temporary help industry fits the model well. With its emphasis on low-skilled workers, the industry finds new employees quickly, thus ramping up capacity in a short time. Supply that is dependent on bricks and mortar is a different story. Capital-intensive industries, such as steel and packaging, require three to five years to build new plants that add supply. Industries that use highly skilled workers, such as the software industry, face short-term constraints as they wait for training courses to provide new programmers.

Projecting Supply Availability

Supply is a function of unused capacity and the ability to bring on new capacity. Interpreting these variables well enough to make a reasonable forecast is complicated. That's why few analysts attempt the job. Ideally, a supply forecast dovetails

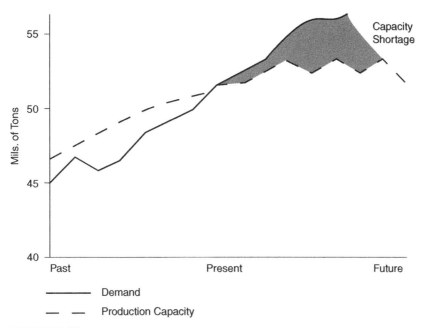

EXHIBIT 6.16 Demand/Supply Graph: Hypothetical Industry

with a demand forecast, and the analyst has an idea about future market equilibrium. If future supply and demand appear to be out of balance, prices for the industry's products will be affected, unless the suppliers change their behavior in time. The ideal research report has a supply/demand graph like Exhibit 6.16. In this case, the graph shows a future supply problem since capacity fails to meet demand.

The supply projection is easiest when the industry has only a few competitors, producing output at a discrete number of sizeable facilities. It also helps if the industry's economics make imports prohibitively expensive, so the analysts can ignore foreign capacity. The cement industry is a good example of this model. First, only large plants, with long construction lead times, make cement. A few plants handle the needs of a large city. Second, the low value per ton makes transportation uneconomical beyond a 250-mile radius from the plant. Thus, it is a simple matter to forecast available supply: An analyst counts nearby capacity and adds planned additions for the next three to five years. In Mexico, this process is straightforward. The cement market is dominated by two companies operating 21 out of 31 total plants, and their expansion plans are public knowledge. All plants have ample reserves of raw materials. A supply calculation appears in Exhibit 6.17.

The forecast demand was then matched against the supply trend, as shown in Exhibit 6.18. The chart showed a capacity utilization rate exceeding 86 percent by 2010, which is considered *high* for the industry, and it suggested that additional capacity should be initiated.

EXHIBIT 6.17   Mexican Cement Market: Future Supply Calculation, 2007–2010 (millions of tons per year)

	2007	2008	2009	2010
2007 capacity	53.2	53.2	53.2	53.2
2008 additions, net	—	1.0	1.0	1.0
2009 additions, net	—	—	1.6	1.6
2010 additions, net	—	—	—	1.2
Total estimated capacity	53.2	54.2	55.8	57.0

Note: Additions are net of closures.

EXHIBIT 6.18   Mexican Cement Industry: Supply/Demand Forecast 2007–2010

	2007	2008	2009	2010
Available capacity	53.2	54.2	55.8	57.0
Expected demand	41.5	44.0	46.7	49.5
Capacity utilization	78.0%	81.2%	83.7%	86.8%

PROFITABILITY, PRICING, AND THE INDUSTRY STUDY

The key to industry selection is future profitability. What's the point of investing in growth if sales go up but profits go down? A good supply/demand forecast gives an indication of the prospects for industry profitability. If supply appears to be reasonably in line with demand, industry earnings will probably stay on their trend line. Profitability is vital if an industry is to make the investment needed to increase supply. An oversupply retards investment since it augurs lower prices. Indeed, a study by Uranium One Corporation predicted lower prices for copper (from $130/lb to $90/lb), resulting from prospective increases in mining capacity and run-downs in inventory.

In an ideal world, the free interplay between supply and demand sets the price for an industry's products. In real life, however, there's a lot of interference in this process. Common factors contributing to pricing include:

- Industry product segmentation.
- Degree of industry concentration.
- Ease of industry entry.
- Price changes in key supply inputs.

To begin, many industries effectively segment their product offerings by brand name, reputation, or service, even when the products are quite similar. Over-the-counter medicines are one example. The ingredients of the store brand and the name brand are identical, yet the name brand has a 40 percent price premium.

An industry with a high degree of concentration inhibits price movements. Assuming that demand and supply are in reasonable balance, the major players have every incentive to engage in monopolistic behavior. They can sustain artificially high prices by price signaling, confidential agreements, and other means. Outside analysts obviously have problems learning what's going on. In Mexico, for example, the two major cement producers control 80 percent of the market, and they barely hide the fact that collusion exists. In the United States, similar behavior occurs, but it's kept behind closed doors.

Monopolies promote artificial pricing, and an industry's ease of entry is a key variable in holding prices to the free market model. Semiconductor production poses an obvious problem; the entry ticket—a new plant—costs $2 billion. Specialty retailing, in contrast, is wide open. An entrepreneur can rent store space, lease fixtures, and stock inventory for less than $100,000.

Some industries rely heavily on one or two inputs. Price changes in these inputs affect costs. Sometimes, the affected industry passes increased costs through in the form of higher prices. Other times, competitive pressures stand in the way. In 2007, for example, the price of diesel fuel, a key supply item for truckers, reached historical highs. Trucking companies such as YRC Worldwide and Vitran were unable to raise prices enough to compensate.

Industry Profitability Is Important

Supply/demand analysis, cost factors, and pricing are critical elements in determining future industry profitability. Without earnings, an industry can't finance the commitment to personnel, plant, and R&D that are needed to prosper. An industry with a poor profit outlook is an unlikely investment candidate indeed.

INTERNATIONAL COMPETITION AND MARKETS

Competition

Competitive analysis is the topic of many books. Michael Porter of the Harvard Business School is a leader in the field and approaches competition from multiple directions, as set forth in Exhibit 6.19. Security analysis synthesizes the approaches of experts like Dr. Porter, and this section provides a general treatment of the subject.

A first step in the competitive analysis is defining the industry. This task was discussed earlier, but it is helpful to remember that some analysts, for example, cover the chemical industry; some follow the chemical fertilizer industry; and still others research the specialty chemical industry. *Institutional Investor* magazine segments the media industry into five subindustries: cable and satellite, entertainment, publishing, advertising agencies, and radio and TV broadcasting. Placing your company into its subindustry and identifying its competitors becomes the second step in your competitive analysis.

For each competitor, the analyst develops an appreciation of its business strategy and how it affects the company under study. For example, in the supermarket business, Safeway pursues a national program; Publix focuses on the Southeast region; and Wegmans sticks to the mid-Atlantic region. In the jewelry industry, Tiffany targets the carriage trade; Zales looks to Middle America. An attempt by Zales to go upscale would impact Tiffany's results.

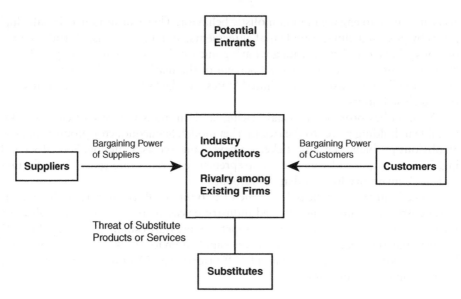

EXHIBIT 6.19   Competition: Five Competitive Forces That Determine
Industry Profitability
Source: Michael Porter, "The Five Competitive Forces That Shape a Strategy,"
Harvard Business Review, January 2008.

Finally, the analyst is advised to outline the strengths and weaknesses of industry participants. Designed by David Aaker, Exhibit 6.20 illustrates many of the items that are considered in such an outline. Financial track record and balance sheet strength are top priorities for most analysts, but a review of other factors reveals whether favorable financial results can be maintained by the competition, perhaps at the expense of the subject company. Similarly, if the subject company's strengths dominate areas where the competition is weak, a higher degree of confidence is embedded in the forecast.

Each industry has a few dominant success factors which can be drawn from Exhibit 6.20. Many analysts (and corporate strategists) inventory these items and the relative positions of competitors. Exhibit 6.21 presents this comparative analysis in tabular form.

A firm's ability to sustain its sales and earnings is highly dependent on the status of the competition. Does the subject company have the ability to be aggressive— to take the offense? Or does it have to protect market share and husband financial resources—play defense? The competitor profile facilitates game theory for the practitioner.

International Competition

The world is becoming a smaller place and industries reflect a globalization theme. This characterization is most advanced with commodity industries such as oil, metals, and basic foodstuffs, but it also dominates intermediate sectors such as light manufacturing, semiconductors, and chemicals. Indeed, about 40 percent of the S&P 500's earnings are connected to international activities.

EXHIBIT 6.20 Competitive Analysis: Analysis of Strengths and Weaknesses of Each Industry Participant

Innovation	Management
Technical product or service superiority	Quality of top and middle management
New product capability	Knowledge of business
Research and development	Culture
Technologies	Strategic goals and plans
Patents	Entrepreneurial thrust
	Planning/operation system
	Loyalty—turnover
	Quality of strategic decision making

Manufacturing	Marketing
Cost structure	Product quality reputation
Flexible production operations	Product characteristics/differentiation
Equipment	Brand-name recognition
Access to raw material	Breadth of product line—systems capability
Vertical integration	Customer orientation
Workforce attitude and motivation	Segmentation/focus
Capacity	Distribution
	Retailer relationship
	Advertising/promotion skills
	Sales force
	Customer service/product support

Finance—Access to Capital	Customer Base
From operations	Size and loyalty
From cash on hand	Market share
Ability to use debt and equity financing	Growth of segments served

Source: David Aaker, *Developing Business Strategies* (New York: John Wiley & Sons, 1995). Reprinted with permission of John Wiley & Sons, Inc.

EXHIBIT 6.21 Sample Competitor Analysis for a Research Report

	Major Competitors			
Competition Indicators	**A**	**B**	**C**	**D**
Market position	Vulnerable	Prevalent	Strong	Vulnerable
Profitability	Low	Average	Average	Average
Financial strength	Low	High	Unknown	Low
Product mix	Narrow	Broad	Narrow	Narrow
Technological capability	Average	Strong	Average	Weak
Product quality	Minimum	Good	Satisfactory	Minimum

Source: Milton Leontiades, *Management Policy, Strategy and Plans* (Boston: Little Brown & Company, 1982).

The United States is the leading economy, has the greatest number of publicly traded securities, and operates the most developed financial market. For these reasons, the security analysis profession has made great strides here. The primary downside of this situation has been a nearsightedness on the part of many practitioners. Even though most industries extend globally, Wall Street research reports often stop at the U.S. border, and analysts frequently give short shrift to corporate foreign operations and international trends. As more institutions emphasize global research and investing, this situation is gradually changing.

SUMMARY

The industry analysis is a continuation of the top-down approach. By conducting a study of the industry, its external environment, demand and supply trend, likely profitability, and competitive situation, the security analyst confirms whether the industry is an appropriate investment. The written research report presents a limited amount of information and practitioners highlight a few key factors in an industry review. Many times, their audience prefers a one-word summary in the review, such as *growth*, *mature*, or *decline*. With a knowledge of the industry, the analyst proceeds to a specific stock selection. Which of the participants are the winners? Which are the losers? Company-specific analysis and valuation are covered in the next few chapters.

CHAPTER 7

Company-Specific Analysis

Having covered macroeconomic, capital market, and industry factors affecting the subject company, the analyst next proceeds to studying the firm's operations and finances. This chapter outlines the steps involved in a company-specific analysis.

For many practitioners, company-specific analysis is where the fun starts. At this level the stock selection process begins in earnest. The foundation of economic forecasting, capital markets analysis, and industry study is in place, and their research now focuses on the attributes of a single business (Exhibit 7.1).

Model Research Report

1. Introduction
2. Macroeconomic Review
3. Relevant Stock Market Prospects
4. Review of the Company and Its Business ✓
   - Industry Analysis ✓
   - Company-Specific Analysis ✓
5. Financial Analysis
6. Financial Projections
7. Application of Valuation Methodologies
8. Recommendation

The first step of the analysis begins with a written review of the subject company's business, which is included under section 4 of the research report. This review is both *descriptive* and *analytical*. Its purpose is twofold: (1) to ensure that the practitioner follows the discipline of placing relevant information on paper; and (2) to convey to the reader the analyst's understanding of the company's operating environment. As noted in Exhibit 7.1, the business review, along with the historical financial analysis, provides the basis upon which financial projections are realized. Financial projections are an important determinant of valuation.

The business review outline set forth in Exhibit 7.2 covers many of the same topics included in an IPO prospectus. Unlike a prospectus, the research report includes the analyst's interpretation of the facts and trends set forth in the official documents, along with whatever additional data the analyst believes is relevant. Furthermore,

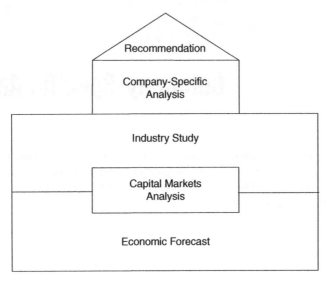

EXHIBIT 7.1   The Building Block of a Business Valuation
Note how the company-specific analysis rests on the
foundation of industry study, capital markets analysis, and
economic forecast.

EXHIBIT 7.2   Business Review Section of
the Company-Specific Analysis

General Information
   Overview and Business Description
   Corporate Strategy
   Life Cycle
   Financial Summary

Products and Markets
   Product Line and New Products
   Market for the Company's Products
   Marketing Strategy and Customer Support
   Significant Customers

Production and Distribution
   Manufacturing Process and Costs
   Distribution
   Suppliers and Raw Materials

Competition
   Competitive Environment
   Comparative Analysis of Competition

Other Topics
   Research and Development
   Foreign Sales and Earnings
   Government Regulation
   Personnel
   Properties
   Management

the report places the appropriate emphasis on matters meriting special attention. In contrast, the business review contained in a prospectus fails to highlight the critical factors upon which a valuation should rely.

Topics covered in this chapter include competitive advantage, corporate strategy, life cycle position, products and markets, production and distribution, suppliers, and competitors. We also review niche subjects such as R&D, foreign operations, government regulations, and management.

SYSTEMATIC APPROACH OF A BUSINESS ANALYSIS

The review is designed to be systematic. In a step-by-step fashion, the analyst plows through each important element of a firm's business. Along the way, he (and the reader) is forced to focus on the company's abilities in every aspect of its operations. Is the product line good enough to garner new customers? Is the distribution system better than the competition? Examining these areas separately enables the analyst to piece together that combination of assets, skills, and innovation which enables the firm to maintain its position.

In the previous chapter, we figured out how the industry made money. Now we must determine how the firm accrues sales and earns profits. Business strategists call this exercise a search for the firm's *sustained competitive advantage* (SCA). Without an SCA, a company's customers are ready for the taking. Competitors can close in and the firm's ultimate survival is in question. The business review hones in on the elements supporting a company's SCAs.

Business scholars ascribe sustainable competitive advantages to three basic strategies:

1. *Low costs*. The firm's cost of producing its goods and services is lower than the competition. Infosys's low-cost programmers are based in India. That gives it a leg up on competing IT-service businesses based in the United States.
2. *Differentiation*. The customer perceives that the firm offers something that is unique in the industry. LifeCell Corporation, for example, offers innovative surgical products that other surgical supply firms can't match.
3. *Focus*. The firm selects a narrow customer base that is underserved by the industry. Wal-Mart started by building stores in small rural towns that Sears and Kmart avoided.

These advantages occur in various parts of a profitable operation, encouraging the practicing analyst to pursue the segmented study outlined in Exhibit 7.2. In his book *Competitive Advantage*, Michael Porter echoes a similar approach:

> *Competitive advantage cannot be understood by looking at a firm as a whole. It stems from the many discrete activities a firm performs in designing, producing, marketing, delivering, and supporting its product. Each of these activities can contribute to a firm's relative cost position and create a basis for differentiation. A cost advantage, for example, may stem from such disparate sources as a low-cost physical distribution system, a highly efficient assembly process, or superior sales force utilization. Differentiation can stem from similarly diverse factors, including the procurement of high quality raw materials, a responsive order entry system, or a superior product design.*[1]

EXHIBIT 7.3   Franchise Values of Major Corporations

Company	Perceived Life of Competitive Advantage
Coca-Cola	Over 20 years
Disney	Over 20 years
Budweiser	10 years
Marriott	10 years
Dell	4 to 6 years
Netflix	2 to 3 years

Many individual investors would be surprised at the number of times profession-als buy a stock, yet fail to pinpoint the company's competitive advantages. Dozens of fast-food chains have gone public, but only a handful prosper under the continuing onslaught of McDonald's and a few other major players. In 1989, there were 56 companies making disk drives in the United States; 10 years later only 11 survived. Breaking into an established market is difficult. Take the breakfast cereal market. The latest brand to make the top 10 was Honey Nut Cheerios in 1979, 30 years ago. Since deregulation, multiple airlines have gone public and then disappeared, unable to hold up against the entrenched participants.

Sometimes the ability to ward off the competition is referred to as a firm's *franchise value*. Strong consumer brands like Coca-Cola and Disney top the list of companies with long-term advantages. Technology firms have shorter terms. A partial list appears in Exhibit 7.3.

Maintaining a competitive advantage is essential to the corporation's survival, but it shouldn't be an end in itself. If developing new products or holding on to market share is too expensive, for example, the firm damages its equity value by maintaining an SCA. For example, Eastman Kodak, a large producer of photographic products, lost market share and store shelf space to digital photography when it stuck to its traditional film business. Running a major ad campaign, obtaining a better product, and renting sufficient shelf space to reverse this mistake might seriously weaken Kodak's shareholder value.

Corporate Strategy

Many analysts are content to extrapolate a company's historical sales into the future, but enterprising practitioners examine a business plan to determine what drives revenues in the long run. Clearly, the credibility of a plan rests on management matching corporate advantages and resources against likely competitor moves.

Internal Growth

In some industries, the strategy appears simplistic. The Ruth's Chris Steak House business model is straightforward. Revenues from a base of 60 owned restaurants are expected to grow by 6 percent annually. With existing resources, 17 restaurants, providing $90 million in annual revenues, can be added in 2008 and 2009. Sev-eral companies duplicate the premium steakhouse dining concept, and other theme restaurants compete for the dining dollar. See Exhibit 7.4.

EXHIBIT 7.4 Ruth's Chris Steak House, Inc., Summary Expansion Strategy (in millions, except for restaurants)

	Year Ending December 31		
	2007	2008	2009
Number of Owned Restaurants			
Existing restaurants	53	64	78
New restaurants	7	8	9
Total	60	72	87
$3 million capital expenditure per new restaurant: total capital expenditures	$ 21.0	$ 24.0	$ 27.0
Projected Revenue			
Existing restaurants at December 31, 2006	$280.0	$297.0	$315.0
Restaurants opened in 2007	17.5	35.0	37.0
Restaurants opened in 2008		20.0	40.0
Restaurants opened in 2009			22.5
	307.5	352.0	414.5
Franchising revenue	15.5	17.0	19.5
Total revenue	$323.0	$369.0	$434.0

Source: Ruth's Chris SEC filings and equity research reports.
Note: Ruth's Chris restaurant opening program should provide higher sales.

In other industries, the process is infinitely more complicated. Pharmaceutical drug companies, for example, own a catalog of drugs. As technology advances and new drugs predominate, the drug sales from the catalog decline. Similarly, when an established drug goes off patent, corporate sales of the drug fall in the face of generic competition. Management estimates the rate of lost sales, and then it plans new drug innovations to replace sales lost from the off-patent products. The large American drug firm Pfizer faces this dilemma. It is dependent on sales of the cholesterol-lowering drug Lipitor, the world's biggest selling prescription medicine, whose patent expires in 2010. Thirty percent of Pfizer's $48 billion in sales are from Lipitor, and revenues will decline when Lipitor's patent expires.

In reviewing a drug company's plans (see Exhibit 7.5), the pharmaceutical analyst has to convince himself that the management has the ability to maintain a new product pipeline. He must also be assured that catalog sales declines follow management's estimates, rather than a more negative scenario.

Other companies are one-trick ponies. DynCorp International, a pricey defense stock, derived 50 percent of its 2007 revenues from Iraq War projects. Such activity involves logistical support, international policing, and contract management. DynCorp's stock was trading at 30 times earnings in early 2008, greater than the P/E multiples of broad-based defense companies. It seemed as if DynCorp investors thought the Iraq War would last forever.

Acquisition Growth

Many companies combine internal growth and acquisitions. At Mantech International Corp., a federal government IT contractor, baseline sales (i.e., *organic growth*)

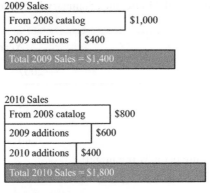

EXHIBIT 7.5 Pharmaceutical Drug
Company: Sample Business Plan
(in millions)

increase 8 percent annually. By carrying out a successful program of acquisitions, management boosts total growth to 20 percent annually. Mantech now has yearly sales exceeding $1.4 billion. Finding sizable deals that meaningfully increase revenue becomes more difficult. In 2008 the analyst decides whether Mantech's strategy can be continued without the firm paying unreasonable prices to buy businesses. See Exhibit 7.6.

Portfolio Approach

With multiline companies, the strategic framework incorporates a *portfolio approach*. For example, Akzo Nobel segments its portfolio into three industry segments: decorative paints, specialty chemicals, and performance coatings. Under Akzo's discipline, the disparate operating businesses are nothing more than a collection of assets. Any business units having similar operational characteristics are combined, leaving little operating synergy between the divisions, which act more or less independently. The holding company acts as the repository of excess cash generated at

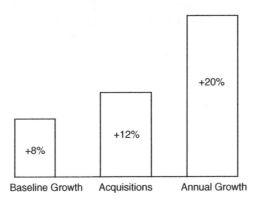

EXHIBIT 7.6 Mantech International Corp.:
Strategy of Combining Internal Growth and
Acquisitions (2000–2007)

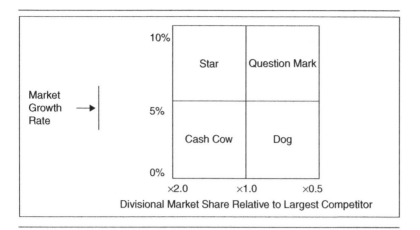

EXHIBIT 7.7   How to Define an Operating Division by the BCG Growth/
Share Matrix

the divisional level, and it dispenses financing, legal advice, personnel guidance, and accounting service to the divisions. The holding company is the divisional bank, and the division managers apply to the bank to obtain new capital. New business ideas are appraised by the bank, which considers whether the divisional applicant has researched its request properly and whether it has the necessary skills to use the capital efficiently.

Besides evaluating the respective *business strategies* of the divisions, the analyst considers the *allocation process* of the divisional bank. Is it placing money into the most deserving operations? Frequently, security analysts resort to the famous Boston Consulting Group (BCG) growth/share matrix (see Exhibit 7.7) to gain insights.

The growth/share matrix enables holding corporate managers (and security analysts) to classify each *division*, each *business*, or each *asset* into a quadrant. The manager then considers whether to implement the recommended strategy for assets falling into that respective quadrant. According to the strategy, the cash thrown off by divisions with strong market shares in low-growth markets (*cash cows*) is reinvested in *stars* to support their growth and market share objectives. Alternatively, the cash cows assist *question marks* in their push to become stars. So-called *dogs* (mature divisions with small market shares in low-growth markets) receive little capital, even if they are profitable; they are candidates for divestiture, as a means to generate cash for the question marks and stars. The BCG framework is simple but effective, and it has influenced a generation of corporations and stock analysts.

The growth/share matrix approach prompts companies to spin off dogs and question marks. The remaining operation is thus easier to pigeonhole as a *growth stock* or a *mature business*. Witness IBM's 2005 spin-off of its $12 billion PC division, considered by Wall Street to be a drag on IBM's growth.

Life Cycle

The corporate life cycle theory provides an easy way to categorize a stock. At the business level, there are four stages, which mirror the definitions covered in the industry discussion in Chapter 6. Exhibit 7.8 summarizes the cycle.

EXHIBIT 7.8   Corporate Life Cycle

Stage	Expected Sales Performance
Pioneer	Unpredictable and volatile sales movements.
Growth	Steady growth in sales as product acceptance widens.
Stable	Moderate sales increases as the market for the company's product matures.
Decline	Sales decrease as customers are attracted to newer, innovative products.

Individual companies can proceed through the entire cycle while their respective industry remains in one stage. This phenomenon is apparent with many growth stocks.

One memorable round-trip was Global Crossing, one of many telecom network firms founded in the 1990s Internet boom. Global began in 1997 and went public in 1998. By 2001, the company registered $4 billion in annual sales and sported a $47 billion market value. It was a growth company in a growth industry, competing with the likes of Corning and Ciena. In late 2001, the shakeout began, and by early 2002, Global declared bankruptcy, just before the networking industry began a new growth phase. John Wagner, a marketing executive who hadn't experienced Wall Street hype, invested in the stock. After his shares became worthless, he wryly remarked, "I got an expensive education from Global Crossing!"

OVERVIEW AND BUSINESS DESCRIPTION

To begin the business review, the analyst provides a brief history of the company and a summary description of its operations. He outlines ownership and corporate structure and he relates the investment theme behind the shares.

Summary financial data is presented in tabular form, and for diversified companies, this information is broken down by line of business. Selected statistical data on unit sales, capacity utilization, and similar operating items are provided. A brief example appears as Exhibit 7.9.

PRODUCTS AND MARKETS SECTION

Product Line and New Products

In this section, the analyst identifies the company's products and/or services. Bear in mind that many product-oriented firms have a heavy service component. Dell manufactures a reputable line of personal computers, but the clincher is often the company's post-purchase service contracts. Alternatively, the subject business sells status. Johnnie Walker Red is a fine scotch, but is it worth 50 percent more than its competitors? Thus, besides a simple description of the product line, this section provides the reader with an understanding of why the company's products are well-received by its customers.

If available, statistics related to sales volume by product line (dollar and unit volume) are presented here. Estimated gross margins by product line are included. Three to five years of data show trends and complement the analyst's interpretations. Increasing dependence on one product line or a declining margin is a warning signal.

EXHIBIT 7.9   Research Report Summary Page, Constellation Energy Group

Country: United States of America
Industry: Power and Utilities
Symbol: CEG
Exchange: NYSE
Description: CEG is merchant energy provider and electric utility, based principally in the
    middle-Atlantic states.
Investment Rationale and Conclusion: CEG is in the midst of an operations turnaround and
    streamlining of the business after a difficult 2008. The impending sale of a 50 percent
    interest in its nuclear unit will raise cash and cut financial risk. Low valuation multiples
    and conservative 2009 earnings estimates suggest the stock is oversold. Conclusion is buy,
    overweight, and market outperform.

Securities Information

Common Stock

Price	$22	Target Price	$30
52-week high/low	$13–26	Dividend	1.91
Market capitalization	$4,651	Yield	8.4%
Shares outstanding	199	Float	166

Selected bond issue:	Ratings S&P/Moody's:	Spread:
CEG 6.125%	BBB/Baa3	341 bp

Valuation/Financial Data

Fiscal Year Ending *December 31*	2007 *(Actual)*	2008 *(Actual)*	2009 *(Estimated)*	2010 *(Estimated)*
EPS—excluding extraordinary items	$4.60	$3.57	$2.95	$3.12
Price/earnings ratio			7.8×	7.3×
EBITDA (millions)	$1,983	$2,273	$2,045	$1,953
EV/EBITDA			4.5×	4.7×
Revenue	$21,193	$19,975	$20,760	$22,000
EV/revenue			0.4×	0.4×
Free cash (after dividends)	–$470	–$1,090	–$1,200	$200

Balance Sheet Data 12/31/08

Net debt	$4,600	Total debt/ EBITDA	2.6×
Total debt	$5,300	EBITDA/ interest	6.5×
Net debt/capital	34%	Price/book	0.8×

Recent Developments
- Reducing dividend to save cash.
- Selling 50 percent of nuclear unit for $4 billion cash and repaying debt.
- Selling several trading divisions to cut risk metrics.
- Management lowered 2009 earnings forecast by 7 percent.

For example, Crocs, Inc., the innovative footwear manufacturer, receives 90 percent of its income from one brand, Crocs, but it wants to diversify.

New products and services are usually extensions of established offerings, but true innovations are mentioned if they have the potential to impact results. The market rationale for the new product and any evidence of satisfactory test studies provide credibility to this discussion. Pharmaceutical firms provide details in this regard and software companies do the same. Retailers sometimes release the results of new store concepts to investors.

The industry study covers the general market for the company's products and services, but it is likely that the firm segments its larger markets into submarkets, by virtue of a cost differentiation strategy. For example, in setting prices, Global Payments looks at the revenues derived from three submarkets: large corporations, medium-size businesses, and individuals. Optimally, the analyst knows dollar sales and unit sales by submarket, and he examines the firm's relative position. Does it have a leading share? Is it the number 2 player? Are certain submarkets growing faster than others? Answers to these questions enable the analyst to judge the business plans.

In evaluating airline securities, Standard & Poor's places market share and market position at the top of the list. See Exhibit 7.10. These two elements form the core of S&P's business evaluation.

Marketing Strategy and Customer Support

The research report describes the company's marketing strategy and presents the tactics that make the selling effort effective. Tactical areas include:

- Price
- Service
- Reputation
- Geographic coverage
- Product warranties
- Technology
- Credit terms
- Return policy

Pricing policy goes hand in hand with marketing. It also involves large corporate objectives. Does the company hold down prices to increase share, or does it maintain high prices to increase margin? The analyst needs to understand the how and why of product pricing.

Advertising is sometimes an important facet of marketing. At the high end, a cosmetic company such as Estee Lauder spends a remarkable 24 cents out of each sales dollar on advertising. Heavy machinery manufacturers spend less than 1 percent. For companies where advertising expense is a significant item, this section shows advertising costs for the past three years and estimates costs for the coming year. If a consumer business is spending ad dollars yet not increasing sales, this is a problem, as evidenced by Vonage, the VoIP service, since 2008.

Customer support is tied to product *and* service offerings. How many sales end the minute the customer walks out the door or receives delivery? Follow-up service, warranties, repairs, and return policies are critical parts of the product-selling package. Auto manufacturers, such as Toyota Motor Company, offer cradle-to-grave

EXHIBIT 7.10 Company-Specific Analysis Example: Standard & Poor's Important Rating Factors for Airlines

Market Share
Share of industry traffic, measured by revenue passenger miles or revenue ton miles for airlines with significant freight operations
Share of industry capacity, measured by available seat miles or available ton miles
Trend of overall market share
Market share among travel agencies of computerized reservation system (CRS) owned by or shared by airline (Travel agencies tend to book a disproportionate number of tickets on airlines whose CRS they use.)

Position in Specific Markets
Geographic position of airline's hubs for handling major traffic flows; position of competing hubs of other airlines
Share of enplanements and flights at hubs
Share at major origination and destination markets; economic and demographic growth prospects of those markets
Strength of competition at hubs and in major markets served
Barriers to entry/infrastructure constraints
    Gates
    Terminal space and other ground facilities
    Air traffic control; takeoff and landing slot restrictions
Position in international markets
    Growth prospects of markets
    Treaty and regulatory barriers to entry
    Strength of foreign and U.S. competition

Revenue Generation
Utilization of capacity, measured by "load factor" (revenue passenger miles divided by available seat miles)
Pricing
    Yield (passenger revenue divided by revenue passenger miles)
    Yield adjusted for average trip length (Airlines with shorter average trips tend to have higher yields.)
Unit revenues, measured by passenger revenue per available seat mile (yield times load factor)
Effectiveness of revenue management—maximizing revenues by managing trade-off between pricing and utilization
Service reputation; ranking in measures of customer satisfaction
Productivity, measured by revenues or revenue passenger miles per employee or per dollar of assets

Cost Control
Operating cost per available seat mile
    Adjusted for average trip length
    Adjusted for use of operating leases and differing depreciation accounting
Labor
    Labor cost per available seat mile
    Structure of labor contracts; existence and nature of any "B-scales" (lower pay scales for recent hires)
    Flexibility of work rules; effect on productivity
    "Scope clauses" limits on outsourcing
    Status of union contracts and negotiations; possibility of strikes
    Labor relations and morale

(Continued)

EXHIBIT 7.10   (*Continued*)

Fuel costs and impact of potential fuel price hikes, given fuel efficiency of fleet and nature of
  routes flown
Commissions, marketing, and other operating expenses
Aircraft Fleet
Number and type of aircraft in relation to current and projected needs
Status of fleet modernization program
      Average age fleet; age weighted by seats
      Proportion of aircraft meeting "Stage III" noise requirements
      Fuel efficiency of fleet
      Aircraft orders and options for future deliveries

---

service. When purchasing a Toyota, the customer receives warranty protection, and
the dealer records the car's service calls in a database. Software producers attach service calls to their product sales, and the accounting period for a software sale extends
several years, reflecting the ongoing obligation. As part of its business, Nordstrom,
the upscale department store, provides a no-questions-asked return policy. Meanwhile, Wartsila Diesel's customer support system is global. Wartsila technicians fly
in on 48 hours notice to solve customer problems, even when the respective engines
are located in remote areas such as Malawi or Honduras.

In addition to describing the customer support component of the subject company's business, the analyst also identifies its competitive advantages in this regard.
A follow-up step is measuring the company's customer support structure against that
of the competition.

Significant Customers

A company's market position is classified by the prestige of its customers. If a firm
sells services to Royal Dutch Shell and Exxon, most investors perceive it as a stronger
business than one selling to Murphy Oil and Tesoro. Blue-chip customers lend a sense
of solidity to an operation, giving it instant credibility on Wall Street. Of course, big
corporations have better bargaining power than smaller firms, so prestige business
is sometimes a loss leader. Suppliers of Wal-Mart, a tough client, attest to this fact.

A diversified sales base is an asset because it diminishes the impact of losing
any one customer. Investors get nervous when one customer represents more than
10 percent of sales. If the customer selects another supplier, revenues suffer quickly.
For example, auto parts maker Visteon gets 45 percent of its revenue from Ford.

Creditworthy customers are a plus. Sprint Nextel, the third largest cell phone
carrier, incurred a billion-dollar loss in 2008 when tens of thousands of customers
abandoned its service, many because they couldn't pay their bills. In the previous
year, the business recruited people with poor credit to boosts its subscriber base.

PRODUCTION AND DISTRIBUTION

Manufacturing Process and Costs

Here, the research report highlights the economics of the manufacturing process.
The principal determinants of product cost are explained and production bottlenecks

are exposed. For example, natural gas is the principal raw material of a methanol producer, amounting to 30 percent of variable cost. This fact is useful to mention. Likewise, a bottleneck in the methanol process is pipeline throughput and cracker capacity.

A typical service company follows a repetitive process to deliver its product to the customer. For a service business, the analyst understands the stages of production and the costs attached thereto.

A proper examination of manufacturing enables the analyst to discover whether the company can fulfill the production side of its business plan. If more facilities are needed, or if the existing plants require upgrading, the related cash investment is factored into the financial analysis.

As Exhibit 7.11 illustrates, the competitive ability of a pulp and paper producer is dependent on its manufacturing cost position. That's why Standard & Poor's devotes significant emphasis to production costs at the mill level.

Distribution

In certain industries, where the distribution function is important, the research report explores this topic. According to conventional wisdom, a business should control its distribution network once a certain sales volume is achieved. The rise of specialized distribution firms and integrated logistics providers has changed this accepted notion. A thorough research report considers the competitive merits of the company's distribution choices.

Suppliers and Raw Materials

The analyst's investigation into suppliers and raw materials is a search for weakness. A company with access to numerous suppliers is less of a risk than a firm that relies on one or two. If the production process involves just a few inputs, this dependency raises a red flag, particularly if the price of one of the inputs is volatile. A newspaper publisher, for example, buys huge amounts of newsprint, which exhibits a wide price cycle. Publishing margins drop when newsprint prices jump, because ad rates and newsstand prices can't be increased quickly enough to make up the difference.

COMPETITION

Competitive Environment

With competition covered by the industry study, a general treatment is unnecessary in the company section. An appropriate use of this section is a narrow discussion of competitive tactics in the firm's submarkets. When Jet Blue Airlines entered the New York to Los Angeles market, research reports focused on the likely reactions of United Airlines and American Airlines, the dominant providers. A review of the strengths and weaknesses of Jet Blue's tactics—and the probable outcomes—represented a large portion of this section.

Anticipating competitive moves is helpful. For example, the market value of Starbucks fell in 2008 when McDonald's announced a move into specialty coffee.

EXHIBIT 7.11   Company-Specific Analysis: Standard & Poor's
Important Rating Factors for the Pulp and Paper Industry

Manufacturing Cost Position
Low-cost status
   Operating margins
   Return on assets
   Mill margins
   Mill cash cost/ton
   Mill total cost/ton
   Man hours/ton
Modern efficient asset base
   Capital expenditures as a percent of net fixed assets over last 10 years
   Repair and maintenance expenditures as a percent of net fixed assets
      over last 10 years
   Ratio of capital expenditures to inflation-adjusted depreciation
   Are facilities "built-out" or is there room for additions?
   Are facilities integrated (on-site pulping)?
   Are machines new, in good running order?
   Mill site configuration and layout
   Process control and computer utilization
Mill location
   Closeness to growth markets
   Closeness to major metropolitan regions
   Closeness to deep seaports for export
   Freight advantages
   Harvest costs
Labor Relations
   Union vs. nonunion mills
   History of labor disruptions
   Advantageous wage rates and work-rule flexibility
   Union contract expiration schedules

Customer Satisfaction
Quality, service, customer loyalty
   Independent surveys
   Evaluation by commercial printers and publishers, and customers

Product Mix
   Value-added vs. commodity grades
   Sales revenue per product ton
   Diversity of mix
   Breadth of products: full line or one-product supplier?
   Consumer vs. nonconsumer end markets
   Relative pricing sensitivity in key grades

Self-Sufficiency
Fiber self-sufficiency and long-term adequacy
   Fiber sources: internal sources vs. long-term private cutting contracts
      vs. government contracts vs. outside market purchases
   Fiber mix: softwood vs. hardwood vs. recycled paper
   Reforestation programs

EXHIBIT 7.11 (*Continued*)

Energy mix and self-sufficiency
    Fuel mix: internal sources vs. oil vs. coal vs. gas
    Cogeneration, hydropower
    Ability to quickly convert or change to alternative energy source

Marketing Prowess
    Gain or loss of market share
    Distribution channels
    Ratio of advertising cost to sales
    New product introductions
    Degree of influence on pricing
Forward integration
    Percent of in-house paper used by converting facilities
    Wholesale and retail distribution

Comparative Analysis

Because companies do not operate in vacuums, their operating performance—sales growth, profit margin, asset turnover, and so on—is judged in comparison to similar firms. At some point in a research report, a practitioner includes side-by-side statistical tables summarizing these comparisons. A 2007 review of five federal IT contractor companies appears in Exhibit 7.12.

From data such as that in Exhibit 7.12, the analyst reaches conclusions on the comparative ability of the subject company in financial and operating performance. For example, SRA has the best ranking in backlog and sales per employee. Inevitably, such relative measures impact the valuations of equities, as we discuss in later chapters.

EXHIBIT 7.12 Comparative Analysis: 2007 Federal IT Contractors

	Financial Results			Operating Data	
				Backlog as	
		EBITDA		Percentage of	Sales per
	Annual Sales	Profit	Return on	Projected 2008	Employee
Company	Growth (%)	Margin (%)	Equity (%)	Revenue	($000)
CACI	8.0	9.5	9.7	62	186
MTC					
Technologies	6.1	9.6	8.3	51	151
SI International	13.4	9.9	8.4	44	126
SRA					
International	10.0	9.0	11.1	72	202
Stanley	15.6	7.6	17.1	49	167

Note: SRA scores well in most categories.

OTHER TOPICS INCLUDED IN THE BUSINESS REVIEW

Research and Development

Some new products are obtained through acquisition, but the lion's share of innovation is realized through internal research and development. The amount of effort devoted to R&D is situational. A high-tech company like Genzyme deserves more attention than a low-tech business like Caterpillar.

R&D expense trends explain a firm's emphasis on developing new revenue (although it should be said that R&D is also used for cost-saving ideas). A decline in R&D expense may signify that the firm robs future growth to prop up current earnings.

Foreign Sales and Earnings

Publicly traded companies report sales and earnings on a consolidated basis. Foreign sales and earnings are not segregated in the financial statements. Relevant information is set forth in the footnotes.

Foreign sales fall into two categories: exports and local operations. Exports represent products and services created in the United States and sold abroad. Sales proceeds arrive in the United States and are denominated in dollars. A local operation, in contrast, has its infrastructure in a foreign country, including inventory, accounts receivable, and plant and equipment. To illustrate, Colgate Palmolive's subsidiary in Brazil is a self-contained business. Its local assets and related sales are denominated in reals, and then translated into U.S. dollars for the parent company's financial statements.

A foreign presence is considered a healthy sign. It demonstrates an outward-looking firm with a global sophistication. Furthermore, in many industries, foreign markets are growing faster than the U.S. market, so an international presence is a vehicle for increasing sales. Coca-Cola, the quintessential American company, now derives more growth overseas than in the United States. The problem with foreign earnings is the lower degree of certainty as compared to domestic income, leading investors to place a reduced value on companies with a heavy reliance on foreign activities.

This *foreign discount* arises from several factors. First, the information on the foreign business is less forthcoming than the U.S. counterpart. Investors hedge because they have fewer facts from which to draw conclusions, on both exports and local sales. Second, many of the related economies experience volatile swings, heightening the uncertainty of operating results. Third, foreign assets expose the subject firm to exchange rate fluctuations, which have a negative impact when the local currency devalues against the U.S. dollar. Finally, outside of the 15 to 20 most developed countries, U.S. foreign subsidiaries run political risks. Local government policies on taxes, tariffs, and worker benefits can turn on a dime when new administrations assume power. In some circumstances, the local authorities prohibit the subsidiary from exchanging local currency into dollars, and cash dividends to the U.S. parent cease. In 2007, for example, Venezuela nationalized the local subsidiaries of several U.S. oil companies. In extreme cases, the government takes over, leaving foreign investors with losses on their investments.

General Bearing historically produced and sold ball bearings in the United States. In recent years, it expanded into China and Thailand. Over time, analysts boosted their risk assessment of General Bearing stock to reflect the emerging market exposure.

Government Regulation

Most businesses have aspects that involve regulatory oversight. For example, Long Island Lighting's (LILCO) Shoreham nuclear-powered electric generation facility was declared operational by the federal government, but state authorities blocked its start-up. Eventually, LILCO wrote off the $5 billion investment. Calgon Carbon faced low-cost Chinese competition in 2006 for its activated carbon business. In 2007 the federal government instituted 63 percent tariffs on the Chinese product, and the stock price doubled.

Personnel

A corporate executive talks about employees being his firm's "greatest resource," but security analysts downplay the people side of the value equation. Often this is done for good reason. Despite their talk of "valued employees," most firms have high annual turnover rates; 20 to 25 percent is not uncommon. And Wall Street frequently applauds downsizing, despite the outward flow of experience and knowledge.

In the research report, the personnel section discloses the number of employees and the proportion in hourly, commission, or salaried jobs. It may also state the percentage of employees represented by a union. Wall Street figures a low union percentage is good and a high percentage is bad. A description of recent work stoppages is appropriate here.

For certain companies, the compensation system merits discussion. A novel employee ownership plan, profit-sharing system, or bonus scheme represents a competitive edge. Likewise, if the corporate culture is unusual, the analyst mentions it here. For example, in *The Microsoft Way*, Randall Stross, a business professor, concludes, "The deliberate way in which (Chairman Bill) Gates has fashioned an organization that prizes smart people is the single most important, and most deliberately overlooked, aspect of Microsoft's success."[2]

Properties

The properties section is relevant for companies that maintain a large asset base relative to sales and earnings. Dozens of industries fall into this category, including utilities (phones, electricity, gas), petrochemicals, building materials, and autos. Because a company's plant and equipment are vital to its progress, this section reviews the age and efficiency of the existing plant, the state of production technology, and the cost of maintenance. Exhibit 7.11's emphasis on fixed assets of the pulp and paper industry exemplifies this attitude. From a financial point of view, the practitioner considers the adequacy of maintenance expenses and depreciation charges. Are these costs large enough to support the production base? Field visits by the analyst are useful in answering this question.

For firms with a strong real estate or natural resources bent, the properties section is renamed *income earning assets* or *reserves*. It takes a front and center position in the report. With such businesses, the cultivation and harvesting of the physical asset is the primary contributor to income. Oil companies pump oil out of the ground, real estate firms lease buildings, and so on.

Again, there's nothing wrong with the analyst doing some personal tire-kicking to make sure the properties reflect balance sheet values. If possible, a field visit should be conducted, *without* management's assistance, so a true picture is developed. Even the pros get tripped up in their due diligence efforts. Thomas Lee & Company, the $10 billion buyout firm, lost hundreds of millions when Refco, a portfolio company, collapsed in 2007. In performing due diligence, Thomas Lee employed prestigious investment banks (First Boston), accountants (KPMG), consultants (McKinsey & Co.), law firms (Weil Gotshal), insurance brokers (Marsh & McLennan), and a private investigative firm at a cost of $10 million to study Refco. In its lawsuit against Refco's former owners, Thomas H. Lee & Co. stated, "Beginning sometime prior to 2004, the defendants had embarked on a secretive and willful scheme designed to misrepresent Refco's true financial picture by falsifying its books and records."[3] This experience underlies the importance of careful study.

Management

In evaluating management, the analyst must answer the critical question, Can the executives do what they say they're going to do?

The executives of a public company speak in optimistic platitudes: "We're going to grow this company," "Sales and earnings should improve over last year," "This management team is turning the business around!" Yet talk is cheap and poor investment choices are expensive. For this reason, practitioners are keen to know personally the top managers of the firms they cover. They need to know how these executives distill information, how they anticipate strategic moves, and how they implement decisions. The grading of a manager is subjective—given the complex operating environment of most businesses—but experienced industry watchers separate the wheat from the chaff.

Over time, an analyst learns to distinguish between executives with realistic agendas versus those with wishful approaches. Management teams earn credibility with the investor community, and analysts compare one management group versus another. Sometimes the choice appears easy. For example, most investors would select Sam Palmisano (IBM) over Donald Trump (Trump Hotels & Casinos) for the CEO post of a large business. At times, the Street takes these differences to extreme lengths. On the day Anthony Terracciano was appointed Sallie Mae's new chairman in 2007, the company's market value rose $1 billion. Terracciano, of course, was instrumental in enhancing Wachovia's shareholder returns.

Management depth is important. A large, established company like 3M Corporation could lose its top 10 managers and I suspect it would keep operating like a well-oiled machine. Meanwhile, a business dominated by one individual, such as Rupert Murdoch at News Corporation, would suffer repercussions if the executive left suddenly.

It's often the small company that has a thin management team. Additionally, small firms have several other risks related to size. Almost by definition, they lack customer, product, and market diversification. In addition, because optimal financing is achieved through size, smaller companies suffer from cost handicaps vis-à-vis their larger competitors.

Many small to medium-size public companies are family-controlled. Since family succession is frequently a higher priority than professional management at these concerns, family control is a negative for outside shareholders. Furthermore, keeping the business in the family stifles a firm's growth potential, as the equity financing needed to finance new projects is frequently rejected due to the family's worries over ownership dilution.

The analyst makes judgments about management's integrity. Self-dealing, lavish perks, and huge salaries are not evidence of a management whose interests are aligned with those of the shareholders. Prior legal problems of executives are a tip-off to investors in the integrity area.

Board of Directors

Occasionally, the board of directors is reviewed in the management section. For most public companies, the board is not worth mentioning because the average director has so little input into the business. The primary qualification of a director is being one of the CEO's golfing buddies, and the chief responsibility is rubber-stamping the CEO's initiatives and pay packages. The new SEC rules on director independence intend to reverse this situation, but progress is slow.

Board evaluation plays a meaningful role in investment selection in two situations: a speculative stock and a distressed company. In the first instance, a prominent director lends a patina of respectability to the stock, giving the analyst another reason to lend his own confidence. In the distressed company, the directors hopefully play a true watchdog role. In some instances, they fire the CEO and bring in a replacement. Experienced and independent directors are an obvious asset to a troubled business.

SUMMARY

The proper evaluation of a corporate investment requires a thorough assessment of the business fundamentals, and security analysis provides a methodical, step-by-step framework promoting this objective. For each principal aspect of the company's operations, the practitioner gathers data, furnishes a description, and forms a judgment about the firm's sustained competitive advantage (SCA). The basis for industry success determines which factors are emphasized for a particular business.

For any given company, one or more factors can hold special significance, even if that factor is not common to the industry. For example, a strong market share in a specific geographic hub is a huge asset in the airline industry. In other sectors, such as paper and pulp, below-average production costs at one or two facilities can spell the difference between superior profitability and mediocre results. Reliance on one product line, like Croc's dependence on its signature shoe line, is fine when product demand is hot, but the business needs replacement products for the inevitable cooling-off period. Similarly, a focus on one customer is a corporate vulnerability since relationships can change through no fault of the management.

Most segments of the business review have a subjective element, but the evaluation of strategy and management is particularly judgmental. Business environments change and companies adjust tactics, yet the analyst is asked to opine on the strategy's effectiveness over time. Assessing management talent is difficult. When an executive's track record is identifiable, the analyst must decide whether the results were attributable to the manager's skills. Strong subordinates, competitors' mistakes, and plain luck play a large role in an executive's success. To the extent possible, the practitioner's opinion of management reflects reality, rather than wishful thinking.

In sum, the business review is a tool for understanding the company and identifying its operational strengths and weaknesses. From the review's multiple parts, we form a composite picture of the firm's prospects and categorize its business as pioneer, growth, mature, or declining. Many sections of this study are grounded in historical fact, but the analysis also relies on judgment as the practitioner gauges those forces that guide the sales and earnings of the business. Combined with the industry study, the review provides the analyst (and his audience) with the proper foundation from which to begin the financial analysis.

CHAPTER 8

Financial Statement Analysis of an Established Business

With the knowledge gained from the company-specific review, the practitioner commences his financial statement analysis. This chapter examines the mechanics of real-life financial statements and considers numerous examples. The use of ratios and comparable-company statistics help establish a firm's earnings power.

The stock selection process involves a large component of expectations. The investor is usually a student of the *intrinsic value* and *relative value*, and he incorporates projections routinely into stock evaluations. In order to form a reasonable basis for predicting corporate performance, however, the investor must understand historical financial results. The business review set forth in the previous chapter enables the practitioner to attach product innovations, competitive struggles, and other qualitative items to changes in sales and earnings. As the numerical complement to the business review, the financial analysis provides a statistical summary of the company's past by boiling it down to the common denominator of all profit-seeking enterprises—dollars and cents.

Model Research Report

1. Introduction
2. Macroeconomic Review
3. Relevant Stock Market Prospects
4. Review of the Company and Its Business
5. Financial Analysis ✓
6. Financial Projections
7. Application of Valuation Methodologies
8. Recommendation

To a large extent, financial statement analysis is a lost art. Few business schools stress the topic, and MBA students who major in finance graduate with only a rudimentary knowledge of accounting, the nuts and bolts of financial statement analysis. Wall Street and the institutional community deemphasize a careful study of prior financial results. Research departments are so preoccupied with predicting future earnings that they don't take time to scrutinize past accounting data. Furthermore, extensive analysis is an expensive proposition. With most institutions owning hundreds of stocks and turning over their portfolios two to three times annually, placing a lot of effort in studying the financial statements of a single holding is not worthwhile.

In this chapter, I cover the step-by-step approach to financial statement analysis beginning with organizing the raw information, calculating ratios, and interpreting them. The financial analysis is then integrated with the industry-specific performance ratios to make conclusions about a firm's earnings power moving forward. The historical analysis sets the stage for projections, an important component of business valuation that I cover in Chapters 11, 13, and 14.

BEGINNING THE INVESTIGATION

Financial statement analysis is the beginning of an investigation, and many practitioners liken it to detective work. Why did sales go up or down? Why did profit margins change? Is there a reason for the increase in the inventory-to-sales ratio? The answers to these sorts of questions are put to practical use when the analyst prepares financial projections.

An analysis of a company begins with the assumption that the statements provided to the investor are not misleading or fraudulent. The risk of material misstatement is small if the statements are audited by a certified public accounting firm—a requirement for publicly traded firms. Even under the supervision of CPAs, however, firms have flexibility in their use of accounting methods, which may, at times, promote earnings inflation. Additionally, when new business models develop or new finance methods proliferate, the accounting profession frequently plays catch-up in modifying its conventions, a situation that recently cost Internet and financial industry investors dearly. By permitting liberal techniques when the conservative approach is justified, CPAs risk exaggerations in audited data. Even as they police fraudulent reporting, CPAs are fooled by crafty clients. Indeed, the stock market is replete with stories of investors suffering from the effects of inaccurate financial statements certified by accountants unable to detect faulty ledgers. The investor's best protection against this problem is a thorough study of the company's financial trends and accounting policies, which can provide evidence of problems. Details on accounting policy are often left out of the footnotes to the financial statements, so this research involves telephone calls to the firm's finance department and investor relations personnel.

Having accepted the possibility of inaccurate financial data, the analyst studying the historical statements aims at preparing an estimate of current earnings power. This estimate is used as the platform for future earnings projections. For example, suppose the analyst concludes that Rainwell Corporation earned an average of $40 million per year in each of the past three years, after stripping out the effects of extraordinary items and asset sales during the period. If the business review presented nothing unusual, and all factors were equal, he has a logical basis for assuming that $40 million is a reasonable earnings objective *in 2008*, as indicated in Exhibit 8.1.

Exhibit 8.1 notwithstanding, basing earnings forecasts solely on past performance is akin to driving your car by looking in the rearview mirror. Many investors

EXHIBIT 8.1   Rainwell Corporation (US$ millions)

| | Year Ended December 31 | | | |
| | Actual | | Projected | |
	2005	2006	2007	2008
Sales	$720	$745	$770	$780
Net income[a]	38	42	40	40

[a]Adjusted to eliminate one-time items.

fall into this trap and pay dearly for their mistake. But a total separation of the future from the past is equally illogical. Most businesses have fairly stable elements that are readily predictable, so the present and immediate past are good first steps in departing for the future.

THE RAW MATERIALS OF AN ANALYSIS

What are the raw materials from which a financial analysis is created? Start with the three financial statements and the attached footnotes:

1. The Income Statement
2. The Balance Sheet
3. Statement of Cash Flows
4. Notes to Financial Statement

The data from these statements provides a wealth of information for discerning trends and patterns. The four primary tools for evaluating corporate performance are as follows:

1. Absolute amount changes.
2. Percentage changes in growth.
3. Common size percentage statements.
4. Financial ratios.

These tools are applied over a three- to five-year period, since interyear comparisons are the best means of facilitating the discovery of trends, patterns, or anomalies. But be forewarned: This sort of analysis is a lot of work. Exhibit 8.2 shows that if you apply the preceding four analytical tools to each of the three financial statements for a one-year period, you have 12 snapshots of the company's finances for that year. This means plenty of number crunching.

Luckily, the advances of technology reduce the effort involved in preparing raw data. Off-the-shelf analysis software packages can assist in the process, Internet-based services can offer solutions, or the practitioner can create custom-made programs.

EXHIBIT 8.2   Financial Statement Analysis Matrix of Accounting Data and Analytical Tools

	Absolute Amounts	Percentage Changes	Common Size	Ratios
Income Statement	1	4	7	10
Balance Sheet	2	5	8	11
Source and Uses of Funds	3	6	9	12

Note: One year of analysis leads to 12 snapshots of the financial statements.

EVOLUTION OF THE APPROACH TO FINANCIAL STATEMENTS

Most analysts begin with the income statement because it provides the best indicator of profitability. Generating profits is the key to a firm's survival, enabling it to attract the resources, client base, and management talent needed to prosper.

In the early days, the balance sheet, rather than the income statement, was the focus of security analysts. Remembering the Great Crash, they brought a defensive posture to stock selection. Serious investors avoided shares at prices in excess of book value. Furthermore, they were cautious about leverage and looked closely at the number of times assets covered liabilities. Over time, the balance sheet landscape changed dramatically (see Exhibit 8.3). Years of inflation, rapid advances in technology, a jump in mergers and acquisitions, and recognition of the value of intangible assets diminished the interpretive worth of accounting-based balance sheet data, which focused heavily on tangible assets like accounts receivable, inventory, and plant and equipment. Nowadays, the stock market places high values on tangible as well as intangible assets. By way of illustration, the Dow Jones Industrials traded at 1.5 times book value in March 2009.

An intangible license to operate a cellular phone system can have the same value as the billions of dollars of copper pipe, telephone poles, and switching stations

EXHIBIT 8.3   Modern Business Valuation

Deemphasizing the Balance Sheet
- *Inflation.* Years of inflation upset the relationship between the historical accounting value and the respective market value of tangible assets. The depreciation account is misleading in many financial statements.
- *Technology.* The rise in technology firms, whose businesses rely on intellectual capital, undercuts balance sheet–based valuations.
- *Mergers and acquisitions.* Most acquisition prices exceed book value, giving the buyers large goodwill and intangible asset accounts. If operating earnings continue to grow, economic goodwill increases in value, rendering the noncash amortization expenses less meaningful.
- *Intangible asset recognition.* Savvy investors accept the notion that intangible assets are no less valuable than tangible ones.

owned by a hardwire phone company. A famous brand name such as Chanel No. 5 can be more valuable than all the manufacturing facilities used to make the product. As a result, balance sheet analysis today examines liquidity and leverage concerns. When are debts coming due? What has been the behavior of the current accounts and their effect on cash flow?

Free cash flow is seen by some analysts as a better measurement of corporate performance than reported earnings in certain industries and high-leverage situations. Although there is usually a strong relationship between profitability and cash flow, many accounting entries affect one and not the other. Thus, an analysis of the statement of cash flows can reveal a level of corporate performance that is either stronger or weaker than might be apparent from earnings. Indeed, some valuation consultants tell investors to forget earnings per share entirely—use price/cash flow ratios instead of price/earnings data. And importantly, lenders are more eager to lend against cash flow rather than hard assets.

The statement of cash flows is a helpful summary of where the company's cash is going, and it gives an indication of how much cash investment is needed to produce new sales and earnings. Furthermore, along with the income statement, it provides insights into the firm's debt-carrying capacity through the calculation of debt service coverage ratios.

ILLUSTRATION OF THE BASIC APPROACH

As an illustration of the recommended approach to financial analysis, consider Neiman Marcus's results for the three years ended July 30, 2005. Neiman Marcus is an upscale department store chain, which at that time was operating 37 stores in 15 states. Sales for fiscal year 2005 totaled just under $4 billion. It is a useful case study because management published projections in 2005, which we compare later with actual results. Summary income statement and balance sheet data are shown in Exhibit 8.4.

A cursory glance at this information enables the reader to reach the following conclusions: (1) Neiman Marcus was profitable and growing; (2) its principal expense was cost of goods sold, which is expected for a retailer that resells products made by others; (3) the company was conservatively leveraged, with cash exceeding long-term debt; and (4) one-time charges reduced earnings in each year.

Normalizing Results for One-Time Items

Like most companies, Neiman Marcus had a number of charges (net of gains) that were unlikely to be repeated, and these one-time items were segmented from recurring expenses. From an analyst's viewpoint, these items obscured the normal results of Neiman Marcus. Our historical analysis of the company's earnings power eliminates the one-time items, so as to make 2003–2005 data *normalized*. See Exhibit 8.5.

Having normalized the historical data, the analyst proceeds to the next step, which is a review of changes expressed in absolute dollar amounts. Most practitioners prefer to eyeball such changes, rather than to make the calculations set forth in Exhibit 8.6.

EXHIBIT 8.4   The Neiman Marcus Group, Inc., Summary Financial Data (in millions)

	Fiscal Year Ended July 30		
	2003	2004	2005
Income Statement Data			
Net sales	$3,080	$3,525	$3,822
Cost of goods sold	1,995	2,228	2,386
Selling, general, and administrative expense	780	848	907
Depreciation	83	99	108
One-time items, net[a]	15	4	9
Earnings before interest and taxes (EBIT)	$ 207	$ 346	$ 412
Interest on debt and other, net	19	19	16
Earnings before taxes	188	327	396
Income taxes	79	121	146
Net income	$ 109	$ 206	$ 250
Earnings per share	$ 2.30	$ 4.19	$ 5.02
Balance Sheet Data			
Cash	$ 207	$ 368	$ 854
Working capital, net	716	978	1,092
Total assets	2,105	2,618	2,661
Long-term debt	325	325	250
Shareholders' equity	1,146	1,370	1,574

[a]To reflect items associated with division closing, accounting change, goodwill impairment, and sale of private-label credit card operation.
Note: Earnings increased faster than sales. The balance sheet improved, with more cash and less debt.

EXHIBIT 8.5   The Neiman Marcus Group, Inc., Normalized Income Statement Data (in millions)

	Fiscal Year Ended July 30		
	2003	2004	2005
Original EBIT	$ 207	$ 346	$ 412
Add back: One-time items	15	4	9
Normalized EBIT	222	350	421
Interest on debt	(19)	(19)	(16)
Normalized earnings before taxes	203	331	405
Income taxes[a]	(85)	(122)	(149)
Normalized net income	$ 118	$ 209	$ 256
Normalized EPS[a]	$2.49	$4.25	$5.14
Original EPS[b]	$2.30	$4.19	$5.02
Difference[b] (normalized EPS divided by original EPS)	+8%	+1%	+2%

[a]Income taxes are assumed to increase proportionally to the higher normalized earnings.
[b]Normalized EPS shows increases over original EPS.

EXHIBIT 8.6 The Neiman Marcus Group, Inc., Normalized Financial Data, Absolute Amount Changes (in millions)

	Fiscal Year Ended July 30		
	2003	2004	2005
Income Statement Data			
Net sales	+150	+444	+297
Cost of goods sold	+74	+233	+158
Selling, general, and administrative expense	+26	+68	+59
Depreciation	−3	+16	+9
Earnings before interest and taxes (EBIT)	+53	+128	+71
Interest on debt	+1	0	−3
Earnings before taxes	+52	+128	74
Income taxes	+18	+37	+27
Net income	+34	+91	−47
Earnings per share	+0.39	+1.76	−0.89
Balance Sheet Data			
Cash	+28	+161	+486
Working capital, net	+118	+262	+114
Total assets	+127	+513	+43
Long-term debt	+20	0	−75
Shareholders' equity	+112	+224	+204

Note: The gains in sales translated into higher earnings. Cash balances rose and debt declined, indicating excess cash flow.

Absolute Amount Analysis

The jump in sales in 2004 and 2005 was the result of three factors: (1) the continuing economic recovery that encouraged luxury spending; (2) the acceptance of the company's merchandise selections by its customers; and (3) the maturation of two new stores opened in 2003. Operating income (EBIT) increased in line with sales, with a slight gain in profit margins. The addition to cash in 2005 reflects the sale of the company's credit card subsidiary. Excluding the cash increase of $675 million from the gain in total assets ($683 million) indicates that Neiman Marcus boosted sales with a minimal increase ($8 million) in operating assets.

Percentage Changes

Percentage growth statistics in revenues, profits, and cash flow are key drivers in establishing business values. The analyst's ability to predict with confidence future earnings is heavily influenced by his ability to determine constant relationships between sales, expenses, and the additional investment required to produce growth. Financial statements expressed in terms of percentage changes are quite helpful in making these determinations. The related information for Neiman Marcus appears in Exhibit 8.7.

EXHIBIT 8.7   The Neiman Marcus Group, Inc., Normalized Financial Data
Percentage Changes

	Fiscal Year Ended July 30		
	2003	2004	2005
Income Statement Data			
Net sales	+5%	+14%	+8%
Cost of goods sold	+4	+12	+7
Selling, general, and administrative expense	+3	+9	+7
Depreciation	−3	+19	+9
Earnings before interest and taxes (EBIT)	+28	+58	+20
Interest on debt	+5	0	−16
Earnings before taxes	+29	+63	+22
Income taxes	+37	+43	−22
Net income	+27%	+77%	+22%
Earnings per share	+26%	+71%	+21%
Balance Sheet Data			
Cash	+16%	+78%	+132%
Working capital, net	+14	+37	+12
Total assets	+8	+24	+2
Long-term debt	+7	0	−23
Shareholders' equity	+11	+20	+15

Considering that inflation was only 3 percent annually over the 2003–2005 period, Neiman Marcus appeared to be a growth company, since it recorded annual sales changes of 5 percent, 14 percent, and 8 percent. Reflecting a small earnings base in 2002, as well as a retailer's operating leverage, earnings advances far outpaced sales gains. Those three-year results, however, mask the cyclical nature of luxury goods retailing.

Common Size Analysis

Another popular tool in financial analysis is the common size statement. In this presentation, the analyst expenses income statement and balance sheet items as a percentage of sales and total assets, respectively. Since all accounting results are reduced to percentages of the same line item, the data arranged in this way is referred to as *common size*. Information for Neiman Marcus appears in Exhibit 8.8.

The common size data facilitates (1) comparisons of operating results between years, and (2) the evaluation of Neiman Marcus against its peers. Exhibit 8.8 shows that profitability increased as a percentage of sales. EBIT rose from 7.2 percent to 11.0 percent, and net income climbed from 3.8 percent to 6.7 percent. A primary contributor to the increase was cost of goods sold, which fell from 64.7 percent to 62.4 percent. The balance sheet data indicates a large gain in cash and a decline in debt. Working capital, as a percentage of assets, rose from 34.0 percent to 41.0 percent, but if cash is excluded, working capital decreased on the rise in sales, dropping

EXHIBIT 8.8   The Neiman Marcus Group, Inc., Normalized Common Size Data

	Fiscal Year Ended July 30		
	2003	2004	2005
Income Statement Data			
Net sales	100.0%	100.0%	100.0%
Cost of goods sold	64.7	63.2	62.4
Selling, general, and administrative expense	25.3	24.1	23.7
Depreciation	2.7	2.8	2.8
Earnings before interest and taxes (EBIT)	7.2%	9.9%	11.0%
Interest on debt	0.6	0.5	0.4
Earnings before taxes	6.6	9.4	10.6
Income taxes	2.8	3.5	3.9
Net income	3.8%	5.9%	6.7%
Balance Sheet Data			
Cash	9.8%	14.0%	32.1%
Working capital, net	34.0	37.3	41.0
Total assets	100.0	100.0	100.0
Long-term debt	15.4	12.4	9.4
Shareholders' equity	54.4	52.3	59.2

Note: A lower cost of goods sold increased earnings; cash rose as a percentage of assets.

from 24.2 percent in 2003 to 8.9 percent in 2005. This change suggested a more efficient use of assets.

Statement of Cash Flows

The statement of cash flows is a blueprint for seeing how cash is generated and where it goes. Because it has no common size items like sales or total assets, the statement of cash flows is interpreted differently than the income statement and balance sheet. Furthermore, a number of the accounts have no true baseline from which to measure year-to-year changes. As a result, the cash flow statement tends to confirm (or deny) opinions reached in the analysis of the first two statements.

The cash flow statement has three sections:

1. *Cash flows from operating activities.* This section summarizes the cash generated from selling a product or service, including the changes in working capital supporting the business.
2. *Cash flows from investing activities.* This is a review of the cash investment in (or disposition of) fixed assets and acquisitions.
3. *Cash flows from financing activities.* The finance function is considered separately from the day-to-day operations of the business. This section indicates how the business is funded or, in certain cases, how excess monies are utilized.

EXHIBIT 8.9   The Neiman Marcus Group, Inc., Summary Statement of Cash Flows (in millions)

	Fiscal Year Ended July 30		
	2003	2004	2005
Net cash provided by operations	$164	$ 53	$845
Net cash used in investing activities	130	(117)	(229)
Cash flow from running the business	34	(64)	616
Net cash provided by financing	(7)	226	(131)
Net increase (decrease) in cash	$ 27	$162	$485

For Neiman Marcus, the cash flow statement illustrates that the firm produces cash from operations, although most of the excess cash originated in 2005 from the sale of private-label credit card business. See Exhibit 8.9

A negative cash flow is not automatically a danger signal for a business evaluation. Many growing companies exhibit thin or negative cash flow because growth requires added investment. Mature and declining companies can have strong cash flow, but the analyst weighs whether this attribute is sustainable in the face of competitive threats. In either case, the analyst considers the following question: Does the business produce an acceptable rate of return on new investment, or should it simply pay a higher dividend? By way of example, in 2007, some activist investors called on management to run McDonald's as a cash flow business to pay dividends, instead of investing money to facilitate dubious growth prospects.

Analysts often promote the use of *free cash flow* (FCF) measures which, depending on the methodology, integrate various items from the funds from operations, investment activities, and financing sections. These measures are of best use in a three- to five-year moving average. Over a one- or two-year period, large differences in working capital accounts, major investments, and specific one-time financings diminish the usefulness of FCF, as demonstrated by the variations in Neiman Marcus' cash flow results. See Exhibit 8.10.

Ratio Analysis

Ratio analysis relates income statement, balance sheet, and cash flow statement items to one another. Like the other forms of analysis reviewed herein, ratio analysis provides clues in evaluating a firm's current position and in spotting trends toward future performance. Ratios fall into four categories:

1. *Profitability ratios* measure the return on assets and equity investments. Profit margins, expressed as a percentage of sales in the common size income statement, are also defined as profitability ratios.
2. *Activity ratios* measure the efficiency with which the firm manages its assets.
3. *Credit ratios* measure the firm's ability to repay its obligations, its existing leverage, and its resultant financial risk.
4. *Growth ratios* measure the firm's performance in expanding its business, a key valuation criterion.

EXHIBIT 8.10   The Neiman Marcus Group, Inc., Statement of Cash Flows (in millions)

	Fiscal Year Ended July 30		
	2003	2004	2005
Cash Flows from Operations			
Net income	$109	$205	$249
Adjustment to reconcile net income to net cash provided by operations:			
Depreciation	83	99	107
Sale of credit card division	—	—	534
Other, net	49	64	40
	241	368	930
Changes in Operating Assets and Liabilities			
Increase in receivables	(36)	(287)	(71)
Increase in inventory	(30)	(33)	(38)
Increase in payables	18	40	35
Other, net	(28)	(35)	(11)
(1) Net cash provided by operations	165	53	845
Cash Flows from Investing Activities			
Capital expenditures	(130)	(120)	(203)
Other, net	—	3	(26)
(2) Cash used in investing activities	(130)	(117)	(229)
Cash Flows from Financing Activities			
Borrowings	—	225	—
Repayment of borrowings	—	—	(112)
Cash dividends	—	(12)	(27)
Other, net	(7)	12	9
(3) Cash provided from financing activities	(7)	225	(130)
(1) + (2) + (3) = Net increase (decrease) in cash	28	161	486
Cash at beginning of year	179	207	368
Cash at end of year	$207	$368	$854

Note: Cash flow from operations was reinvested in the business, prompting a need for external financing.

Most industries record consistent financial ratios over time, and ratio analysis shows when results become out of sync. The causes for disproportions or extreme variations in a company's ratios become the focus of further study. Fifty years ago, John Myer, an accounting professor, described an investigation methodology that is still in use today:

Investigating Changes in a Financial Ratio

1. Compare subject company ratios with industry standards and historical norms.
2. Examine the ratio's past trend.
3. Analyze the performance of the components of the ratio.
4. Look at qualitative changes in the underlying business that impacts the components.

EXHIBIT 8.11   Three Firms with a Decrease in Sales/Receivables Ratio (in millions, except for ratios and percentages)

	Sales	Receivables	Sales/Receivables
Growth Company			
2007	$600	$100	6.0×
2008	700	140	5.0×
2007 Index = 100%	100%	100%	
2008	117	140	
Mature Company			
2007	$600	$100	6.0×
2008	590	118	5.0×
2007 Index = 100%	100%	100%	
2008	98	118	
Decline Company			
2007	$600	$100	6.0×
2008	500	100	5.0×
2007 Index = 100%	100%	100%	
2008	83	100	

For example, Exhibit 8.11 shows three firms that experienced a decrease in the ratio of sales to receivables, from 6.0 in 2007 to 5.0 in 2008. In each case the ratio changed, but for different reasons.

The analyst studies notes about the 6.0× ratio in 2007 for the three companies, as well as the 2008 drop to 5.0×. The first action is step 1: a quick comparison to standards. The industry norm for the sales/receivables ratio is 5.5×. The second step is observing changes. The negative trend in the ratio from 2007 to 2008 is apparent. Finally, in step 3, the analyst figures out the rationale for the changes:

> *Growth company:* There was a rise in both sales and receivables, but the receivables rose at a higher rate.
>
> *Mature company:* There was a decline in sales but a rise in receivables.
>
> *Decline company:* There was a decline in both sales and receivables, but sales declined faster.

The analysis then passes to the business reasons behind the ratio differences. Both the industry analysis and company-specific review outlined the causes for revenue changes—differences in unit volume and/or prices—and the qualitative elements contributing to revenue movements. Variations in receivables require inquiry in two areas: (1) external factors such as the customers' ability to pay because of a recession, for example; or (2) internal factors such as collection policy changes or more liberal credit terms. Finding answers to these questions is step 4.

From this illustration, we see that ratio analysis is more than just the compilation of statistics. Ratios provide evidence of the manner in which a business is being administered, and significant variations to a company's trend or the industry norm require study.

Neiman Marcus Ratio Analysis

Exhibit 8.12 shows selected Neiman Marcus' ratios, segmented into the four categories: profitability, activity, credit, and growth.

The financial ratios paint a picture of a business enjoying solid performance. The profitability ratios show the return on equity climbing from 10 percent to 17 percent. With AA corporate bonds yielding 5 percent at the time, Neiman Marcus provided a premium return. The activity ratios indicate progress in boosting inventory turnover, an important element of a retailing operation, and the credit ratios illustrate financial strength. The current ratio rose from 2.4 to 2.8 and debt service coverage ratio improved. The growth ratios demonstrate the firm's investor attraction. Sales grew at a moderate 6 percent compound annual rate, but EPS increased at a rapid 21 percent. In sum, the ratio analysis provides a flattering portrait of Neiman Marcus.

In part, the positive trends convinced lenders to participate in the $5 billion leveraged buyout of the company, which was completed in October 2005.

EXHIBIT 8.12 The Neiman Marcus Group, Inc., Selected Financial Ratios (normalized data)

	Year Ended July 30			
	2003	2004	2005	Trend
Profitability Ratios				
Net profit/average equity	10%	16%	17%	Up
EBITDA/average assets	11%	19%	20%	Up
Activity Ratios				
Sales/average assets	1.5×	1.5×	1.4×	Stable
Average inventory/cost of goods sold	3.0×	3.2×	3.2×	Stable
Credit Ratios				
Current assets/current liabilities	2.4	2.3	2.8	Up
Total debt/stockholders' equity	0.2	0.3	0.2	Stable
EBIT/interest	12×	18×	26×	Up
EBITDA/average debt service	6×	6×	8×	Up

Growth Ratios 2001–2005	
Sales	6%
EBITDA	17%
Net income	23%
Earnings per share	21%

Note: Ratio trends were stable to up as the company benefited from an economic recovery.

EXHIBIT 8.13   The Neiman Marcus Group, Inc., Industry-Specific Statistics

	Year Ended July 30			
	2003	2004	2005	Trend
Growth in same-store sales	4.1%	14.4%	9.9%	Up
Growth from acquisitions and new stores	$ 79.6	—	—	Down
Sales per store (in millions)	$ 67.8	$ 77.0	$ 86.2	Up
Sales per square foot of selling area	$475	$528	$577	Up
Growth in sales per square foot	(1.2)%	11.1%	9.3%	Up
Sales per employee (in thousands)	$195	$206	$220	Up
Number of stores	37	37	36	Down

Industry-Specific Indicators

In the preceding analysis, we reached conclusions through the evaluation of data arranged in specific ways for Neiman Marcus, but remember that each situation is unique. Part of the art of interpreting financial performance is selecting which information is the focus of the investigation. Which ratios are meaningful? What trends are important? What are the best comparative indicators? How reliable are the past results in predicting future performance? A consideration of these questions prior to the start of a financial analysis represents a huge time savings in completing the research report.

Complementing financial statement analysis is the evaluation of a company's results in industry-specific terms. Most firms provide industry-specific statistics that have proven to be useful performance indicators (or the analyst calculates them with the information available). The retailing industry is no exception. Exhibit 8.13 shows selected industry-specific data.

Because retailers can increase sales volume easily by opening new stores, practitioners developed a statistic that isolates the sales growth accruing from established properties from the sales growth resulting from new stores. This statistic is termed the growth in same-store sales. An examination of this statistic shows the strength of a retailer's underlying growth, without the capital expense of new stores and acquisitions. In the case of Neiman Marcus over the 2003–2005 period, same-store sales growth was higher than the inflation rate, signaling good prospects for the firm's base business. Sales efficiency—measured by sales per store, sales per square foot of selling area, and sales per employee—is also a monitor of performance. If inflation is excluded from the data, Neiman Marcus showed real growth. The only negative indicator was a 1.2 percent drop in sales per square foot in 2003, which was attributable to two store openings in 2003. As those stores matured, the sales per square foot reached the mean.

Comparable Company Performance

The historical financial analysis of a business is not conducted in a vacuum. Statistics, ratios, and profit margins are not meaningful numbers in and of themselves; they must be compared with something before they are useful. Much depends on the type of industry involved. For example, a brokerage firm, with a preponderance of liquid assets, operates with a much higher degree of leverage than a department store chain, whose primary assets are merchandise inventories and fixed assets. Evaluated within the same industry, however, single-company data takes on new meaning, as it provides the basis for comparisons and thus facilitates conclusions. For this reason, the ratios used to measure firm performance are compared to ratios for companies operating in the same industry. The company that is the object of study is measured against its peer group. Has it done better, or worse, than the competition? Do its yardsticks meet industry averages? Do its results trend with those of the industry? The answers to these questions are useful in appraising the relative merits of a business.

In addition to Neiman Marcus, two other luxury department store chains were publicly traded in 2005: Nordstrom, Inc. and Saks, Inc. A description of the two firms follows:

1. *Nordstrom, Inc.* Nordstrom operated 101 upscale department stores. Sales and net income for the fiscal year ending January 29, 2005, were $7.1 billion and $393 million, respectively.
2. *Saks, Inc.* Saks operated 54 Saks Fifth Avenue department stores. Sales and net income for the fiscal year ended January 29, 2005, were $6.4 billion and $61 million, respectively.

Because Neiman Marcus, Nordstrom, and Saks were similar in size but not identical, comparable data was helpful when evaluated in common size percentages and ratios. Relevant information is set forth in Exhibit 8.14.

EXHIBIT 8.14 Luxury Department Store Chains Comparable Common Size Data, Normalized Financial Results, Fiscal 2005

	Neiman Marcus	Nordstrom	Saks
Income Statement Data			
Net sales	100.0%	100.0%	100.0%
Cost of goods sold	62.4	60.2	65.2
Selling, general, and administrative expense	23.7	28.3	27.6
Depreciation	2.8	3.7	3.6
Earnings before interest and taxes (EBIT)	11.0%	7.8%	3.6%
Interest	0.4	(1.0)	(1.7)
Other income	—	2.4	—
Earnings before taxes	10.6	9.2	1.9
Income taxes	3.9	3.6	0.8
Net income	6.7%	5.6%	1.1%
Balance Sheet Data			
Cash	32.1%	7.8%	2.2%
Working capital	41.0	28.9	24.2
Total assets	100.0	100.0	100.0
Long-term debt	9.4	22.3	34.6
Shareholders' equity	59.2	38.8	44.3

Note: Neiman Marcus's net margins were higher than the competition, and its balance sheet was less leveraged.

EXHIBIT 8.15   Comparable Financial Ratios, Normalized Data, Fiscal 2005

	Neiman Marcus	Nordstrom	Saks
Profitability Ratios			
EBITDA/average assets	17%	17%	10%
Net profit/average equity	20%	24%	4%
Activity Ratios			
Sales/average assets	1.4×	1.6×	1.3×
Average inventory/cost of goods sold	3.2×	4.5×	2.7×
Credit Ratios			
Current assets/current liabilities	2.8	1.9	2.2
Total debt/stockholders' equity	0.2	0.6	0.7
EBIT/interest	8.1×	7.2×	2.0×
Growth Statistics—Latest Five Years			
Sales	6.3%	6.6%	(0.6)%
EBIT	16.4	43.2	(9.8)
Net income	23.1	34.2	(1.0)
Earnings per share	21.4	31.1	(12.0)

Note: Neiman Marcus is above the competition in credit ratios. It underperforms in activity ratios and ranks second in growth, generally Wall Street's most important category.

Referring to the income data, Neiman Marcus ranked better than its two competitors in terms of the EBIT/sales ratio. Cost of goods sold for Neiman Marcus was in the middle at 62.4 percent, but the company had relatively low selling, general and administrative (SG&A) expense. Bottom-line performance for Neiman Marcus, as summarized in the net income to sales ratio, was the highest of the group. The balance sheet data shows Neiman Marcus's low leverage. Both Nordstrom and Saks had lower working capital/assets and higher debt/assets ratios.

Comparable ratio analysis indicated that Neiman Marcus ranked second in profitability and first in credit quality. Its activity ratios were the lowest, reflecting the relatively high-end nature of its inventory, which tends to turn over less than the slightly less expensive products offered by its competitors. See Exhibit 8.15

The five-year growth statistics demonstrate the operating leverage inherent in retailing. With moderate sales growth of 6 percent annually, Neiman Marcus and Nordstrom showed EPS growth of 21.4 percent and 31.1 percent, respectively. Saks was beset with digestive problems related to acquisitions and exhibited flat growth.

The industry-specific data pinpointed Neiman Marcus as an overperformer in 2005. Same-store sales growth exceeded that of its rivals, and the company's sales per square foot were much higher at $577. See Exhibit 8.16. In part, the sales per square foot differential resulted from Neiman Marcus selling higher-priced goods than either Nordstrom or Saks. It paid for this attribute by having lower inventory turnover than Nordstrom, so its return on investment was lower.

EXHIBIT 8.16 Industry-Specific Statistics

| | Latest Fiscal Year: 2005 | | |
	Neiman Marcus	Nordstrom	Saks
Growth in same-store sales	9.9%	8.5%	5.3%
Growth from acquisitions, new stores, or store closings	(1.5)	2.0	1.0
Sales per square foot of selling area	577	347	274

REVIEW OF NEIMAN MARCUS FINANCIAL ANALYSIS

Any comparable analysis suffers from the fact that few companies are totally the same. Another drawback is the different accounting practices of similar firms. Finally, a review of past performance is only one guide to the likelihood of future success. Historical financial analysis is a base from which financial projections and corporate valuations are determined, but it's not the end-all for the practitioner.

In the case of Neiman Marcus, we reached the following conclusions:

- *Sales growth* reflected good same-store performance, rather than acquisitions. Sales rose, in part, due to the U.S. economy rebounding from a 2000–2001 slowdown, as luxury retailing is a cyclical business.
- *Earnings growth* was much stronger than sales growth, showing the operating leverage of the company.
- *Liquidity and credit ratios* ranked high, and Neiman Marcus had substantial cash reserves.
- *Comparable analysis* placed Neiman Marcus between two competitors.

The evidence indicated that Neiman Marcus was a solid operator with a conservative balance sheet. Reflecting this fact and the company's low-tech nature, management received a leveraged buyout offer in early 2005 for $100 per share. Private equity firms and institutional lenders eagerly funded the transaction later that year.

Management's Projections

To consider the interplay between historical results and future projections, we examine management forecasts provided in 2005. Post-buyout, the new Neiman Marcus had a debt-to-equity ratio of 3:1, demonstrating lenders' willingness to loan against future cash flow. A key element of the $4 billion debt financing was a management forecast, which exemplified the optimism found in the vast majority of Wall Street projections: historical trends continue, sales go up, operating margins increase, and working capital shrinks. Neither a recession nor a new competitor is contemplated. See Exhibit 8.17.

EXHIBIT 8.17   The Neiman Marcus Group, Inc., Projected Statement of Operations Data (in millions)

	For the Fiscal Year Ended July				
	2006	2007	2008	2009	2010
Sales	$4,082	$4,375	$4,779	$5,191	$5,549
Gross profit	1,793	1,921	2,099	2,278	2,438
EBITDA	543	602	665	729	779
EBIT	433	478	526	577	618

Forecast Assumption: No Recession   *The economy will continue to prosper.*

Importantly, the forecast assumes no U.S. recession, despite the fact that the U.S. economy experiences downturns every 7 to 10 years. During the 2000–2002 slowdown, for example, Neiman Marcus's sales rose an anemic 1 percent annually and earnings fell 26 percent.

Forecast Assumption: Sales   *Compound annual sales growth is 8 percent, reflecting inflation, same-store increases, and several new stores.*

For 2006 and 2007, sales growth is higher than projected.

Forecast Assumption: Gross Profit Margin   *Gross profit margin is stable at 44 percent and is consistent with prior years.*

In reality, the gross profit margin was slightly higher over the projected period.

Forecast Assumption: EBITDA Margin   *EBITDA margins rise about 1 percent over the five-year period, reflecting the operating leverage of the luxury retailing business.*

EBITDA rose higher than forecast as gross margin increased, as SG&A costs (as a percent of sales) fell under the new ownership.

Actual Results: 2006–2008

It is interesting to compare management's projections with what really happened. After all, who can predict a company's future better than its management? Exhibit 8.18 compares the projected data with the firm's actual results for the three years ended July 2008.

EXHIBIT 8.18   The Neiman Marcus Group, Inc., Condensed Financial Data (in millions)

	Fiscal Year Ended July 30		
	2006	2007	2008
Projected sales	$4,082	$4,375	$4,779
Actual sales	4,029	4,390	4,600
Projected EBITDA	543	602	665
Actual EBITDA	514	685	515

Actual sales approximated management's targets. Actual EBITDA exceeded management's objectives in 2006 and 2007 as assumptions regarding gross margins and SG&A expense proved conservative. In this case, management had an incentive to lowball projections to ensure that the private equity firm's price (and management's buy in) were below market. The ability of Neiman Marcus to exceed its projections led its private equity owners to consider an IPO in 2007. With the unfolding of the subprime crisis, that offering was shelved, as economic conditions forced consumers to retrench, contributing to the fall-off in 2008 EBITDA.

SUMMARY

An evaluation of an established company's future prospects is based on prior events. Thus, a historical financial analysis precedes a projection of future results. An analysis is conducted systematically using the firm's financial statements as the raw materials and using the four primary analytical tools: absolute amounts, percentage changes, common size statements, and financial ratios. The would-be investor also prepares industry-specific statistics to measure the firm's operating health. All of this information is used in comparison with data from similar businesses.

Experienced practitioners approach financial statements with a critical eye. Accounting firms are far from perfect and managements have an incentive to use liberal accounting methods, which may hide true economic returns. Furthermore, accounting profits are superseded by cash flow measures in certain situations.

Analysts sometimes fall in love with a company and prepare projections while looking through rose-colored glasses. All forecasts benefit from a comparison with recent results and a realistic view toward the likelihood of future economic downturns.

CHAPTER 9

The Limitations of Accounting Data

Accounting scandals have affected some of America's largest corporations and have caused major losses for investors. Executive compensation at most firms is tied to financial targets, so managers are motivated to manipulate accounting results in order to increase their personal income. Because the corporate managers and the public auditors who facilitate misleading statements are rarely punished, accounting problems are a recurring theme.

As shown in the previous chapter, intelligent financial analysis combines a thorough understanding of a business with a detailed review of its financial statements. Because the financials are constructed from accounting data, the practitioner must appreciate the limitations of accounting as a means of describing a firm's financial condition. The complexity of the modern corporation and the advance of new technologies, industries, and financial instruments make the auditor's job a continuing challenge. These factors emphasize the business evaluator's need for diligence and skepticism.

Many beginning students of security analysis regard financial statements as snapshots of absolute monetary values. After all, the statements are usually audited by a Big Four accounting firm, reviewed by a corporate board of directors, and passed through SEC scrutiny. They carry the imprimatur of expertise and officialdom. The notion of exactitude is further supported by the fact that the statements fit each other like a glove. The income statement carries over to the balance sheet, and both statements supply the raw information for the cash flow tables. All the accounts balance in a tidy symmetry, and the package is nicely prefaced with an accountant's formal letter, which is followed by voluminous footnotes explaining accounting policies and disclosure items.

This appearance of numerical accuracy belies the fact that many accounting entries are not based on actual transactions, evidenced by certifiable records of money changing hands. Rather, a number of accounts rely heavily on the educated judgment of management and the corporate auditor. Ideally, these judgments provide financial statement users with a fair mathematical interpretation of a firm's financial condition.

A perfect example of historical accounting's shortcomings is the fixed asset account. The economic life of specific asset classes varies widely among companies, and the depreciation charge attached to an asset represents simply a best guess on the auditor's part, particularly as the asset takes on unique attributes within its class.

Likewise, the stated value of the asset (net of depreciation) on the balance sheet has curiosity value to the reader interested in original cost, but it typically has little economic meaning. Yet alternatives are lacking. Replacement cost is of minimal use if the firm has no plans to replace the asset in the near future. Liquidation value has little relevance if the business is a going concern, and "value in use" is difficult to separate from the totality of operations. The practicality of traditional accounting wins out over the alternatives.

The accounting profession readily acknowledges the limitations of today's system, and it strives to update the methodology to respond to changing circumstances. Nevertheless, the profession often plays catch-up in confronting new situations, and accountants caution analysts against taking financial statements literally. They repeat the following precepts:

> *Financial statements are prepared for the purpose of presenting a periodic report on progress by the management. They deal with the status of the investment in the business and the results achieved during the period under review.*
>
> *They reflect a combination of recorded facts, accounting conventions and personal judgments; and the judgments and conventions affect them materially. The soundness of the judgments necessarily depends on the competence and integrity of those who make them and on their adherence to generally accepted accounting principles and conditions.*[1]

As these statements imply, an appropriate financial investigation of a company extends past a review of the financial statements. It involves a meticulous study of the footnotes to the statements and an intelligent dialogue with the company's executives.

Time and time again, investors have been burned because a casual study of a firm's reports indicated a satisfactory condition, yet the actual situation was marginal. If a quick review reveals warning signals, the analyst is well advised to conduct a deeply probing investigation without cutting corners. Unfortunately, this doesn't happen as often as it should. Most analysts lack extensive accounting training, and they are under pressure to focus singularly on future growth. As a result, Wall Street doesn't police accounting issues well. Corporations frequently get away with presenting a rosy scenario where none exists.

Accounting irregularities are a regular occurrence in the public markets, and recent trends suggest that affliction is spreading from smaller speculative firms to larger blue-chip companies where management is supposed to know better. In December 2006, for example, Fannie Mae, the gigantic mortgage lender, reduced its earnings for 2002, 2003, and 2004 by $5 billion, capping an earlier announcement that caused the company's market value to drop by $35 billion. In 2007 and 2008, multiple top-tier banks and brokerage firms took huge write-offs on mortgage-booked securities, corporate loans, and structured investment vehicles that they and their accountants had trouble evaluating. Stockholders lost billions, but few managers were fired. Almost none were fined or arrested.

A number of post-Enron rule changes, such as the Sarbanes-Oxley bill, were supposed to limit this irresponsible behavior, but they represent Band-Aid solutions to the broad problems set forth by Penn State accounting professor Edward Katz as "the fragility of accounting, the underauditing by the Big Four, and the lack of real enforcement by the SEC."

BASIC ACCOUNTING ISSUES

The current system works pretty well, but practitioners repeatedly confront six issues that complicate their work. The first three items are global problems that affect many analyses. The other three elements are company-specific.

Global Issues	Company-Specific Issues
1. Accounting for financial companies and instruments.	4. Management discretion.
	5. Disclosure.
2. Growth in mergers and acquisitions.	6. Potential for fraud.
3. International accounting differences.	

This chapter covers these issues and looks at how they apply to selected accounting entries.

GLOBAL ISSUES

Accounting both for financial companies' mergers and acquisitions and for international firms presents generic problems for issuers worldwide. We cover key issues in this section.

Accounting for Financial Companies and Instruments

Financial companies have represented the largest accounting scandals, costing investors and guarantors (such as the federal government) hundreds of billions of dollars. The repetitive nature of the problem—stretching from the savings and loan collapse of the early 1980s to the subprime blow-up of 2008—shows that the accounting profession lacks a good set of models to evaluate financial companies. Commercial banks, brokerage firms, insurance companies, and similar businesses own complex arrays of loans, public securities, private investments, and custom derivative instruments. These assets are difficult for financial professionals to value properly. The task is harder for auditors, who don't participate in the markets on a regular basis.

To lend transparency to the valuation of financial assets and to provide objective yardsticks for auditors, the Financial Accounting Standards Board (FASB) in 2008 required financial firms to "mark to market" their assets and to classify them into one of three levels. Each level indicates the degree of freedom with which the asset can be bought or sold.

Level 1: Easy to trace pricing; the assets have quoted prices in active markets (e.g., U.S. Treasury bonds, gold futures, or large-cap stocks).

Level 2: An intermediate stage for assets that are not traded but where there is a quoted, public market for similar assets (e.g., a private equity investment in a chemical company that has publicly traded comparables).

Level 3: Private, custom-tailored securities for which there is no publicly quoted equivalent (such as many derivative contracts and certain securitized loans) or where the public market is inactive. These valuations contain assumptions of the party "fair valuing" the asset, and it may involve discounted cash flow modeling, a methodology that has much subjectivity.

This outline of three levels of classification is an improvement over earlier practices, but as Ron Everett of Business Valuation Center says, "It puts the auditor in the role of valuation expert, which is frequently inappropriate." Furthermore, as others have noted, the auditing firm is paid by the corporate client and there is pressure to bend the mark-to-market process in management's favor. Hiring independent consultants to appraise complex securities is another option, but companies are reluctant to do so because of the cost involved.

A derivative financial instrument represents a contractual agreement between counterparties and has a value that is *derived* from changes in the worth of some other underlying asset, such as the price of another security, interest rates, or currency exchange rates. Examples of derivatives include stock options, futures, and interest rate swaps. Once relegated to a small group of sophisticated financial institutions, the use of derivative instruments has spread rapidly throughout corporate America. Commonly used as hedging devices that make income flows more predictable, derivatives can have unforeseen side effects. If used for speculative purposes, they can result in disaster. That's because a derivative's price tends to be more volatile than the price of the underlying security. The billion-dollar Aman hedge fund closed when rising interest rates caused its derivative portfolio to plummet in value.

The accounting profession and the SEC are updating disclosure standards for the increasing variety of new and exotic derivatives, but for now, the information is typically off balance sheet and scattered throughout the footnotes. For corporations such as banks and insurance companies, which use these instruments on a regular basis, the required disclosure is unintelligible to anyone but the most tenacious practitioner. Furthermore, derivative values are quite volatile, changing dramatically in days or weeks, yet the security analyst relies heavily on quarterly reports that are released only every three months.

Growth in Mergers and Acquisitions

Since the 1980s, there has been an explosive growth in mergers and acquisitions. In 90 percent of the transactions, the acquirer pays in excess of the seller's tangible book value (defined as net tangible assets minus liabilities). When buyers use purchase accounting, there is a significant upward revision of the seller's asset value. Usually, such revisions don't account for the entire premium over book, and large amounts are registered as "goodwill" and "identifiable intangible assets." The existing asset write-ups and new intangible assets are each assigned amortization periods that hopefully match their economic lives. The resulting charges are deducted from the buyer's income. A firm that undergoes multiple transactions has more inconsistencies between depreciable life and economic life than one whose business is internally grown. Practitioners deal with this problem by evaluating results above the line. They look at earnings before interest, taxes, depreciation, and amortization (EBITDA) instead of net earnings as the primary measurement of performance; thus, the impact of artificial depreciation and amortization charges is eliminated. Other substitutes for net earnings are free cash flow and economic value added (EVA).

Exhibit 9.1 summarizes the write-ups when Dove Equipment buys Falcon Manufacturing to form Newco. Exhibit 9.2 illustrates the analyst's predicament. How does he compare the EPS of the newly merged Newco with its competitor, Telright Corp? The results are similar, but different. Sales and EBITDA are the same for both firms, but Telright's earnings per share (EPS) are higher because Newco's earnings are depressed by amortization charges.

Acquisition prices for companies are increasingly higher than net tangible assets. In 1988, net tangible assets represented 40 percent of takeover purchase prices. By 2008, this statistic had fallen to just 20 percent. Lowell Bryan of McKinsey & Co. points out that "Historical accounting understates the value of intangibles—people,

EXHIBIT 9.1   Dove Equipment Acquiring Falcon Manufacturing for $1 Billion to Form Newco—Balance Sheet Data (in millions)

	Dove Equipment	Falcon Manufacturing	Adjustments	Newco Pro Forma Combined
Assets				
Current assets	$ 500	$225		$ 725
Fixed assets	500	225	+100[a]	825
Goodwill	—	—	+300[a]	300
Identifiable intangible assets	—	—	+300	300
Total assets	$1,000	$450	$700	$2,150
Liabilities and Stockholders' Equity				
Current liabilities	$ 300	$150	—	$ 450
Long-term debt	100	—	+600[b]	700
			−300[c]	
Stockholder's equity	600	300	+400[c]	1,000
Total liabilities and stockholders' equity	$1,000	$450	$700	$2,150

Adjustments
[a]$1 billion purchase price exceeds $300 million Falcon equity by $700 million. The excess is allocated $100 million to fixed assets, $300 million to goodwill (not amortized), and $300 million to identifiable intangible assets (like customer lists or brand names, amortized over 10 years).
[b]Issuance of $600 million of new debt for finance acquisition.
[c]Elimination of Falcon equity and issuance of $400 million of new Dove equity.

EXHIBIT 9.2   Similar Companies, Different Accounting (in millions except per share data)

Comparative Balance Sheet Data		
	Newco Combined	Telright Corp.
Assets		
Current assets	$ 725	$ 725
Fixed assets	825	825
Goodwill	300	—
Identifiable intangible assets	300	—
	$2,150	$1,550
Liabilities and Equity		
Current liabilities	$ 450	$ 450
Long-term debt	700	700
Stockholders' equity	1,000	400
	$2,150	$1,550

Comparative Income Statement Data		
	Newco Combined	Telright Corp.
Revenues	$3,000	$3,000
EBITDA	$ 250	$ 250
Depreciation	100	100
Intangible asset amortization	30	—
EBIT	120	150
Interest	50	50
Pretax income	70	100
Income taxes	42	40
Net income	$ 28	$ 60
EPS	$ 2.80	$ 6.00
Shares outstanding	10	10

Note how Newco and Telright are similar with the exception of merger and acquisition items that affect earnings per share.

patents, brand, software, customer bases and so forth—that contribute to earnings."[2] By way of illustration, General Mills, Kellogg, and Kraft Foods collectively have a net tangible asset base of *minus $30 billion*, yet their collective stock market value is $80 billion!

Of course, the value of brands, goodwill, and other intangible assets can change. That's why companies are required to revalue such assets on an annual basis. The Schwinn brand used to represent excellence in bicycles; now it is a distant memory to consumers. Credit Suisse bought Donaldson, Lufkin & Jenrette (DLJ) for its sterling reputation, client base, and banking experience, but most of DLJ's experienced personnel left to join competitors after the deal, often taking the clients with them. McClatchy Newspapers bought the Knight Ridder chain for $4.5 billion in 2004, only to take a $3 billion intangible write-off in 2007. Besides the stated values, the analyst considers the depreciable lives attached to identifiable intangible assets. A firm boosts near-term earnings by using unrealistically long lives. The analyst must take extra care in reviewing the financials of active acquirers.

International Accounting Differences

With finance becoming increasingly global, it's important for investors to know the differences between U.S. and international accounting. Foreign firms trading on U.S. exchanges typically have statements adhering to U.S. accounting principles. Many of the larger firms trading on the major, non-U.S. exchanges use International Financial Reporting Standards (IFRS). IFRS is similar to U.S. generally accepted accounting principles (GAAP) in many ways, and the goal of the accounting profession and the SEC is to have a convergence over time. In the emerging markets, companies use local standards, which may depart from U.S. GAAP in a number of ways. For now, professionals familiarize themselves with the differences.

COMPANY-SPECIFIC ACCOUNTING ISSUES

Accounting for financial instruments, for acquisitions, and for international businesses are generic problems encompassing many industries, and practitioners know to ask questions and make adjustments to conform the accounting to economic reality. This same diligence must be applied to specific company statements, as large variations occur among similar companies, even within the accounting conventions. A principal source of these differences is management discretion. Generally accepted accounting principles permit economic transactions that receive accounting treatment to be recognized in different ways by different statement preparers. As a result, the analyst examines not only the economic relevance of a given accounting method but also the manner in which the managers and the auditors apply it in a given situation.

Management Discretion

Management discretion in the selection of an accounting policy is the enemy of the security analyst, who needs consistency of method over time and within industries. As shown in the Neiman Marcus example in Chapter 8, financial statement analysis concentrates on a series of consecutive statements. Particular attention is paid to observing changes from period to period. If management varies accounting methods over time, this data interpretation has less meaning. Likewise, an important part of the Neiman Marcus financial analysis was the comparison of that firm with similar enterprises. It follows that the accounting values used as a comparison should be based on similar methodologies. Substantial differences within an industry diminish the basis for a good comparison. Consider the interindustry example in Exhibit 9.3. Continental's choice of 30 years for aircraft life is more liberal than the others.

This isn't to say that every business doesn't have its own idiosyncrasies that deserve special treatment, but the fundamental elements of a company's accounts should conform to its competitors. Unfortunately, some managements use this flexibility to present results in a way that reflects neither economic reality nor industry

EXHIBIT 9.3   Airline Industry
Longest Depreciable Lives of Aircraft

Company	Years
Alaska	20
American	25
Continental	30
Southwest	23
U.S. Air	20

Source: Center for Financial Research and Analysis.

convention, and it can be stated that management is not an innocent observer in the setting of such policy. Executives actively participate with the independent auditor firm in putting together financial statements, and they exercise influence in the selection of accounting benchmarks. Should 100 percent of revenue be recognized immediately, or should 20 percent be withheld as future service and guaranty revenues? For a percentage-of-completion project, is the job 50 percent finished, or 60 percent? What is the estimated profit margin? Even experienced auditors need management's assistance in answering such questions intelligently.

Furthermore, the accounting profession has undergone an evolution, which, in the eyes of many practitioners, undercuts their objectivity. In the 1960s and 1970s, accounting was like a gentlemen's club where boorish behavior resulted in expulsion. Standards were very high. Firms didn't advertise and they didn't directly solicit business. With the application of U.S. antitrust laws in the early 1980s, accounting firms advertised and grew other businesses, which sought fees from the same auditing clients. Some of these businesses were spun off in recent years, but the resulting potential for conflicts of interest remains, as does the pressure on accounting firms to increase their bottom lines. The securities analyst knows that auditors don't operate out of an ivory tower; they are susceptible to the same foibles as other businesspeople, like bending the rules once in a while. Thus, while the vast majority of financial statements are done properly, the practitioner cannot place blind faith in management's judgment and an auditor's report. He must look behind the numbers.

Corporate Management versus the Security Analyst

Given the flexibility inherent in GAAP, it is inevitable that corporate managers sometimes succumb to the temptation of providing misleading results to the public. Usually, the objective is to portray the business in a more favorable light than would otherwise be the case. In a minority of instances, the company may understate income statement and balance sheet values, either to save money on taxes or to keep earnings in reserve for later years. More often, management's tactics take the form of liberal accounting, such as using unrealistically long asset lives for depreciation purposes or deliberately underestimating bad debt expenses. At other times financial statements mislead by way of omission. An off-balance-sheet support arrangement is

EXHIBIT 9.4 Management Devices for Exaggerating Corporate Financial Performance

Accounting method selection	GAAP permits corporations, working with auditors, to have latitude in the way in which certain revenues and expenses are recorded. Management may deliberately select methods that don't reflect economic reality.
Asset valuations	Financial assets and intangible assets can be hard to value. Auditors may lack the expertise to assess these assets on a regular basis. UBS wrote down $37 billion of subprime mortgages in a mere six months in 2008.
Liability valuation	Certain liabilities, particularly for pension and health care benefits, are subject to a variety of assumptions that involve subjectivity on the part of management. GM's $70 billion in such liabilities can rise or fall by billions on changes in assumptions.
Off-balance-sheet items	GAAP has complex rules governing what items a company can keep off-balance-sheet and what disclosure is necessary. In 2008, HSBC, the global banking giant, shut down two supposedly independent structured investment vehicles (SIVs) it had set up and put their $40 billion in subprime mortgages on its balance sheet, exposing HSBC shareholders to billions in future losses. How did the SIVs escape prior scrutiny?
Disclosure	Footnote disclosure and management discussion may be vague, misleading, and suffering from omissions. The analyst is thus deterred from finding the truth.
Fraud	In extreme cases, management cooks the books by creating sales and earnings through fraudulent means such as forged receipts and double invoicing. Even skilled auditors have trouble detecting clever schemes, as suggested by Chris Nunn, risk management partner of Arthur Andersen. In response to an $80 million profit overstatement by Wickes, the English retailing chain, he said, "We were the victims of what is every auditor's nightmare—a skillfully executed, collusive fraud which deceived everybody."

forgotten or a nettlesome lawsuit is dismissed as immaterial. In the severe situation, this manipulation leads to fraud, and managers conceal items from auditors and forge accounting documentation. See Exhibit 9.4 for a few examples.

Disclosure

Why are managers tempted to inflate corporate financial results? One reason is that they can get away with it. Bill Berkley, chairman of W.R. Berkley Corporation and a veteran of many public offerings, summarized it in a simple fashion: "Wall Street doesn't respect conservative accounting." Independent public accountants, the supposed keepers of the flame of financial objectivity, are good, but less than perfect. Meanwhile, the institutional investor community, the bond rating agencies, and the SEC have a difficult time in assigning sufficient resources to police the problem. Finally, it is an unusual set of financial statements that contains sufficient information for a comprehensive analysis. For verbal explanations and additional disclosures, the practitioner is forced to call the same managers who are motivated to exaggerate their performance.

Potential for Fraud

Major accounting scandals, such as those involving Enron, WorldCom, and Fannie Mae, are often triggered by inside whistleblowers or outside parties, rather than by Wall Street practitioners. Even when caught red-handed, the majority of participants escape jail time and serious fines.

Two books, *Financial Statement Analysis* by Martin Fridson (John Wiley & Sons, 2002, 3rd ed.) and *Financial Shenanigans* by Howard Schilit (McGraw-Hill, 2002, 2nd ed.), cover well the incentives managers have to boost corporate financial results. A summary of these incentives appears in Exhibit 9.5.

The stage is thus set for the battle between corporate managers and security analysts. Managers try to convey the impression that their business is going well and getting better. Sure, risks are present in the business, but we have crafted plans to deal with them, so prospective investors needn't worry. Taken at face value, such words are reassuring, but the practitioner knows he cannot accept them blindly,

EXHIBIT 9.5   Management Rationales for Exaggerating Corporate Financial Performance

Rationale	Comments
Increase or maintain stock market valuation	A healthy stock price is helpful for several reasons: 1. *Obtaining equity finance.* Positive financial results (and continued expectations thereof) are critical to a company accessing the equity markets. 2. *Optimizing equity finance.* Access is important, but so is the pricing of a company's equity. Companies prefer receiving the greatest amount of money for the least relinquishment of ownership. The appearance of good financial results provides a better valuation and a higher P/E ratio. 3. *Maximizing management compensation.* Most high-level corporate managers receive stock options as part of their compensation. Inflating the underlying stock price increases these option values.
Promote access to the debt markets	Banks, institutional lenders, bond markets, trade creditors, commercial paper investors, and rating agencies rely on financial statements to judge a firm's creditworthiness. Managers may choose to exaggerate results to maintain the flow of finance and to keep pricing at reasonable levels. Consider an example of the cost of even a small change in perception. When Standard & Poor's dropped the debt rating of Merrill Lynch from AA to A in 2007, the change cost the firm $100 million annually.
Job preservation	Even when the financial markets aren't a big factor in corporate operations, management may have a temptation. A board of directors likes to see growth in sales and earnings. Keeping the directors happy with a steady stream of improving results may be necessary for a manager to keep his job.

since management has incentives to place a positive spin on any situation. Even the veracity of financial statements is suspect, since auditors and accounting policies sometimes cannot portray properly the economic status of a business—either on a stand-alone basis or in fair comparison with similar companies. The analyst's role as a *financial detective* is thereby cemented alongside his multiple roles as industry expert, business operations specialist, financial analyst, and valuation consultant.

THE FUNDAMENTAL OBJECTIVE OF PUBLIC COMPANIES

In its quest to increase shareholder value, a public company management should be cognizant of the valuation methodologies outlined in this book. At a basic level, the executives should remember the following three fundamental principles of Wall Street:

1. *Growth in sales and earnings is good.* Growth brings higher valuation ratios, such as a high P/E ratio.
2. *Stability and assurance of these growth objectives is good.* Stability brings higher valuation ratios and lower discount rates.
3. *Unpredictability and volatility in sales and earnings is bad.* Unpredictability and volatility imply risk, which means a lower valuation ratio and a higher discount rate.

Management, therefore, should endeavor not only to achieve higher growth in sales and earnings, but to foster an image of financial stability. Preferably, annual sales and earnings grow in a consistent and seamless fashion from year to year, showing a trend line such as that in Exhibit 9.6.

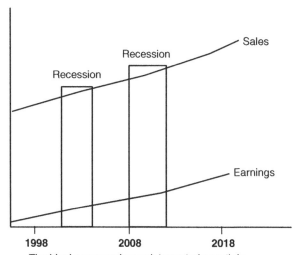

The ideal company has uninterrupted growth in sales and earnings. Recessions don't affect its results.

EXHIBIT 9.6 The Uninterrupted Sales and Earnings Growth of the Ideal Company

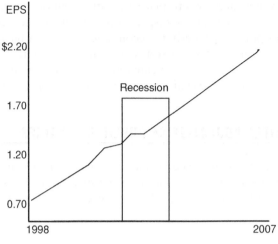

Note the smooth pattern of GE's growth.
1998 EPS = $0.73, 2007 EPS = $2.20

EXHIBIT 9.7   General Electric Company Summary
Track Record

General Electric was one of the all-time champions at displaying uninterrupted earnings growth. Its record was even more remarkable when you realize that the firm's main business lines were quite cyclical. See Exhibit 9.7. General Electric frequently offset one-time gains from asset sales with restructuring charges; this kept earnings from rising so high that they couldn't be topped the following year. GE also timed sales of equity stakes and made divestitures to produce profit gains when needed. In 2001, a recession year that was problematic for most industrial companies, GE's earnings rose 7 percent. In 2009, the company paid a $50 million civil penalty to settle SEC charges accusing the conglomerate of improper accounting, and throwing doubt on prior results.

Sustaining an image of constancy leads to accounting gimmickry at some companies. In the next section, we review income-smoothing techniques employed by management.

CASE STUDY: STABILITY CORPORATION

Consider the income statement and balance sheet of Stability Corporation, an imaginary manufacturer of consumer products. We review the key accounting items in a sequential fashion in Exhibits 9.8 and 9.9, beginning with sales, the top line of the income statement.

Income Statement

The income statement begins with sales and then operating expenses follow. Abuses occur in either category.

EXHIBIT 9.8　Stability Corporation Summary Income Statement (in millions, except per share data)

Sales		$10,000
Cost of Sales		
Labor		
Raw materials	XX	
Finished materials	XX	
Utilities	XX	
Rent	XX	
Depreciation and amortization	XX	
Total cost of sales	XX	$6,000
Gross income		4,000
Selling, General, and Administrative Expense		
Executive compensation		
Marketing	XX	
Insurance	XX	
Research and development	XX	
Other	XX	
Total selling, general, and administrative expense	XX	3,000
Earnings before interest and taxes (EBIT)		1,000
Interest expense		300
Pretax income		700
Income tax		300
Net income		$ 400
Net income per share		$ 3.00

Sales　Typical means of exaggerating sales include the following nine tactics:

1. *Shipping goods before a sale is finalized.* Stability Corporation has ongoing service obligations on some product lines and a liberal return policy, which means that not all revenues are recognized when the product is shipped to the customer.

   Revenue recognition is a big issue in the software industry, where vendors are tempted to book revenues, despite continuing obligations to the customer. MicroStrategy had a problem when it booked major revenue before a software contract was signed. Chip maker Vitesse failed to record credits for returned merchandise.

2. *Selling goods to uncreditworthy customers.* One way to boost revenues is to sell to customers that can't find anyone to sell to them for credit reasons. When sales are booked to these uncreditworthy customers, management downplays loss reserves. This is a short-term strategy for inflating revenues but, over the long term, the inevitable write-off of receivables harms results. Capital One expanded its credit card business dramatically in 2006 and 2007. With many of its new customers unable to pay, earnings fell in 2008 and the stock price dropped by half.

3. *Selling goods on unrealistic terms.* One way of obtaining new customers is to offer liberal repayment terms. If the industry norm is a 2 percent discount for

EXHIBIT 9.9   Stability Corporation Summary Balance
Sheet (in millions)

Assets	
Cash	$ 500
Accounts receivable, net of reserves	800
Inventories	1,200
Other current assets	500
	3,000
Fixed Assets, Net of Depreciation	
Long-term equity investments	2,500
Deferred taxes	300
Goodwill	200
Identifiable intangible assets	1,000
	500
	$7,500
Liabilities and Stockholders' Equity	
Short-term loans	$ 500
Accounts payable	1,000
Other current liabilities	500
Total current liabilities	2,000
Long-term debt	2,000
Post-retirement benefits	500
Stockholders' equity	3,000
	$7,500

10-day payment, and full payment by 30 days (i.e., 2/10, net 30), an aggressive firm generates additional sales by providing 3/30, net 60, for example. Auto companies traditionally boost sales by offering customers zero-interest loans on car purchases. The cost of this tactic shows up in financing expense since the company carries the receivables on its balance sheet.

4. *Pushing sales into a quarter.* The desire for both favorable quarter-to-quarter sales comparisons and smooth sales trends prompts managers to manipulate the timing of revenue. In some cases, the action is as benign as asking a salesman to book a transaction on the first day of the following month instead of the twenty-eighth day of the current month. In other cases, the activity is systematic. It may take an aggressive tack, such as channel stuffing, whereby a company inflates its sales figures by forcing more product onto its distributors than they can reasonably sell in a given quarter. In 2004, Bristol-Myers Squibb paid a $150 million fine for such alleged activity that boosted revenues by $1.5 billion.

5. *Understating warranties and returns.* When Maytag sells a dishwasher, it recognizes a liability for the machine's repair guarantee. A $1,000 sale, therefore, might only appear as $950 in the first year because of the warranty obligation.

$1,000	Sale
(50)	Repair guarantee
$ 950	Net sale

Consider a firm selling a new product with untested warranty experience. The management may be tempted to underplay this obligation, pushing expenses into future years. Similarly, mutual funds, such as Legg Mason, refuse to allow the value of their money management accounts to drop below $1 per share. This de facto guarantee does not appear on financial statements, but it has cost Legg Mason hundreds of millions when covering 2008 investment losses.

6. *Abusing percentage-of-completion accounting method.* Some revenue-generating activities require months and years to complete. Examples include sophisticated computer systems, large defense projects, and long-term construction jobs. Rather than book a huge sale when the contract is finished, the selling company accrues revenues and profits on a gradual basis, as the project meets completion goals. Since the firm is likely to be more knowledgeable about the project's ins and outs than its auditor, the temptation is for management to say the job is 60 percent complete (and book 60 percent of the revenues), when in fact it is only 50 percent done. Electronic Data Systems had a $2.2 billion write-off in 2003, related to improper percentage-of-completion accounting.

7. *Swaps and barter.* During the height of the Internet craze in 2001 and 2002, companies swapped capacity of dubious value and recorded the swaps as if they were cash revenue. Global Crossing and Qwest Communications were notable offenders.

8. *Reseller or product distribution.* If a distribution company decides to book its revenues as "gross" rather than "net," its revenues might be inflated. Pharmaceutical firm Merck booked billions in consumer-to-pharmacy copayments that it never collected. Priceline's selection of gross revenue (instead of net) for a time suggested a sizable customer base that wasn't there.

9. *Fraud.* The preceding eight tactics tend not to approach the level of criminal fraud. One such action is phonying up sales invoices. By creating nonexistent invoices that enter the accounting system, managers achieve the illusion of growth. Another tactic is to hide expenses in the capital investment account, as HealthSouth did for several years. Well-designed schemes avoid detection, even by outside auditors, for some time. Typically, the auditor is lax in spot-checking the veracity of related documents. Technology company NEC noted in 2008 that employees created fictitious orders using the names of subcontractors. Several Qwest executives created a phony paper trail to convince auditors that certain sales contracts were in force.

Cost of Sales   Despite the long history of inflation, a few U.S. firms still record the cost of sales using the first-in, first-out method (FIFO), rather than last in, first out (LIFO). LIFO is more reflective of current costs in an inflationary environment; however, international standards emphasize FIFO for foreign reporting companies.

Labor   A popular tactic for recording a misleading labor expense lies in the calculation of future benefits. Fringes such as pensions, medical care, and vacations add up to one-third of labor costs. The determination of the current cost of future items such as pensions and medical plans is inherently uncertain, and shading actuarial assumptions one way or another makes a big difference. Outside actuaries assist the auditors in many instances, but the corporation can influence numerous actuarial variables. A few such items are as follows:

Variables Affecting Future Medical Costs

- Number of eligible employees in 20 years.
- Cost of future care.
- Number of employees requiring care.
- Annual discount rate for future benefits.

Variables Affecting Future Retirement Costs

- Eligibility assumptions (service time, future layoffs, etc.).
- Future employee salaries.
- Employer versus employee contributions.
- Assumed rate of return on pension assets.

In 2007, Ford Motor assumed annual pay increases of 4 percent, health care inflation of 5 percent, and pension returns of 8.5 percent. PPG Industries and Lehman Brothers used 10.9 percent and 10.8 percent for pension returns, respectively. The higher rates meant lower pension costs.

Raw Materials/Finished Materials   Management has little ability to manipulate raw materials. One exception is the accounting method selection, such as LIFO versus FIFO versus lower of cost or market.

Utilities   It is difficult to mask utility expenses.

Rent   Rent is a large item for firms that lease rather than own. It becomes an accounting issue when the lease is really a noncancelable financing and should therefore be capitalized as debt. For many businesses, access to debt financing is dependent on low leverage, so management struggles to classify lease costs as rent (an operating lease) versus debt service (a capitalized lease).

Depreciation   Independent auditors have benchmarks that match assets with depreciable lives, but there are ranges within the reference points and numerous exceptions. Thus, depreciable lives vary among similar assets of similar companies, because judgment and discretion are involved. The short-term earnings benefit of using a long depreciable life is obvious for a $100 million asset. A five-year life reduces annual income by $20 million; a 10-year life by only $10 million.

$100 Million Asset

Depreciable life	5 years	10 years
Annual income reduction	$20 million	$10 million

Given a new asset with an untested economic life, the issue is never cut-and-dried. When Blockbuster Entertainment went public, analysts complained about the three-year life attached to its primary asset, movie videos. Wall Streeters argued that

(1) few people wanted to rent a video after it had been in the store for one year; (2) most depreciation, therefore, should occur over the first 18 months; and (3) the firm's earnings, therefore, were overstated with the three-year video life. Netflix, the DVD rental company, assigns a one-year life to new-release DVDs and a three-year life to classic titles. Analysts seem to find these lives acceptable.

Identifiable Intangible Assets   The increase in merger and acquisition activity means that corporate income statements are affected by identifiable intangible assets. Acquirers must write off any excess purchase price that cannot be attributed to either the seller's tangible assets (like plant and equipment) or goodwill. The life of the identifiable intangible assets incurred in an acquisition is a subjective determination, set jointly by management, the independent auditors, and, in some cases, outside appraisers. Similar to the depreciation account, a long intangible life represents a smaller impact on earnings. The annual difference between a 5-year life and a 10-year life on a $100 million goodwill account is $5 million annually.

$100 Million Intangible Asset Account

Estimated life	5 years	10 years
Annual charge to income	$20 million	$10 million

Common intangible assets are customer lists, trademarks, technology, patents, and leases. Vishay Intertechnology writes off intangibles over an average period of seven years with the exception of trademarks, which have an indefinite life. It assigns most acquisition values to goodwill. Allocating less value to goodwill and shortening lives to five years would have cut net income by 20 percent.

Selling, General, and Administrative Costs

Executive Compensation   In order to evaluate a firm's true earnings power, an analyst needs to know executive compensation. Top executives at most public companies are well paid by any measure. It is not unusual for the compensation of the top dozen executives in a business to represent 5 to 10 percent of corporate profits. The compensation comes in a number of forms, including cash salaries and bonuses, stock options and grants, corporate jet privileges, tax-deferred payments, and generous bankruptcy-proof pension plans. Historically, firms obscured the sizeable pay packages through various means, but their ability to do so has declined with mandated disclosures. In 2004, a study by Professor Erik Lie of the University of Iowa sparked an options backdating scandal that involved over 100 public companies and caused the resignations of dozens of executives.[3] The companies had misled investors by issuing stock options at prices that were lower than the market price at the time of the option grant. The hidden executive compensation totaled in the billions.

Marketing   In addition to media print and Internet advertising, companies use dozens of schemes to promote their products. Rebates, allowances, credits, shelf space payments, and long-term commissions are a few marketing practices that complicate accounting, and they have served as the basis for many earnings restatements over the years.

A common practice in the United States is for companies to capitalize a portion of the monies used to attract new customers. By capitalizing such costs and amortizing them over the expected customer life, firms avoid big up-front expenses. The question is: Do the customers keep coming back? In 2007, IAC, a leading Internet company with a consumer emphasis, began to capitalize and amortize the cost of customers obtained through Web access points. The policy reduced expenses by $17 million annually.

Insurance   The analyst needs to ensure that the firm under study carries adequate insurance for its operations. Management may try to pinch pennies (and thus increase earnings) by not buying enough coverage.

Research and Development   A lot of companies capitalize a portion of their research and development costs and amortize them over a period of years. This policy attempts to match costs against future revenues, much like the depreciating value of a paper factory is allocated to each ton of paper produced. The problem with placing R&D on the balance sheet is the uncertainty attached to whether the R&D will actually produce earnings. Many innovations fail and others are minimally profitable. A disclosure item in the auditor's report for a high-tech firm is vague: "The establishment of technological feasibility and the ongoing assessment of recoverability of development costs require considerable judgment by management with respect to certain external factors, including, but not limited to, anticipated future revenues, estimated economic life, and changes in software and hardware technologies." With this kind of elusive disclosure, the analyst must evaluate R&D accounting carefully, particularly when high-tech stocks play a large role in the stock market.

Nonoperating Items

Interest   Managers have a variety of means to disguise debt financings. Interest costs can be hidden in the rent expense category. Debt can be squirreled away in nonconsolidated subsidiaries and project finance vehicles. Enron was a prime example, but there have been many other offenders.

Income Taxes   A company with a heavy fixed asset component typically pays less in cash income tax than the tax accrual indicates. Federal income tax depreciation schedules have shorter lives than GAAP, meaning that true taxable income is less than GAAP pretax income. Financial statement footnotes provide details on cash tax payments.

Earnings per Share   The plethora of equity-linked securities, such as options, convertible bonds, and hybrid debts, distort the economic meaning of earnings per share. A number of high-tech firms that I evaluated had outstanding stock options equivalent to more than 10 percent of shares outstanding. A determination of value per share must incorporate an analysis of these equity-linked securities.

At some point, firms that rely on accounting machinations to achieve a bottom line must yield to economic reality. That worried certain accountants, such as Sam Rajappa, head of Fannie Mae's internal audit department. He e-mailed his staff in 2000 before the firm's massive write-offs as follows: "As Frank (Raines, the CEO) navigates the ship, we are the ones who stand on the deck, who look for icebergs far and near, to the right, to the left, small ones, medium ones, big ones . . . and warn the office of the chairman well in advance to steer clear."[4] Mr. Raines left the firm with a $120 million severance package, even as the stock price fell 80 percent.

The Balance Sheet

Assets   Assets comprise many categories that present challenges in evaluating a business. This section begins with cash and continues through intangibles.

Cash   Stability Corporation can do little to inflate this account short of fraud. A few firms have been caught commingling the operating cash account with dedicated cash accounts (i.e., those set aside for lenders, landlords, and other special parties).

Marketable Securities   Often aggregated with cash, marketable securities represent high-quality, short-term debt obligations, such as prime certificates of deposit and commercial paper. In 2008, this conservative characterization came into question when dozens of public corporations took write-downs. They had invested billions in spare cash in auction-rate securities that proved to have both limited liquidity and poor credit standing. For example, MIND CTI, Ltd., a growing software firm, wrote down $20 million of its $30 million in cash and equivalents. Not one analyst caught the auction rate problem in advance.

Accounts Receivable, Net of Reserves   The receivables from many sales are not reflected at 100 percent face value. A reserve is established for the possibility of nonpayment, returns, warranties, and other items. Of particular note are health care providers, who frequently have a large number of nonpaying customers. Health South had significant nonpayment issues prior to its billion-dollar restructuring.

The proper level of reserves is a major issue for any finance company, whose principal assets are loans and receivables from others. Auto lenders increased reserves in 2009 as difficult economic conditions hurt consumers' repayment ability.

Bad debt reserves are important issues with banks and insurance companies. The former's voluminous bad debts cost the U.S. government billions during the subprime crisis.

As noted earlier, the counterfeiting of invoices has been used to jigger financial statements. The analyst relies on the independent auditors to police this fraud, although a studied examination of receivables' performance against revenue can present clues to such shenanigans.

Inventories   Fashion changes, product innovations, and technological advances can quickly reduce the value of a firm's inventory. After the Internet boom, many Internet equipment suppliers endured sizable inventory markdowns. Demand for the equipment dried up and selling prices fell. Cisco Systems' charge-off was $2.2 billion. Inventory valuation is an ongoing challenge in the apparel and retailing industries because of fashion changes.

Not being experts in all products, many accountants have trouble identifying diminished value, so the analyst has to ask questions if inventories seem high by historical standards.

Verifone's 2007 inventory write-down reduced profits for the prior three years by 80 percent. The firm specialized in third-party credit cards and authorization devices.

Fixed Assets, Net of Depreciation   If Stability Corporation deliberately understates depreciation, the economic value of the fixed assets may be less than the accounting value. At times, an asset is worth far more than its balance sheet number, particularly as an alternative use. Such is the case with real estate, which tends to increase in value with inflation. In one of my merger transactions, the seller operated a printing plant in an area that featured tony office buildings. After the deal, the buyer relocated the plant and sold the property for a large profit.

Rather than depreciate fixed assets in an orderly fashion, managers are tempted to take the occasional big-bath write-off, so future earnings are enhanced while past earnings are history. In other instances, a company husbands a hidden value, waiting to offset down earnings with a profitable sale. A. H. Belo owns a sizable piece of Dallas real estate that has little mention in the firm's reports.

Natural Resource Reserves   Historical accounting for the ownership of natural resources, such as timber and mineral reserves, is practically meaningless from the analyst's standpoint. The practitioner is only interested in the statistical compilations of these reserves and the estimated cost of extraction so he can attach market values to them. A useful piece of accounting data is the tax basis of the reserves, but this information is usually unavailable to the public.

Natural resource reserve accounting is usually done in consultation with an independent third party, but nevertheless, problems do arise. Shell Oil, among other firms, was caught overstating reserve values, the effect of which was to enhance its stock price temporarily.

Long-Term Equity Investments   Analysts should try to mark-to-market long-term equity investments, since management cannot be relied upon to perform this task. Most companies wait too long to write down impaired investments, while profitable equity sales are deferred until normal operations incur problems.

Overstating the value of a securities portfolio—particularly hard-to-value private securities—is a common practice. In a study of private equity firms, Professor Ludovic Phalippou found that many such firms overstated the value of their investments in order to hype returns.[5]

Derivatives   Many manufacturers use derivatives to hedge supply costs. These derivatives are generally marked-to-market if the underlying commodity changes in price.

Deferred Taxes   Usually when a business loses money, it incurs tax losses that can be carried forward to reduce taxable income in future years. However, if the likelihood of future profitability is dim, this asset should be written off, along with a corresponding downward revision in equity.

Goodwill   The economic value of goodwill is a subjective decision. Acquired goodwill is an accounting item, but the value of internally generated goodwill is decided in the stock market on a day-to-day basis. Most companies trade at a multiple of net tangible accounting value. Trademarks, reputations, patents, customers, distribution systems, employees, and production processes are just a few items lending goodwill to a business.

Firms assess the value of goodwill on an annual basis. The typical practice is a big-bath write-down when goodwill is impaired, rather than gradual charge-offs. In 2008, Sprint posted a $30 billion loss upon writing down the value of its Nextel Communications acquisition.

The trick for active acquirers is to place acquisition value mostly in goodwill, rather than identifiable intangible assets, because goodwill is not amortized. The SEC has gotten wind of the practice, and it has an informal guideline that goodwill not represent more than 60 percent of the excess purchase price over a target's book value.

Identifiable Intangible Assets   Under GAAP, as noted earlier, firms capitalize the value of an acquisition's customer relationships, mailing lists, research and development costs, leasehold interests, contractual rights, software, patents, and shelf space, among other items. Even with the help of professional appraisers, companies and auditors have problems in establishing fair value and economic life for these assets.

Liabilities and Stockholders' Equity   Hidden liabilities and lowball estimates present problems in business valuations. We cover major liability categories here.

Short-Term Loans   This is a difficult item for executives to manipulate.

Accounts Payable   Short of outright fraud, accounts payable balances are difficult to manipulate.

Long-Term Debt   To reduce perceived financial risk and to enhance access to debt financing sources, corporations like to understate their true leverage positions. Direct debt financing often has the lowest cost, but it appears prominently on the balance sheet. Accordingly, companies seek alternative sources of debt-like financings such as long-term operating leases, supplier credits, and off-balance-sheet transactions. The analyst can get a grip on operating lease exposure by investigating the footnotes, but off-balance-sheet deals are harder to figure out.

Lenders to securitization and project financings typically turn to a specific asset base when things go bad, but in many deals lenders have subsequent recourse to the lead sponsor (i.e., the analyst's subject of study). Rather than outright guarantees, the support arrangements involve nomenclatures that mean the same thing (e.g., a project may have a working capital maintenance agreement, "first loss" coverage protection, or take-or-pay contract). Due to legal and accounting nuances, many supports don't qualify as outright debt, but in judging the economic value of the sponsor, the analyst must consider their potential impact on corporate performance. Debt rating agencies, for example, usually capitalize leases and consolidate off-balance-sheet financings (along with related assets) in calculating a firm's total debt picture.

From time to time, management is able to hide debts and keep them from appearing on the balance sheet. Scandals at Italian food conglomerate Parmalat and at cable TV giant Adelphia Communications involved billions in undisclosed loans.

Reputational Guarantees—The Halo Effect   Many times, a shaky business obtains premium loan terms through its affiliation with a larger and stronger entity. Lenders extend credit under the belief that the business will be bailed out by the stronger entity if problems arise, even when there is no formal guarantee. The idea is that the stronger entity will protect its reputation by preventing the failure of an affiliate. There have been many examples of this "halo effect," from the Russian government bailing out partially-state-owned firms to money center banks assuming the debts of off-balance-sheet affiliates. At this writing, Wall Street was surprised at the United Arab Emirates' refusing to backstop the $26 billion loans of Dubai World, a large conglomerate closely intertwined with UAE rulers, despite the fact an explicit guarantee was never offered.

Postretirement Liabilities: Pension and Medical   The analyst wants to verify that (1) the actuarial assumptions for pension funding are reasonable, and (2) the pension plan is fully funded. Given the difficulties in estimating pension and medical liabilities, the objective here is to ensure that the calculations have a safety margin. The corporate investor relations officer may provide information in this regard, as do the footnotes to the financial statements.

Undisclosed Liabilities   In addition to project financing arrangements, a firm may have undisclosed liabilities that affect its value. Auditors have a hard time catching these items if management is not forthcoming. Potential damages from lawsuits are difficult to quantify, for example. Environmental liabilities are open-ended in certain industries.

Deferred Taxes   The deferred income tax reported on the balance sheet does not have the attributes of a liability. It lacks legal obligation, relative certainty of amount, and estimation of payment date. Moreover, unlike pension liabilities, the amount shown is not a present value computed using a discount rate. For 99 percent of going concerns using accelerated depreciation on the tax return, this tax payment is deferred indefinitely.

Preferred Stock   Preferred stock used to be a simple quasi-debt obligation, but more corporations issue unusual preferreds. Toxic private investments in public equities (PIPEs) are preferreds that drastically increase equity dilution if a certain share price is not achieved. Private-equity-based preferreds sometimes force the issuer to pay two times the face amount upon maturity if preset financial goals are not achieved. The analyst must be on guard for these instruments.

Statement of Cash Flows

The statement of cash flows is a collection of (1) income statement data, and (2) selected changes in balance sheet items, as set forth in Exhibit 9.10. Liberal accounting methods in the first two statements thus flow through to the statement of cash flows. Because of the leeway in accounting rules, net income can be reported in different ways, but cash in the bank is hard to fake. As a result, analysts increasingly consult the statement of cash flows to verify that cash follows reported earnings. Furthermore, many a junior analyst has pondered this question: "My target company's accounts show profits, but it has problems paying bills and cash is getting

EXHIBIT 9.10 Stability Corporation Statement of Cash Flows (in millions)

Cash Flows from Operating Activities	
Net income	$ 400
Adjustments to reconcile net income to net cash provided by operating activities:	
Depreciation	250
Deferred taxes	50
Changes in Operating Assets and Liabilities	
Accounts receivable	(100)
Inventories, net	(150)
Other current assets	(50)
Accounts payable	150
Other current liabilities	50
Net cash provided by operating activities	600
Cash flows from investing activities	(400)
Capital expenditures	(50)
Acquisitions, net of liabilities	(450)
Cash Flows from Financing Activities	
Proceeds from loans	350
Payments on loans	(200)
Proceeds from equity sales	50
Dividends paid	(150)
Net cash provided by financing activities	50
Net increase in cash	$ 200

Note: Stability dedicates most of its operating cash flow to capital expenditures.

smaller and smaller." Are capital investments increasing for the firm, or is cash being absorbed by unsold inventories and unpaid receivables?

Footnotes to the Financial Statements

The footnotes describe accounting policies and provide additional information. They are indispensable to a financial analysis. Most practitioners prefer to obtain more disclosure, and investor relations officers are usually agreeable to answering questions, particularly if the questioner works for a large institutional investor. Many accounting entries involve management, and the footnotes provide information on assumptions used and policies considered by the firm. For example, a footnote might disclose a contingent debt obligation that does not have to appear in the balance sheet. The footnotes also supply detail on revenue and expense breakdown by line of business, currency, and geography in many cases.

Big-Bath Write-Offs, Restructuring Charges, and One-Time Write-Offs

Over the past 20 years, companies have become enamored with taking one-time charges to earnings in lieu of properly matching periodic costs to the revenues. One tactic is to use liberal accounting methods for several years, thus boosting earnings performance. Perhaps depreciation lives are understated; R&D expenses are capitalized, rather than expensed; goodwill is exaggerated. Eventually economic reality sets in: The fixed assets, R&D, and goodwill aren't producing sufficient income.

Management can admit its financial errors and restate past earnings or, with the auditor's consent, they post a large nonrecurring charge that marks down values in one fell swoop. This popular tactic has several benefits: (1) It negates the need to show restated earnings, which would give the analyst a true picture of past earnings power; (2) by exaggerating the one-time write-off, future depreciation and amortization expenses are reduced, thus providing an artificial bonus to future earnings; and (3) several one-time charges can be lumped together in a big-bath restructuring loss, complicating investors' ability to ferret out the impacts of each charge. The big-bath announcement gets the bad news out in one big chunk. Earnings are not penalized year by year in a Chinese water torture style, and the overall negative impact on the firm's share price is lessened. See Exhibit 9.11.

EXHIBIT 9.11   Two Companies Amortizing the Same Identifiable Intangible Asset (in millions)

The Scenario
- On January 1, 2009, Conservative Corporation and Liberal Corporation each place a $60 million intangible asset on their respective balance sheets.
- Conservative Corp. chooses a three-year economic life and Liberal Corp. selects a six-year life.
- Both companies have 2009 earnings before interest, taxes, and amortization (*on this asset only*) of $100 million.
- Liberal Corp. incurs a special charge in 2011, after deciding the asset's value has been impaired. The data appear in the following table.

	Accounting 2009–2014					
	2009	2010	2011	2012	2013	2014
Conservative Corp.						
EBITDA	$100	$110	$120	$130	$140	$150
Amortization	(20)	(20)	(20)	—	—	—
EBIT	$ 80	$ 90	$100	$130	$140	$150
Liberal Corp.						
EBITDA	$100	$110	$120	$130	$140	$150
Amortization	(10)	(10)	(10)	—	—	—
EBIT before nonrecurring charge	90	100	110	130	140	150
Nonrecurring charge[a]	—	—	(30)	—	—	—
EBIT	$ 90	$100	$ 80	$130	$140	$150

[a]2011 write-down of asset from remaining $30 million value to zero.

The Result
- Liberal Corp.'s EBIT *exceeds* Conservative Corp.'s EBIT for the first two years. After 2011, Liberal Corp.'s EBIT matches Conservative Corp.
- Liberal Corp's short-term earnings record (2009–2010) appears better, possibly helping its stock price over this time.

The acceptance of the nonrecurring charge is reaching absurd levels. Over the past six years Eastman Kodak took 40 so-called one-time restructuring charges totaling $4 billion, which exceeded the company's reported earnings during that time. Cisco Systems, Procter & Gamble, and Verizon recorded large nonrecurring charges in each of the five years from 2002 to 2007. How does the analyst determine the normal earnings power of a company like Kodak that takes repeated write-offs? He tries to adjust reported results to accounting that reflects economic reality.

SUMMARY

In recent years, the financial markets have been rocked by accounting-based scandals that have cost equity investors, bondholders, and government insurers hundreds of billions of dollars. Such events are recurring themes, as unscrupulous executives find new ways of exaggerating their firms' financial performance in the face of lackluster enforcement efforts and moderate penalties.

Accounting rules permit a company to represent its financial condition in a number of ways. The pressure for management to tinker with earnings is intense. Rising earnings mean a higher stock price, while missed growth targets send stock prices into a free fall. Firms are thus tempted to base a financial statement presentation on overoptimistic assumptions and sporadic one-time charges. In determining earnings power, practitioners check the veracity of a firm's accounting policies, substitute their own assumptions if need be, and recalculate the reported financial data. If the situation doesn't inspire confidence, a proper investigation might reveal misrepresentations, concealed losses, and window dressings. Unfortunately, this type of analysis costs money, and many institutional investors are reluctant to commit the dollars to study individual stocks intently.

There remains a fundamentally adverse relationship between security issuers and analysts. Professional investors are resigned to the fact that companies take liberties with accounting policy. Alert to the need to question accounting policies and the assumptions behind them, practitioners hope for progress in the movement toward uniform reporting and meaningful enforcement.

Financial Analysis and Company Classification

What is a growth company? A mature firm? A cyclical business? Wall Street and the financial media use these terms regularly, but what do they mean? Chapter 10 provides the tools for making these classifications.

In Chapter 8 we studied the results of Neiman Marcus, an established business in a mature industry. In Chapter 9, we looked at accounting data with a critical eye. In this chapter, we consider markers that place a business in its corporate life cycle. Historical financial analysis thus complements industry and company research in classifying a business within the pioneer, growth, mature, and declining phases. This chapter also defines the cyclical firm and notes how management-directed changes in shares outstanding and leverage alter earnings per share.

Model Research Report

1. Introduction
2. Macroeconomic Review
3. Relevant Stock Market Prospects
4. Review of the Company and Its Business
5. Financial Analysis ✓
6. Financial Projections
7. Application of Valuation Methodologies
8. Recommendation

Most valuation textbooks focus on the mature, established business. This is appropriate for the university environment, where the student is getting accustomed to financial analysis. Examining a business with minor variances from year to year is a good place to start. As the student transforms into the practitioner, though, he is subject to a rude awakening. The public company landscape is littered with firms that fall outside of the teaching model. Many firms exhibit sharp changes in year-to-year operating performance—for both positive and negative reasons. Others complicate the analyst's job by completing numerous acquisitions, so one doesn't know where the real business ends and the new acquisition begins. A healthy percentage of listed firms lose money. Section 5 of the research report covers the requisite tasks.

COMPANY CLASSIFICATIONS

Wall Street likes to summarize a company's attributes in a shorthand manner, preferably within six classifications. The analyst pigeonholes firms within those classifications by completing a financial analysis.

The Stock Market's Six Business Classifications

1. Mature company
2. Growth company
   - Classic growth
   - Market share growth
   - Consolidator
3. Cyclical company
   - Business cycle is dominant
   - Other cycles
4. Declining company
5. Turnaround
6. Pioneer

In this chapter, we discuss these classifications.

THE MATURE COMPANY

As our study of Neiman Marcus illustrated, the prototypical mature business exhibits steady, if unspectacular, gains in sales and earnings. The standard ratios show small year-to-year changes, and the impact of acquisitions and divestitures is easy to distinguish. With a few adjustments derived from the footnotes, the analyst evaluates the progress of the base operation separate from acquisitions. An example appears in Exhibit 10.1 for Thomas & Betts, an electrical components manufacturer.

EXHIBIT 10.1   Mature, Established Company: Thomas & Betts Corporation
(in millions, except ratios)

	2006	2007	2008 (Estimated)
Sales			
Base business	$1,827	$2,016	$2,118
New acquisitions	42	120	530
Total sales	$1,869	$2,136	$2,648
EBIT	$ 246	$ 289	$ 346
Ratios			
Operating margin	13.2%	13.5%	13.1%
Asset turnover	1.1×	1.0×	1.1×
Current ratio	3.5×	1.9×	1.7×
Base sales growth	8.3%	10.3%	5.1%
Total sales growth	10.2%	14.3%	24.0%

Source: SEC reports.
Note: Thomas & Betts complements its base business with acquisitions to spur growth.

In classifying a business as *mature*, the practitioner likes to see a moderate up-trend in base revenues and stability in profit margins. From this predictable pattern, he forms an opinion on annual earnings power, absent acquisitions.

THE GROWTH COMPANY

A growth company shows consistent above-average growth in sales and earnings. The definition of *above average* shifts with the times, but a 15 to 20 percent annual rate (or higher) in the base business qualifies as a growth trajectory. Profit margins are stable or increasing, yet the business consumes cash, since investment in new facilities, accounts receivable, inventories, and acquisitions outstrips internal cash generation. The company issues debt and equity regularly to fuel the expansion. Because management is learning the business and competitors are jockeying for position, the growth company hits a bump in the earnings road from time to time. Overly generous sales promotions, excess inventories, and supply bottlenecks are three common problems.

SunPower fit well the description of a growth company in 2008. Without the use of acquisitions, sales rose at a rapid pace, but earnings were uneven. The firm required common stock offerings in 2005, 2006, and 2007, and new debt issues in 2007 and 2008. SunPower used the funds to finance a $230 million jump in accounts receivables and a $120 million increase in capital expenditures, as the demand for solar power equipment quickly climbed. Exhibit 10.2 shows selected income statement data and financial ratios.

Not all growth companies expand from the same set of underlying factors. There are three types, described briefly here:

1. *Classic growth company.* This business offers a new product that no one (or no firm) knew they needed before the product's invention. These products are

EXHIBIT 10.2   Classic Growth Company: SunPower Corporation, Selected Financial Data (in millions, except for ratios and percentages)

Income Statement Data	Year Ended December 31		
	2005	2006	2007
Revenues	$79	$237	$775
(% growth)	82%	200%	127%
Net income	$(15)	$26	$9
(% growth)	N.A.	N.A.	(65)%
Ratios			
Operating margin	Negative	8.6%	0.3%
Asset turnover	0.3×	0.6×	0.7×
Current ratio	6.2×	4.8×	1.1×
Cash Flow Data			
Increase in receivables	$21	$26	$160
Capital expenditures	72	108	193

Note how the growth company generates accelerating levels of receivables and capital expenditures. (N.A. means not applicable because of negative number.)

EXHIBIT 10.3   Market Share Growth Company (in millions, except for percentages)

	2007	2008	2009
Market revenues	$1,000	$1,060	$1,125
Percent growth in the market	6%	6%	6%
Company revenue	$ 200	$ 233	$ 270
Percent of market share	20%	22%	24%
Percent increase in company sales	15%	17%	16%
Result: Amount by which company's growth exceeded market growth	9%	11%	10%

frequently the result of technological innovation (e.g., iPods and GPS systems). SunPower is a classic growth company, offering solar power equipment that competes with conventional energy generation systems. The classic growth company often is part of a new industry comprised of similar firms.

With many new product offerings, the practitioner has no comparable companies against which to analyze the subject firm. The industry is too new to have more than one or two publicly traded stocks. For example, in 2007 there were no true comparables for Blackstone Group, the private equity firm. In this case, analysts consulted the results of growing companies in related fields, such as hedge funds and mezzanine lenders. Thus, they didn't conduct valuation analysis for Blackstone in a vacuum.

2. *Market share growth company.* This company participates in a mature industry, with GNP-like unit sales growth. Due to superior marketing or a better mouse-trap, the business grabs market share from its competitors. The mathematics appears in Exhibit 10.3.

Nokia was a good example of a firm increasing its share in a mature market. Its sales rose 53 percent from 2005 to 2007, as its market share in cell phones rose from 34 percent to 39 percent. Its principal competitor, Motorola, saw its share decline from 22 percent to 15 percent.

3. *Consolidator.* A consolidator operates in a mature industry that is highly frag-mented. Rather than achieving share through internal product and marketing developments, the consolidator buys numerous mom-and-pop firms in its indus-try. Each acquisition of a competitor means more market share. In addition, there are synergies resulting from the combinations. The technique is discussed fully in one of my previous books, *M&A: A Practical Guide to Doing the Deal* (John Wiley & Sons, 1994).

A summary of the three types of growth companies can be found in Exhibit 10.4.

The key to the consolidator's business is twofold: (1) acquiring companies at a reasonable price, and (2) achieving cost savings and revenue gains through the acqui-sitions. Due to the number and frequency of acquisitions consummated by the con-solidator, the accounting is complex and the security analysis is difficult. Reviewing the financials, the practitioner needs to confirm several aspects of the consolidator:

- *Base businesses are stable.* The acquired businesses prosper after being brought under the consolidation umbrella. One big risk in acquisitions is poor integra-tion, causing a corresponding loss in customers.

EXHIBIT 10.4   Three Kinds of Growth Companies

Classic growth company	Offers a new product for which there was no established demand. The product is typically the result of new innovation and technology.
Market share growth company	Participating in a mature industry, this company grows quickly because it boosts market share through better product quality, image, or service.
Consolidator	Operating in a fragmented and mature industry, the consolidator grows by acquiring numerous other firms. Paying the right price and realizing synergies are critical factors for success.

EXHIBIT 10.5   Sales Growth of a Consolidator: Gatehouse Media, Inc. (in millions, except acquisitions)

	2004	2005	2006	Compound Annual Growth Rate
Sales	$205	$315	$588	69%
Acquisitions	6	10	18	

Source: Gatehouse Media SEC filings.

■ *Purchase prices are reasonable.* In its zeal to expand, the consolidator is tempted to pay high purchase prices, particularly when other consolidators are at work. The analyst's research should show that acquisitions provide a fair return on investment.

■ *Realistic synergies exist.* In order to attract financing, consolidators sometimes inflate the cost savings and revenue enhancements that a transaction realizes. The analyst casts a critical eye on the consolidator's assumptions.

Developing a consolidator is a favorite tactic of the private equity industry. At any given time there are dozens of consolidators trying to build sufficiently large businesses that can go public or attract a strategic buyer. Set forth in Exhibit 10.5 is summary data for Gatehouse Media, a small-town newspaper consolidator controlled by the private equity firm Fortress Investment Group.

Note how multiple acquisitions promote sales growth for the consolidator.

THE CYCLICAL COMPANY

Both mature businesses and growth companies exhibit stable trends that lend confidence to earnings power estimates. Without a strong argument to the contrary, practitioners continue these trends in their projections. After all, will people stop drinking Coca-Cola or eating McDonald's hamburgers? Cyclical companies pose another problem. Since their earnings exaggerate the movement in the business cycle, boom times are followed by bust times, and this pattern repeats every cycle. Exhibit 10.6 shows earlier data from Chapter 6, where cyclical firm Paccar Truck was highlighted.

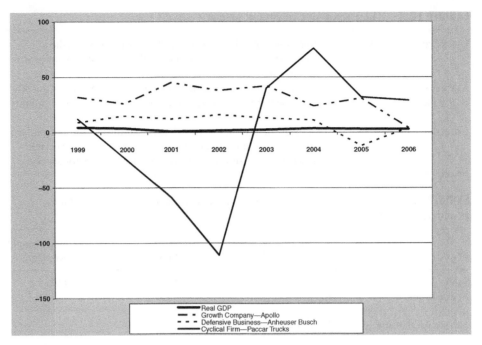

EXHIBIT 10.6   Business Cycle Comparison, GNP versus Earnings per Share Percentage Changes

Given the ups and downs of a cyclical business, there is no point in using current earnings as a base, since that performance level is only temporary. If the cycle is peaking, the analyst knows that earnings declines are just around the corner. Similarly, particularly poor performance may signal a bottom, and one is justified in anticipating a recovery. Accordingly, the historical analysis considers the firm's earnings over the last full business cycle. Of particular interest to the analyst are average performance, operating leverage, and debt service capability. There items are examined for each year in the most recent cycle.

Average Performance and the Cyclical Company

Determining the average annual earnings power for the cyclical company complements the standard analytical strategies. The average is computed over the entire cycle, which includes one or two bad years and three or four good years. Analysts average EBITDA, return on equity, and other performance measures, which calculations are then used in valuation estimates. Selected data for Con-Way, Inc., a cyclical trucking firm, appears in Exhibit 10.7. Cyclical companies encourage the averaging practice by maintaining dividends over the cycle.

Operating Leverage and Cyclical Companies

Operating leverage is the degree of earnings volatility associated with sales movement. For example, a business whose earnings climb 30 percent for each 10 percent increase in sales has high operating leverage. A firm that registers only a 10 percent

EXHIBIT 10.7 Averaging Cyclical Performance: Con-Way, Inc.

	Peak		Recession		Peak					
	1999	2000	2001	2002	2003	2004	2005	2006	2007	Average
EPS	2.98	2.79	0.42	1.28	1.67	2.57	3.85	4.04	3.39	2.55
Cash dividends/ share	0.40	0.40	0.40	0.40	0.40	0.40	0.40	0.40	0.40	0.40

Note: Recession began in 2001 and continued through 2002.

earnings gain on a 10 percent sales boost lacks such leverage. Firms with high fixed costs generally have high degrees of operating leverage.

Most cyclical businesses have high fixed costs, resulting from the substantial infrastructure needed to operate. Automobile manufacturers, cement producers, and paper mills are examples of firms that have major overhead in plant depreciation, maintenance, and capital costs. In the cement industry, fixed costs in a recession year are 50 percent of sales, as compared to 5 percent in the temporary help industry. Furthermore, most cement employees are retained in the down cycle, since retraining new workers during the rapid up cycle is impractical. This overhead is a drag in a recession, when unit sales volumes fall, because the fixed costs per unit are high. As demand picks up, per unit costs decline as fixed overhead is spread over more units. Profit margins increase along with sales volumes, thus providing a double impetus to earnings growth. Cyclical businesses can multiply net earnings on a relatively small sales gain (but the opposite occurs with a sales decline). Exhibit 10.8 shows two examples of this phenomenon.

As the practitioner examines cyclical performance, he refers to the industry study, which provides a link between the firm's revenues and key macroeconomic factors, such as GNP growth, housing starts, or capital goods demand. Knowing the drivers for corporate sales, he then looks for those aspects of operating leverage that strongly influence earnings. If the firm has a limited product line, the analysis sometimes

EXHIBIT 10.8 Volatility of Cyclical Company Performance

	Peak		Recession		Recovery				
	1999	2000	2001	2002	2003	2004	2005	2006	2007
Mueller—copper tube									
Sales (billions)	$1.2	$1.2	$1.0	$0.9	$1.0	$1.4	$1.7	$2.5	$2.7
EPS	2.51	2.43	1.80	1.58	0.95	2.15	2.40	4.26	3.10
Cooper Industries— electrical equipment									
Sales (billions)	$3.9	$4.5	$4.2	$3.9	$4.0	$4.5	$4.7	$5.2	$5.9
EPS	1.75	1.90	1.38	1.30	1.42	1.79	2.06	2.55	3.14

Source: SEC filings.
Note how net income for these firms suffered during the recession, only to bounce back during the recovery.

synthesizes changes in profit margins and earnings into a few relationships. For example, Agnico-Eagle Mines is a $10 billion gold mining play. A $100 per ounce change in the gold price causes a change in annual EPS of $0.38, according to CFO David Garofalo. Gold prices are linked to inflation and currency movement. Plum Creek Timbers sells logs and processed wood. As a result, I calculated that a $2 variation in log prices per ton affected the bottom line by $0.20 per share. Naturally, this number factored in elements affecting the timber industry like housing starts, shipments, and transportation costs, but quantifying operating leverage is difficult. Most firms participate in multiple lines of business and it's hard to separate expense items by segment. Also, many public filings don't disclose enough details on unit volumes and prices to facilitate the determination. Gaining insights involves telephone calls to management.

Cyclical Companies and Financial Leverage

Lenders must be repaid, whether or not the borrower endures a recession. The debt service issue takes center stage for cyclical firms that rely on leverage. Most are obligated to pursue sizable capital programs because growth requires capacity expansions. In this way, the firms combine financial leverage with operating leverage, and the combination adds to earnings volatility. Accordingly, the cyclical company review assesses prior cash flow carefully. Did cash flow cover debt service and capital expense over the cycle? Did the firm borrow to pay dividends? Were cash reserves sufficient to fund shortfalls if credit dried up? Exhibits 10.9 and 10.10 show conservative and aggressive debt service approaches.

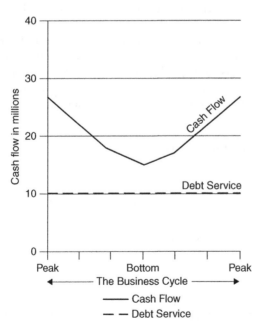

The Conservative Business exceeds its debt service at the bottom of the cycle.

EXHIBIT 10.9 Cyclical Firms and Debt Service Coverage— Conservative Approach

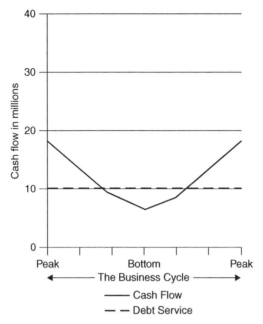

The Aggressive Business pays debt service out of cash reserves at the bottom of the cycle. It should plan for a cash reserve to cope with the bottom of the cycle.

EXHIBIT 10.10 Cyclical Firms and Debt Service Coverage—Aggressive Approach

Another evaluative method is forecasting debt service coverage. Low coverage suggests that management risks credit problems. On a forward-looking basis, the practitioner must be confident that the business can fulfill debt obligations during a downturn; otherwise, it may go bankrupt before the upturn! Trinity Industries, the railroad car maker, survived the 2002–2004 recession in its industry by dipping into its cash reserves. (See Exhibit 10.11.)

Other Cycles

As noted in Chapter 6, besides the general business cycle, there are other phenomena that promote cyclical performance. Brokerage firms, for example, show cyclicality

EXHIBIT 10.11 Trinity Industries Corporation—Interest Coverage

	2001	Downturn			2005	2006
		2002	2003	2004		
EBIT (millions)	$151	$11	$13	$14	$204	$383
Interest coverage	7.2×	0.3×	0.4×	0.3×	4.9×	6.0×
Interest expense	$21	$36	$35	$42	$42	$64

Note: Excluding captive finance operations and special charges. Trinity survived the 2002–2004 downturn by dipping into cash reserves and working capital.

EXHIBIT 10.12   S&P 500 Index versus Merrill Lynch's EPS

	2000	2001	2002	2003	2004	2005	2006
S&P 500 Index	1,320	1,150	880	1,110	1,210	1,250	1,420
S&P Index	100	87	67	84	92	95	108
Merrill Lynch	$4.11	$2.40	$2.83	$4.05	$4.38	$5.16	$6.63
Merrill Lynch Index	100	58	69	98	107	126	162

Note how the stock price index and Merrill Lynch's EPS track each other.

based on the ebb and flow of stock prices. Product cycles in the computer industry lead to prominent swings in semiconductor demand. Some volatility arises from predictable supply variations in commodity-based products, which result in repetitive price trends that are independent of the business cycle. Exhibit 10.12 shows a recent stock price cycle, and Exhibit 10.13 illustrates Merrill Lynch's earnings record.

Commodity-type industries rely on gigantic production facilities. Examples include iron ore mining ($1 billion per mine), petrochemical processing ($2 billion plus for a large plant), and paper production ($1 billion for a paper mill). Producers tend to construct new facilities during the middle to end of the cycle when times are good and lenders are flush. The facilities start up at the same time, and new supply floods the market, depressing prices until demand catches up. The paper industry is a perfect example of this pattern of capacity expansion and retrenchment. Changes in pulp prices indicate the extent of the problem: $840 per ton in 2000, dropping to $450 per ton in 2004 before jumping to $880 per ton in 2008.

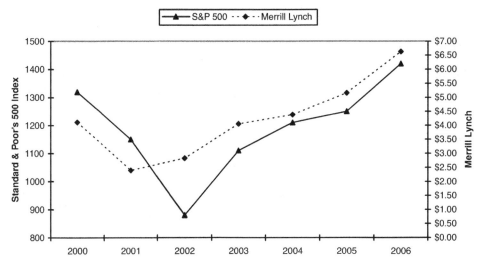

EXHIBIT 10.13   Merrill Lynch EPS versus S&P 500 Index

THE DECLINING COMPANY

It's important to distinguish between a cyclical company in the down cycle and a business in a permanent state of decline. Sometimes, purely cyclical factors are hard to differentiate from coincidental changes in business fundamentals, such as shifts in customer preferences or changes in product technology. The industry study provides guidance in this area, but the firm may be operating in a submarket that functions separately. Declining unit volumes and lower profit margins are stark evidence of a failing business. Forecast earnings power should be a continuation of this downward spiral, all things being equal. Few people want to invest in a modern-day buggy whip manufacturer. Cash flow and balance sheet analysis are helpful in determining sustainability.

A current buggy whip candidate is the newspaper industry. As more people get their news from cable TV and the Internet, fewer read newspapers, and the industry's secular decline in readership is now 3 percent annually. Newspaper stock prices fell on average by 70 percent from 2006 to 2008, as investors grappled with the changes.

THE TURNAROUND

In every mature industry and every growth business, there is a firm whose star has fallen. Once a profitable enterprise with rising sales, the turnaround is now a laggard. Sales growth is flat to negative, and profit margins lag behind the competition. Reasons behind the collapse are many and varied, and while historical financial analysis synthesizes the problems in statistical form, it offers little in the way of predictive ability. Typically, management has a plan to revitalize the business (i.e., the turnaround), but the implementation requires time and money. The practitioner focuses on historical cash flow patterns and existing leverage concerns, to determine whether the company has the time and resources needed for management to pull off the plan. Chapter 25 reviews valuing turnaround candidates.

One well-known turnaround was Waste Management. A highflier in the later 1990s, this waste services firm saw its share price plummet from $58 to $15 in 2000. Ill-fated acquisitions, heavy debts, environmental liabilities, and accounting issues cast a cloud over the business. From 2001 to 2008, a new management and a new restructuring brought back profits, investor confidence, and the stock price. One key item ignored by investors in the dark days was the firm's vast base of customer contracts and landfills. These assets provided Waste Management with the financial foundation from which to fix its business.

THE PIONEER

Historical financial analysis is almost useless for the pioneer company. With few sales and no earnings, the business is a poor candidate for the tools of absolute amount, percentage change, common size, and ratio analysis. Valuations of these stocks, in fact, are tied mostly to projections that have little connection with the firm's past.

EXHIBIT 10.14   Calculation of Microvision's Burn Rate

Twelve Months Ending June 30, 2008	($ millions)
Cash operating expenses	$25.0
Capital expenditures	2.0
	27.0
Divided by months per year	÷12.0
Burn rate	$2.3 per month
Cash on hand at June 30, 2008	$23.0
Divided by burn rate	÷2.3
Number of months	10 months

With a $2.3 million per month burn rate, Microvision has 10 months
of financing-free operations.

With little track record to go on, investors use hopeful projections to justify prices,
and they're willing to absorb losses for the chance of a big payoff. Waiting for the
earnings to arrive, practitioners sometimes emphasize one statistic—the *burn rate*.

In the process of establishing itself, the pioneer company runs negative cash
flows. Operating expenses, R&D, and capital investment exceed the cash derived
from operations. Using the somewhat naive assumption that outside financing is
unavailable, the analyst calculates *monthly negative cash flow*. This is called the
burn rate because the business burns through that much cash in a typical month.
This amount is then divided into the cash on hand, and the analyst has a rough
idea of how long the firm can last without outside assistance. For example, $24
million in cash divided by a $1 million burn rate implies a two-year window. During this time, the enterprise can avoid selling equity securities, which might dilute
existing shareholders' claims on future earnings. This figure also gives an indication
of management's flexibility in concentrating on R&D, instead of selling stock.

Exhibit 10.14 shows the calculation of Microvision's burn rate, and indicates
that the business has funding for 10 months. Microvision develops miniature imaging
systems. It has few sales and no earnings, but offers a promising technology with
enthusiastic supporters.

FINANCIAL GAMES

Much of a public company CFO's job is the consideration of tactics to manage
earnings per share. In this section, we discuss the three popular maneuvers:

- Issuing new shares to finance growth.
- Repurchasing shares to increase EPS results.
- Boosting leverage to accelerate EPS growth.

For much of this book so far, financial analysis has been discussed in terms
of total corporate performance. Higher sales and net income were naively assumed
to translate into higher earnings and dividends per share. In numerous instances,

EXHIBIT 10.15 Higher Earnings, But Lower EPS: Redwood Corporation, Selected Income Statement Data (in millions, except per share data)

	2007	2008	2009	Compound Annual Growth Rate
Sales	$100.0	$120.0	$144.0	20%
Net income	20.0	24.0	29.0	20%
Average shares outstanding	10.0	13.0	17.0	30%
Earnings per share	2.00	1.85	1.70	(8)%

A higher number of shares meant EPS went down, even as net income went up.

this logical progression is not the case. Instead, companies issue more shares to finance the innovative products, market expansions, and acquisitions that provide growth. If earnings from the new initiatives aren't sufficient to cover the added shares, stockholders suffer a diminution of their investment's earning power.

Since we are discussing the purchase of common shares in this book, performance statistics on a per share basis take precedence. Consider hypothetical Redwood Corporation, for example. It prefers to grow sales rather than earnings per share. As shown in Exhibit 10.15, net income increased 20 percent annually from 2007 to 2009. To the casual observer, Redwood qualifies as a growth company. The experienced practitioner, however, continues his inspection to *earnings per share*, which dropped 8 percent annually. Income growth failed to travel to the bottom line—earnings per share. To achieve the income gains, Redwood issued too many new shares.

Cleco Corporation, an energy company, is a good example of the Redwood phenomenon. Since 2003, sales and net income increased 4 percent and 7 percent, respectively, on a compound annual basis, but EPS failed to keep up, rising only 1 percent annually. Over that time period, Cleco boosted the number of shares by 28 percent. See Exhibit 10.16.

An analysis revealed the faulty financial mechanics of Cleco in achieving growth. The follow-up question, of course, is whether more share issuances will be needed to support Cleco's future performance.

With some companies, the analyst notices that top-line growth is moderate or nonexistent, yet earnings per share keep rising. The culprit in this case is either (1) a share repurchase program or (2) a larger financial leverage.

EXHIBIT 10.16 Top-Line Growth without Corresponding EPS Gains: Cleco Corporation (in millions, except earnings per share)

	2003	2004	2005	2006	2007	Compound Annual Growth Rate (%)
Revenues	$875	$746	$920	$1,001	$1,091	4
Net income	61	66	75	75	80	7
Earnings per share	1.26	1.32	1.42	1.36	1.32	1
Common shares	47	49	50	57	60	6

The Share Repurchase Program

When net income is flat to moderately up, a business can often *increase* EPS by *decreasing* the number of shares. The firm buys its shares and places them into a treasury account, so they aren't counted as outstanding. The EPS numerator is therefore divided by a smaller denominator:

$$EPS = \frac{\text{Net Earnings}}{\text{Number of Shares Outstanding}}$$

The effectiveness of a share buyback is dependent on a number of variables, such as the opportunity cost of cash, the cost of debt, the share price, the tax rate, and the P/E ratio.

Papa John's practiced this technique. As shown in Exhibit 10.17, the firm's income growth was moderate over the three years displayed here (2005–2007), but EPS rose 17 percent. The reason was the firm's repurchase program, which reduced shares outstanding from 34 million in 2005 to 29 million in 2007.

In many cases, the function of share repurchases is to return excess cash to stockholders in a manner that is more tax efficient than paying dividends. Some businesses generate excess cash and lack attractive investment options.

Increasing Leverage

When faced with mediocre earnings prospects, some companies prop up EPS by increasing debt. Rather than financing additional investment by issuing new shares, these firms opt to use debt exclusively for cash needs. Shareholder dilution is thus avoided because the number of shares remains constant, but this objective is achieved at the expense of making the earnings stream more volatile and, therefore, more risky.

Consider the plight of Industrial Distribution Company. In December 2008, it had to decide how to raise $100 million to fund the completion of a new warehouse, along with the associated inventory. At a board meeting, the chief financial officer pushed an all-debt option, and trotted out his projections showing how EPS increased faster with leverage.

"Projected EPS growth is now below-average," he said. "We can't afford equity." In contrast, the chief operating officer argued for the conservative all-equity option: "We're sensitive to the business cycle," he argued, "and EBIT doesn't go up in

EXHIBIT 10.17   Boosting EPS with Share Repurchase Program: Papa John's International (in millions, except for per share data)

	2005	2006	2007	Compound Annual Growth Rate
Revenues	$970	$1,002	$1,064	5%
Net income	42	47	50	9
Earnings per share	1.21	1.42	1.66	17
Average shares outstanding	34	33	29	(8)

Papa John's 17 percent EPS growth rate was almost double the 9 percent net income growth rate. Share repurchases decreased shares outstanding and boosted EPS.

EXHIBIT 10.18   Industrial Distribution Company—Three Financing Alternatives

Capital Structure	Alternatives		
	Do Nothing	Issue Long-Term Debt	Sell Equity
Short-term debt	$100	$ —	$ —
Long-term debt	100	200	100
Equity	200	200	300
Total capitalization	$400	$400	$400
Average shares outstanding	20	20	26

Projected 2009 EBIT: $50 million
Income tax rate: 40%
Stock price: $17.00
Estimated 2009 EPS: $1.00

a staircase fashion. Debt stands at $100 million already." An assistant controller prepared the numbers and presented the board with three alternatives, as set forth in the hypothetical case in Exhibit 10.18.

Which financing alternative should the board select?

The debate boiled down to management's appetite for risk and their perception of future operating results. In the "sunny day" forecast, the all-debt option was the clear winner: EPS increased 11 percent on a compound annual basis versus 8 percent under the all-equity alternative. The "rainy day" forecast assumed a cyclical downturn in the middle of the period, threatening the firm's ability to pay cash dividends and service debts. Rainy day EPS was higher under the equity scenario. Exhibit 10.19 provides the details.

EXHIBIT 10.19   Industrial Distribution Company—Financing a New Warehouse (in millions, except per share data)

	2009	2010	2011	2012	2013
Sunny day forecast					
Sales	$1,000	$1,100	$1,150	$,250	$1,350
EBIT	50	54	58	63	68
Earnings per share					
Debt financing	$1.02	$1.14	$1.26	$1.41	$1.56
Equity financing	1.00	1.09	1.18	1.29	1.38
	All-debt EPS is higher in the sunny day forecast.				
Rainy day forecast					
Sales	$900	$800	$700	$800	$900
EBIT	40	35	30	35	40
Earnings per share					
Debt financing	$0.75	$0.60	$0.45	$0.60	$0.75
Equity financing	0.76	0.65	0.53	0.65	0.76
	All-equity EPS is higher in the rainy day forecast.				

With a shift in financing strategy, Industrial Distribution Co. changes its projected EPS performance. Other corporations perform similar sleight of hand to remedy poor prospects. Some firms incur huge amounts of debt to complete large acquisitions. Others incur debt to fund share repurchases, thus increasing leverage and cutting outstanding shares simultaneously. A proper financial analysis uncovers such EPS-building strategies in short order.

EXTRA SHARES OUTSTANDING?

Another thing to look for is the ownership dilution attributable to hybrid securities. Besides convertible bonds and employee stock options, financial technology has created equity-oriented hybrids that are difficult to figure. A studied review of the financial statement footnotes and the proxy statements provides the answers.

SUMMARY

Wall Street likes to summarize a company's attributes in a shorthand manner, preferably within six classifications. The analyst pigeonholes firms within those classifications by completing a financial analysis:

1. Mature company
2. Growth company
3. Cyclical company
4. Declining company
5. Turnaround
6. Pioneer

After the analyst clarifies a firm's earnings origin and defines its classification, he confirms that top-line revenue performance is in sync with bottom-line EPS. Abrupt increases in leverage and sizable issuances of equity upset the traditional relationship between revenue, EBIT, net income, and EPS.

Companies divorce the top and bottom lines in the following ways:

- Going overboard in issuing new shares to finance growth.
- Repurchasing shares to increase EPS results.
- Boosting leverage to accelerate EPS growth.

Security analysis would be a lot easier if all public companies exhibited steady upward trends in sales, net income, and earnings per share. Unfortunately, the real world doesn't operate that way. As a result, the practitioner is confronted with a bewildering variety of performance patterns. Now that you have a good comprehension of the factors underlying historical results, we proceed to the financial forecast. In today's market, forming a view on the future is more important than describing the past.

CHAPTER 11

Financial Projection Pointers

Most research reports incorporate sales and earnings projections of the company under study. Before jumping into the business of making projections, the analyst should know popular approaches and common pitfalls. Moderating optimistic assumptions with reality checks is an important part of this work.

Constructing accurate financial projections is a difficult task. As the top-down approach in Chapter 5 illustrated, so many variables affect a firm's performance—and they originate in so many sectors of the economy, the industry, and the company itself—that the forecasting process appears well nigh impossible. The academic literature is full of studies showing the inaccuracy of earnings estimates. Even one-year forecasts have a mean error of 25 to 30 percent, but what choice do we have? Everyone knows the Graham and Dodd approach of picking cheap stocks on the basis of low price/earnings (P/E) and low price/book ratios, so these opportunities are scarce. Relative value analysis identifies pricing inefficiencies, but the investor risks plunging into an already overvalued sector. Notwithstanding the problem of forecasts, the basis for stock prices tends to be forward looking, and there remain rationales for why this should be the case. That's why section 6 of the research report is critical.

Practitioners aren't seers, so it's fortunate that no one seeks perfection in security analysis. As noted earlier, the analyst who is right 60 to 70 percent of the time is considered a superstar. And being right doesn't mean predicting earnings per share down to the penny year after year. Just detecting when the consensus forecast falls out of the bounds of common sense is a great service to investors, who then use this information as a buy or sell signal.

In this chapter, we cover projection methodology at the company-specific level and review principles that make you a better forecaster. The nuts and bolts of projections, such as assigning growth percentages to revenues and applying inventory-to-sales ratios, are covered in Chapter 8 (the Neiman Marcus case), this chapter (the Huntsman Chemical case and the William Wrigley case), Chapter 15 (the Temporary Staffing Services case), and Chapter 19 (the Ruddick Corporation case).

Model Research Report

1. Introduction
2. Macroeconomic Review
3. Relevant Stock Market Prospects
4. Review of the Company and Its Business
5. Financial Analysis
6. Financial Projections ✓
7. Application of Valuation Methodologies
8. Recommendation

THE CASCADE OF PROJECTIONS

As Chapter 5 illustrated, the top-down approach isolates the important macroeconomic, capital market, and industry variables that affect a firm's performance. Generally, these relationships tie into each other in a sequential fashion, leading to the cascade of projections summarized in Exhibit 5.5 and reproduced here as Exhibit 11.1.

THE TYPICAL FINANCIAL PROJECTION

The typical financial projection relies heavily on what happened in the past. The Neiman Marcus case was a classic illustration. Key statistics such as same store sales, gross margins, and selling, general, and administrative (SG&A) expenses were anticipated to improve modestly over historical results, and neither a recession, a new competitor, nor a major market change was predicted. The vast majority of projections follow this pattern of the future reflecting the immediate past. Indeed,

EXHIBIT 11.1   Cascade of Forecasts: Home Building Company

Top-Down Analysis	Sample Forecast for Home Builder
Economy	GNP will increase 3 percent.
	↓
Capital markets	Interest rates will decline.
	↓
Industry	Housing starts to increase.
	↓
Home builder	Home building company will gain market share, so its sales rise 15 percent instead of the 10 percent industry average. Steady profit margins signify a 15 percent earnings increase.

EXHIBIT 11.2   Huntsman Chemical Corporation: Cyclical Company Forecast without the Cycle (revenue in billions, EBIT in millions)

	2008	2009	2010	2011	2012
Revenues	9.7	9.9	10.2	10.9	11.2
EBIT	655	9,087	1,009	1,201	1,255

Source: Huntsman 2008 Proxy Statement.
Note how there is no business cycle in this projection, even as the economy entered a downturn.

it is difficult for investors to argue against the rearview mirror approach. Analysts, economists, and other investment experts are notoriously poor at gauging when a reasonably stable business, such as Neiman Marcus, faces either a serious downturn or a rejuvenating upturn. As a result, most forecasts involving established businesses extend historical performance into the future, usually via a loosely derived mathematical model such as a regression, moving average, trend line, or exponential smoothing.

A clear exception to this convention should be the cyclical business, yet most practitioners are loath to predict downturns, a fact noted by many observers. Accordingly, many published forecasts of cyclical firms move upward in lockstep, like the projections of stable companies. Huntsman Chemical provided one example in 2008, even as the U.S. economy entered a downturn. See Exhibit 11.2.

ALTERNATE MEANS OF FORECASTING

To prevent total reliance on historical data for established concerns—and to construct projections from the ground up for new companies—analysts consider alternatives to trending past history. These approaches are most popular for businesses that either have a short track record or participate in a volatile industry. Examples of the former are start-up ventures. Examples of the latter are firms dependent on changing technology or fashion-oriented businesses.

The base component of any forecast is the revenue projection. Most expenses and balance sheet items flow directly from sales. Your first assignment is thus determining which technique is best for estimating sales. The initial reaction of the average analyst is to look at past sales as the anchor for predicting future revenues. While this technique is valid for many businesses, it must be tempered with a review of prospective changes in the company's product offerings, product prices, competitive environments, and technologies. Even when firms operate in the same industry, they contain unique elements that make each projection a situational exercise. Many of these elements contain a strong historical bias, while others require an independent interpretation.

A common approach to sales forecasting is placing the business in the now-familiar corporate life cycle chart. Alternatively, the candidate is designated as falling into a certain industry type. Both the corporate life cycle positions and industry categories carry sales growth patterns that are now well-known to the reader. (See Exhibit 11.3.)

EXHIBIT 11.3   Defining the Candidate for Sales Forecasting

Corporate Life Cycle	Expected Sales Performance
Pioneer	Unpredictable and volatile sales movements.
Growth	Steady growth in sales as product acceptance widens.
Mature	Moderate increases in sales as market for the company's product matures.
Decline	Sales decrease as customers are attracted to newer, innovative products.

Industry Characterization	Expected Sales Performance
Growth	Steady growth in sales as product acceptance widens.
Cyclical	Established business in sector where sales are dependent on the economic cycle (e.g., autos, home construction).
Defensive	Sales movements are resistant to changes in the economic cycle (e.g., bread, beer, and cigarette companies).

When the analyst establishes the fit between the candidate, its industry, and its life cycle position, he is in a position to select the appropriate projection technique. Sales projections are segmented into three categories: (1) time series, (2) causal, and (3) qualitative.

Time Series Forecast Techniques

The basic assumption underlying time series analysis is that the future will be like the past. Analysts prepare sales forecasts, therefore, by examining historical results, which are then brought forward through the use of moving averages, exponential smoothing, or trend lines. Using this technique, a company with a five-year growth rate of 10 percent likely has an estimated future growth rate around 10 percent. This rearview mirror approach is difficult to counter effectively unless someone has a fresh reason for promoting a dramatic reversal.

The time series analysis has proven itself well in basic industries such as food, electricity, and medical care. As a result, it is popular in projections of stable and defensive concerns. Accurate projections in these industries can be difficult at the firm-specific level, but they become easier when the business controls a significant market share. Dominant firms, like Budweiser in the beer business, are a proxy for the entire industry.

The weakness of the time series technique is its inability to predict turning points in a company's performance. Turning points are often the result of hard-to-predict new competition or product innovation. How could a time-series analysis forecast the demise of SUV sales after 15 years of dominating the auto sector? Or, the explosive growth of software-on-demand providers? How about the complete turnaround in Apple Computer's fortunes?

The time series technique also encounters a problem with business cycles. These phenomena do not appear on a preset schedule, and they vary considerably in their duration and magnitude. Other predictive measures are required.

Causal Forecast Techniques

The causal methods forecast a company's sales by establishing relationships between sales and certain variables that are independent of the corporation. At times these relationships involve broad economic statistics such as gross national product (GNP) or employment. To illustrate, cement demand is tied closely to GNP growth, so a cement industry projection relies heavily on GNP estimates. In other instances, demographic factors influence a firm's future sales. For example, the graying of America inevitably leads to predictions that the nursing home business is a growth industry. With other companies, industry-related factors drive revenue. Housing starts drive furniture sales.

Company-specific factors may be causal. In lodging, a hotel chain's future sales are influenced by a new hotel construction program. A computer chip maker's revenues are impacted by a new production plant.

Quantifying these causal relationships involves the use of regression formulas or econometric calculations. Complementing the results are customer surveys and feasibility studies connecting future revenue to variables that are not observable from the past. For example, hotel room rates went down in Las Vegas after 2007. A tourist survey would have quantified that future link to the supply of rooms from new hotel openings.

Causal forecasting is used for firms in the stable and decline phases of the corporate life cycle. It is also applied to established firms in cyclical or defensive industries. A firm in the later stages of its growth phase is a causal candidate, since it, like the others mentioned, has a track record that is long enough to relate to external variables.

Qualitative Forecast Techniques

Qualitative projection techniques are applied to pioneer and growth companies offering new products and services. With little history to act as a guide, the sales forecaster is left with expert opinions, market research studies, and historical analogies as his analytical tools. Sometimes the result is nothing more than educated guesswork. The market reaction of truly new products is hard to gauge. Questions such as what will be the level of acceptance, and what price will the consumer pay, are difficult to answer, even for experienced professionals. Direct satellite radio services and wearable computers, for example, confounded Wall Street prognosticators.

Any would-be analyst is well advised to use qualitative techniques in developing projections, even if the business in question has a consistent sales record. The added work is another part of an effective research report, and it might reveal an inflection point unnoticed by the investment community. Important qualitative methods for predicting sales are described in Exhibit 11.4.

CRITIQUING THE HUNTSMAN CHEMICAL PROJECTION

Confronted with a historically derived projection from an established business like Huntsman Chemical, the careful analyst weighs causal and qualitative means. First, in 2008 the U.S. economy was slowing down, and the company's unit growth rate was probably going to fall with the economy. Second, the firm's revenues in its

EXHIBIT 11.4   Qualitative Forecasting Methods

Experts	The practitioner consults with an industry expert(s) to develop assumptions on sales projections.
Market research	Consumer studies are performed to estimate future demand and pricing for a potential or existing product line.
Historical analogy	The analyst makes a connection between the company's potential sales and those of firms that offered a related concept in the past. For example, BlackBerry manufacturers examined the introduction of the cell phone and Gameboy into the American household.
Futurists	A long view, say 5 to 10 years into the future, may require an unconventional interpretation. The force, intensity, and speed of contemporary business bring unpredictable change. Every industry has its visionaries who look beyond the likely near-term developments.

petrochemical line were tied to oil prices that trended higher; this argued for scenarios with more flow-through revenue but with less profit margin than management forecasts. Third, the dollar's weakness seemed unsustainable, affecting the amount of export revenues assumed in the firm's projection. In sum, higher revenues, but lower profit, seemed a more reasonable prediction.

Accompanying the preparation of top-line sales projections are future assessments garnered from your historical review. Is it likely that the gross margin will change in the future? Will SG&A expense stay constant as sales rise? Will inventory turnover jump in the coming years? Applying the answers provides the analyst with a framework for making his projection. In the case of Huntsman Chemical, an objective practitioner would have prepared a forecast that was less sanguine than the data provided in the 2008 merger proxy. For example, high oil prices would have hurt profit margins and the subprime crisis would have kept interest rates high, curtailing prospective expansions and acquisitions. Exhibit 11.5 shows management's numbers alongside hypothetical data developed by a sensible analyst.

PREPARING PROJECTIONS

With Huntsman Chemical, or any projection, the practitioner should follow these seven steps:

Seven Steps to Making Projections

1. Complete a historical financial analysis.
2. Match company classification with appropriate sales forecast technique.

Pioneer	Time Series
Growth	Causal
Mature	Qualitative
Decline	

EXHIBIT 11.5 Huntsman Chemical Corp.: Condensed Forecast Financial Data (revenue in billions, EBIT in millions)

	2008	2009	2010	2011	2012
Proxy			**Optimistic Forecast**		
Sales	9.7	9.9	10.2	10.9	11.2
EBIT	655	908	1,009	1,201	1,255
Sales growth	1%	2%	3%	7%	3%
EBIT margin	7%	9%	10%	11%	11%
Rational Investor			**Realistic Forecast**		
Sales	11.0	10.8	10.5	10.8	11.5
EBIT	430	360	475	668	947
Sales growth	13%	(2)%	(3)%	3%	6%
EBIT margin	4%	3%	5%	7%	8%

Source: SEC filings and author estimates.
The proxy contained optimistic projections that didn't fit Huntsman's likely results. A rational investor uses realistic data.

3. Select reasonable assumptions for other relevant top-down variables.

Macroeconomic
Industry
Company-Specific

Establish Linkages

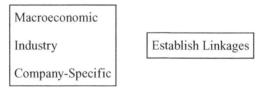

4. Prepare income statement down to the EBIT line.
5. Estimate external cash needs, if any, and structure future finances, such as debt and common stock.
6. Complete all forecasts down to earnings per share.
7. Perform reality check.

Steps 1, 2, and 3: Focus on Top-Down Study and Historical Financial Analysis

The first three steps draw from the analyst's top-down study and his historical research. Experience dictates that he focus on the critical assumptions and linkages. For the average publicly traded stock, such items can be summarized in one or two pages. A normal forecast period is 5 or 10 years.

Step 4: Project the EBIT Line First

As noted in the previous chapter, the corporate financing decision influences per share earnings. More debt means more interest cost. If more shares are issued, EPS can fall behind net income growth. Before predicting pretax income, net income, and EPS, the analyst's assumptions about future debt use must be balanced against new equity finance. That's why EBIT is a good stopping point.

The capital structure assumptions are intertwined, of course, with the firm's forecasts for property and equipment, inventory, receivables, and other requirements. These items change in tandem with sales.

Step 5: Structure Future Finances

The firm's operating performance, stock market value, and creditworthiness play an important role in the formulation of the forward capital structure. A company with a strong track record and conservative balance sheet, like Campbell Soup, raises debt financing more easily than a technology business like Amazon. The analyst can logically assume that the latter firm is more likely to use equity instead of debt.

A common mistake among junior analysts (and MBA students) is naively assuming that debt is available to fill in the gap between future cash flows from operations and cash needs for growth. This beginner's mistake avoids unwanted earnings per share dilution in the future, but it doesn't fit the real world. Only a small minority of publicly traded firms qualify as investment-grade credits (i.e., the elite corporate group that has an easy time accessing the debt markets). Most publicly traded firms are junk bond credits, and their debt financing options are limited. Presumed leverage parameters have to be realistic, even if that means the subject firm issues more shares in the projection.

Step 6: Complete the Earnings per Share Forecast

With the financing scheme in place, the analyst estimates interest expense and outstanding shares over the projected period. He then calculates pretax income, net income, and earnings per share for the income statement. The last step is filling in the balance sheet and the statement of cash flows.

Step 7: Reality Check

With the final projection in hand, it's time for the analyst to step back, perhaps for a few days, and consider whether his numbers are sensible. From my experience, many a practitioner gets swept up in running endless scenarios on his personal computer, when he should be taking a second look at the fundamental assumptions driving his forecast. Sometimes another set of eyes helps spot obvious inconsistencies, and I recommend that analysts show abbreviated data to a disinterested third party, such as a colleague or an industry observer.

On the sell side, I've noticed that the reality check leans heavily on the subject company's management. Even after doing painstaking research and financial modeling, the brokerage firm analyst feels insecure. Anxious to have the benefit of the in-house projections and competing analyst opinions, he lays out his forecast in front of the firm's executives, who then have the opportunity to dissuade him of any P/E-deflating assumptions. Managers are an important source of information, but their opinions are obviously biased and should be taken with a grain of salt. Yet the sell-side analyst feels pressure to conform to the consensus of others.

EXHIBIT 11.6   William Wrigley Jr. Company: Three Forecast Scenarios (in billions)

	Forecast				
	2008	2009	2010	2011	2012
Upside Case					
Sales	$6.1	$6.8	$7.7	$8.6	$9.6
EBIT	1.2	1.4	1.6	1.7	2.0
Base Case					
Sales	$6.0	$6.6	$7.2	$7.9	$8.6
EBIT	1.1	1.2	1.3	1.4	1.6
Downside Case					
Sales	$5.9	$6.4	$6.9	$7.4	$8.0
EBIT	1.0	1.0	1.1	1.2	1.3

Source: SEC filings and author estimates.
The financial projection exercise often calls for three scenarios. Here sales growth and profit margin are modified ±2 percent in each scenario.

Three Scenarios

During the refinement of steps 1 through 6, the practitioner runs alternative scenarios, testing the earnings and cash flow effects of different assumptions. These scenarios produce many forecasts to consider, but the process usually boils down to three versions: (1) the upside case (optimistic), (2) the base case (best guess), and (3) the downside case (pessimistic). For the established business in a mature industry, the initial EBIT spread is typically ±10 percent off the base case, and future EBIT moves off this level. Goldman Sachs used this approach for its forecasts of William Wrigley Jr.'s $22 billion takeover by candy-maker Mars, Inc., in 2008. Exhibit 11.6 is illustrative.

The upside case of the average research report assumes no recessions, smooth product introductions, and moderate competition. Included in the downside case are the effects of recessions, price wars, and turning points. Many gunslinging portfolio managers pooh-pooh downside cases as too pessimistic, but thoughtful investors need to examine the financial cushion of a business if things go bad. For long-term forecasts, such as 7 to 10 years, a practitioner should include at least one recession.

CYCLICAL COMPANY FORECAST

Because of the inevitability of a recession, it should be mandatory that practitioners include a one- or two-year down period in the base case of any cyclical business. Nevertheless, most analysts ignore this advice, as evidenced by the Huntsman Chemical base case, which showed earnings climbing in lockstep fashion for five years. Even a cursory review illustrated the industry's deep cycles over the past 20 years—three periods of strong revenue growth, followed by three periods of steep declines—but

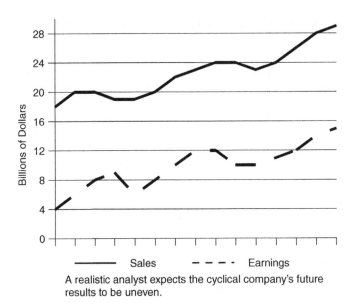

A realistic analyst expects the cyclical company's future results to be uneven.

EXHIBIT 11.7   Long-Term Cyclical Company Forecast

the 2008 projection maintained that things were different this time. Entertaining the notion that Huntsman can escape the chemical commodity cycle is speculative indeed.

A more practical approach is provided by a veteran steel analyst Jim Rudolph: "You know there's going to be a downturn for these capital-intensive companies, so your forecast has to show the effects of the waves (of economic prosperity) coming in and out." Thus, while the overall sales trend over the future cycles moves upward, it is interrupted periodically with a couple of down years. If one assumes a repetitive seven-year cycle for aircraft orders, then Huntsman's revenue tops out in 2008, to be followed by a couple of years of 15 percent declines.

The same rationale is appropriate for the larger universe of cyclical enterprises, which includes most capital goods and consumer durables companies. Assuming the underlying business shows promise, the relevant sales and earnings forecast should look something like Exhibit 11.7.

HOCKEY STICK PHENOMENON

The hockey stick phenomenon occurs as follows: (1) A professional evaluates a steadily growing business and makes a financial projection; (2) in order to justify an investment recommendation, he kick-starts the company's earnings the year after the investment starts; and (3) others use his forecast to sign off on the recommended stock, which otherwise appears overpriced. Graphically, the optimistic projection resembles a hockey stick. See Exhibit 11.8.

Hockey sticks are most prevalent in the latter stages of a bull market, since investors make increasingly optimistic assumptions in order to rationalize the

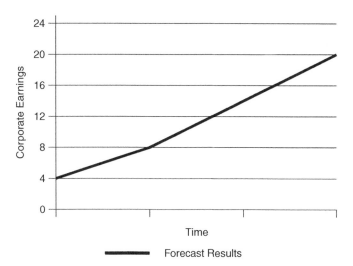

EXHIBIT 11.8 Hockey Stick Projections
Note how results suddenly get better in the hockey stick
projection.

high prices they're paying for stocks. Professors Becchetti, Hasan, Santoro, and
Anandarajan proved this assertion in a 2007 study.[1] Hockey sticks are also endemic
to the merger and acquisition business and the leveraged buyout industry. Consider
the April 2008 comments of Yahoo! CEO Jerry Yang, in justifying the rejection of a
$40 billion Microsoft takeover offer: "We believe we can significantly accelerate our
revenue growth, return to our historically high margins and double our operating
cash flow by 2010."[2] CEOs and merchant bankers often use inflated numbers to
promote debt, financings, IPOs, and M&A deals. Common sense is left behind.

This is exactly what happened in the $1.7 billion acquisition of Linens 'n Things,
a specialty retailer of home textiles, by Apollo Management, a leveraged buyout
firm, in 2005. In outbidding two industry players, the firm assumed a jump in
earnings, which never happened. Instead, the economic downturn hurt consumer
spending and heightened textile price competition. Unable to pay its debts in this
unexpected environment, Linens 'n Things filed for bankruptcy. The deal showed
how even experienced investors succumb to overly optimistic thinking. Exhibit 11.9
summarizes the situation.

A 2008 research paper by Professors Cusatis and Woolridge of Penn State
showed that over long periods, sell-side analyst forecasts are overly optimistic.[3]
Furthermore, analysts rarely project negative EPS growth, even for cyclical companies. The Wall Street hype mentality contributes to this sell-side bias, but my
experience in private equity and institutional lending shows that these two sectors
also favor steady, upward forecasts, rather than the choppy patterns that are evident
in corporate track records. Because so many common stock and corporate loan professionals move from job to job, their careers face little disruption when a former
employer suffers losses from a poorly valued transaction in which they participated.
Accordingly, investment approval committees at institutions must resist efforts to

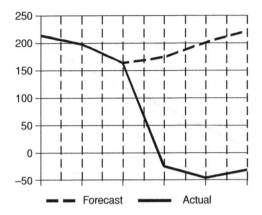

	2003	2004	2005	2006	2007	2008
Actual	214	199	164	(24)	(46)	(31)
Forecast	—	—	—	175	201	222

EXHIBIT 11.9   Hockey Stick Projection: Linens 'n Things EBITDA
Source: SEC filings.

approve transactions that have not been thoroughly vetted, even if their short-term results are impacted.

SUMMARY

The critical variable for most projections is sales, and practitioners emphasize three techniques to forecast this item—times series, causal, and qualitative. Once a methodology is selected, the analyst follows a seven-step process to round out the remainder of his financial projection. Common missteps during this task include naively filling in debt financings and using overoptimistic assumptions. Positive thinking is an occupational hazard in the investment business, and practitioners are advised to prepare multiple scenarios and seek independent counsel from time to time.

Valuation and the Investment Decision

At the conclusion of the evaluation report, the practitioner answers two questions: (1) Is this business fairly valued? and (2) Based on the previous response, should I recommend buying or selling an equity interest? Part Three provides the framework to answer these questions.

Valuation Methodologies

Chapter 12 reviews the principal valuation methodologies. Subsequent chapters discuss the methodologies in more detail and provide examples.

Now that we have studied historical financial analysis and financial projections, it's time to gain an understanding of the methods by which investors justify public stock prices, which in turn form the basis for valuing many private equity deals and corporate acquisitions. In this chapter and subsequent chapters, we review the four approaches that instill a discipline in the equity market and form the basis for section 7 of the research report.

Model Research Report

1. Introduction
2. Macroeconomic Review
3. Relevant Stock Market Prospects
4. Review of the Company and Its Business
5. Financial Analysis
6. Financial Projections
7. Application of Valuation Methodologies ✓
8. Recommendation

Recall the five broad approaches to business valuation (reiterated in Exhibit 12.1). Of these, only the first four lend themselves to the quasi-scientific method outlined in this book. They forecast stock prices on the basis of historical economic,

EXHIBIT 12.1   Business Valuation Methodologies

---

1. *Intrinsic value.* A business's intrinsic value equals the net present value of its dividends. Intrinsic value is sometimes called fundamental value or discounted cash flow (DCF).
2. *Relative value.* A firm's value is determined by comparing it to similar companies' values.
3. *Acquisition value.* Calculate a company's share price by considering its worth to a third-party acquirer.
4. *Leveraged buyout.* One prospective price for a business is its value in a leveraged buyout.
5. *Technical.* Share prices can be divined from prior trading patterns.

---

capital market, industry, and company statistics, which are then used to establish predictive trends for a firm's operating performance and stock price.

ASSESSING EACH METHODOLOGY

The four methodologies covered in this book have positive and negative attributes that are summarized here:

Intrinsic Value (Discounted Cash Flow, or DCF)

+ Intrinsic value is theoretically appropriate and the subject of many textbooks.
+ Corporate lenders use DCF on a regular basis for pricing loans and fixed-income securities.
− Equity professionals are reluctant to emphasize DCF. It is heavily reliant on 5- to 10-year projections. Forecasts are notoriously inaccurate past 1 year, much less 5 to 10 years.
− Practitioners have difficulty in reaching a consensus on the right discount rate for the future cash flows.
− Small changes, such as 1 percent, in the earnings growth or discount rate assumptions produce sizable value differences, damaging DCF's credibility.
− The terminal value often represents more than half of the DCF estimate, reducing the importance of the cash flow forecast.

Relative Value

+ The valuations of the similar public companies are indisputable, since their stock prices are published daily.
+ The calculations involving the enterprise value (EV)/sales, EV/EBITDA, P/E, and similar ratios have substance, since the underlying firm's financial results are audited.
− Many subject businesses lack a set of true comparable firms, so there is little to which to relate them.
− There is no yardstick to indicate whether the entire group of comparables is properly valued. During the dot-com boom, the pricing of the entire Internet sector was inflated.
− Relative value relies on past track records and current prices, when investors should focus on a firm's future.

Acquisition Value

+ Like relative value, the acquisition prices (and price multiples) of similar public firms are a matter of public record.
+ The public acquisition prices can be supplemented with private deals.
− Generally, there are fewer mergers and acquisitions (M&A) comparables than public comparables, diminishing the validity of the acquisition approach.
− Private M&A deals lack the information provided in public transactions, so the resulting conclusions are less definitive.
− Like relative value, acquisition pricing is backward-looking and reflective of market hype, rather than set in a commonsense approach to future fundamentals.

Leveraged Buyout

+ The principal assumptions behind the leveraged buyout (LBO) analysis—degree of permissible debt, interest cost, and payment schedule—can be verified by private equity participants.
+ Private equity firms have a long history of closing LBOs, lending credence to the methodology.
− Many subject companies lack the characteristics of an LBO candidate, such as a low-tech business, consistent earnings record, and near-debt-free balance sheet. This approach is thus unworkable for these companies.
− Strategic buyers and public market investors typically pay more than private equity firms, so this approach is sometimes a bottom price.

APPLYING MULTIPLE METHODOLOGIES

The uncertain nature of the valuation process, and the situational aspect of many assignments, frequently requires that the analyst use the four valuation methodologies in concert. Part of his job is to apply different weights, or degrees of emphasis, in reaching an investment decision. Based on my experience in different finance venues, the weighting attached by institutional equity investors, M&A professionals, and business appraisers to the four methodologies is as follows:

Valuation Methodologies	Institutional Equity Investor Weighting
Intrinsic value/discounted cash flow	20%
Relative value	60
Acquisition value	20
Leveraged buyout value	10
	100%

In other words, in 100 random assignments, relative value is the principal approach 60 times out of 100 (i.e., 60 percent). Or, in a task where the analyst combines methodologies to achieve the optimal result, he frequently gives relative value a 60 percent weighting.

If applied objectively, the methodologies can represent a good double check or reality check on each other. For example, when Internet stocks traded at 10 times annual revenue in 1999, many portfolio managers were reluctant to use relative value because they thought the sector's pricing was inflated. When they ran their DCF models on Internet stocks, their base case forecasts produced valuations of just two to three times revenue. A similar phenomenon hit Chinese equities a few years later. That is why I recommend that analysts use multiple approaches for most valuation assignments.

The application and weighting of the methodologies improves with experience, which is one reason beginning analysts are apprenticed to senior practitioners during the first few years of their careers.

SUMMARY

Wall Street has four principal approaches to valuing equity securities:

1. Intrinsic value (discounted cash flow).
2. Relative value.
3. Acquisition value.
4. Leveraged buyout value.

The relative value approach receives the most emphasis on Wall Street, but it is far from foolproof. Most investors use a combination of methodologies to get the best answer.

These four approaches are each featured in subsequent chapters. Specific numerical examples are presented as well as relevant commentary covering the positive and negative attributes discussed earlier in this chapter.

The goal of a valuation report is not process, but decision. After completing the chapters on the process of using methodologies, I close Part Three with a case study on how to apply multiple approaches to an actual company, to synthesize your conclusions, and to make a decision: buy or sell.

CHAPTER 13

Intrinsic Value and Discounted Cash Flow

Discounted cash flow is the student's first introduction to valuation. It involves multiyear forecasts and firm-specific discount rates. Analysts often refer to it as intrinsic value.

A company's intrinsic value is the present value of its stream of future cash dividends. This value is calculated with different formulas, depending on the situation at hand. The simplest formula is used for firms that have a stable capital structure and growth rate:

Discounted Cash Dividend Valuation Approach: Constant Growth Model

$$P = \frac{D_1}{k - g}$$

where $P =$ Intrinsic value (i.e., correct price)
$D_1 =$ Next year's cash dividend
$k =$ Annual rate of return required by shareholders
$g =$ Expected annual growth rate of dividends

To calculate the intrinsic value, the practitioner plugs in the numbers for D_1, k, and g. He derives D_1 and g from his financial projections. We discuss k later.

For companies that are not expected to have anything approaching a constant growth rate, such as a cyclical business, a start-up venture, or a firm with a history of special dividends and spin-offs, the formula is modified. The practice is to predict dividends for a 5- or 10-year period, after which time the business is assumed to pay out dividends in a constant fashion. A 10-year time horizon is shown here:

| | | | Year 1 | Year 2 | Year 3 | Year 4 | Year 5 | Year 6 | Year 7 | Year 8 | Year 9 | Year 10 | Year 11 | Year 12 |

Rate of Return

30%							
25%	Post-Venture Stage						
20%	Assume stock is priced so that first two years' explicit cash flows, plus stock price at end of year two, return 25% annually.	Market Share Accumulation Stage	Earnings Growth Stage	Approaching Maturity Stage
15%				
10%		Assume stock is priced so that next three years' explicit cash flow, plus stock price at end of year five, return 20% annually.	Assume the stock is priced so that next five years' cash flow, and stock price at end of year 10, return 17% annually.	At year 10, assume stock is priced to return 15% annually.
5%				
0%				

EXHIBIT 13.1 Multistage Discounted Cash Flow Analysis, Speculative Growth Stocks

Discounted Cash Dividend Valuation Approach: Two-Step Growth Model

| Step 1: Variable Growth Rates (Years 1 to 10) | Step 2: Constant Growth Rate (Year 11) |

$$P = \frac{D_0\,(1+g_1)}{(1+k)^1} + \frac{D_1\,(1+g_2)}{(1+k)^2} + \cdots + \frac{D_9\,(1+g_{10})}{(1+k)^{10}} + \frac{D_{10}\,(1+g_{11})}{k - g\,(1+k)^{10}}$$

where P = Intrinsic value
   D = Current year's dividend
   k = Annual rate of return required by a shareholder (which is the sum of the risk-free rate plus a premium for risk)
   g = Yearly growth rate
   g_{11} = Constant growth rate after year 10

In the two-step model, g_1 is the growth rate of the dividend in year 1, g_2 in year 2, and so on until year 11 when the model becomes steady state. Alternative dividend models value stocks that don't pay dividends, consider situations involving short-term holding periods, and allow for periods of varying discount rates. Large institutions often use multiple discount rates for speculative growth stocks. See Exhibit 13.1.

ISSUES IN APPLYING DISCOUNTED CASH FLOW

The inability of businesspeople to predict accurately the future growth rate of a firm's dividend, and the lack of a market consensus on the right discount rate for almost any stock, combine to generate an enormous amount of trading activity based simply

EXHIBIT 13.2 Atlas Gas Company (AGC) Common Stock, October 2008

Compound annual dividend growth	8.0%
Next year's dividend rate	$1.50
Expected constant dividend growth rate (*g*)	8.0%
Dividend payout ratio	50.0%
Earnings per share	$3.00
Compound annual earnings per share growth	8.0%
AGC stockholders' required annual rate of return (*k*), given a choice of alternative investments	11.0%

on differing views regarding these two fundamental aspects of a stock's worth. Even if there appears to be an underlying consensus on future dividends and on what an equity holder's expected return should be, minuscule differences in the D_1, g, and k estimates provide a broad band of trading values.

An analysis of the fictitious Atlas Gas Company (AGC) is shown in Exhibit 13.2. The AGC stockholder's 11.0 percent rate of return objective is reasonable. Alternative investments with less risk provide expected returns that are below 11 percent, so the AGC stockholder gets paid for the extra risk. Exhibit 13.3 shows alternative investments.

AGC stock (and any corporate stock) is a riskier investment than a U.S. government bond or a high-quality corporate bond. For this reason, AGC offers shareholders the potential for a superior return.

Using the information in Exhibit 13.2, the analyst applies the constant dividend discount formula to derive a $50 share value:

$$\text{AGC price} = \frac{D_1}{k - g}$$

$$\text{AGC price} = \frac{\$1.50}{0.11 - 0.08}$$

$$\text{AGC price} = \$50.00$$

An investor who disagrees just slightly with the 11 percent k and 8 percent g estimates has a substantially different price. For instance, if one concludes that the growth rate is 7.5 percent annually (versus 8 percent) because of a slowdown in the

EXHIBIT 13.3 Sample Alternative Investments, October 2008 Annual Expected Rates of Return

U.S. government bonds	6.0%
A-rated bonds	7.0
BB-rated bonds	9.0
AGC stock	11.0

firm's service area, this small 0.5 percent deviation places AGC shares at $43 (i.e., $1.50/[0.11 − 0.075]), a 14 percent difference. If the shares trade at $50, the investor is a seller.

Small differences in opinions on k and g move a stock price up or down, so a public company pays attention to how its growth rate and required return are perceived by outsiders. Even a minor decline in the consensus view of a firm's growth rate is damaging, as is a small increase in k, the investor's desired rate of return (i.e., the discount rate). For example, an increase in k from 11 percent to 11.5 percent drops the stock price to $43 again. Thus, in addition to implementing strategies that actually achieve higher dividends, companies foster an image of predictable growth. This image of constancy is quite valuable, because complacent investors view the firm's shares in a less risky light. They award a lower discount rate to its cash flows, resulting in a bigger present value.

This portrait of stability is in obvious contrast to the volatile environment that is endemic to a market economy. Nevertheless, in an effort to defy economic gravity, public companies avoid cutting dividends, notwithstanding earnings declines, and seek to *smooth out* or *manage* the natural variability in annual income by timing revenue recognition, incurring special charges, or taking one-time gains. This feigned stability provides confidence to investors, who then consider the stock as having a lower risk profile than reality might indicate.

Once you determine a stock's intrinsic value, your job is monitoring the situation for developments that change D, k, or g significantly. Separating short-term factors from truly fundamental issues is the real challenge here. Large acquisitions, for example, demand immediate attention. Their size, balance sheet, diversification, and growth implications influence dramatically the value equation. A large deal causes a security analyst to revise the buyer's dividend prospects. After completing what-if projections, he looks to the quality of the dividend stream being forecast. Did the buyer finance the deal entirely with debt? If so, the combined company's leverage indicates that future dividends are subject to greater volatility, thereby mandating a higher required rate of return than before the deal. Likewise, a diversification acquisition might lead to a lower k by reducing the buyer's risk. For example, if an erratic high-tech firm purchases a stable food business, investors consider the combined earnings stream as less risky than the high-tech enterprise on a stand-alone basis, assuming no change in leverage. This sentiment of less risk results in a lower k for the surviving business. If a water utility buys a biotech firm, the opposite happens since the risk profile goes up.

The use of k and g as individual firm statistics independent of the broader market is a key tenet of the intrinsic value crowd, but the sheer difficulty of forecasting corporate dividends and determining the discount rate spawns many arguments. Discussions among intrinsic value investors typically involve comments such as the following:

- "How can you assign an 11 percent growth rate to the stock's dividends when the historical growth rate is 14 percent?"
- "Other firms in the industry are growing at 12 percent; why is your projected growth rate only 8 percent?"
- "Your 18 percent discount rate is too high; if we drop it to 16 percent, we can justify buying the stock."

- "How can our estimates of $g = 12$ percent and $k = 17$ percent be correct? They indicate a $14 stock price when the market price is $25. Our numbers must be wrong!"

DISCOUNTED CASH FLOW VERSUS RELATIVE VALUE

The variables k and g are popular subjects in business schools, but the inability of investors and analysts to agree on exact estimates for individual stocks, and the huge price differences that small differences in these statistics make, reduce their relevance in the real world. Indeed, both the U.S. tax court and the IRS often reject DCF-based valuations because of the concern about manipulation of both forecasts and discount rates. While believing that the intrinsic value concept is intuitively correct, a large portion of the investment community abandons it as unworkable from a practical point of view. In its stead has risen the relative value concept, which uses comparisons as the basis for establishing value. The theory is simple enough: If they participate in the same industry, companies with comparable track records and balance sheets should have comparable valuation yardsticks. Since k and g statistics are indeterminate, the relative value school adopts substitute measures, the most popular being the price to earnings (P/E) and enterprise value (EV) to EBITDA ratios.

Relative value adherents can be spotted when they are saying things like "Merck's stock is undervalued at a 19 P/E ratio, yet it is growing faster than Pfizer, which has a 22 P/E ratio," or "Union Pacific is overvalued. Its 20 P/E is one-third higher than the industry's 15 P/E, but its growth is only 15 percent higher than the industry."

DISCOUNTED CASH FLOW AND THE P/E RATIO

Wall Street synthesizes the k and g variables of the dividend discount model into one statistic, the price/earnings ratio. Business publications constantly print statements such as

- "AT&T is trading at a 16 P/E ratio, 10 percent over the market average."
- "Dow Chemical looks cheap at a 15 P/E ratio."
- "Cisco is overpriced at a 22 P/E ratio."

Individual P/E ratios are expressed in relative terms. When a firm's P/E ratio exceeds the P/E ratio of the stock market as a whole, that business is considered to have growth potential exceeding the prospects of the average listed company. Conversely, a low P/E indicates a below-average profile.

In the case of either a high-growth business or a low-growth business, the P/E ratio is a function of two perceptions: (1) What is the future growth rate, and (2) how much should this stock return relative to other investments? Consider the interrelationships involved in the following two formulas:

Dividend Discount Model	Price/Earnings Multiple
$P = \dfrac{D_1}{k - g}$	P/E multiple $= \dfrac{P_A}{\text{EPS}}$

where
$$P = \text{Intrinsic value (i.e., appropriate stock price)}$$
$$P_A = \text{Actual market price}$$
$$D_1 = \text{Expected dividend rate}$$
$$k = \text{Investors' required rate of return}$$
$$g = \text{Expected growth rate in dividends}$$
$$\text{EPS} = \text{Current earnings per share}$$
$$\text{P/E multiple} = \text{Price/earnings ratio}$$

For every publicly traded stock, its actual price, dividend rate, and earnings per share are known facts, which cannot be disputed. These statistics are available in many business media. The variables that are open to interpretation and educated guesswork are k and g; these same media provide only estimates of these statistics. It's up to the analyst to decide whether his DCF calculation matches the market price. Changes in the perception of a stock's risk or growth characteristics alter the P/E ratio. Exhibit 13.4 shows substitution of $D_1/(k - g)$ for P_A in the P/E multiple calculation for Atlas Gas.

Assume that AGC announces a major new contract, unanticipated by investors. If the Street decides the deal increases the growth rate, the P/E ratio goes up. Suppose AGC's growth rate increases to 10 percent from 8 percent. The stock price reaches $150 and the P/E ratio climbs to 50× (see Exhibit 13.5).

After the initial exuberance, analysts learn that AGC will incur substantial debt to build capacity for the new contract. The perception is now one of increased

EXHIBIT 13.4   Atlas Gas
Company P/E Calculation Using
Intrinsic Value Variables

$$\text{P/E} = \frac{\left(\dfrac{D}{k - g}\right)}{\text{EPS}}$$

$$= \frac{\left(\dfrac{\$1.50}{11.0\% - 8.0\%}\right)}{\$3.00}$$

$$= \frac{\$50.00}{\$3.00}$$

$$= 16.7$$

EXHIBIT 13.5   Atlas Gas
Company Adjusted P/E Calculation
for New Contract

$$\text{P/E multiple} = \frac{\left(\dfrac{\$1.50}{11.0\% - 10.0\%}\right)}{\$3.00}$$

$$= \frac{\$150.00}{\$3.00}$$

$$= 50.0$$

EXHIBIT 13.6   Atlas Gas
Company Adjusted P/E Calculation
for New Contract and New Debt

$$
\text{P/E Multiple} = \frac{\left(\dfrac{\$1.50}{12.0\% - 10.0\%}\right)}{\$3.00}
$$

$$
= \frac{\$75.00}{\$3.00}
$$

$$
= 25.0
$$

leverage and risk. Investors demand a higher rate of return (i.e., 12 percent versus 11 percent), thus reducing the $50\times$ P/E to a more reasonable number, like $25\times$. Exhibit 13.6 shows the calculation.

The P/E ratio is a statistic that incorporates the *growth* and *risk* aspects of a stock. The P/E ratio climbs when investors boost a stock's indicated growth rate. Likewise, the P/E ratio increases or decreases with changes in the perception of a stock's risk. (The same can be said for the EV/EBITDA ratio.) This having been said, Wall Streeters focus on growth rates far more than on perceived risks, which is why investors have to be doubly careful when buying speculative issues.

THE DISCOUNTED CASH FLOW VALUATION PROCESS

The DCF approach involves four steps:

1. *Projections.* Using your research up to this point, prepare 5- to 10-year projections for the subject firm;
2. *Terminal value.* Estimate the firm's public trading value (or its acquisition value) at the end of the projected time period (i.e., terminal value).
3. *Discount rate.* Calculate the appropriate discount rate and apply it to the forecast cash flows to common stockholders.
4. *Per share value.* Divide the company's net present value of cash flows by the number of outstanding common shares.

Let's consider a brief example, Sample Manufacturing Company.

Step 1: Projections

A proper projection includes the income statement, balance sheet, and sources and uses of funds. From these items, you prepare a summary of free cash flow that is available to stockholders. Using his top-down research, an analyst prepared Exhibit 13.7 for Sample Manufacturing Company data. This business generates positive cash flow over the forecast period and suffers an income downturn in the fourth year.

Step 2: Terminal Value

Step 2 encompasses the terminal value. Analysts estimate a firm's terminal value (TV) in one of two ways: DCF or relative value.

EXHIBIT 13.7   Base Case: Free Cash Flow Projection, Sample Manufacturing Company (in millions)

		Downturn		
	2010	2011	2012	2013	2014
Net income	$100	$115	$130	$120	$140
Plus: Depreciation and amortization	30	35	40	40	45
Gross cash flow	130	150	170	160	185
Less: Capital expenses	40	45	50	30	40
Less: Incremental working capital	10	12	13	5	20
Less: Incremental debt paydown[a]	—	30	50	45	25
Free cash flow available for dividends	$ 80	$ 63	$ 57	$ 80	$100

[a]The projection assumes no changes in shares outstanding, due to share buybacks or new issuances.

DCF   The first option assumes Sample becomes a steady-state business in 2015 and, therefore, the constant dividend growth equation can be applied to the 2015 parameters. For example, five-year compound annual income growth (2010 to 2014) is 9 percent, so the DCF approach conservatively uses 7 percent, a lower number, for constant growth. (*Note:* Here we use income growth as a proxy for dividend growth because of the dividends' choppy track record.) The presumed discount rate is 15 percent, and the terminal value calculation appears in Exhibit 13.8 below.

Relative Value   Alternatively, the analyst uses value multiples gleaned from similar public companies and comparable acquisitions. If similar public companies trade at an average P/E of 12×, he applies 12× to Sample's 2014 net income in order to obtain a terminal value.

Final year (2014) net income = $140 (a)

P/E of similar firms = 12 (b)

Terminal value = $1,680 (a × b)

EXHIBIT 13.8   Sample Manufacturing Company Terminal Value Calculation: Constant Dividend Growth Model (DCF) (in millions)

$$TV_{Year\ 5} = \frac{D_6}{k - g}$$

$$= \frac{\$106}{15\% - 7\%}$$

$$= \$1,325$$

EXHIBIT 13.9 Sample Manufacturing Company Terminal Value Calculation: Weighting of Methodologies (in millions)

Methodology	Weighting	Value	Weighted Value
Constant dividend growth	50%	$1,325	$ 663
Relative value	50%	1,680	840
			$1,503

To resolve differences between terminal value methodologies, it is not uncommon for practitioners to apply weightings. For this case, we assign 50 percent to each methodology, and reach a conclusion of $1.5 billion. See Exhibit 13.9 above.

Step 3: Discount Rate

With the base case projections in hand, we apply the 15 percent discount rate selected for Sample's future cash flows. For each succeeding year, the rate is compounded: 1.15 for year 1; 1.32 for year 2 (i.e., 1.15^2); and so on. Thus, a dollar of cash flow in the initial years has more value than a dollar in later years. In Exhibit 13.10 below, we determine the present value of Sample's free cash flow and terminal value. Note how three-quarters of Sample's present value is attributable to its terminal value. This is not unusual in DCF calculations.

Step 4: Per Share Value

The final step is dividing the net present value of equity by the number of common shares outstanding. Sample has 100 million shares outstanding and, unlike most companies, it has neither stock options, convertible bonds, nor warrants. As a result, the $10 per share computation is simple division, as set forth in Exhibit 13.11 on page 208.

We prepared a $10 estimate of Sample's per share value. As discussed earlier, a reasonable margin of safety is ±15 percent, setting a decision range of $8.50 to

EXHIBIT 13.10 Applying the Discount Rate to Sample Manufacturing Company Forecast (in millions)

	Cash Dividends					Terminal Value
	2010	2011	2012	2013	2014	2014
Net present value =	$\frac{\$80}{1.15}$ +	$\frac{\$63}{1.32}$ +	$\frac{\$57}{1.52}$ +	$\frac{\$80}{1.75}$ +	$\frac{\$100}{2.01}$ +	$\frac{\$1,503}{2.01}$
Net present value =	$70 +	$48 +	$38 +	$46 +	$50 +	$748
Net present value =	$1,000					

Sample Manufacturing's common equity has a net present value of $1 billion. The terminal value represents 75 percent of the net present value.

EXHIBIT 13.11   Sample Manufacturing Company Calculation of
Net Present Value per Share

$$
\begin{aligned}
\text{Net present value per share} \;\; &= \;\; \frac{\text{Net present value of company equity}}{\text{Outstanding shares}} \\[2mm]
&= \;\; \frac{\$1\ \text{billion}}{100\ \text{million shares}} \\[2mm]
&= \;\; \$10\ \text{per share}
\end{aligned}
$$

Note: If Sample's common stock trades at $5 per share, the $10 per share NPV calculation suggests the stock is inexpensive relative to its intrinsic worth.

$11.50. A trading price below $8.50 is a *buy* signal, and a price above $11.50 is a *sell*. A price between $8.50 and $11.50 is a *hold*. Practitioners run multiple scenarios with differing assumptions to refine such work.

SUMMARY

Of all the valuation methods used in the stock market, the discounted cash flow method is the most valid from a theoretical point of view. It also makes common sense. Particular care must be given to the terminal value calculation, which represents a substantial portion of DCF estimates.

The large number of assumptions and calculations involved in devising a firm's intrinsic worth limit this method's use on Wall Street. Professionals prefer short, concise value indicators, such as the P/E and EV/EBITDA ratios, which summarize the relevant DCF statistics into one number. The subject firm's ratios are then compared with those of similar businesses, just as the historical financial analysis used comparable company ratios to study a firm's financial condition.

CHAPTER 14

Discounted Cash Flow:
Choosing the Right Discount Rate

The credibility of the discounted cash flow approach is dependent on an accurate projection and an appropriate discount rate. The discount rate is a representation of what a reasonable investor would expect from the subject investment, in terms of an annual rate of return. This book emphasizes the equity rate of return on a publicly traded common stock, rather than the weighted average cost of capital (WACC), which incorporates both a firm's debt and equity returns.

Investors base a stock's required rate of return on a relative analysis of the returns being offered by competing investments, taking into account the respective risks involved. Investments perceived as risky because of checkered track records or questionable prospects should provide a high expected rate of return relative to those thought of as conservative. Exhibit 14.1 illustrates a risk/return matrix for different investments and Exhibit 14.2 shows the matrix in graphic form.

The notion that the risks of competing investments can be (1) measured and then (2) priced comes from the capital asset pricing model (CAPM), a financial concept refined in the 1960s. The principal measure of risk under CAPM is beta (β), a statistic that measures the historical volatility of a given investment's rate of return with the return of the U.S. stock market. The beta of an individual stock is calculated empirically, and lists of corporate betas are available from many data services.

The logic of the CAPM is simple. Unpredictability and volatility in returns is bad. Stability and assurance of returns is good. The required return of any stock should equal the rate of return on a relatively riskless investment, such as a U.S. government bond, plus a premium for the added risk incurred for holding a non-government-guaranteed security. The premium is obtained in a two-step process. First, the government bond rate is subtracted from the return of the stock market. Second, the result of this subtraction, which is defined as the *market premium* for risk, is multiplied by the stock's beta in order to determine the applicable risk premium. If government bonds yield 6 percent and *people believe* the stock market has an expected rate of return (i.e., dividends plus capital gains) of 13 percent, the market premium is 7 percent (13 percent minus 6 percent). If the *relevant beta of the stock is*

EXHIBIT 14.1   Risk and Return October 2008

Investment	Annual Expected Return
U.S. government bond	6%
A-rated corporate bond	7
S&P 500 index fund	8
High-tech common stock	15
Emerging market index fund	20
Venture capital investment	30

1.50, this means that the risk premium for the investment is 1.50 times the 7 percent
market premium, or 10.5 percent. The calculation appears in Exhibit 14.3.

Once the individual stock risk premium has been calculated, you compute k by
adding the government bond yield to the individual stock risk premium (ISRP).

$$k = \text{Government bond yield} + \text{Individual stock risk premium}$$

$$= 6\% + 10.5\%$$

$$= 16.5\%$$

Based on the preceding information, a rational investor purchases the stock when
he believes he can achieve a 16.5 percent return. Projected cash returns from the stock
are discounted at 16.5 percent and the resultant present value is then compared to the
stock price. If the present value is higher than the market price, the stock is a buy. This
is the exercise we completed for Sample Manufacturing Company in Chapter 13.

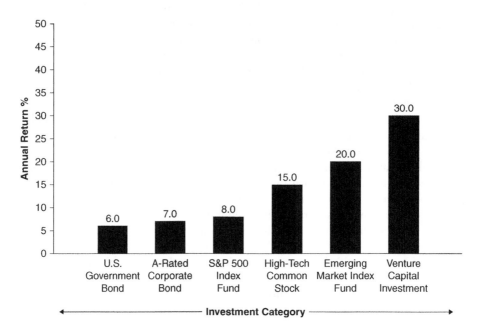

EXHIBIT 14.2   Risk and Return Graph for October 2008

EXHIBIT 14.3 Calculation of Risk Premium for an Individual Common Stock

Market premium × Beta = Individual stock risk premium (ISRP)

(Expected return on stock market − Yield on government bond) × Beta = ISRP

$(13\% − 6\%) × 1.5 = $ ISRP

$10.5\% = $ ISRP

BETA

Beta is, by itself, a mathematical calculation involving a comparison of a stock's historical returns to that of the market. The beta of a security whose return just matched the return of the broad market is 1.0. If the stock market is forecast to provide investors with capital gains and cash dividends equivalent to a 13 percent return, the 1.0 beta stock has a 13 percent expected return. Should the market forecast drop to negative 5 percent, the stock's forecast drops to −5 percent to mirror the market movement. A stock with a beta of 1.5, in contrast, moves one and one-half times the market's movement. So if the market is projected to return 10 percent in the next year, the 1.5 beta stock has a 15 percent forecast return (or −15 percent on a 10 percent downward market move). To endure the greater swing in returns, investors demand higher payment.

A stock's beta is only a measure of its *past* sensitivity to market moves. For any stock, beta's applicability as a predictor of future price sympathy with the market is limited. All stock prices have a tendency to go up and down with the market, but individual share prices are heavily influenced by nonhistorical factors peculiar to that one company: a management change, a new product, and so on. A portfolio largely eliminates firm-specific risk by accumulating 20 or more stocks. The diversification achieved thereby brings the portfolio's returns more into line with what its weighted average beta would predict, as aberrant individual returns cancel each other out.

Beta and the CAPM have achieved wide acceptance with portfolio managers. Indeed, the CAPM makes common sense: Corporate investments should yield more than U.S. government bonds, and risky firms should offer investors higher returns than conservative businesses. The CAPM offers distinct advantages for practitioners, who need a framework with which to compare and contrast risks. The CAPM allows them to grade the risk of competing investments and discount the cash flows accordingly. For example, because the stock prices of high-tech companies rise and fall more sharply than the stock prices of consumer companies, high-tech firms have traditionally provided higher returns.

Besides wide acceptance, the CAPM has another advantage: Its primary elements are easy to find. The government bond yield is readily available and the stock market's historical return is a given fact. Betas are found in multiple business media, such as Value Line and Standard & Poor's. Two exercises appear in Exhibit 14.4 for Exxon-Mobil and Goodyear Tire.

These two *k* calculations involve prominent public companies, but many times professionals study new public offerings that don't have betas. Alternatively, a public business may have undergone a recent change, such as a leveraged recapitalization,

EXHIBIT 14.4   Sample k Calculations, October 2008

$$\text{Corporate dividend discount rate} = k = \text{Government bond rate} + \text{Beta} \left(\text{Expected market return} - \text{Government bond rate} \right)$$

ExxonMobil (1.1 beta)
  $k = 6\% + 1.1 \ (13\% - 6\%)$
  $k = 13.7\%$
Goodyear Tire (1.6 beta)
  $k = 6\% + 1.6 \ (13\% - 6\%)$
  $k = 17.2\%$

where   10-year government bond rate $= 6\%$
         Expected market return $= 13\%$ (market premium of 7% plus the 6% bond rate)

that renders its historical beta obsolete. For such investments, the beta of a similar publicly traded firm is a good proxy. If a close match cannot be found, the median beta of a group of comparable public companies provides a substitute, or, as another guide, you might look at the yields on the firm's debt to establish a risk classification. To illustrate, a large for-profit education business with a consistent record and good balance sheet would have a 1.1 beta estimate as a public company, given the median of similar firms found in Exhibit 14.5.

THE BUILDUP METHOD FOR THE EQUITY RATE OF RETURN

The process just discussed is helpful in determining the beta and, thus, the equity rate of return for a new public company (or soon-to-be public company) that has numerous comparables. For those firms with fewer comparables, the analyst turns to the buildup method for estimating a discount rate. Ibbotson Associates popularized

EXHIBIT 14.5   Beta of Public For-Profit Educators Summary Information, October 2008

Company	Beta	Twelve Months	
		Revenue (billions)	Debt/Total Equity
Apollo	0.8	$3.0	No debt
Career Education	1.1	1.7	No debt
Corinthian College	1.4	1.1	0.2×
DeVry	1.0	1.2	No debt
ITT	1.2	0.9	1.6×
Strayer	1.0	0.4	No debt
Median	1.1		

The 1.1 median beta is used as a proxy for a nonlisted education company that is soon to go public and that has a leverage ratio close to the median.

the buildup method and publishes an annual yearbook (as does Duff & Phelps) that provides useful statistics for making the calculations.

Fundamentally, the methodology states that a stock's required return begins with a risk-free *foundation* to which are added succeeding levels of risk premiums. The ultimate return is thus constructed as a set of building blocks. The premiums are based on rates of return recorded for the classes of public equity securities that match the subject investment.

As a formula, the buildup method is expressed as follows, with four risk premiums:

Public common stock's required = Risk-free rate
    rate of return   + Equity risk premium (1)
                   + Industry premium (2)
                   + Size premium (3)
                   + Company-specific risk premium (4)

The buildup equity risk premium (1) corresponds to the same term outlined earlier in the CAPM. The industry premium (2) is positive or negative, depending on the industry's return performance over time. For example, the defense industry has a negative industry premium, while the computer components industry has a positive premium. The size premium (3) accounts for the fact that smaller companies historically provide higher returns than larger companies in the same business. Ibbotson segments industry and size premiums into many different classifications in order to help analysts fit the relevant statistics to a prospective investment. Finally, some computations include a company-specific risk premium. Such a premium is included "to the extent the subject company's risk characteristics are greater or less than the typical risk characteristics of the companies from which the industry premium and size premium are drawn," according to Shannon Pratt and Roger Grabowski, authors of *Cost of Capital* (John Wiley & Sons, 2008, 4th ed.). In my experience, positive company-specific premiums result from factors such as single-customer dominance or high leverage, whereas a negative premium derives from no leverage or formidable patent protection.

In Exhibit 14.6, an analyst estimates a discount rate for a new public firm with few comparables. The firm participates in the plastics industry and has a $1 billion equity market capitalization (a *small-cap* business in Ibbotson terminology). Its revenue is concentrated among six customers. The resultant discount rate is 14.6 percent.

As noted in Chapter 11, when preparing financial projections, the practitioner uses several scenarios to reflect the uncertainty of any forecast. Similarly, the practitioner typically utilizes several discount rates centered closely around a base number. There are thus multiple combinations of forecasts and rates.

SPECIAL CASES

Speculative businesses, private companies, and international companies require modification to the formulaic approach discussed in this chapter. I cover these situations in more detail in later chapters and provide selected commentary here.

EXHIBIT 14.6   The Buildup Method for Equity Rate of Return, Hypothetical Plastics Firm, October 2008

	(Rounded)
Risk-free rate[a]	6.00%
+ Equity premium[b]	+7.10
+ Industry premium[c]	−2.30
+ Size premium[d]	+1.80
+ Individual company premium[e]	+2.00
Estimated discount rate	14.60%

[a]10-year U.S. government bond.
[b]Premium for investing in stocks rather than government bonds.
[c]The relevant industry has less risk, and less return, than the broad equity market.
[d]The firm's small size dictates a higher return.
[e]Concentrated customer base.

Publicly Traded Speculative Firms

A large number of publicly traded firms are speculative investments, with minimal track records and uncertain prospects. A small portion are high-tech companies with major institutional backers, while the majority are obscure firms listed through small IPOs or reverse mergers. In effect, most of the speculative public firms have similarities to private venture capital investments, and their rate of return should approach venture capital returns, adjusted for the greater liquidity of a publicly traded security.

QED Research is an economic consulting firm that has sampled institutional venture capital investors on the range of discount rates required for early stage companies. A summary appears as Exhibit 14.7 for six stages with a range of discount rates from 26 percent to 75 percent.

Private Firms and International Companies

Only a handful of American businesses are publicly traded. Developing an appropriate discount rate for a private firm requires minor modifications to the formula

EXHIBIT 14.7   Venture Capital Discount Rates

Development Stage	Summary Description	Mean Discount Rate
Start-up	Less than one year old	49–75%
First stage	Technology almost proven	41–60%
Second stage	Product shipping begun	35–49%
Third stage	Sales growth, no profits	31–46%
Fourth stage	Some debt financing possible	28–41%
Bridge	IPO or sale candidate	26–37%

Source: QED Research.

approach used here, mainly to provide a premium for the illiquidity of a stockholder's shares. Additionally, investors increasingly look overseas to acquire equity securities and entire companies. To evaluate the discount rates for international firms, analysts adjust the CAPM and buildup methods. I discuss such modifications in later chapters.

2008 Market Crash and Discount Rate

The 2008 stock market crash was the second major bear market in 10 years. Evidence is mounting that equity investors will demand rates of return that exceed those determined by the CAPM and equity buildup methods by several percentage points. The additional return will compensate them for the risk of another crash, which is less than fully reflected in the calculations discussed here.

Investors, however, have short memories and this excess return requirement may dissipate over time.

SUMMARY

Selecting the right discount rate is pivotal to developing a good DCF valuation. For public equity investments, practitioners emphasize the CAPM and buildup methods. Both approaches are essentially backward-looking for any given security, so the analyst must be alert to (1) situational aspects concerning the industry or company under study; (2) how these aspects involve the future deviating significantly from the past; and (3) whether these circumstances warrant adjustments to the formulaic calculations.

The Relative Value Approach

Wall Street favors the relative value approach. Chapter 15 takes a close look at this popular valuation technique and offers a methodology for implementing it.

The reliance of the fundamental school on uncertain projections and arguable discount rates reduces its relevance in the real world. Indeed, hedge fund manager Madhav Dhar suggests there's no such thing as the intrinsic value of a stock. "You have to figure out where you are relative to everybody else," he says. "It's an investment decision overlaid by game theory." With most institutions sharing this view, practitioners increasingly turn to relative values to price companies. Instead of a fair price based on discounted cash flows, practitioners use relative value analysis where the positive and negative aspects of a stock are evaluated against those characteristics of similar stocks falling in the same industry. Value parameters are then compared and contrasted, resulting in statements such as "Kroger is undervalued relative to Safeway because Kroger's growth rate is higher, yet its P/E ratio is lower." Other popular ratio comparators are EV/EBITDA, EV/sales, and price/book.

Professionals generally relate equity values to these and other standard ratios. In fact, intrinsic value is something rarely discussed. With the exception of speculative stocks, which have no earnings (E) or earnings before interest, taxes, depreciation, and amortization (EBITDA), you hardly ever see intrinsic values in research reports. Inevitably, a stock price is characterized as "20× earnings," "11× EBITDA," or "3× book value." When the analyst is asked how he justifies this valuation, the response is invariably something like, "Comparable companies are trading at 20× earnings, 11× EBITDA, or 3× book value." If the subject company's multiples are higher than the comparables, the investor asks the obvious question: Why is this company's price higher than its peers? The answer is a recitation of the firm's positive attributes, such as a better growth outlook, a better track record, or a better balance sheet. These value-defining characteristics are important elements of the relative value process.

Model Research Report

1. Introduction
2. Macroeconomic Review
3. Relevant Stock Market Prospects
4. Review of the Company and Its Business

EXHIBIT 15.1 Summary Relative Value Analysis, Temporary Staffing Services, October 2008

Company	Value Ratios				Equity Market Value (millions)	Five-Year EPS Growth Rate
	P/E	EV/EBITDA	EV/Sales	P/Book		
CDI	11.9	5.8	0.3	1.4	$ 474	19%
Kforce	12.3	6.0	0.4	1.4	423	21
Kelly Services	12.6	5.4	0.1	0.8	629	23
On Assignment	16.1	7.2	0.7	1.5	292	(12)
Robert Half	13.5	6.6	0.8	4.0	3,980	22
Volt	11.5	5.0	0.2	0.6	212	42

A relative value analysis compares and contrasts value ratios among similar businesses.

5. Financial Analysis
6. Financial Projections
7. Application of Valuation Methodologies ✓
8. Recommendation

Exhibit 15.1 above provides a summary relative value table for the temporary help industry.

REAL ESTATE ANALOGY

For people with little exposure to relative value for businesses, a good analogy is real estate appraisal. Anyone who has bought a house has seen an appraisal. The real estate appraisal lists comparable sales within the subject house's neighborhood. Alongside each comparable sale is a summary of the attributes that make the comparable *better* or *worse* than the subject house; *discounted cash flow is never used* in such appraisals. For example, if the subject house has three bedrooms, two baths, a two-car garage, and a swimming pool, it has a $780,000 value relative to a similar $800,000 property. See Exhibit 15.2.

WHAT'S THE RIGHT P/E RATIO?

As demonstrated in Exhibit 15.2, residential real estate appraisal has accepted additions (or deductions) for specific attributes, like an extra bedroom, bathroom, or parking space. In the relative value approach for companies, unfortunately, there isn't a gold standard that says how many P/E multiples you knock off when your subject firm lacks certain characteristics. Life would be easier if a 2 percent standard growth rate mechanically reduced a P/E multiple by 3 (e.g., from 17× to 14×), but it doesn't work that way. Too many extraneous variables enter the process, particularly those hard-to-define future expectations. Nevertheless, investors constantly contrast and compare attributes such as growth rate, profit margin, leverage, and productivity among companies, both public and private.

EXHIBIT 15.2 Relative Value in a Real Estate Appraisal

Subject House Price: $?	Comparable Sale $800,000	Attributes of Subject House, Net Relative to Comparable Sale	Comments
Three bedrooms	Four bedrooms	$−25,000	Subtract $25,000 for fewer bedrooms
Two baths	Three baths	−15,000	Subtract $15,000 for one less bathroom
Two-car garage	One-car garage	+10,000	Add $10,000 for extra garage space
Swimming pool	No pool	+10,000	Add $10,000 for swimming pool
	Relative difference, net	−20,000	
	Comparable sale price	$ 800,000	
	Appraisal of subject house relative to comparable sale	$ 780,000	Based on its attributes, the subject house is worth $780,000

As one means of quantifying the performance of similar businesses, historical rankings are an important part of the process. To set the stage for a quantitative comparison, I rank companies according to a few ratios germane to the industry. If the firm with the best ranking has a low valuation multiple, I search for concrete reasons that explain the discrepancy. Finding none, I conclude the stock is cheap on a relative basis. In the next section, I conduct one such analysis.

CASE STUDY: TEMPORARY STAFFING SERVICES

In this case, let's look at the relative values of six temporary staffing services stocks. Our goal is to determine whether one of the share prices is out of sync with the group. Exhibit 15.3 is the list of firms and their P/Es.

The P/E rankings suggest that On Assignment has the best investment prospects, since it has the highest P/E ratio.

EXHIBIT 15.3 Temporary Staffing Services Ranking by P/E Ratio

Company	P/E	Ranking by P/E
CDI	11.9	5
Kforce	12.3	4
Kelly Services	12.6	3
On Assignment	16.1	1
Robert Half	13.5	2
Volt	11.5	6

To gauge relative performance, we select a few ratios from the following categories, set forth in Chapter 8:

Four Ratio Categories	Selection for Temporary Staffing Comparison
Profitability	EBIT margin, net profit margin, return on total capital, return on equity
Activity	Asset turnover, capital turnover
Credit	Debt to equity ratio, interest coverage ratio
Growth	Sales per share, cash flow per share, earnings per share, dividends per share

We then construct a database that has the normalized results for the six firms. We look at trends in the ratios and run a series of averages for the group. Changing trends merit special attention and are highlighted by boxes. A small section of the calculations appears as Exhibit 15.4.

Exhibit 15.4 illustrates several facts about the industry:

■ Over the past 10 years, the industry's return on equity declined.
■ Asset turnover and debt to equity ratios within the industry were stable.
■ Over the past 10 years, EPS and sales growth were moderate, barely exceeding inflation.
■ The five-year growth record was more robust, reflecting a rebound off cyclically induced lows.

After reviewing the many ratios, we grade each company. Rapidly improving (or declining) results are given extra weight, and we develop the rankings in Exhibit 15.5.

A quick glance at the rankings shows two companies with the top spots in several categories: Robert Half and Kelly Services. Indeed, these two firms have the second and third highest P/E multiples. (On Assignment has the highest P/E multiple, because the market is optimistic over a recent acquisition that doubled its revenue.) However, your evaluative system should emphasize growth, and in this case, we assign a 40 percent weighting to a firm's ranking in that important category (i.e., 20 percent to sales growth and 20 percent to EPS growth). The other categories receive 20 percent weightings. To illustrate, I calculate CDI's overall score as follows:

$$
\begin{aligned}
\text{CDI's overall rank} = \text{ The sum of:} & \\
\text{Profitability rank} \times 20\% & \\
\text{Activity rank} \times 20\% & \\
\text{Credit rank} \times 20\% & \\
\text{EPS growth rank} \times 20\% & \\
\text{Sales growth rank} \times 20\% & \\
= 3(0.2) + 3(0.2) + 1(0.2) + 5(0.2) + 6(0.2) & \\
= 3.6 &
\end{aligned}
$$

EXHIBIT 15.4 Temporary Staffing Services Company Historical Results and Rankings by Ratio

	CDI	Kforce	Kelly Services	On Assignment	Robert Half	Volt
Profitability ratio						
Return on equity						
1998	19%	Neg.	17%	21%	25%	10%
2008	10	13%	7	9	29	8
Rank	3	2	6	4	1	5
	Negative trend	Positive trend	Negative trend	Negative trend		
Activity ratio						
Asset turnover						
1998	2.9×	2.1×	3.9×	2.1×	3.2×	3.1×
2008	3.2	2.4	4.0	2.4	3.3	3.1
Rank	3	5	1	5	2	4
Credit ratio						
Debt to equity						
1998	0.3	0.0	0.1	0.0	0.0	0.3
2008	0.0	0.2	0.1	0.3	0.0	0.2
Rank	1	3	2	4	1	3
Growth ratio						
Earnings per share						
10 years	(3)%	8%	5%	1%	10%	2%
5 years	19	21	23	(12)	22	29
Rank	5	4	2	6	3	1
				Negative trend		
Sales ratio						
10 yrs.	(2)	5	4	17	11	4
5 yrs.	3	22	6	25	20	5
Rank	6	2	5	1	3	4
		Positive trend				

A table of weighted rankings is prepared, and shown alongside P/E multiples (see Exhibit 15.5).

Exhibit 15.5 indicates that Robert Half, Kelly Services, and Kforce are fairly valued on a relative P/E basis. Volt and CDI rightly belong in the bottom half of the P/E ratios, based on historical performance, but Volt seems a better relative value. Volt's performance ranking is greater than CDI, but Volt's P/E ratio is lower. On Assignment has the lowest historical performance, but the highest P/E ratio. This disparity, as noted earlier, reflects market optimism over a large acquisition. All things being equal, an investor might buy Volt stock (or sell CDI) based on this

EXHIBIT 15.5   Temporary Staffing Service Relative Value Analysis: Weighted Rankings by Historical Performance October 2008

Company	Historical Performance		Valuation Performance		Comments
	Score	Ranking	P/E Ratio	Ranking	
Robert Half	2.0	1	13.5	2	P/E in line with relative historical performance
Kelly Services	3.2	2	12.6	3	Same as above
Kforce	3.2	3	12.3	4	Same as above
Volt	3.4	4	11.5	6	P/E seems low compared to CDI
CDI	3.6	5	11.9	5	P/E seems high compared to Volt
On Assignment	4.0	6	16.1	1	P/E is inflated due to optimism on recent acquisition

information. A more sensible practice, however, is to use such a chart as an initial point of inquiry and then to dig down for explanations.

Hedge funds, portfolio managers, and traders utilize complex software to run endless variations of the desired ratios, weighting, value multiples, and rankings set forth in Exhibits 15.1, 15.3, 15.4, and 15.5. For example, many investors emphasize free cash flow per share rather than EPS (and EV/EBITDA rather than P/E) and inject forward EPS and sales projections into the growth statistics.

Alternatively, because the temporary staffing services industry has cyclical elements, prospective investors might examine value ratios based on average performance over the cycle.

VALUING AN INITIAL PUBLIC OFFERING

For a temporary staffing firm planning an IPO, its underwriters rely heavily on relative value techniques to establish a proposed stock price. They place the firm's historical performance loosely within the ranking scheme previously set forth, adding and subtracting the firm's positive and negative attributes from the others in determining a P/E (or EV/EBITDA) ratio. Growth is the most important variable. The process is slightly less quantitative, and more subjective, than Exhibit 15.5, but the logic is similar. As a result, if the IPO's historical ranking falls between Kforce and Volt, the proposed P/E should fall between 11.5 (Volt) and 12.3 (Kforce), unless there are evident factors pushing the IPO's P/E in one direction or the other.

As noted earlier in this book, underwriters tend to price IPOs at a discount to their peers, in an attempt to guarantee institutional customers a quick profit and to minimize the underwriter's risk. Such discounted IPOs tend to move up to their appropriate relative value in short order.

EXHIBIT 15.6   Growth Expectations and High P/E Stocks

Buy-in P/E	Exit P/E After Five Years	Required EPS Growth over Five Years to Realize Market Return[a] (%)	Required Compound Annual EPS Growth (%)
100	20	820	56
50	20	360	36
40	20	270	30
30	15	270	30

[a]To realize a 13 percent market return; assumes no cash dividends.

BALANCE SHEET ITEMS AND RELATIVE VALUE

Relative value multiples are income-statement-heavy, with a focus on P/E, EV/EBITDA, and EV/sales multiples. Balance sheet items such as unusually large securities holdings, understated real estate assets, or off-balance-sheet liabilities can sometimes be left out of the equation. Adjusting the calculations to reflect these and other balance sheet items is an important task for the analyst. This is covered briefly in Chapter 18, "Sum-of-the-Parts Analysis."

HOW HIGH IS UP?

The temporary staffing industry had moderate P/E ratios in October 2008, reflecting investors' anxiety about the industry's performance in a possible recession. One year earlier, in mid-2007, tape watchers commented on the high P/Es ascribed to established technology businesses, such as Level 3 and Oracle. Before plunging forward, a smart investor is well advised to consider the mathematics involved in buying a high P/E stock. If you buy a 50 P/E stock today and plan on selling it at a 20 P/E (which is still above average) in five years (when the issuer's business is likely maturing), the earnings per share of the company must quadruple in order for you to realize a market-type return. Exhibit 15.6 above provides a table outlining the EPS growth required by high P/E stocks to achieve market returns.

SUMMARY

Most practitioner debates about stock prices center on relative values. If the auto parts group is trading at 16 times annual net earnings, then this 16× multiple is the starting point for an auto parts stock. If research shows that the subject company is a better performer than its peers, it deserves a higher multiple. If its record is worse and it has fewer prospects, it merits a lower multiple. Non-earnings-based factors, such as hidden asset values or off-balance-sheet liabilities, are then added to or deducted from the benchmark estimate.

The main problem with the comparable company approach is that it doesn't tell you whether the industry as a whole is cheap or expensive at any specific time. Some practitioners look back to historical norms to identify clear aberrations, but staying with this idea requires a contrarian view that endangers one's career prospects. A second problem with relative analysis is the lack of true comparables. Even within the same industry, firms have different characteristics that limit the relevance of such studies. Accordingly, I recommend applying the three alternative approaches as a reality check for every relative valuation. If the calculations are significantly different, the analyst should refrain from making a recommendation until the matter is resolved.

CHAPTER 16

Marginal Performers

Perhaps one-fifth of publicly traded companies record losses, rather than profits, yet they still have significant value. Many firms have choppy track records, recording losses one year and profits the next. Analysts modify the relative value approach from Chapter 15 to fit these companies, and this chapter provides guidance.

Once, I worked as a valuation expert for the stockholders of a sizable money-losing business. They sought compensation in a legal case against a third party whose actions had damaged the stock price. The opposing side argued that money-losing companies had few prospects of turnaround and, therefore, such companies had no intrinsic value. To some, this assertion has appeal at a gut level, but the facts say otherwise. Thousands of publicly traded firms record accounting losses, yet their shares trade at prices suggesting significant worth. Indeed, one valuation assignment I completed in the alternative energy sector featured a comparable-company table where none of the firms made money, but each business had an equity value in the millions. See Exhibit 16.1.

The discounted cash flow (DCF) approach deals with erratic firms by discounting projected cash flows at a higher rate than might otherwise be the case. If steady,

EXHIBIT 16.1 Publicly Traded Alternative Energy Companies: Consistent Money Losers with Substantial Equity Value, October 2008 (in millions)

Company	Latest 12 Months		Equity Market Value
	Revenue	Losses	
Blue Fire Ethanol	$0	$(17)	$36
ECOtality	8	(11)	7
Juhl Wind	1	(23)	70
NewGen Biofuels	0	(15)	55
Ocean Power Technologies	6	(16)	64
ZBB Energy	1	(5)	20

Many money-losing firms have substantial value.

profitable comparables involve a 15 percent internal rate of return (IRR), then a consistent money-loser might have a 30 percent IRR. The high discount rate reflects the uncertainty of current losses evolving into future profits.

Unlike DCF, relative value has a limited ability to peer into the future, since the comparable company ratios on which relative value is based reflect present performance. As a result, for money-losing firms, either practitioners emphasize non-earnings-based ratios in their relative value analysis (such as EV/sales), or they estimate a normal, future earnings power for the business and then apply the conventional profit-based ratios.

Model Research Report

1. Introduction
2. Macroeconomic Review
3. Relevant Stock Market Prospects
4. Review of the Company and Its Business
5. Financial Analysis
6. Financial Projections
7. Application of Valuation Methodologies ✓
8. Recommendation

DEFINING THE PROBLEM COMPANY

If you have to prepare a relative value analysis for a problem company, place the business into one of the following three categories before you begin:

> *Category 1: Eliminating one-time earnings hiccup.* A category 1 business has a good historical trend, but it suffered a recent one-year earnings hiccup. The analyst presumes this year was an aberration and modifies the track record accordingly.
>
> *Category 2: Choppy past performance is smoothed out.* Erratic performers, cyclical businesses, and consistent money losers fall into category 2. The earnings potential of such firms is suspect. The analyst may smooth out the history or use a large discount before applying the comparable-company ratios. For example, instead of utilizing a normal-company median EV/sales ratio of 10×, the analyst might use 6× for the category 2 prospect, a 40 percent haircut.
>
> *Category 3: Natural resource firms.* Category 3 firms have dormant natural resource assets, such as oil reserves, metallic ore reserves, or timberlands. In order to generate income, the natural resource must be extracted, harvested, and then sold. An investor calculates the likely future costs of oil drilling, ore mining, or timber cutting, and compares these costs to estimated revenues.

Harvesting such assets can be capital intensive. For example, a business with substantial iron ore faces considerable expense in order to exploit the reserves. Mining equipment, rail spurs, utility connections, and start-up costs represent huge investments. Constructing this infrastructure on time and within budget is uncertain, as are the risks that the reserves, after some development work, are not what they appeared to be at the time of the initial discovery. The behavior of future ore prices is another matter for study.

Analyzing Category 1 Candidates

One-Time Gains or Losses   By definition, a *one-time* event is something that happens on rare occasions. In recent years, corporate America has gotten into the habit of labeling many operating miscues as one-time items in an effort to make management look good. The accounting profession takes a dim view of the practice, but it does little to instigate reform. Investment practitioners consider which of these items are truly occurrences that won't happen again, and then they eliminate such gains or losses from the calculation of a firm's net income and EBITDA, providing normalized data (i.e., as if the event had never occurred). They adjust the data of similar companies in the same fashion to facilitate a comparison.

Exhibit 16.2 shows how eliminating a $20 million one-time charge increases a firm's net income by $12 million, or 50 percent.

One-Time Discontinued Operation Sell-Off   Corporations regularly sell off divisions that do not fit in with their long-term goals. Following the divestitures, the sales and profits (or losses) of these discarded businesses are included in a separate part of the income statement for accounting purposes, such as the "Discontinued Operations" section. For valuation purposes, practitioners eliminate discontinued operations from historical results, thereby producing pro forma data that is used in a comparative analysis.

Analyzing Category 2 Candidates

Uneven Track Records   Companies that do not exhibit smooth upward earnings trends are nevertheless valuable commodities, primarily because investors believe existing management (or a new management) can reform the inconsistent pattern.

EXHIBIT 16.2   Category 1 Firm: One-Time Loss Adjustment, Year Ended December 31, 2009 (in millions)

	As Reported	Adjustments	Pro Forma
EBITDA	$100	—	$100
Depreciation and amortization	(30)	—	(30)
One-time charge	(20)	+20	—
EBIT	50	+20	70
Interest	(10)	—	(10)
Pretax income	40	+20	60
Income taxes	(16)	−8	(24)
Net income	$ 24	+12	$ 36

Experts realize that a simplistic *estimated corporate value*, computed by multiplying a one-year earnings statistic (*x*), such as EPS or EBITDA, by the comparable company median multiple (*y*), has less meaning for an erratic performer than that same calculation performed for a consistent moneymaker. Several averaging methods exist to moderate the problematic effects of uneven track records. A common remedy is to smooth out the candidate's spotty performance by averaging three to five years of results. Instead of using the previous year's earnings (or next year's estimated earnings), one calculates an average of the past three years' results. This average is multiplied by the one-year EPS ratios applicable to the industry, thereby creating a sensible yardstick.

Cyclical Firms   As we have discussed, many firms have earnings streams that are highly sensitive to the business cycle. Boom times for these firms are followed by bust times, and their historical results show a repeated pattern of peaks and troughs. Other cyclical firms experience earnings changes that do not correlate well to the general economy, but trend against other economic variables. Brokerage firms, for example, show cyclicality based on stock and bond prices, while agricultural firms exhibit earnings tied to the crop cycle. Security analysts are hard pressed to place precise relative values on these enterprises. In practice, one-year and average earnings multiples are complemented by other methods, including the following:

- *Value as a multiple of earnings power over the cycle.* Average the company's EPS over an entire cycle, which can last from five to eight years. Assume reasonable secular growth in the next cycle and multiply estimated EPS over the next cycle by an appropriate P/E.
- *Value as a multiple of the most recent peak year results.* Consider the P/E for similar firms in the subject company's industry. Apply this multiple to the subject's peak year EPS in order to determine a reasonable valuation.
- *Value as a multiple of the most recent bottom year results.* Repeat the same exercise for bottom-of-the-cycle earnings.
- *Value as a multiple of weighted average results.* Apply a 40 percent weighting to current year earnings, 30 percent to prior year, and so on.

Money-Losing Companies   The first reaction of many institutions is to shy away from money-losing firms. The operating, managerial, and financial problems of the money-losers create analytical headaches over and above those that accompany normal equity investments. Furthermore, the institution's risk of overpayment is magnified, since money-losers are difficult to value, and their earnings are notoriously hard to predict. These considerations increase the chances of the stockholder not collecting what was anticipated on the investment.

Nevertheless, hundreds of big money-losing companies trade at substantial equity values, notwithstanding the aforementioned complications, and the stockholders of these underperformers represent a cross section of investors. How does an analyst look for valuation guideposts in these circumstances? Discounted cash flow analysis is helpful for the analyst's own work, but few institutions place much stock in DCF. Earnings-based multiples are of minimal use in appraising a money-losing business since there are no earnings to multiply. The primary attraction of the underperformer

EXHIBIT 16.3   Value Multiples for Companies with Negative EPS

- *EBITDA multiples.* Suppose the company has negative EPS, yet it has positive EBITDA because of depreciation, amortization, and interest expenses. The latest year's EBITDA per share is then multiplied by a benchmark, such as 5 or 6, to set a rough estimate of enterprise value. The analyst then subtracts debt and adds excess cash to develop an equity value.
- *Book value multiples.* The money-losing firm doesn't generate profits, but its shareholders' equity account is positive, indicating that the accounting value of assets exceeds liabilities. The price/book value ratio of profitable manufacturing companies is usually 2× to 4×. Similar ratios for money losers are 1× or less.
- *Sales multiple.* A business with a high sales volume may have the potential to make money. Perhaps unneeded expenses can be cut, or prices raised. Recognizing this possibility, Wall Street says something like, "Well, the enterprise value is only one times sales," as if this is a bargain for a money-losing business. To make sense out of this comment, investors examine enterprise value to sales ratios of comparable publicly traded firms. A discount is then applied to establish a reasonable value for the underperformer.

is its potential to make money. How do investors measure this potential in the real world, where *all* projections are suspect?

They consider valuation benchmarks besides those derived from historical earnings. Many of these tools are based on accounting statistics, while others rely on operating data. Popular accounting-based ratios for valuing a money-losing firm are shown in Exhibit 16.3.

EBITDA Multiples   The idea of valuing a company as a multiple of EBITDA, rather than net earnings, became popular with the increase in M&A activity. Corporate acquirers, particularly private equity firms, relied heavily on EBITDA to evaluate a takeover target's ability to repay acquisition debts. The practice spread to security analysts, who used it to gauge the likely acquisition pricing of companies, as well as the economic value of businesses reporting losses. Most of Wall Street defines operating cash flow as EBITDA (that is, earnings before interest, taxes, depreciation, and amortization). Depreciation and amortization (D&A), of course, are noncash accounting charges reflecting assumed drops in the value of corporate assets.

Accounting theory implies that D&A cash should be plowed back into the business if net earnings are to be maintained, but the theory isn't always right. From 2000 to 2008, for example, real estate prices rose far above depreciated values. Also, many non-real-estate acquirers registered large amortization costs over the same time period, but nevertheless had big gains until the 2008 stock market crash.

The EV/EBITDA ratio is used to appraise many industries, including the cable TV, cellular phone, oil, hotel, real estate, and gambling industries. It is sometimes apparent that equity value holds up without the full reinvestment of depreciation and amortization. This worked well for many media stocks over the past 10 years, despite many never recording an annual net profit. Now, new Internet technology threatens the prospects of TV, radio, and newspaper concerns. Likewise, real estate firms skimp on refurbishments and tenant improvements when the office market is tight, but the cost of such items mushrooms when tenants have multiple leasing options.

EXHIBIT 16.4 Medical Software Comparable—2007 (in millions)

	Latest 12 Months			
	Revenues	EBITDA	EV/Revenues	EV/EBITDA
Subject Company	$17.7	$(1.0)	1.5×	Neg.[a]
Public Comparables				
A	53.0	4.4	2.6	N.M.[a]
B	108.0	16.2	2.2	14.7
C	74.0	3.2	3.0	N.M.[a]
D	49.0	6.3	1.2	10.9
E	63.0	8.1	1.5	11.7
	Median		2.2	11.7

[a]Neg. means a negative ratio; N.M. indicates an artificially high ratio.
The subject company was evaluated on an EV/revenues basis since it had negative EBITDA.

Book Value Multiple This calculation is computed as current share price divided by book value per share. Book value is based on historical accounting data, and it has shortcomings as a measurement device. Besides excluding the extra value of the business as a going concern (along with related intangible assets), book value fails to write up increases in tangible assets, such as real estate. The price/book ratio is most meaningful for a troubled business, where liquidation is an option and book value helps define downside risk. Financial companies are often quoted in price/book terms since their principal assets (corporate bonds and loans) have little intangible value.

Enterprise Value to Sales Multiples Measuring the relationship of enterprise value to sales is useful when the money-losing company (1) has turnaround potential, (2) introduces a new product, or (3) develops a franchise. The idea is that sales translate into earnings down the road. You see this ratio a lot with speculative, high-tech businesses. Their sales accelerate rapidly, but they lack sufficient economies of scale to realize a profit. For example, set forth in Exhibit 16.4 are statistics from a medical software valuation. With EBITDA-positive firms having a median EV/sales ratio of 2.2×, I assigned a 1.5× ratio (a 30 percent discount) for the money-losing subject company.

Shorthand Relative Value Ratios For the most part, money-losing firms do not lend themselves well to valuation multiples based on accounting data, which work better for profitable firms with steady earnings trends. Nevertheless, comparable-company enterprise value/EBITDA, price/book, and enterprise value/sales are factored into most distressed stock research reports. The lack of similar money-losing firms (or M&A transactions) limits the usefulness of this data, but practitioners try to make lemonade out of lemons by applying a money-loser discount from profitable firm ratios. Projected cash flow analysis is also of questionable use with the problem firm because of the uncertainty attached to its prospects.

Uncomfortable relying totally on either (1) value multiples based on historical results, or (2) cash flows derived from doubtful projections, practitioners use numerous shorthand value ratios. These ratios depend on something other than historical and forecast financial data. Typically, they are calculated quickly, using asset and production statistics related to the candidate's business. Shorthand indicators provide another value estimate for the problem company, and analysts want to employ multiple approaches before reaching a conclusion.

Most shorthand value ratios use industry-specific operating criteria. For example, the value of a money-losing retailing company is expressed in terms of its enterprise value divided by the number of stores. The money-loser's enterprise value per store statistic is then compared to other retailing firms. Shorthand calculations are unscientific, yet they are in everyday use as part of the Wall Street landscape. Most appropriate for erratic, cyclical, or money-losing firms, they also enter the reports for businesses with successful track records, to ensure the completeness of an appraisal and to showcase possible discrepancies in the accounting-derived techniques. Set forth in Exhibit 16.5 are common shorthand value ratios, segmented by industry.

EXHIBIT 16.5   Shorthand Value Ratios Used in Security Analysis

Restaurants

$$\frac{\text{Enterprise value}}{\text{Number of restaurants}} = \text{Value per restaurant in operation}$$

Telephone Services

$$\frac{\text{Enterprise value}}{\text{Number of phone lines}} = \text{Value per phone line}$$

Cable Television

$$\frac{\text{Enterprise value}}{\text{Number of subscribers}} = \text{Value per subscriber}$$

Cement, Steel, Petrochemical

$$\frac{\text{Enterprise value}}{\text{Tons of annual production capacity}} = \text{Value per ton of capacity}$$

Hotels

$$\frac{\text{Enterprise value}}{\text{Number of rooms}} = \text{Value per room}$$

Average nightly room rate × Number of rooms × 1,000 = Enterprise value

Airlines

$$\frac{\text{Enterprise value}}{\text{Annual passenger miles}} = \text{Value per passenger mile}$$

$$\frac{\text{Enterprise value}}{\text{Number of annual seats filled}} = \text{Value per seat filled}$$

Movie Theaters

$$\frac{\text{Enterprise value}}{\text{Number of movie screens}} = \text{Value per movie screen}$$

Category 3 Companies

Natural resource companies have a distinct shorthand, relative value ratio that places a price on reserves. The calculation is as follows:

Oil, Gas, Timber, and Mining—Shorthand Relative Value

Equity value = The sum of:
+ Net working capital
+ Fixed assets
− Accounting liabilities
+ Value of natural resource reserves based on recent prices paid solely for such reserves (e.g., 2008 price for oil-in-the-ground reserves were $20 per barrel, versus above-the-ground price of $75 per barrel)

After working with the ratio, an analyst might say something like "Goldcorp stock trades at $230 per ounce of gold reserves versus Barrick Gold, which trades at $280 per ounce." I cover natural resource firms in greater depth in Chapter 21.

SMALL COMPANIES AND RELATIVE VALUE

Small-capitalization stocks often trade at a discount to the multiples of large-capitalization issues. Two factors support the continuation of this practice. The first is technical. Small company shares, by definition, have a limited float so the big institutions don't invest. Demand for the stock is thus diminished. Second, small companies have higher operating risks than most larger enterprises. In comparison to the bigger firms, they exhibit greater earnings fluctuations, rely on fewer customers, and have less management depth. Small business discounts can be as much as 30 percent off large company multiples.

SUMMARY

Wall Street institutions, private equity firms, and large M&A corporations emphasize the relative value approach, which compares equity prices to performance-based valuation ratios, such as price/earnings and EV/EBITDA. These ratios are particularly appropriate for firms with steady earnings trends, but they are less helpful in evaluating companies with erratic performance records. Should the subject company have an uneven track record or earnings shortfall, practitioners turn to averaging, peak year, and shorthand value indicators. These statistics stress the potential of the business to make money, as opposed to its actual profit history. Many of them are industry-specific and include ratios based on revenue, production capacity, or mineral reserves.

The Mergers and Acquisitions Market, Security Analysis, and Valuation

To complement DCF and relative valuation, practitioners examine corporate takeover pricing. Chapter 17 integrates merger and acquisition (M&A) values into your analysis.

Despite cyclical downturns, merger and acquisition activity has accelerated at a rapid pace in the United States and abroad. Large and small companies alike recognize the importance of buying versus building in the attainment of corporate objectives. As operating firms build up their businesses through acquisitions, they compete with thousands of private equity firms and hedge funds seeking to buy companies. And neither size nor diversification makes a business safe from this phenomenon. Of the businesses appearing on the original Fortune 500 list in 1955, less than 100 operate independently today. Most have been merged out of existence.

In my role as an investment banker and a private equity executive, I closed over 60 M&A transactions. My experience showed that corporate buyers use all of the processes set forth in this book in determining a takeover price. The principal differences between an M&A evaluation and a security analysis lie in three domains: control, synergy, and leverage.

1. *Control.* An investor buying 1,000 shares of a publicly traded company has no power to change corporate affairs, directors, or objectives. An entity buying a controlling interest obviously has that power. Traditionally, a controlling interest costs 30 percent more per share than a minority interest in a publicly traded company.

2. *Synergy.* A corporate acquirer justifies a takeover by assuming that its skills and resources, once applied to the seller's business, will ratchet up the seller's sales and earnings. When Google bought YouTube, the inclusion of YouTube's community into Google's marketing and distributing system propelled YouTube's revenues. Wells Fargo's acquisition of Wachovia didn't increase the combination's revenue, but the cost savings from eliminating duplicative headquarters,

EXHIBIT 17.1   Projecting Synergies in a Takeover (in millions)

	Acquirer	Seller	Adjustments	Pro Forma Combined
Sales	$1,000	$500	$+30[a]	$1,530
Operating expenses	(850)	(425)	+25[b]	1,300
Cost reductions	—	—	−20[c]	(20)
Operating income	$ 150	$ 75	$+25	$ 250

[a] $30 million in sales enhancements from cross-selling customers.
[b] $25 million in operating expenses related to $30 million sales gain.
[c] $20 million reduction in seller's costs, related to diminution of duplicate overhead and other efficiencies.

marketing programs, and branch functions increased the combined firms' earnings. In many deals in which I participated as an investment banker, cost synergies alone boosted the acquisition's bottom line by 10 to 20 percent. As a result, it follows that an operating company can afford to pay more than a target's public market price for control. See Exhibit 17.1 above.

3. *Leverage.* Management teams of established public companies are reluctant to use heavy leverage, despite its cost-of-capital and tax advantages. In contrast, the private equity firms that facilitate leveraged buyouts (LBOs) are unafraid of high debt, and they turn the advantages into a premium purchase price from time to time.

You can set a minimum takeover price for an enterprise by applying the LBO method described in this chapter. I refer to the *minimum* price because a private equity (PE) firm tends to pay a lower multiple for a target than does an operating business. The PE firm can't realize the operating synergies that come from combining two similar companies, so its pricing tends to be lower. The maximum price of what one operating business can logically pay to acquire another is beyond the scope of this book (the reader can refer to my earlier work, *M&A: A Practical Guide to Doing the Deal*, John Wiley & Sons, 1994).

Since operating corporations are active buyers of equities—usually for the purpose of gaining 100 percent control over the investment—analysts must be cognizant of what price level stirs takeover interest in a business. Thus, M&A complements the DCF and relative values found in section 7 of the research report and covered in previous chapters.

Model Research Report

1. Introduction
2. Macroeconomic Review
3. Relevant Stock Market Prospects
4. Review of the Company and Its Business
5. Financial Analysis
6. Financial Projections
7. Application of Valuation Methodologies ✓
8. Recommendation

For diversified businesses, the first two M&A valuation approaches are used with the sum-of-the parts approach, which is set forth as the third bullet point.

- *LBO valuation.* A company's minimal worth in the takeover market is its value to a financial buyer that can't realize operating synergies. The analyst applies a 25 percent discount to the leveraged buyout value in order to gauge a reasonable price for a publicly traded minority position.
- *Takeover pricing.* Optimum takeover prices are achieved when one operating business buys another. Firms trading at substantial discounts to industry acquisition multiples can be good investment opportunities.
- *Sum-of-the-parts analysis.* The various divisions of a diversified company are valued separately. The collective values are then added together. This technique is covered in Chapter 18.

UNDERSTANDING LEVERAGED BUYOUTS

The basic principle behind the leveraged buyout is simple: OPM, which stands for "other people's money." The private equity (PE) firm specializing in LBOs acquires companies while investing as little as possible of its own money. The bulk of the purchase price is borrowed from banks or other knowledgeable lenders. The PE firm does not guarantee the related debt financing, which is secured solely by the assets and future cash flows of the target business. Nor does the PE firm promise the lenders much in the way of operating expertise, since it is staffed mainly with financial professionals who know little about how to run a large manufacturing or service business. The PE firm is basically a transaction promoter, which is a full-time job in and of itself. Finding an acquisition candidate, pricing the deal, performing due diligence, finding financing, and negotiating documentation is a lengthy and complex process, requiring combinations of contacts and skills that are not easily duplicated.

Over 1,000 PE firms specialize in arranging leveraged buyouts. Hundreds of hedge funds, investment banks, and general investment funds dabble in the field. Collectively, these buyers control large chunks of American and European industry. Despite academic studies that show that LBO investments do not outperform the broad market, net of fees, many blue-chip state, corporate, and employee pension plans participate in the field, and they are now the primary funding sources behind the vast equity pools commanded by the PE firms. Like all M&A activity, LBO volume declines sharply during troubled economic times, and early 2008 saw the peak of the 2002–2008 cycle.

By using large amounts of leverage, the PE firm enhances its returns because lenders share little or none of the increase in value of the corporate assets. The PE firm can only lose its initial investment, perhaps 25 percent of the deal's purchase price, and enjoy practically 100 percent of the upside, if any. Since corporate earnings have upward tendencies because of inflation and economic growth, the LBO tactic of using lots of borrowed money to buy corporate assets is sensible, particularly if the acquisition prices are in line with historical standards.

Buying right is the second linchpin of the PE firm because a premium price can spell failure. Overpaying is costly for two key reasons. First, like any corporate

EXHIBIT 17.2 Three LBO Principles

1. *Other people's money.* Use as much leverage as possible in deals, thus enhancing prospective equity returns.
2. *Buying right.* Search for businesses that can be acquired at relatively low value multiples.
3. *Improve operating performance.* Shift management's orientation to acting as owners, rather than employees.

acquirer, a PE firm faces smaller returns with each extra dollar it pays for a deal. Second, it operates with a small margin for error, even when it buys a deal right. When the PE firm overpays, the acquisition is loaded up with more debt than is normally the case. If the deal's operating earnings come in lower than forecast, the target's ability to pay debt service is jeopardized.

The third leg of the LBO table is enhancing the target's performance. After acquisition, the PE firms seek above-average efficiencies from their management teams. Top executives are provided with equity participation and they are expected to run the business like owners, instead of employees. Many respond by cutting expenses that they would otherwise tolerate under the public ownership model. The result for the PE firm might be an acquisition that exceeds its projections. See Exhibit 17.2 for these three foundational elements of LBOs.

LBO MECHANICS

The mechanics of implementing an LBO are well-known and center around finding a business that can support the debt needed to finance about 75 percent of its purchase price. See Exhibit 17.3. This degree of leverage is typical in real estate, banking, and airlines—to name a few categories—but it is uncommon in most industries that manufacture a product or provide a service. Why? Because operating company values fluctuate widely from year to year. Even the values of big-name corporations exhibit wide ranges. In 2008, the price of General Electric stock traded between $17 and $40, a 58 percent difference in just 12 months. Wal-Mart shares moved within a $42 to $64 range, a 35 percent difference.

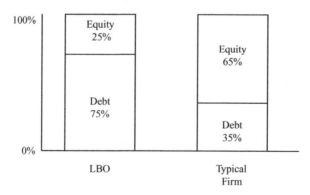

EXHIBIT 17.3 Leveraged Buyout Capitalization

To justify the risk of a significant value drop, LBO lenders look for borrowers with a few key characteristics:

- *Low-tech.* Lenders prefer businesses relying on technology that is not subject to rapid change.
- *Solid track record.* Lenders prefer low-tech businesses with a history of consistent profitability and a pro forma ability to cover debt service.
- *Hard assets.* As an insurance policy against potential operating problems, lenders prefer borrowers with lots of tangible assets, such as real estate, plant and equipment, inventory, and receivables.
- *Low indebtedness.* To support acquisition debt, the target company needs to have low leverage in the first place.

In reviewing potential buyout candidates, PE firms balance these lender preferences against likely purchase prices. They perform basic calculations to determine a would-be acquisition's attractiveness to lenders.

CASE STUDY: KEANE, INC.

Take the example of a PE firm's 2007 consideration of a buyout of Keane, Inc., a provider of information technology and business process services. Keane had a consistent record of profitability and participated in a moderately low-tech business. Keane had ample debt servicing capabilities. During 2006, the stock traded between $10 and $16 per share. Exhibit 17.4 sets forth selected information.

HOW MUCH CAN THE PE FIRM PAY?

Keane is a good LBO candidate, but how much can a PE firm pay in an LBO? The lenders provide most of the money and their initial thoughts on debt incurrence provide a good indication of a minimum takeover price. In reviewing LBO candidates, lenders use a few benchmark ratios: total debt/EBITDA, annual debt service/EBITDA, and EBIT/interest. The size of the ratio changes with the state of the capital markets, but in early 2007, the benchmarks approximated 6.0×, 1.7×, and 1.3×, respectively. In this analysis, we base a buyout price on the 1.3× EBIT/interest ratio.

For 2006, Keane's EBIT was $52 million. The required 1.3× EBIT/interest ratio indicates that a Keane LBO can support $40 million of annual interest costs (i.e., $52 million ÷ 1.3 = $40 million). Figuring a 7.00 percent interest rate on LBO debt (2.50 percent over the 10-year U.S. Treasury bond), Keane can shoulder about $570 million of debt (i.e., $40 million ÷ 0.07 = $570 million). Applying a debt/equity ratio of 75/25 to the transaction means the PE firm can assign Keane an enterprise value of $760 million. (See Exhibit 17.5.)

Keane's total debt in early 2007 totaled $150 million. This existing debt must either be assumed or repaid by the LBO, so it is subtracted from the enterprise value as cash is added back. The net amount is Keane's acquisition equity value, which is divided by shares outstanding to provide an LBO per share price (see Exhibit 17.6).

EXHIBIT 17.4   Keane, Inc.: Selected Financial Information
(in millions, except per share data)

	Year Ended December 31		
	2004	2005	2006
Income Statement Data			
Revenue	$ 801	$ 912	$ 956
EBITDA	69	79	80
EBIT	42	51	52
Net earnings	29	32	33
Earnings per share	$0.44	$0.52	$0.55

	At December 31, 2006
Balance Sheet Data	
Cash	$166
Other current assets	180
Total assets	807
Current liabilities	113
Long-term debt	150
Shareholders' equity	440
Share Data	
2006 price range	$10 to $16
Shares outstanding	60 million

EXHIBIT 17.5   Keane LBO Enterprise Value

	Millions	Percent
LBO debt	$570	75
Equity	190	25
LBO enterprise value	$760	100

EXHIBIT 17.6   Keane LBO Per Share Value
(in millions, except per share data)

Enterprise value	$ 760
Less: Existing debt	(150)
Add: Cash on hand	166
Acquisition equity value	776
Divided by outstanding shares	÷60
LBO per share value	$12.93

EXHIBIT 17.7   Keane Hypothetical $760 Million LBO Summary, Financial Projections (in millions)

	Actual	Projected[a]		
	2006	2007	2008	2009
Income Statement Data				
Revenue	$956	$1,002	$1,052	$1,105
EBIT	52	56	59	62
Assumed LBO interest	40	40	38	34
EBIT/Interest ratio[b]	1.3×	1.4×	1.6×	1.8×

[a]Projections are from Keane's SEC filings in connection with a takeover offer.
[b]Minimum acceptable ratio is 1.3×. Ratio assumes selected debt repayment in 2008 and 2009.

This $12.93 per share value is a guide to affordability. Given that it is higher than the bottom of Keane's 2006 trading range of $10 to $16, it holds open the possibility of the company selling out to a PE firm. The number, however, is a rough estimate. A prospective buyer's due diligence might uncover hidden assets or liabilities that change the value.

Corporate projections made available to the public indicated that Keane was in a position to support an LBO-type debt load. Exhibit 17.7 provides projected data for a $760 million deal.

The projections reflect the usual seller's optimism with respect to future results. If management's EBIT projections are trimmed by 20 percent, Keane still covers its debt service on a pro forma basis. Accordingly, the LBO price of $12.93 is the bottom for an acquisition. In fact, after an auction conducted by Morgan Stanley, Keane received multiple bids, including several from PE firms. Cantor, Inc., a global consulting firm, bought Keane for $14.30 per share, an 11 percent premium to the LBO value.

LBO VALUATION AND THE SECURITY ANALYSIS OF A PUBLICLY TRADED COMPANY

For manufacturing and service firms that fit the lenders' criteria, the practitioner computes an LBO equity value, following the steps of the Keane example.

Step 1: Verify low- to moderate-tech business and a solid track record. These attributes attract lenders.

Step 2: Determine the affordability quotient of an LBO buyer by using prevailing benchmarks, such as a 1.3× EBIT/interest ratio.

Step 3: Develop projections with a top-down analysis and make sure that future debt service is covered.

Step 4: Calculate the per share value as an LBO.

When a stock is trading at less than 75 percent of its LBO value, practitioners consider the underlying firm as ripe for a takeover bid. If the shares are widely held and the corporate charter has little takeover protection, an activist hedge fund or hostile buyer might take note, providing an impetus to a higher stock price.

STRATEGIC TAKEOVER VALUES

From 2005 to 2008, LBOs represented about 30 percent of M&A deals, and their pricing parameters were easier to surmise than the other 70 percent. Operating company–to–operating company mergers have so many situational variables that estimating one given firm's value to another—and the likely timing of a deal—is difficult. Nevertheless, a healthy business trading at less than 75 percent of the multiples of comparable acquisition transactions (or, as Warren Buffett would say, "private market values") is fundamentally cheap. For example, prior to mid-2007, four nursing home operators accepted takeover bids at EV/EBITDA ratios ranging from 11.5× to 13.0×. A nursing home trading at 9 times EBITDA (or 75 percent of the median) would have been considered a good investment, all things being equal. See Exhibit 17.8.

Identifying M&A comparables is more difficult than tracking publicly traded comparables. Generally, the number of deals is smaller than the number of the public participants. Moreover, the M&A information that the analyst compiles at any given time is dated, since developing a representative sample of transactions requires going back a year or more. Practitioners maintain a running inventory of transaction data, which are amended as new deals crop up. Analysts wanting to track industry pricing can buy M&A data from a number of services, such as Mergerstat, Capital IQ, Thomson Financial, Done Deals, and SDC Platinum. To the extent possible, you should compare the financial and operating attributes of the acquisitions to your subject business, and then make the appropriate adjustments to the median ratios before applying them to the subject's results. For example, if your company is growing faster than the comparables, you may want to assign a slightly higher value multiple than would otherwise be the case.

EXHIBIT 17.8   Selected Nursing Home Takeovers 12 Months Prior to August 2007

Seller/Buyer	Date	Enterprise Value (in billions)	Enterprise Value to EBITDA	Sales
Carlyle/Manor Care	July 2007	$6.6	12.9×	1.1×
Formation/Genesis HealthCare	Dec. 2006	1.8	11.5	1.0
Sun Healthcare/Harborside Healthcare	Oct. 2006	1.2	13.0	1.1
JER/Tandem Health Care	August 2006	0.8	12.0	1.0
	Median		12.5×	1.1×

SUMMARY

Including M&A transactions in a security analysis is a good idea. Firms trading substantially below their private market values are better-than-average takeover candidates, which suggests the possibility of the investor receiving a takeover premium on his stock. The takeover value of a business is a data point that complements the DCF and relative calculations of prior chapters.

Nevertheless, industries go in and out of fashion in the M&A business, and recessions dry up LBO lending sources. Recognizing the vagaries of the financial markets, the analyst uses top-down research to verify whether the future of an industry justifies its M&A pricing.

CHAPTER 18

Sum-of-the-Parts Analysis

A multiline business poses an extra challenge for the practitioner. Breaking it down into its component parts and valuing each separately is discussed in this chapter.

One of the problems with business valuation is the diversity of public corporations. Many are engaged in disparate product lines, which means the evaluation of one stock turns into the study of a series of businesses. The painstaking methodologies of discounted cash flow and relative value are thus repeated for each and every business. As a result, the proper analysis of a conglomerate involves two or three times the effort of evaluating a one-industry company. This chapter examines the valuation of a multiline business.

Model Research Report

1. Introduction
2. Macroeconomic Review
3. Relevant Stock Market Prospects
4. Review of the Company and Its Business
5. Financial Analysis
6. Financial Projections
7. Application of Valuation Methodologies ✓
8. Recommendation

BACKGROUND

Because the main operations of a truly diversified enterprise have little to do with one another, a practitioner does not appraise the company as one large going concern. Rather, he views it as a collection of separate units, each of which can be peeled off to realize value.

Sum-of-the-parts analysis is applied best to conglomerates with divisions in unrelated businesses. The term *breakup* originally described this type of analysis. Takeover artists performed such research and then bought diversified public companies at prices below their collective divisional values. Afterward, they sold off the companies division by division, thereby unlocking value not recognized by the market. The larger operation was thus broken up into its component parts. A conglomerate trading at $25 per share might have a breakup value of $35 per share. My earlier book, *M&A: A Practical Guide to Doing the Deal*, covers this technique.

Actual breakup transactions are rare these days. Responding to an upsurge in this activity, the government closed tax loopholes promoting such transactions. Now, the tax burden makes most breakups uneconomic. In its place, a diversified public company realizes the value of a noncore business by registering its shares with the SEC and distributing them to the parent's shareholders. In such a spin-off, the parent declares the business's shares as a noncash dividend, after gaining an IRS ruling saying that such distribution is tax-free. Subsequent to the spin-off, the parent's stockholders own two sets of shares: those of the parent, and those of a newly created public firm. Hopefully, the dual stockholding trades at a higher price than the original position.

Contemplating spin-offs at the time of this writing were several conglomerates, including Motorola, Time Warner, and Media General. Motorola studied the spin-off of its troubled cell phone manufacturing business, in order to achieve greater visibility for its rapidly growing mobile network and mobile solutions divisions. Time Warner evaluated the spin-off of both its mammoth cable TV operation and its underperforming AOL subsidiary. Investors complained the two businesses dragged down Time Warner's stock price. Media General researched the idea of splitting the business into two public firms: broadcast television and newspaper publishing, much like other media companies had done.

TAXES FAVOR SPIN-OFFS VERSUS CASH SALES

When told of the spin-off technique, many financial people ask: "Why doesn't the parent company just sell the noncore division to the highest bidder for cash, which can then be applied to general corporate purposes?" The answer: The tax burden of a cash sale is so onerous that parent stockholders are better off receiving new spin-off shares, rather than having the parent receive the cash and use it for debt repayment, cash dividends, or stock buybacks. For many enterprises, a noncore division has a long history, and therefore, the tax basis of the parent's investment in the division is quite low relative to its market value. In a cash sale, the parent might pay taxes that exceed a third of the proceeds. By way of illustration, when the McClatchy Company sold $2 billion worth of newspapers in 2006, the income tax bill was $700 million.

Consider this example: A noncore subsidiary is 40 years old and its stock has a tax basis of $100 million. The parent company ("Parent") sells the stock for $1 billion, paying a 35 percent tax on the $900 million gain. Parent has a tax bill of $315 million, representing 31.5 percent of the price. The stockholders' realized value is just $685 million on the $1 billion sale (or $1 billion minus $315 million). See Exhibit 18.1.

EXHIBIT 18.1 Parent Selling Low-Tax-Basis
Subsidiary Tax Bill on Cash Divestiture (in millions)

Cash sale price	$1,000
Tax basis of noncore subsidiary stock	(100)
Taxable gain	$ 900
Income taxes	×35%
Income taxes payable	$ 315

Alternatively, if Parent spins off the noncore subsidiary stock to shareholders, the stock trades in the public markets at a slight discount to its $1 billion takeover value. Using a minority discount of 20 percent, the noncore subsidiary shares trade at $800 million (i.e., 80 percent times $1 billion), which is a 17 percent premium to the $685 million after-tax cash sale proceeds (i.e., $800 million ÷ $685 million = 117 percent). By Parent affecting a spin-off, rather than a sale, its stockholders come out ahead by $115 million (i.e., $800 million minus $685 million). See Exhibit 18.2 below.

SAMPLE SUM-OF-THE-PARTS ANALYSIS

As an example of how to implement a sum-of-the-parts analysis, let's examine Honeywell International, Inc. In March 2009, Honeywell owned four businesses—aerospace, automation, specialty materials, and transportation—which had little operating synergy. Despite the varied nature of its operations, Honeywell's formula worked. Earnings trended higher over the previous 10 years, and occasional downturns in one business line were offset by growth in the others. The balance sheet was strong and return on equity was favorable. Summary operating and market data at March 2009 are shown in Exhibit 18.3.

BUSINESS DIVISION VALUATION

The first step in my sum-of-the-parts analysis was to value each of Honeywell's business divisions (or segments) as a stand-alone company. Summary performance

EXHIBIT 18.2 Comparing the Public Trading Value of a
Noncore Subsidiary to the Cash Sale Proceeds Available to
Parent Stockholders (in millions)

Trading value of noncore subsidiary stock	$800
Net cash proceeds to Parent from sale	(685)
Extra value to Parent stockholders from spin-off	$115

EXHIBIT 18.3 Honeywell International, Inc.: Summary of Financial and Market Data (in billions, except per share data and ratios)

Income Statement	Year Ended December 31, 2008	2003–2008 Compound Annual Growth Rate (percent)
Revenues	$37.1	10%
EBITDA	5.4	16
EBIT	4.6	17
Net income	2.8	16
Earnings per share	3.70	19

Balance Sheet	At December 31, 2008
Cash	$2.3
Net working capital	1.4
Fixed assets	5.0
Total debt	9.1
Stockholders' equity	9.5

Market Data	At March 15, 2009
Share price	$32
P/E multiple	8.6×
Price/book value	2.3×
Enterprise value/EBITDA	5.6×
Dividend yield	3.4%

Notes:
One-time items excluded from net income calculations.
Note the company's strong growth rate, solid balance sheet, and moderate valuation multiples.
EPS growth exceeded net income growth because corporate share repurchases decreased shares outstanding.

of the divisions appears in Exhibit 18.4. Often, when an analyst seeks to determine the worth of a corporate division, he faces a business that does not report a true net income, since its capitalization structure is artificial or nonexistent. The business unit, however, reports an operating earnings figure, which is roughly equivalent to the EBIT of a publicly traded firm. He thus has an indicator from which to begin a valuation.

Large corporations like Honeywell use a holding company to segment their businesses for legal, tax, and accounting purposes. Each business line is encapsulated in a subsidiary, a separate corporation that receives its permanent capital in the form of equity (and sometimes debt) from the mother company. The subsidiaries own inventory, receivables, plant, and equipment, while the mother company's primary assets are the common shares of these subsidiaries. Its primary liabilities are the debt it issues to finance its subsidiaries' operating activities (i.e., the subsidiaries actually make the product or provide the service that is sold to an outside party). The mother company accesses large sums of financing at a cheaper cost than its subsidiaries

EXHIBIT 18.4   Honeywell International, Inc.:
Business Segment Information for the Year
Ended December 31, 2008 (in billions)

	2008
Net Sales	
Aerospace	$12.7
Automation and Control Solutions	13.8
Specialty Materials	5.5
Transportation Systems	5.1
Corporate	—
	$37.1
Division Operating Profit (EBIT)	
Aerospace	$ 2.4
Automation and Control Solutions	1.6
Specialty Materials	0.7
Transportation Systems	0.5
Corporate	(0.2)
	$ 5.0
Interest charges	(0.5)
Stock option expense	(0.1)
Pension expense	(0.2)
Pretax income	4.2
Income taxes	(1.4)
Net income	$ 2.8

can obtain on a stand-alone basis; and furthermore, it has the finance, legal, tax, accounting, human resources, and IT experts required to administer services to the operating businesses. Exhibit 18.5 presents a diagram showing an organization structure for a holding company.

The relevant subsidiary (or division, as the case may be) does not have an independent capital structure. Its few long-term debts are owed to the mother company, which also owns its common equity. The concept of subsidiary net income does not exist on a stand-alone basis, since income tax obligations are consolidated at the parent company level.

Because the Honeywell divisions were consistently profitable, earnings-based multiples and DCF were appropriate valuation tools, but first I needed to construct individual income statements for each division, as if it was independent. Each division received a corporate overhead allotment and a 35 percent income tax rate. With the divisional depreciation estimated from the financial statements, I thus had pro forma EBITDA, EBIT, and net income numbers to use as a base for DCF forecasts and relative values. Exhibit 18.6 summarizes this procedure.

The remainder of the divisional valuation process follows the DCF and relative value techniques described earlier. Due to the lack of full balance sheet

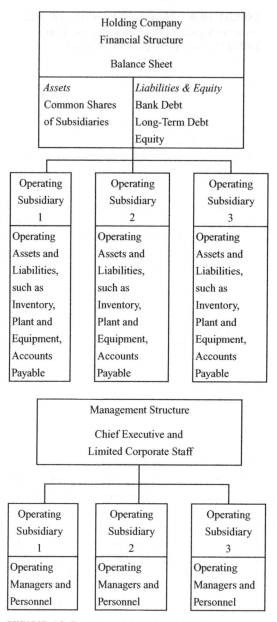

EXHIBIT 18.5 Financial and Management Structure of a Holding Company with Three Subsidiaries

EXHIBIT 18.6   Honeywell International, Inc.: Pro Forma Divisional Net Income and
EBITDA for Year Ended December 31, 2008 (in millions)

	Aerospace	Automation	Specialty Materials	Transportation
Operating income	$2,400	$1,600	$700	$500
Allocated overhead	(70)	(80)	(30)	(20)
EBIT (A)	2,330	1,520	670	480
Divisional interest	—	—	—	—
Pretax income	2,330	1,520	670	480
Pro forma taxes (35%)	(820)	(530)	(220)	(170)
Net income	$1,510	$ 990	$450	$310
Depreciation (B)	320	360	120	100
EBITDA (A + B)	$2,650	$1,880	$790	$580

Note: Allocating corporate overhead and income taxes provides stand-alone profitability by
division.

and footnote data, the divisional analysis relies mostly on relative value multiples, as opposed to classical cash flow forecasts. Highlights of the work are as
follows:

Value (billions)	Division
$19.0–$21.0	*Aerospace.* Aerospace suppliers traded publicly at EV/EBITDA ratios of 7× to 8×. Honeywell's aerospace division performance was in line with comparables, so I assigned the same range.
$9.5–$11.3	*Automation.* In early 2009, the automation business was sensitive to the downward capital cycle, with prospects of falling revenue. Similar public firms traded at 5 to 6 times EBITDA.
$6.3–$6.3	*Specialty Materials.* This division sold high-performance chemicals and related products to a broad range of customers, including many in the profitable energy industry. As a moderate size, stand-alone firm in a niche business, it would be a likely takeover target. A public trading value of 8 times EBITDA was higher than comparables, owing to the division's premium growth record.
$2.2–$2.2	*Transportation.* The economic downturn in 2008 depressed the earnings outlook for the division, with its exposure to the auto industry. I assigned a 4.0 times EV/EBITDA multiple.
$37.0–$40.8	*Total enterprise value of divisions*

NONOPERATING CORPORATE ASSETS AND LIABILITIES

The Honeywell analysis evaluates the worth of divisional assets (and liabilities) that actually create sales and earnings. Each division is a separate value unit. From this $37 billion to $41 billion total (in Exhibit 18.6) must be added or subtracted extraneous assets and liabilities that are not directly involved in operations.

In my experience, nonoperating items tend to be centered in the holding company and have a financial orientation. Sometimes they are valuable assets, such as real estate parcels, that have little operating importance. This is referred to as a *hidden value*. In one 2007 transaction, a private equity firm acquired Central Parking Corporation for $700 million. Central Parking operated over 3,000 parking lots across the country and owned the underlying real estate of many lots. The appreciation of the real estate did not appear in accounting EBITDA, and the buyer modified the takeover price accordingly.

In the case of Honeywell, the largest nonoperating items were excess cash ($1.5 billion) and outstanding debt ($9.1 billion). Long-term investments, insurance recoveries, pensions, and other defined liabilities netted out to $2.0 billion. The breakup value before income taxes (if any) was $37 to $42 per share, slightly above the $32 market price. See Exhibit 18.7.

UNLOCKING SUM-OF-THE-PARTS VALUES

Unlocking sum-of-the-parts values can be accomplished in three ways: (1) a corporate takeover, (2) a cash sale of certain divisions, or (3) a spin-off of shares to corporate equity holders. Being taken over isn't the first option of most managements, but

EXHIBIT 18.7 Honeywell Sum-of-the-Parts Value as of March 2009 (in billions, except per share)

	Value Range (in billions)
Aerospace	$19.0–21.0
Automation	9.5–11.3
Specialty Materials	6.3–6.3
Transportation	2.2–2.2
	$37.0–40.8
Add:	
Corporate excess cash	+1.5
Less:	
Corporate debts	−9.1
Other, net	−2.0
Sum-of-the-parts value before taxes	$27.4–$31.2
Sum-of-the-parts value per Honeywell share	$37.00–$42.00
Premium to actual market price ($32) on New York Stock Exchange	16–31%

many companies consider the other two choices. As noted, a spin-off is beneficial if it is ruled tax-free by the IRS. Selling a division for cash often means heavy income taxes for the parent company, although it does put cash into management's hands. Some corporate boards blend the tactics by having the division borrow money prior to the spin-off, and then the division pays an intercorporate cash dividend to the parent. Under this scenario, stockholders receive shares in a more leveraged business than would normally be the case.

With Honeywell, the sum-of-the-parts value per share was higher than the market price. As a result, there was an incentive to buy the stock on the basis of a presumed discount to its component values. Many professionals like to acquire shares of companies trading at 70 percent to 80 percent of breakup value, thus preserving upside potential while minimizing downside exposure. Aggressive investors, such as Carl Icahn, Mario Gabelli, and numerous hedge funds, build ownership positions in such businesses and pressure management to unlock the values, thus providing an impetus to a higher stock price.

SUMMARY

An analyst estimates the value of a diversified business by calculating the sum of its individual parts. Because of the lack of information available on divisional operations, such research emphasizes relative valuation rather than discounted cash flow. Sum-of-the-parts, or breakup, analysis is a good reality check for the other techniques discussed in this book. Tracing hidden values and discounts to sum-of-the-parts values are common avocations of practitioners.

The Investment Recommendation

Chapter 19 presents a case study whereby the four approaches to valuation are applied to a real-life company. The investment recommendation concludes the chapter.

Chapters 12 to 18 covered the four principal approaches to equity valuation. To review, they are:

1. *Intrinsic value (or discounted cash flow).* A business is worth the net present value of its dividends.
2. *Relative value (or comparable companies).* Determine a company's value by comparing it to similar firm's values.
3. *Acquisition value.* Calculate a company's share price by determining its worth to an acquirer, such as another operating business or a leveraged buyout firm. Then apply a 25 percent discount for a passive minority investment.
4. *Sum-of-the-parts analysis.* One values a multiline business by segmenting its components and valuing each separately. The whole is thus the sum of its parts.

In a business valuation, it is critical for the analyst to apply multiple approaches. Each approach has its pluses and minuses from the standpoint of accuracy, and substantial differences in valuation estimates between approaches provide evidence of mistaken assumptions or flawed application. One approach is thus a reality check on another. A discounted cash flow model (using reasonable projections), for example, might identify a stock price bubble that a relative value analysis would miss, since all the comparable stocks would be inflated.

In this chapter, we apply each technique to Ruddick Corporation, a successful business with two divisions, Harris Teeter and American & Efird:

- *Harris Teeter* operates a grocery chain in the southern United States with a leading position in the North Carolina market. Sales and operating income for the year ended September 30, 2008, were $3.7 billion and $178 million, respectively.

■ *American & Efird* (A&E) produces industrial sewing thread for use by apparel, automotive, and home furnishing manufacturers. A&E is the largest producer in the U.S. industrial thread market with a 35 percent share, and has a sizable international presence. A cyclical business, A&E's sales and operating income totaled $328 million and $2 million, respectively, for the year ending September 30, 2008.

Ruddick's two divisions have nothing in common, so the company is a good breakup candidate. Furthermore, Ruddick's profitable history, low-tech operation, and conservative balance sheet make it a potential leveraged buyout. In sum, the firm is a good case study for the valuation tools set forth in the earlier chapters. Financial and market data as of December 2008 appear in Exhibit 19.1.

EXHIBIT 19.1   Ruddick Corporation, Summary Financial and Market Data (in millions, except per share and percentage data)

Income Statement	Year Ended September 30			10-Year Compound Annual Growth Rate
	2006	2007	2008	
Net sales				
Harris Teeter	$2,922	$3,300	$3,665	5%
American & Efird	343	340	328	(1)
Total net sales	3,265	3,640	3,993	4
Operating profit				
Harris Teeter	128	154	178	12
American & Efird	2	1	2	(27)
Corporate	(6)	(7)	(6)	
Total operating profit	124	148	174	
EBITDA	213	249	288	2
Net income	72	81	97	8
Earnings per share	1.52	1.68	2.00	7

Balance Sheet	At September 30, 2008
Cash and investments	$174
Fixed assets	967
Total assets	1,696
Total debt	332
Stockholder's equity	824

Market Data	At December 19, 2008
Ruddick share price	$27
P/E multiple	13.5×
Price/book	1.6×
Enterprise value/EBIT	5.1×
Dividend yield	1.8%

SUMMARY TOP-DOWN ANALYSIS

A proper top-down study can fill 20 to 30 pages in a typed format. For the sake of illustration, I present a few remarks regarding (1) the study's conclusions and (2) the assumptions for the financial projections.

Macroeconomy

The U.S. economy began a recession in early 2008, and economic activity was stymied further by the subprime financial crisis. Forecasters indicate a recovery by 2010. Accordingly, the operating income of Harris Teeter and A&E will decrease in 2009, before rebounding in 2011.

Capital Markets

Forecasting the stock and bond markets is a hazardous exercise. This case assumes no gain in share prices through 2009, responding to the drop in corporate earnings and a decline in P/E ratios.

Industry

Supermarkets   The grocery store industry is mature within the corporate life cycle framework. From the business cycle viewpoint, it is a defensive industry. The low-tech nature of supermarkets indicates few rapid changes, and the basic need for food ensures continued demand for the industry's products. The primary threat to the industry's growth in the Southeast was the entry of Wal-Mart into the grocery business, which has run its course. Grocery sales in the region rose faster than in other areas, reflecting above-average population growth. Expected sales increase thus exceeds nominal GNP growth (real growth + inflation = nominal growth) by 2 percent annually. Profit margins fall in 2009 and recover in 2011.

Thread Industry   With a large share of the industrial thread market, A&E is a proxy for the industry. Within the corporate life cycle, the U.S. industry is in decline due to foreign competition; in the business cycle model, it is cyclical. The low-tech aspect of industrial threads and the nature of the customer base suggest few important developments over the medium term. Sales growth falls below nominal GNP.

The Company

Harris Teeter   The leader in its core North Carolina market, Harris Teeter is expanding gradually into adjacent areas. Besides name recognition, a key Harris Teeter differentiation is its upscale image relative to the competition. Cultivating this image requires an emphasis on perishable areas, such as produce, deli, bakery, and seafood. Capital expenditures are substantial, reflecting ongoing renovation, improvement, and expansion.

American & Efird   A leader in a niche market that is facing low-cost foreign participants, A&E's profit margins have declined as sales flatten out.

Historical Financial Analysis

Ruddick is an ideal candidate for a historical financial analysis. With the exception
of the 2001–2002 recession, sales and earnings have trended upward. Most of its
growth was derived from internal sources, rather than acquisitions. Management
didn't play financial games to enhance earnings per share performance. Leverage
declined over the period and the number of shares outstanding was stable.

By today's standards, the company's accounting is straightforward. Unlike many
publicly traded firms, Ruddick incurred few special charges over the past 10 years.
The balance sheet is clean with no hint of hidden liabilities. Other assets consist
primarily of undeveloped real estate (for new stores) and whole life surrender values.

Financial Projections

From Chapter 11, there are three projection techniques:

1. *Time series.* This method suggests that the future will be like the past. It is well
   suited for basic industries such as food, brewing, and electricity.
2. *Causal.* The causal techniques forecast a firm's results by establishing relationships between corporate sales and certain external variables, such as housing
   starts or interest. Supermarket sales, for example, are dependent on population
   growth, among other factors.
3. *Qualitative.* Qualitative projection techniques are applied to pioneer companies, which have little history to act as a guide for the future. The forecaster is left with expert opinions, market research, and historical analogies as
   his predictive tools. High-tech companies frequently use qualitative projection
   techniques.

The Ruddick forecast relies heavily on the time series methodology. Causal
techniques assisted me in developing the new store opening program.

Key Forecast Assumptions

Harris Teeter   Given the Southeast's healthy economy and the division's ability to
capture new store sites, nominal sales growth should exceed the presumed 7 percent
nominal GNP growth rate by three percentage points over the long term. Hannaford
Bros., Food Lion, and Wal-Mart continue to encroach upon the division's market,
fostering competition that prevents a significant rise in profit margins. Working
capital and capital expenditure needs track sales gains. The initial years of the forecast
are affected by the U.S. recession.

American & Efird   The division's downward slide continues at a moderate pace.
Break-even results are maintained.

EXHIBIT 19.2 Ruddick Corporation Condensed Forecast Financial Data (in millions, except per share data)

	For the Fiscal Year Ended September 30					
	Actual	Forecast				
Income Statement	**2008**	**2009**	**2010**	**2011**	**2012**	**2013**
Net sales:		Recession	Recession			
Harris Teeter	$3,665	$3,550	$3,650	$3,870	$4,140	$4,430
American & Efird	328	300	290	280	270	270
	3,993	3,850	3,940	4,150	4,410	4,700
Operating profit:						
Harris Teeter	178	148	167	180	196	213
American & Efird	2	(2)	(1)	—	—	—
Corporate	(6)	(6)	(6)	(7)	—	2
	174	140	160	173	196	215
EBITDA	288	254	272	288	315	336
Net income	97	80	91	96	108	118
Earnings per share	2.00	1.65	1.89	1.97	2.20	2.40
Cash dividends	0.48	0.48	0.48	0.52	0.56	0.60
Balance Sheet						
Cash	$ 174	$ 142	$ 138	$ 151	$ 160	$ 166
Fixed assets	967	951	947	983	1,077	1,168
Total assets	1,696	1,640	1,653	1,714	1,825	1,939
Total debt	322	290	254	266	324	387
Stockholders' equity	824	768	835	908	991	1,080

Corporate Corporate overhead, expressed as a percentage of sales, declines over the projected period. Management cuts back capital investment during the recession and then restores it to previous levels in 2011. The dividend is stagnant for two years and then rises thereafter.

Summary forecasts appear in Exhibit 19.2.

DISCOUNTED CASH FLOW VALUATION

The critical components of a DCF valuation are (1) cash dividend forecast, (2) discount rate, and (3) terminal value. The dividend projections are available from Exhibit 19.2. The first discount rate calculation uses the capital asset pricing model (CAPM), Ruddick's 0.9 beta, a 4 percent 10-year U.S. Treasury bond yield, and an 11 percent market return. The CAPM provided a 10.3 percent required return rate. The equally valid equity buildup method suggested a 10.8 percent discount rate. We use the 10.5 percent average here. See Exhibit 19.3.

The third variable—the terminal value—is problematic. Projections on EPS and P/E multiples become more inaccurate as the time period lengthens, and our dividend discount model requires a stock price prediction in 2013, five years after the initial purchase date. In Ruddick's case, most practitioners would figure

EXHIBIT 19.3   Two Options for Determining Ruddick's Discount Rate—December 2008

Capital Asset Pricing Model

Ruddick Dividend Discount Rate	$= k =$	Government Bond Rate $= 4\% + 0.9\ (11\% - 4\%)$ $= 10.3\%$	+ Beta	(Market Return – Bond Rate)

Equity Return Buildup Method	**Rounded**
Risk-free rate[a]	4.00%
+ Equity premium[b]	+7.10
+ Industry premium[c]	−1.00
+ Size premium[d]	+0.70
+ Individual company premium[e]	+0.00
Estimated discount rate	10.80%

[a]10-year government bond.
[b]Premium for investing in stocks rather than government bonds.
[c]The supermarket industry has less risk, and less return, than the broad equity market; hence, the negative premium. The thread business is more risky.
[d]The firm's moderate size warrants a higher return.
[e]No special risks.

a terminal value by applying an average historical supermarket P/E multiple to the company's 2013 EPS. Others might consider a modified sum-of-the-parts approach, achieved through determining the 2013 values of Harris Teeter and A&E. A small minority might utilize the constant-growth dividend discount model (DDM). Exhibit 19.4 illustrates the P/E multiple and DDM methods. (We'll cover the sum-of-the-parts valuations shortly.) Note that the terminal values are $36 and $21, respectively.

EXHIBIT 19.4   Terminal Value Computation, Ruddick Corporation

P/E Approach	Constant-Growth Dividend Discount Model
2013 EPS = $2.40 Estimated 2013 P/E multiple = 15×	2014 dividend = $0.64 Constant growth rate = 7.5% Discount rate = 10.5%
Terminal value 2013 = P/E × EPS $\qquad = 15 \times \$2.40$ $\qquad = \underline{\underline{\$36.00}}$	Terminal value 2013 $= \dfrac{D_{2014}}{k - g}$ $\qquad = \dfrac{\$0.64}{10.5\% - 7.5\%}$ $\qquad = \underline{\underline{\$21.33}}$

Notes: I recommend using multiple forms of terminal value calculation. In complete appraisals, practitioners complement the P/E approach with the EV/EBITDA multiple. The DDM constant growth tends to provide unrealistically low terminal values. In this case, $21.33 is only 9 times EPS in 2013.

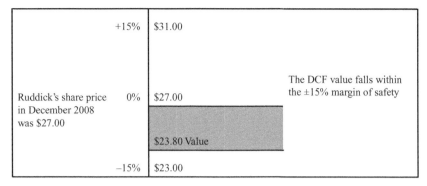

EXHIBIT 19.5   Ruddick's Share Price, DCF Value, and the Margin of Safety, December 2008

With terminal values in hand, the rest of the DCF exercise consists of filling in the variables of the two-step dividend discount model, which we reviewed in Chapters 13 and 14.

The next computation applies the data.

$$
\begin{aligned}
\text{Ruddick 2008} \atop \text{share value}
&= \frac{D_1}{1+k} + \frac{D_2}{(1+k)^2} + \frac{D_3}{(1+k)^3} + \frac{D_4}{(1+k)^4} + \frac{D_5 + \text{Terminal Value}}{(1+k)^5} \\
&= \frac{\$0.48}{1.105} + \frac{\$0.48}{(1.105)^2} + \frac{\$0.52}{(1.105)^3} + \frac{\$0.56}{(1.105)^4} + \frac{\$0.60 + \$36.00}{(1.105)^5} \\
&= \underline{\$23.80}
\end{aligned}
$$

Using the $36.00 terminal value from Exhibit 19.4, the DCF equation produces a $23.80 Ruddick share value.

As set forth in Exhibit 19.5, Ruddick's share price at the time of this writing was $27.00 per share, about 13 percent higher than the $23.80 per share value determined by the DCF method. By itself, such a value does not stimulate an investment decision because it falls within the 15 percent margin of safety. In my experience, this no-action event occurs in 90 percent of valuations. Sensible people perform similar analyses, resulting in reasonable prices for most shares. *We consider relative value next!*

RELATIVE VALUE/SUM-OF-THE-PARTS VALUATION APPROACH

Because of the differing nature of Ruddick's two divisions, the relative valuation approach necessarily adopts the sum-of-the-parts technique. We value each division separately by looking at comparable company multiples, add nonoperating corporate assets, and subtract nonoperating corporate liabilities. The net result is then divided by the number of shares outstanding, as outlined in Chapter 18.

EXHIBIT 19.6   Regional Supermarket Comparisons

Company	Beta	Annual Sales (billions)	Compound Annual Growth	EV/EBITDA	Debt/Equity
A&P	0.7	$8.6	(2)%	5.6×	2.4×
Arden Group	0.9	0.5	5	6.9	0.1
Ingles Market	0.8	3.2	7	5.7	2.0
Village Supermarkets	0.9	1.2	6	6.0	0.3
Weis Markets	0.6	2.3	2	6.6	0.0
Winn Dixie	0.8	7.3	(6)	5.9×	0.0
Median	0.8	$2.8	4%	5.9×	0.2×

Company	Region of Operations
A&P	Northeast
Arden Group	California
Ingles Markets	Southeast
Village Supermarkets	New Jersey
Weis Markets	Mid-Atlantic
Winn-Dixie	Southeast

Note: We use these comparisons to value the Harris-Teeter division of Ruddick Corp. The division's growth record and prospects suggest a premium value multiple.

Harris Teeter Relative Valuation

To start the Harris Teeter relative valuation, I prepared Exhibit 19.6, which shows data for publicly traded supermarket chains. The median EBITDA ratio for the group was 5.9. Based on a comparative study of the industry, Harris Teeter merited an EV/EBITDA multiple that was higher than the median. A 6.3 EV/EBITDA multiple for Harris Teeter produced a $1,695 million value.

$$\text{Harris Teeter value} = \text{Divisional operating income} + \text{Divisional D\&A}$$
$$- \text{Allocated corporate overhead} \times \frac{\text{EV}}{\text{EBITDA}}$$
$$= \$178 \text{ million} + \$96 \text{ million} - \$5 \text{ million} \times 6.3$$
$$= \underline{\$1.695 \text{ million}}$$

American & Efird Relative Valuation

The American & Efird division had no direct comparables, but certain textile and accessory manufacturing firms were similar in several respects. Comparable EBITDA multiples were in the 4 to 5 range. With its declining performance, A&E deserved an inferior multiple, but the division's marginal performance suggested the use of any EBITDA multiple undervalued the business. As a result, this analysis also considered the comparable firms' median EV/revenues and equity market value/book value ratios, which are often used for distressed companies. The end result was a $100 million valuation. See Exhibit 19.7.

EXHIBIT 19.7 American & Efird Valuation at December 2008 (in millions)

Measurement	2008 Divisional Results	Relevant Multiple[a]	Implied Public Company Value (rounded)
EBITDA	$ 20	3.5×	$ 70
Revenue	328	0.3	100
Book value	195	0.5	100
		Median	$100

[a]The relevant multiple for American & Efird is lower than the comparable company medians because of the division's relatively poor performance.

Corporate Assets and Liabilities

Ruddick's two divisions had an aggregate value of $1.8 billion (i.e., $1,695 million plus $100 million). To this amount, I *added* nonoperating corporate cash and investments, and I *subtracted* corporate debt, unfunded pension liability, and minority interest. The sum-of-the-parts value was $1,508 million, as illustrated by Exhibit 19.8. The resulting per share value was $31.10, 15 percent higher than the $27 market price. This estimate fell within the 15 percent margin of safety, indicating no investment action.

ACQUISITION VALUE

To determine Ruddick's value in the M&A market, I considered two methods: (1) industry acquisition multiples, and (2) leveraged buyout value.

Since Harris Teeter and American & Efird are so different, I calculated the value of each division separately, using industry acquisition multiples. The heavy

EXHIBIT 19.8 Ruddick Corporation, Sum-of-the-Parts Value, December 2008 (in millions, except per share data)

	Valuation
Relative values:	
Harris Teeter	$1,695
American & Efird	100
Subtotal	1,795
Add:	
Corporate cash and investments	+174
Subtract:	
Corporate debt	− 332
Unfunded pension liability	− 44
Other	− 95
Sum-of-the-parts value	$1,508
On a per share basis	$ 31.10

Note: The $31.10 sum-of-the-parts value was 15 percent higher than the $27 per share market price.

EXHIBIT 19.9 Ruddick Corporation, Comparable Acquisition Value Multiples at December 2008

Industry	Number of Transactions	Date	Median EV/ EBITDA Multiple	20% Adjustment[a]
Supermarkets	4	July 2007 to May 2008	9.0×	7.2×
Textiles and Accessories	3	November 2007 to June 2008	6.8×	5.4×

[a]The downward adjustment reflects rapid equity market decline from July 2008 to December 2008.

amortization accounts of several acquisitions suggested that EBITDA was the appropriate multiplier, rather than net earnings. The median EBITDA multiples were 9.0 and 6.8, respectively. See Exhibit 19.9 for median results. All of the transactions occurred prior to August 2008, the beginning of a sharp equity market decline, but our appraisal date was several months later. To reflect this fact, the multiples were reduced by 20 percent to incorporate lower M&A prices in December 2008. As a result, Harris Teeter's private market value was $1,937 million. This number was higher than the public comparable company appraisal ($1,695 million) because of the control premium inherent in M&A prices. The calculation is as follows:

$$\text{Harris Teeter private market value} = \text{Divisional operating income} + \text{Divisional D\&A}$$
$$- \text{Allocated corporate overhead} \times \frac{\text{EV}}{\text{EBITDA}}$$
$$= \$178 \text{ million} + \$96 \text{ million} - \$5 \text{ million} \times 7.2$$
$$= \underline{\underline{\$1,937 \text{ million}}}$$

A similar exercise for A&E provided a private value of $108 million.

At a minimum of 75 percent of acquisition value, Ruddick has a $25.50 per share price, as indicated in Exhibit 19.10. This estimate was 6 percent below the actual $27 market trading value, indicating no investment action.

LEVERAGED BUYOUT METHOD

To estimate Ruddick's per share value in a leveraged buyout, we follow the steps outlined in Chapter 17.

Step 1: Approximate the Company's Maximum Interest Carrying Ability

At December 2008, the LBO market was at a standstill, with few deals closing. In this environment, LBO lenders wanted a 1.5 EBIT/interest coverage ratio, to

EXHIBIT 19.10 Ruddick Corporation, Private Market Value
Approach, December 2008 (in millions, except per share)

	Valuation
Private market values × 75 percent:	
Harris Teeter ($1,937 × 75%)	$1,453
American & Efird ($108 × 75%)	81
Subtotal	1,534
Add:	
Corporate cash and investments	+ 174
Subtract:	
Corporate debt	– 332
Unfunded pension liability	– 44
Management options	– 95
Private market value approach	$1,237
On a per share basis	$ 25.50

Note: The $25.50 per share value derived from the private market value
approach was 6 percent lower than the $27 per share market price.

the extent they would do a transaction at all. Ruddick can carry $116 million of
annual interest.

$$\text{LBO interest carrying ability} = \frac{\text{EBIT}}{1.5}$$

$$= \frac{\$174 \text{ million}}{1.5}$$

$$= \$116 \text{ million}$$

Step 2: Gauge LBO Debt Capacity

The debt of an LBO is often divided between banks and junk bond investors. In
normal times, the banks, as senior lenders, charge about 1 percent over the U.S.
Treasury bond. As subordinated lenders, junk bondholders incur more risk. They
charge the U.S. Treasury bond rate plus 2.5 percent and sometimes require an equity
participation. The normal yield spread is thus 2.00 percent (i.e., 1.5 percent plus
2.5 percent divided by 2). LBO debt yields in December 2008 indicated a widening
of spreads, and this analysis uses 4 percent instead of 2 percent.

In December 2008, the 10-year Treasury bond yield was 4 percent. Assuming
a 4 percent yield spread, the LBO interest cost was 8 percent (i.e., 4 percent +
4 percent). Dividing 8 percent into the $116 million interest carrying ability meant
a debt capacity of $1,450 million.

$$\text{LBO debt capacity} = \frac{\text{LBO interest carrying ability}}{\text{LBOI interest rate}}$$

$$= \frac{\$116 \text{ million}}{8 \text{ percent}}$$

$$= \$1,450 \text{ million}$$

EXHIBIT 19.11   Ruddick Corporation,
LBO Enterprise Value, December 2008

	Millions	Percent
LBO debt	$1,450	70
Equity	620	30
Enterprise value	$2,070	100%

Step 3: Calculate the LBO Enterprise Value

Typically, banks refuse funds to LBOs unless the sponsor puts up at least 20 percent of the purchase price. In December 2008, lenders required 30 percent. Applying a debt/equity ratio of 70/30 to the hypothetical transaction gave Ruddick a $2,070 million enterprise value, as set forth in Exhibit 19.11.

Step 4: Derive an LBO Per Share Value

In a real leveraged buyout, Ruddick's debt would either be assumed or repaid by the acquirer. The corporate cash would be applied toward the purchase price. The net debt amount is deducted from enterprise value to produce Ruddick's LBO equity value. See Exhibit 19.12. Dividing this amount by the shares outstanding produces a per share LBO price of $36.50.

Step 5: Compare LBO Value to the Market Price

Many investors consider a stock cheap when it trades at less than 75 percent of its LBO value. Ruddick's stock traded at $27 per share, which was about the same as the $27.38 price determined by multiplying the LBO value ($36.50) by 75 percent. Thus, the LBO approach recommended no investment action.

In buoyant stock markets, LBO sponsors are hamstrung by the lofty prices accorded to acquisition candidates. In order to pursue transactions, they (1) commit to a higher equity investment, (2) assume a rise in EBIT from postacquisition cost savings, and (3) ask lenders either to soften the interest coverage ratio, to compute the ratio on forward-year EBIT, or to loosen restrictive covenants. By using such modifications, Ruddick's theoretical LBO value per share jumps from $36.50 to

EXHIBIT 19.12   Ruddick Corporation
LBO Value per Share, at December 2008
(in millions, except per share)

Enterprise value	$2,070
Less: Debt and other liabilities	− 471
Plus: Cash and investments	+174
Adjusted enterprise value	$1,773
Divided by outstanding shares	÷ 48.5
LBO value per share	$36.50

$41.00 (a 12 percent increase!). The 75 percent marker then becomes $30.75 instead of $27.38, and Ruddick stock edges closer to a buy.

INVESTMENT RECOMMENDATION

In this chapter, we appraised Ruddick Corporation shares through multiple approaches, the results of which appear in Exhibit 19.13.

In sum, Ruddick's actual share price ($27) was close to the valuations of the practitioner approaches. The estimates fell within the 15 percent margin of safety; thus, this analysis recommended neither a buy nor a sell. Ruddick's expected investment return was in line with its future prospects and the returns of competing securities.

Even though an equity decision wasn't reached, the effort wasn't wasted. The practitioner can keep it for future reference as the stock price changes, or he can provide it to his fixed-income colleagues (if any), who can use the report to assist in their evaluation of Ruddick's debts and credit default swaps.

In certain applications of valuation, such as business appraisals, a definitive number, rather than a range, is desirable. Thus, a practitioner might attach a weighting to each approach, corresponding to his opinion of the credibility of each approach in a given situation. In the Ruddick case, the acquisition technique suffered in comparison to others because of the lack of recent M&A and LBO deals, so one might assign a proportionately lower weighting. See Exhibit 19.14, which shows the $28.59 value on a weighted average basis.

EXHIBIT 19.13 Ruddick Corporation Summary of Valuation Approach

Approach	Per Share Value Estimate	Recommended Investment Action
1. Intrinsic value: A business is worth the net present value of its dividends.	$23.80	The intrinsic values fall within the 15 percent margin of safety. No action.
2. Relative value: Determine a firm's value by comparing it to similar businesses.	$31.10	Because of the differing nature of Ruddick's two divisions, we used relative values when breaking up the company. The sum-of-the-parts value was within the margin of safety. No action.
3. Acquisition value: A public company's share price should exceed 75 percent of private market values.	$25.50 (comparable acquisitions) $27.38 (LBO) $30.75 (modified LBO)	Given the $27 market price, the comparable acquisitions and modified LBO values were within the margin of safety. No action.
4. Sum-of-the-parts analysis: A diversified firm's value equals the sum of its parts.	$31.10	The relative value approach integrated the sum-of-the-parts analysis. No action.

EXHIBIT 19.14   Ruddick Corporation, Weighting the Valuation Approaches

Approach	Per Share Value Estimate	Percent Weighting
1. Intrinsic value: A business is worth the net present value of its dividends.	$23.80	30%
2. Relative value: Determine a firm's value by comparing it to similar businesses.	$31.10	60%
3. Acquisition value: A public company's share price should exceed 75 percent of private market values.	$25.50 (comparable acquisitions) $26.63 (LBO) $30.75 (modified LBO)	10%
4. Sum-of-the-parts analysis: A diversified firm's value equals the sum of its parts.	$31.10	Included in relative value
Weighted average	$28.59	100%

SUMMARY

Using this book's approach, "No recommended action" is the conclusion of 90 percent of security analyses. This result is a reflection of the market's effectiveness in processing information and the tendency of practitioners to follow similar evaluative methods. In this particular instance, my conclusion didn't mean Ruddick was a poor stock selection. Rather, it suggested that a shareholder couldn't expect to receive a superior return on a relative basis. For those investors who wanted superior performance, this research told them to look elsewhere.

For the 10 percent of research efforts that yield valuations below (or above) the margin-of-safety trading price, the analyst is well advised to double-check the assumptions and applications involved in each approach. If they pass the test of reasonableness, the subject stock price is likely the subject of excessive optimism or excessive pessimism. An investment decision, such as buy, sell, or sell short, is thus appropriate.

Four

Special Cases

In a classroom environment, the model company for business valuation is an industrial manufacturer or service business with a history of improving sales and earnings. Most publicly traded firms don't fit this model. Part Four reviews special cases.

Private Equity

Thousands of practitioners work in the private equity industry, which eval-uates businesses in a manner similar to a security analysis.

My career included dozens of private investment transactions, covering multiple countries, diverse industries, and billions of dollars. In addition to working as an investment banker brokering such deals, I was an executive employed by sizable institutions that actually bought the investments. As a result, you can be reassured that private equity buyers do not rely on a secret formula to make investments; rather, they utilize the same decision-making process set forth in this book, with few exceptions.

Private equity (PE) funds invest primarily in privately owned businesses, as opposed to publicly traded companies. The valuation process used by PE funds is similar to the method discussed in the previous chapters for public common stocks; however, the limited liquidity elements and custom-designed control features of these investments require modification to the public company approach.

As we examine PE funds, it's important to understand just how different types of investment funds operate, how their managers are compensated, and what these funds achieve. These fund managers are extremely well compensated for what they do and, on top of this, receive a tax subsidy for their carried interest profits. Close examination of the industry shows that whatever benefits they provide to their clients or to the broader economy are little different (and often less) than those provided by asset managers focusing on publicly traded stocks.

INDUSTRY SEGMENTATION AND SIZE

The PE industry is divided into four business lines: (1) hedge funds, (2) leveraged buyouts, (3) venture capital, and (4) mezzanine and other funds.

1. *Hedge funds* principally invest in the securities (or derivatives thereof) of publicly traded companies, or in the securities and currencies of sovereign governments. As their businesses expanded, many hedge funds diversified into private-company investments. Allocations to that new asset class made hedge funds sizable players in private equity.

2. *Leveraged buyout funds* acquire profitable established companies, using a combination of their own capital (used as equity) and substantial borrowings from banks and other lenders.
3. *Venture capital funds* invest in young, unproven businesses that often develop new technologies or business concepts.
4. *Mezzanine funds* loan money to highly leveraged companies and risky medium-size firms that have advanced beyond the start-up phase. The *other funds* part of this business line encompasses a variety of specialized groupings, including real estate and distressed debt.

One Trillion-Plus Funds Under Management

In 2009, publicly available databases and industry sources provided a $1.6 trillion estimate breakdown of funds under management by the private equity industry in the United States, but the 2008 market crash prompted many investors to withdraw from hedge funds. Exhibit 20.1 includes an estimate as of December 2009.

Private Equity Fund Investors

The investors in PE funds are institutions and wealthy individuals. The definition of *institution* includes corporate and government pension funds, insurance companies, banks, university endowments, foundations, and sovereign wealth funds. The minimum investment commitment is $1 million for smaller funds and $250 million for larger funds.

FEE STRUCTURE

In investing huge sums on behalf of institutions and individuals, most private equity firms charge fees under a structure known as *2 and 20*. Clients pay an annual fee of

EXHIBIT 20.1   Private Equity Funds under Management in the United States

Hedge funds	$800 billion
Buyout funds	500 billion
Venture capital	140 billion
Mezzanine and other	160 billion
Total	$1.6 trillion

Sources: Venture Expert (Thomson Financial), Private Equity Analyst, Preqin (formerly Private Equity Intelligence), and Hedgefund.net databases. *Institutional Investor, Absolute Return, Financial Times*, and Dow Jones have published articles on these facts.

Note: The assets controlled by the industry are higher than the $1.6 trillion of funds under management because of the leverage employed by the industry. The table excludes non-U.S.-based funds, which add $400 billion to the total.

2 percent of committed monies, plus an incentive fee called a *carried interest*, equal to 20 percent of profits over a fixed rate, such as 8 percent annually (the *hurdle rate*). The 2 percent fee was designed several decades ago, when firms were much smaller, to cover the modest salaries and overhead costs of fund managers. Now, with $1 billion funds being routine, a handful of executives receive $20 million annually (2 percent times $1 billion), whether or not their clients beat the market. Thus, typical fund managers are not entrepreneurs, as depicted by the industry's public relations machine, but cautious, well-paid businesspeople. Indeed, one of the primary concerns of sophisticated investors today is that fund managers care more about their annual fees than about maximizing client returns.

Like a corporate stock option, the future value of the carried interest is not guaranteed, but the potential gain to the managers is enormous. Due to inflation and the long-term trend of rising corporate profits, a carefully selected portfolio of companies should increase in value, absent sizable stock market crashes like that of 2008. With even modest returns such as 12 percent per year, the math of a 20 percent carried interest indicates that executives of a $1 billion fund become wealthy.

Other Fees Charged to Clients

The fund manager fees do not stop at 2 and 20. The managers, particularly LBO funds, charge their underlying portfolio companies yearly monitoring fees, deal closing fees, financing fees, and deal selling fees, all of which reduce client returns. The firms' success in squeezing fees out of their clientele is remarkable in light of the modest historical returns. Total fees reduce a fund investor's internal rate of return by four to six percentage points annually.

PRIVATE EQUITY DOES NOT BEAT THE S&P 500

There is a lot of hype surrounding private equity performance, but most clients do not receive outsized returns. Multiple studies by academics conclude that average returns to private equity investors do not beat a passive strategy of buying an S&P 500 index fund. The high fees are one contributor to this result. Some investors try to avoid this problem by negotiating smaller fees. Others concentrate their monies in fund managers that rank in the top quartile in terms of prior performance, which show demonstrably superior returns. However, the research shows that a top quartile fund only has a 40 percent chance of repeating such performance in a follow-on offering, suggesting a random quality to returns, instead of innate investment skill. The private equity industry has never refuted this research. Unfortunately, the financial media has largely ignored these studies and academics are rarely invited to industry conferences.[1]

PRIVATE EQUITY FUNDS AND INFORMATION COLLECTION

Like institutional public stock managers, PE funds complete research reports that outline the industry and business prospects of a potential investment; however, the quality of the information in a private equity report is generally better than that of a public equity manager. There are several reasons for the difference.

- *More money for research.* Unlike a public stock fund, which may own small positions in dozens (or even hundreds) of companies, the PE fund portfolio is concentrated into 10 or 15 businesses. The related investments are sizable, so a $1 billion fund has between $50 and $150 million committed to a given firm. Extra care is thus spent in examining each prospective investment. A public stock fund might invest $50,000 in researching a new equity, while the comparable expenditure at a PE fund could easily be $500,000 or more, according to Bill Pearce, director of private equity at Overseas Private Investment Corporation. With the added funding, the PE fund can afford to hire industry experts, outside accountants, corporate lawyers, and other consultants to assist it in scouring the business of a possible investment.
- *Better access to management and inside information.* Due to the size of their investments, PE funds receive better access to management than buy- or sell-side analysts obtain from a public company. Furthermore, the PE fund and its consultants have access to internal corporate books and records, enabling them to delve deeply into those attributes contributing to a business's success. Even in the case where a PE fund buys into a public company (i.e., a private investment in a public company, or a PIPE), the fund receives inside information because it signs a nondisclosure agreement.
- *Projections.* Although publicly traded companies are allowed to distribute detailed projections to the market, they rarely do so, as noted earlier, because the corporate executives are afraid of their company being sued if it fails to achieve its projections. In a private equity context, the participants are considered consenting adults, and the fund manager acknowledges that the confidential projections provided to it may not come true.

Similar Accounting Information

Most enterprises large enough to obtain private equity funding have audited financial data. If not, the PE investor requires an audit prior to money changing hands and stipulates that follow-on financial statements be audited. Subsequent to the investment, stockholders reduce outsized owner salaries and prerequisites. Thus, valuation discussions focused on EBITDA and net income multiples eliminate such items, and the participants negotiate around true earnings power. See Exhibit 20.2.

PRIVATE EQUITY CHANGES TO THE PUBLIC COMPANY VALUATION METHODOLOGY

After the PE fund prepares a research report, it applies public company methodologies with a few adjustments:

- *Discounted cash flow.* Private companies do not have a beta that can be used with the CAPM formula. As a substitute, the private equity fund calculates the mean (or median) of the betas of comparable public companies. Alternatively, the fund utilizes the equity buildup method to establish a discount rate. In the

EXHIBIT 20.2 True Earnings Power of a Private
Corporation Pro Forma Calculation (in millions)

Reported pretax income	$10.0
Add back:	
Excess owners' compensation[a]	2.0
Excess personal expenses charged to corporation[b]	1.0
Nonworking relatives on corporate payroll[c]	1.0
Pro forma pretax income	$14.0

[a]In a C corporation, excess owners' compensation is essentially
a nontaxable cash dividend.
[b]Expensive cars, vacation trips, corporate apartments used for
holidays, and so on.
[c]Some owners place nonworking wives and other relatives on
the payroll in a derivation of (a).

case of a leveraged buyout, the indicated discount rate is adjusted by the fund to
reflect the high leverage. See Exhibit 20.3 for an LBO discount rate calculation.
Once a discount rate is set, the terminal value calculation follows the procedure
set forth initially in Chapter 13.

- *Relative value.* The PE fund remembers to make deductions for expenses that
  would not be tolerated in a public company environment, as set forth in
  Exhibit 20.2.
- *Mergers and acquisitions.* Before you apply the M&A multiples to the subject
  company, you make the adjustments shown in Exhibit 20.2.

At the end of the analytical exercise, the PE fund has a value for the prospective
investment target; however, there is no public trading price for comparison purposes
or for margin-of-safety concerns.

LIQUIDITY AND CONTROL ADJUSTMENTS

Once a PE fund establishes a hypothetical public value for a prospective investment,
it adjusts this value for control and liquidity factors that do not arise in a publicly-
traded stock. Let's look at liquidity first.

Value of Liquidity

An investor in a publicly traded stock can sell his position within a matter of hours,
days, or weeks, depending on the stock's trading volume. A private investment
requires more time. For a noncontrol position, the PE investor is usually required
to offer the position initially to other investors and to the company itself. These
entities have two to three months to make a decision. If they refuse, the investor can
offer the position to third parties, who may need another two to three months
to appraise the deal. Alternatively, the PE investor can recruit other investors to
demand that the private company provide liquidity by going public or selling itself.
Either action requires months of preparation and is subject to market forces, like the
receptivity of the IPO market.

EXHIBIT 20.3   LBO Leverage Increases a Firm's Assumed Beta and Required Equity Return

---

General Formula

According to the CAPM, the effect of higher leverage changes a company's beta through this formula:

$$\beta_{\text{Leveraged}} = \beta_{\text{Before Leverage}} \times [1 + (D/S)(1 - T)]$$

where
$$\begin{aligned} \beta_{\text{Leveraged}} &= \text{Beta of a company with leverage} \\ \beta_{\text{Before Leverage}} &= \text{Beta of a company's equity, assuming the business is} \\ & \quad \text{debt-free} \\ D/S &= \text{Company's debts divided by market value of its equity} \\ T &= \text{Income tax rate} \end{aligned}$$

Cost of equity[a] for private firm with assumed 1.2 beta:

$$\begin{aligned} K &= R_F + \beta[E(R)_M - R_F] \\ &= 4\% + 1.2(13\% - 4\%) \\ &= 14.8\% \end{aligned}$$

where
$$\begin{aligned} K &= \text{Required rate of return for LBO shareholder} \\ R_F &= 4\% \text{ (i.e., yield on 10-year U.S. Treasury bond)} \\ \beta &= 1.20 \\ E(R)_M &= 13\% \text{ required rate of return on the broad stock market} \end{aligned}$$

LBO Beta of the Same Firm

$$\begin{aligned} \beta_{\text{Leveraged}} &= \beta_{\text{Before Leverage}} \times [1 + (D/S)(1 - T)] \\ &= 1.2 \times [1 + (70/30)(1 - 0.4)] \\ &= 1.2 \times [1 + 1.4] \\ &= 2.9 \end{aligned}$$

LBO Cost of Equity

$$\begin{aligned} K &= R_F + \beta_{\text{LBO}}[E(R)_M - R_F] \\ K_{\text{LBO}} &= 4\% + 2.9(13\% - 4\%) \\ &= 30\% \end{aligned}$$

The equity in this LBO should have an expected return of 30 percent.

---

[a]As of January 2009.

Value of the Liquidity Private Company Discount

The importance of liquidity is illustrated in repeated studies of discounts for unregistered shares in public or soon-to-be-public companies. The study invariably finds that investors pay more for common shares that are marketable. William Silber of New York University and John Emory of Robert Baird & Co. completed the two most cited studies. Silber found two clusters of discounts for unregistered placements in public companies; the large company median discount was 14 percent while the small company median discount was 54 percent. Emory's repeated tabulations of new issue prospectuses covering the years 1980 through early 2000 found 50 percent to be the mean discount for private sale transactions in prepublic companies, compared to their subsequent public offering price.

In practical terms, business appraisers assign a 30 to 40 percent lack-of-liquidity discount (off the hypothetical public market value) to small interests in private companies, where the minority stockholders have no ability to force an IPO or sale of the business. Thus, if a private company has a hypothetical $1 billion public value, a 1 percent interest is judged to be worth $6 to $7 million, rather than $10 million. A PE investor thus has a rationale to seek its own discount in negotiations where a noncontrol position is involved.

Value of Control and its Liquidity Implications

In contrast, a control position means that the shares in question have sufficient voting power to change officers, directors, or corporate objectives. In the M&A and buyout world that means 100 percent control, and acquirers pay, on average, a 30 percent premium to a public company's stock price for that authority. Total control means the investor can sell his shares at any time, so there is no illiquidity discount for the shareholding.

In many instances, the private equity investor acquires only partial control, such as a one-third ownership, and the ownership is conveyed in a security that is senior to common stock, converts into common, and pays a fixed return prior to conversion. Included in the transaction are multiple legal documents outlining the investor's restrictive covenants, rights, and liquidity options. As a result, the security is substantially different than a plain vanilla common stock.

Suppose a 1 percent minority interest in a $1 billion firm has an appraised value of $6 million, rather than $10 million, because of the implied 40 percent discount for lack of liquidity. The same 1 percent interest on a control basis has a value of $13 million because of the 30 percent control premium. The $7 million difference ($13 million minus $6 million) reflects the application of relevant discounts and premiums. See Exhibit 20.4.

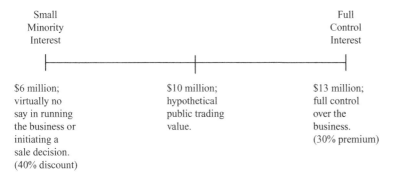

EXHIBIT 20.4 Private Company Valuation Example: 1 Percent Holding

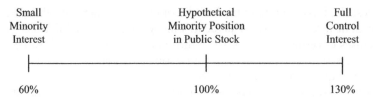

EXHIBIT 20.5   Private Company Valuation Example: Control and Liquidity Features as a Percent of Neutral Value

Exhibit 20.4 can be expressed as percentages over (or below) a neutral value. The neutral value has minimal control facets but full liquidity (such as a small shareholding in a public company). See Exhibit 20.5.

A PE fund buying a significant interest in a private company tries to price its equity below 100 percent of neutral value, after considering the benefits of seniority, fixed return, investor rights agreement, and liquidity potential. The fund manager can thus inform his fund investors that he obtained a relative bargain. Jud Hill, managing partner at Summit Global Management, describes his firm's thinking as follows: "We have illiquidity, but we manage the portfolio investments for a reasonable exit time frame. We like to aim for prices somewhat below the public comparables." By way of illustration, consider a private firm with a hypothetical public value of $1 billion; the PE fund hopes to obtain a 10 percent equity interest for $80 million, rather than $100 million. See Exhibit 20.6 below.

Premium and Discounts for a Convertible Bond

Stated in the form of premiums and discounts, suppose the private equity fund acquires its 10 percent interest through purchasing a 7 percent convertible bond, whereby the conversion price is 10 percent higher than the hypothetical public value. A theoretical determination of the PE fund's 80 percent purchase price (set forth earlier) appears as Exhibit 20.7 on page 277.

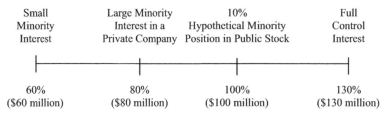

EXHIBIT 20.6 $1 Billion Private Company Control and Liquidity Features versus a Neutral $100 Million, 10 Percent Interest

EXHIBIT 20.7 Premiums and Discounts for a Noncontrol, Convertible Bond, Private Equity Investment

Hypothetical public market value of company, on a minority interest basis	100%
Premium	
Excess of bond conversion price over public value	+10
Value of partial control features in bond covenants and related legal documents	+10
Discounts	
Net present value of the amounts by which bond interest payments exceed common stock dividends over the PE fund's holding period	−15
Value of bond's seniority (over common stock) in a distress scenario	−5
Partial illiquidity discount	−20
PE fund's implied purchase price as a percent of hypothetical public market value	80%

SUMMARY

Private equity funds focus on closely held businesses, but they evaluate a potential investment in a manner similar to the research process described in this book for publicly traded stocks. Unlike public equity analysts, the funds have access to inside information and detailed projections, enhancing the quality of the report.

PE investments are loosely segmented into two categories for pricing purposes: control and noncontrol. A control investment, such as a leveraged buyout, places the deal in the M&A marketplace and involves the PE fund paying a premium above a firm's hypothetical public trading value. A noncontrol position entails a substantial minority ownership, with limited liquidity. To compensate, the private firm provides the PE fund with rights and privileges not given to small, ordinary stockholders. These rights and privileges are sometimes difficult to quantify, but the PE funds attempt to buy noncontrol investments at a moderate discount to a company's hypothetical public market value.

CHAPTER 21

Natural Resource Companies

Natural resource stocks are a proxy on the underlying commodity or mineral. These securities require a separate application of the discounted cash flow and relative value approaches. Replenishing the resource is necessary to corporate survival.

Manufacturing and service companies compete on multiple considerations. Price, quality, reputation, service, brand name, technology, and other differentiating characteristics enable them to compete and succeed. Natural resource companies, in contrast, participate in commodity markets where the basic product—oil, timber, or iron ore, for example—is essentially the same. Furthermore, the success of these firms is dependent on the regular replacement of resource reserves. These characteristics call for a special form of analysis, which we review in this chapter.

GENERAL METHODOLOGY

In evaluating a natural resource stock, the practitioner focuses on four factors:

1. *The appraisal of the company's resource reserves* represents a major component of equity value. In the oil exploration and production (E&P) business, a reserve value to stock price of 70 percent is not uncommon. Oil reserves are the equivalent of long-term inventories, waiting to produce revenues.
2. *The value of other physical assets* is a contributing factor. The extraction, processing, and distribution of a natural resource requires substantial plant and equipment. Furthermore, like any other business, the natural resource business has cash on hand, accounts receivable, and other tangible assets. Most companies also carry substantial acreage that has yet to be explored and exploited.
3. *Net tangible assets* are calculated by subtracting the accounting value of liabilities from the sum of reserve values and physical assets. The result is also known as *net asset value* (NAV) in Street jargon.

4. *Management's ability to replenish the company's reserves* on an economical basis is a nontangible asset, like goodwill. Management engages in a continual search for new reserves that can be exploited and sold. At the time of this writing, most natural resource stocks traded above NAV, indicating confidence in the managers' abilities to find new reserves.

This four-factor approach is different than the DCF method that we used earlier, and the reasoning behind it stems from the importance of reserves to a natural resource business. See Exhibit 21.1. Unlike the brand name of the consumer firm, the reputation of the service provider, or the technology of the software developer, the principal assets of the natural resource firm—its reserves—have a finite life that is easy to calculate. Suppose an oil E&P company has one billion barrels of oil reserves (i.e., oil in the ground) and a production rate of 100 million barrels yearly. Assuming the reserve base is depleted evenly, the company, absent any replenishment, has a 10-year life (1 billion barrels ÷ 100 million barrels/year = 10 years). Assigning an exact economic life to industrial assets is far more complicated (as we discussed in Chapter 9), and this difference accounts for much of the change in valuation technique.

Furthermore, since reserves relate to widely traded commodities, their cash value out of the ground is easy to determine. One need only pick up the *Wall Street Journal* or consult a commodity web site to see the market price of oil, timber, or iron ore. That price is then extrapolated into the future, and multiplied by annual production volumes, to form a sales projection. Projecting revenues for an industrial firm is far more problematic.

In-the-ground values are obtainable for the most visible commodities such as oil and gold. Transactions in such reserves take place frequently and the prices appear in databases. Of course, each reserve transaction has unique elements. Thus, the $20 per barrel of in-the-ground oil statistic used in several 2008 E&P transactions was a value guide, rather than a precise appraisal of a firm's reserve base, particularly since oil prices fell rapidly toward the end of 2008.

In the research report, the practitioner first compares the probable future revenues from reserves against the cost of extracting them (or cutting them down in the case of lumber). In some cases, the firm may sell forward its production at a fixed price in the futures market. A second part of the security analysis is gauging the firm's ability to replace reserves. This skill sustains and grows the enterprise, and a company's record in finding and/or purchasing economical reserves is an important performance measure. Some companies are better at doing this than others, and investors assign such firms the highest intangible values.

EXHIBIT 21.1   Natural Resource Stocks Evaluation Methodology

+	Market value of natural resource reserves.
+	Value of other physical assets, including working capital.
−	Accounting value of liabilities.
±	Intangible value of management's ability to replenish the reserve base.
Net amount	Appropriate equity value of the firm.

This is the four-step approach to valuing a natural resource company.

THE FINANCIAL REPORTING OF NATURAL RESOURCE COMPANIES

As shown in Exhibits 21.2 and 21.3, the income statement and balance sheet of a natural resource firm have historical accounting data that is similar to the industrial company presentation. However, the accounting information set forth in the financial statements has less interpretative value for the natural resource firm, and practitioners use a special set of accounting-based measurements that track reserves and units of production. Encore Acquisition Company (EAC) is an oil and gas exploration and development company.

The accounting profession and the SEC have tried to make financial reporting relevant to the valuation process of a natural resource company, but the end result confuses the inexperienced practitioner. The financial information and operating data needed for a research report are scattered throughout the SEC filings, forcing the analyst to hunker down and methodically examine the public documents to pick out the required statistics. Leading performance criteria for the oil and gas industry are set forth in Exhibit 21.4. Note how net income, EPS, and EBITDA don't appear on the list.

EXHIBIT 21.2   Encore Acquisition Company, Summary Income Statement Data (in millions, except per share data)

	Year Ended December 31		
	2006	2007	2008
Revenues			
Oil and gas production revenues	$493	$713	$1,125
Operating expenses			
Depreciation, depletion, and amortization	113	184	228
Production costs	98	143	175
Production taxes	50	76	112
General and administrative	23	39	48
Exploration, cost of dry holes	31	28	39
Other operating	10	23	15
Operating income	168	220	508
Reserve write-down	—	—	59
Derivatives	(24)	112	(346)
Operating income	192	108	795
Interest	44	86	69
Income before income taxes	$147	$ 22	$ 726
Net income	$ 93	$ 17	$ 430

Encore Acquisition Company explores for, develops, and produces crude oil and natural gas. Its reserves are located in the United States. Using the successful efforts method of accounting, EAC expenses immediately the cost of dry holes. It sells forward a portion of its production, and the related derivative contracts are marked to fair value. In 2008, it sold future production at a high price compared to the year-end value of oil, thus providing a large gain.

EXHIBIT 21.3 Encore Acquisition Company, Summary Balance Sheet Data at December 31, 2008 (in millions)

Assets

Cash	$ 2
Accounts receivable	129
Derivatives	349
Other current assets	34
Total current assets	541
Oil and gas reserves,[a] on the basis of successful efforts accounting:	
Proved properties	3,538
Unproved and properties under development	124
Other property and equipment	25
Less: accumulated depreciation, depletion, and amortization	(784)
	2,902
Other assets	190
	$3,633

Liabilities and Shareholders' Equity

Current liabilities	$ 352
Long-term debt[b]	1,319
Deferred income taxes	417
Other long-term liabilities	61
Minority interest	170
Shareholders' equity	1,314
	$3,633

[a]Most of EAC's assets are represented by its oil and gas reserves.
[b]EAC's ability to incur leverage is dependent on its reserve position. Debt is 37 percent of historical reserve value.

Because historical accounting doesn't do justice to underlying mineral reserve values, a natural resource firm has its reserves evaluated by an independent engineering firm each year. A summary of the engineer's reserve calculations is included with the financial statements. For oil and gas companies, the issuer prepares an abbreviated calculation of the present value of such reserves, using year-end oil and gas prices and a statutory 10 percent discount rate. The engineer's report thus complements the recording and measurement functions of the independent accountant, appraiser, actuarial consultant, and others who weigh in on certain aspects of financial statements.

Because of the prominence of the oil and gas industry, I use a case study to illustrate the evaluation process. To simplify the exercise, we cover Encore Acquisition Company (EAC), a medium-size, independent oil and gas exploration and production company, rather than a large integrated oil business like ExxonMobil. The big firms supplement their exploration and development businesses with substantial downstream operations in chemicals, oil refining, and gasoline retailing. Analyzing such conglomerates is quite complicated.

EXHIBIT 21.4 Oil and Gas Industry Financial Performance Criteria

Reserves Measurement	Comments
Reserve production ratio	Total in-the-ground proved reserves divided by annual production. This ratio provides an indication of expected reserve life, before any new additions. Specific data is provided in the body of the Form 10-K. There is no guarantee that all reserves can be extracted economically.
Estimated quantities of proved reserves	The footnotes to the financial statements have a tabular summary of reserves that engineers have determined are economically viable for exploitation. Proved developed reserves can be recovered through existing wells. Proved undeveloped reserves need to be drilled, so there remains uncertainty about extraction costs. Like other financial statement entries, reserves estimates have a gray area. From time to time, overstatements are apparent and unexpected write-downs occur. Royal Dutch Shell was fined by regulators for exaggerating oil and gas reserves.
Reserves per share	A measure of reserves that can be related to the stock price.
Standardized measure of discounted future net cash flows to proved reserves	Using current energy prices and extraction costs, the company provides a DCF value of proved reserves. To foster standardization, the SEC mandates a 10 percent discount rate (although it doesn't reflect true risk in most cases) and the prices are not escalated.
Underdeveloped acreage and cost per acre	E&P companies acquire mineral rights in promising regions in anticipation of future exploration. Unless there is information available to the contrary, the firm values these assets at historical cost.

Operating Data	Comments
Average prices received in the sale of oil and gas	Either the footnotes or the SEC Form 10-K provide a tabular summary of average prices per barrel of oil and per thousand cubic feet (Mcf) of natural gas. Some E&P companies hedge prices by entering into long-term contracts.
Lifting costs per barrel	In their financial statements, E&P companies separate the cash operating costs needed to extract (i.e., *lift*) the resource from (1) general and administrative expenses and (2) noncash depletion, depreciation, and amortization (DDA) charges. Cash operating costs are then divided by annual barrels of production. Low lifting costs are favorable for the corporation. Note that 6 Mcf of gas equals one barrel-of-oil equivalent (BOE).
General and administrative (G&A) costs	G&A costs are expressed both as (1) a percentage of revenues and (2) cost per BOE production. Low G&A costs indicate efficiencies.
Cash flows and depreciation, depletion, and amortization (DDA)	DDA represents the run-off of the substantial exploration and development expenses that E&P companies capitalize with respect to reserves. DDA is the major expense of an E&P business, and it is generated on a unit-of-production basis. DDA is a noncash charge and represents a significant portion of E&P operating cash flow. In most firms, the bulk of this cash flow is reinvested in the search for more reserves.

(*Continued*)

EXHIBIT 21.4   (*Continued*)

Reserve Replacement	Comments
Reserve replacement ratio	Using footnote data, the analyst divides new reserves by annual production. Obviously, a ratio of 1.0 or higher is necessary to sustain the corporation. High ratios imply favorable search abilities.
Finding costs per barrel-of-oil equivalent (BOE)	In the footnotes or on the 10-K form, the company should summarize the capitalized costs incurred in exploration, development, and reserve acquisition activities. New reserve additions are then divided into the newly capitalized costs. To remain profitable, a company's finding costs per BOE, taken with lifting and G&A costs per BOE, have to be less than the BOE selling price. Low finding costs indicate a capable management. In 2008, for example, average U.S. finding costs were $12/BOE. Lifting costs ($7) and production taxes ($6) presented a $25 cost "out of the wellhead." The average sale price was $80, before other costs were deducted.

CASE STUDY: ENCORE ACQUISITION COMPANY

EAC's historical financial statements don't tell the whole story, but they provide the best starting point. Summary data appears as Exhibits 21.2, 21.3, and 21.5.

As shown in Exhibit 21.2, EAC reported an accounting profit in each of the past three years. Revenues increased sharply in 2007 and 2008 due to increasing oil and gas prices. Profits were impacted by marking to market forward sales contracts (derivatives). The debt to total capitalization ratio was 50 percent, which was higher than most E&P companies. Reserves (net of depletion) represented 80 percent of accounting assets.

Certain Accounting Aspects

The typical E&P company spends huge amounts exploring for oil and preparing reserves for lifting. Many times a well is drilled on the firm's acreage and no oil is found (i.e., a *dry hole*). Participants use one of two accounting methods to capitalize and expense exploration and development costs:

1. *Full cost accounting.* All drilling costs, including those of dry holes, are capitalized on the balance sheet. The resultant capitalized costs are then amortized on the unit of production method.
2. *Successful efforts accounting.* Only successful well expenses are capitalized. Dry-hole costs are immediately charged against earnings. The successful efforts method is more conservative. (The analyst should remember to add back dry-hole costs to capital investments to determine finding costs.) EAC uses the successful efforts method.

EXHIBIT 21.5   Encore Acquisition Company, Summary Cash Flow Data (in millions)

	Year Ended December 31, 2008
Cash Flows from Operating Activities	
Net income	$431
Adjustments to reconcile net income to net cash provided by operating activities:	
Depreciation, depletion, and amortization	228
Deferred income taxes	233
Noncash derivative gain	(299)
Other	166
Changes in operating assets and liabilities, net	(96)
Cash flows from operations	663
Cash Flows from Investing Activities	
Exploration and development expenditures on successful wells	561
Other	25
Purchases of proved reserves	142
Net cash used by investing activities	(728)
Cash Flows from Financing Activities	
Borrowings, net	
Common stock repurchase	200
Other	(67)
Net cash provided by financing activities	(66)
Net change in cash	67
	$ 2

As oil and gas are extracted from the ground, their accounting values on the balance sheet are "depleted." Depletion is a noncash charge. Note EAC's sizable commitment to exploration and development under "investing activities."

Under both methods, the E&P company should write down the capitalized amounts if events indicate that such values cannot be recovered in the future. For example, in 2008 EAC recognized a noncash charge of $59 million, as four wells proved to be uneconomical at year-end prices. (Conoco Phillips had a $25 billion write-down that year.) In 2007, oil and gas prices rose 40 percent, but accounting rules don't permit upward revisions.

Most E&P companies that I examine pay little or no federal income tax. Resource depletion allowances for tax purposes are faster than book depletion rates, so the firm defers income taxes until production falls off. In practice, such obligations can be postponed indefinitely through internal growth or M&A transactions.

Present Value of Reserves

Reserves are essentially underground. See Exhibit 21.6. They can be pumped out of the ground, at differing speeds, to satisfy the need for revenue. Because

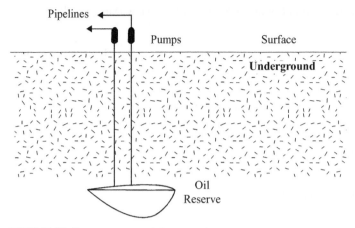

EXHIBIT 21.6 Pumping Oil from Underground Reserves

reserves are such an important component of a company's stock price, U.S. firms disclose the present value (PV) of their reserves, minus the cost of lifting the reserves out of the ground and paying production taxes. The financial model resembles Exhibit 21.7. In an SEC filing, the PV is shown in two ways: (1) the SEC standardized calculation, using prior year average sale prices; and (2) the PV-10 calculation, which includes the impact of certain corporate-level income

EXHIBIT 21.7 Present Value of Reserves on a Per Share Basis: Oil and Gas Company Example

	Oil				Expenses Operations/ Development/ Taxes ($millions)	Pretax Undiscounted Net Cash Flow ($millions)	NPV Pretax Cash Flow @13% ($millions)
Year	Reserves (million barrels)	Production (million barrels)	Pricing ($/barrel)	Revenues ($millions)			
2010	50	8	40	320	168	152	135
2011	42	7	40	280	147	133	104
2012	35	6	40	240	132	108	75
2013	29	5	40	200	110	130	77
2014	24	5	41	205	110	105	57
2015	19	5	41	205	115	90	43
2016	14	4	41	164	92	72	31
2017	10	4	42	168	96	72	27
2018	6	3	42	126	72	54	18
2019	3	3	42	126	72	54	16
		50				970	583

Net present value/BOE	$11.66

Pricing parameters: In this model, oil and gas prices escalate gradually. The SEC Form 10-K standardized calculation does not escalate price or cost. It uses a 10 percent discount rate. A 13 percent rate is utilized here to reflect market conditions better.

EXHIBIT 21.8   Encore Acquisition Company: Two Mandated
Reserve Present Value Calculations at December 31, 2008

Net Present Value	
SEC Standardized	$1.2 billion
PV-10	$1.4 billion
Net Present Value per Barrel	
SEC Standardized	$6.50
PV-10	$7.57
Net Present Value of Reserves per Share	
SEC Standardized	$23
PV-10	$26

taxes. For Encore Acquisition Company, the summary calculations appear in Exhibit 21.8.

Encore Acquisition Company: Performance Criteria

As an illustration of the key criteria used to evaluate E&P corporate performance, consider EAC's statistics for the three years ended December 31, 2008, as shown in Exhibit 21.9. A cursory glance at this information enables the reader to reach the following conclusions:

- *Reserves:* EAC's reserve position declined, due to the 2008 write-off of four oil wells. Reserve life fell to 12.8 years and BOE reserves per share dropped 20 percent to 3.5. The company pumped more oil out of the ground than it replaced with oil reserves for future production. The substantial decrease in the price of energy saw the net present value of reserves per share fall to $23 in 2008 from $62 in 2007.
- *Operating results:* Most of the increase in oil and gas prices occurred in 2008's final quarter, so the average 2008 price was actually $89.30 per barrel, a 48 percent jump from 2007. Lifting costs grew 14 percent, but as a percent of revenues, they declined from 18 percent in 2007 to 14 percent in 2008. Nevertheless, at $12 per barrel, lifting costs were $5 per barrel higher then the U.S. average. G&A costs as a percentage of revenues (4.3 percent in 1996) were higher than those of competing firms, because EAC's small size didn't permit it to spread overhead easily.
- *Reserve replacement:* Reserve replacement performance was below average, and the firm's proved reserves fell from 205 million to 186 million over two years. Oil and gas price increases supported a tripling of the stock price from March 2007 to July 2008, but the reserve drop and rapidly decreasing prices caused the stock price to fall 80 percent within six months.
- *Finding:* EAC had a disastrous year in 2008 as it spent over $600 million to find less than 20 million barrels of new reserves. Finding costs grew from $12.89 per barrel to $30.90, an unfavorable trend. E&P analysts prefer to average finding costs over a three-year period to moderate the effects of such aberrations.

EXHIBIT 21.9   Encore Acquisition Company Key Performance Measures

	2006	2007	2008	Trend
Reserves				
Reserve to production ratio	18.5 years	17.1 years	12.8 years	Unfavorable
Reserves per share (BOE)	3.8	4.4	3.5	Unfavorable
Reserve DCF per share (SEC basis)	$27.55	$62.10	$23.00	Unfavorable
Operating Data				
Sale price:				
Oil (barrel)	$43.40	$58.96	$87.30	Favorable
Natural gas (Mcf)	6.24	6.26	8.63	Favorable
Lifting costs/BOE production	8.73	10.59	12.12	Unfavorable
General and administrative cost/ BOE production	2.06	2.89	3.35	Unfavorable
General and administrative cost/revenues	4.7%	5.5%	4.3%	Favorable
DDA/BOE production	10.10	13.59	15.80	Favorable
Operating cash flow per share	5.02	7.62	13.88	Favorable
Reserve Replacement				
Reserve replacement ratio	178%	125%	(225%)	Unfavorable
Finding costs/new BOE reserves	$12.89	$22.94	$30.90	Unfavorable

Note: Six Mcf of gas approximates one BOE. Excludes EAC's purchase of new reserves.

EAC Value per Share on a Breakup Basis

A thorough research report on an E&P company contains a breakup calculation. The analyst estimates the reserve value by either the DCF approach or the comparable sales method. For the DCF process, he first assumes a future production curve for existing reserves (Exhibit 21.10), and then applies the appropriate selling prices and lifting costs to annual barrels of production. DCF calculations for EAC reserves are provided in Exhibits 21.7 and 21.8. An alternative technique is to examine the recent sale prices of in-the-ground reserves. If the most recent sale price is $10 per barrel, this value can be applied to the firm's reserves, depending on the qualitative nature of the comparable sales.

Once the production curve and financial model are in the analyst's personal computer, he is free to manipulate the assumptions to see the effect of different discount rates, lower prices, and higher extraction costs. To the reserve present value, he adds other assets and subtracts accounting liabilities. The analyst is now ready to estimate EAC's breakup value. Exhibit 21.11 reviews the mechanics of the calculation.

Reaching a Conclusion

The breakup calculation provided a possible liquidation price for EAC, absent the intangible benefits of a management team that knew how to replenish a depleting reserve base and, therefore, grow the business. Such intangible qualities had minor

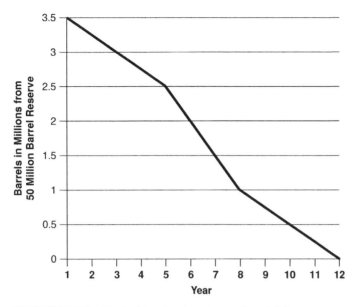

EXHIBIT 21.10 Typical Production Curve of an Oil Reserve

value in EAC's case, since reserves per share fell by 10 percent. In March 2009, the share price was $17, yet the breakup values ranged from $9 to $19 per share. The $8 difference from the bottom of the range (i.e., $17 minus $9) was attributable to either intangible assets or expectations of higher oil prices.

Confidence in a firm's exploration ability leads to premium price/breakup and price/cash flow ratios. Management's experience in generating new reserves at a low

EXHIBIT 21.11 Breakup Value Encore Acquisition Company at March 15, 2009

	Discounted Cash Flow: SEC/PV-10 Average		$10/Barrel Value, In-the-ground[b]	
	Amount	Per Share	Amount	Per Share
Proved oil and gas reserves	$1,300	$24.50	$1,850	$34.91
Undeveloped acreage	124		124	
Property and equipment, net	12		12	
Other assets	190		190	
Net working capital	189		189	
Gross asset value	1,815	34.25	2,365	44.62
Long-term debt	(1,319)	(24.89)	(1,315)	(24.89)
Net asset value[a]	$ 496	$ 9.36[c]	$1,050	$19.73

[a]Depending on the assumptions, the breakup value has a wide range. Here it is $9 to $19.
[b]The $10 per barrel in-the-ground estimate is loosely based on recent reserve sales, adjusted for the late-2008 oil price drop.
[c]The stock price was $17, indicating that investors expected future oil prices to be higher than the SEC/PV-10 forecasts, which provided only a $9.36 stock value.

EXHIBIT 21.12   Ranking E&P Companies

	Oil and Gas E&P Company			
	A	**B**	**C**	**D**
Existing reserve situation	Good	Excellent	Average	Average
Operating performance	Excellent	Good	Good	Average
Reserve finding ability	Poor	Average	Good	Average

The company with the best grades deserves a premium valuation.

finding cost is of paramount concern, but analysts also examine the E&P company's leverage, its control over operating costs, and the qualitative aspects of its existing reserves. How much is oil versus gas? Are the reserves located in a safe location, like the United States, or in a volatile country, like Namibia? And so on.

In assessing *relative* values, the practitioner compares the industry operating statistics across specific companies. Like we did in Chapters 15 and 19 for industrial companies, a good exercise is ranking E&P firms by historical performance. Those firms receiving the best grades have a basis for a premium valuation. Exhibit 21.12 shows a hypothetical ranking for four firms. Depending on the defining characteristics, EAC has between 15 and 20 comparables that can be used in a ranking scheme.

In conjunction with relative value analysis, the practitioner prepares projections that elaborate upon the breakup value calculation. Rather than showing a static production curve, the company is assumed to continue (or improve upon) its record of finding reserves in excess of annual production. By making the requisite assumptions with regard to selling prices, operating expenses, and finding costs, the analyst constructs a 5- to 10-year financial forecast. At the end of the period, a terminal value is assigned to the company, based on a cash flow multiple, rather than a net asset value. Doug Cannon, portfolio manager at Texas First Investment Management, suggests, "5 to 6 times cash flow as a reasonable multiple, because it's a good historical indicator of E&P values."

MINING COMPANIES

Mining company analysts employ several of the techniques used in oil and gas appraisals, but the performance parameters are different. For example, the lifting cost (per sales dollar) of a mining operation tends to be much higher than its E&P counterpart. Tons of ore must be extracted and processed to obtain a few hundred pounds of the lesser grade metals (such as copper and zinc) or just a couple of ounces of the precious metals (such as gold and platinum). This costs a lot of money. Operating expenses for a mining company can exceed 60 percent of sales, whereas a typical ratio for an E&P firm might be 30 percent. However, the mining company has fewer finding and amortization costs (as a percentage of the sales dollar), and its shipping costs are lower due to the higher value-to-weight ratio enjoyed by metals (e.g., $40 per barrel oil equals 15 cents per pound, whereas silver has a value of $200 per pound).

Like the oil and gas industry, mining company valuations are heavily dependent on reserve calculations. Reserve life and replacement experience is important. In addition to examining ore quantities per share, the analyst reviews the grade (or purity) of the reserves. Higher-grade ore implies less processing (i.e., less operating expense) per pound (or ounce) of saleable product. To assist the investors, mining companies disclose reserves, grades, and operating costs per ton in their SEC filings. From this information, one calculates reserve replacement ratios, lifting cost per pound (or ounce), and other statistics.

In the United States, mining company reserve disclosures are verified by independent mining engineering firms. The importance of third-party checking was highlighted by the scandal affecting Bre-X Minerals, a small Canadian gold mining company. From being an obscure penny stock operation with a market value of less than $10 million, Bre-X ran claims of a fantastic Indonesian gold strike into a capitalization of $6 billion. Only independent testing by Freeport-McMoRan, a possible merger partner, uncovered fraudulent reserve calculations by the firms, which suddenly collapsed into bankruptcy, costing investors huge losses.

As the *Washington Post* noted,

> *Bre-X's public statements and official filings frequently noted that estimates of the size of the find had been prepared by a respected engineering firm, Montreal-based SNC Lavalin. Not as publicized was the fact that the engineering company had been hired only to make its calculations based on samples of earth extracted and processed by Bre-X.*[1]

Few sophisticated players thought to ask Bre-X for a legitimate double check of its reserve claims, and the list of those hoodwinked by the management comprise a veritable who's who of finance: Fidelity, the giant fund company; J.P. Morgan, the global banking concern; Nesbitt Burns, Canada's most prestigious investment bank; the Toronto stock exchange, Canada's largest securities market; the NASD, which listed the shares in the United States; and the SEC, which processed the company's U.S. regulatory filings. Nesbitt Burns provided a typically lame excuse for failing to uncover the problem: "Our analysts rely on publicly available information that is released by reputable companies, but in this case there is fraud. Our experts are not experts in uncovering fraud." As the reader now knows, an effective security analysis extends past information spoon-fed to the public by the issuer.

Anglo Gold Ashanti, Ltd.

As an example of mining operations estimate disclosure, Exhibit 21.13 provides summary information regarding the gold operations of Anglo Gold Ashanti, Ltd.

The values of mining stocks reflect the market price of the related commodity. Thus, if gold prices jump 10 percent in a week, the share price of Anglo Gold Ashanti usually rises in sympathy.

EXHIBIT 21.13   Anglo Gold Ashanti, Ltd.

Selected Operating Data	Year Ended December 31, 2008
Gold produced (ounces)	4,928,000
Price per ounce	$702
Production cost/per ounce	
Cash operating costs	444
Noncash costs	123
Total production costs	567
Gross margin per ounce[a]	$135

Ore Reserves[b] Category	Tonnage (million tons)	Average Grade of Gold (ounces per ton)	Contained Gold Tons	Gold Content (million ounces)
		At December 31, 2008		
Proved	341	1.89	646	20.9
Probable	697	2.42	1,683	54.0
Total proved and probable	1,038	2.25	2,329	74.9

[a]From the gross margin, the company pays for corporate administration, market development, and exploration costs, among other items.
[b]Reviewed by independent engineering firm.

SUMMARY

Natural resource firms participate in commodity markets where the basic product—oil, gas, or metallic ore—is essentially the same. With no brand name, service component, or technology to differentiate one company's products from another, the analyst's research focuses on two factors: (1) the net present value of the company's reserves, using the DCF method and the recent transactions approach; and (2) the presumed ability of the management team to find new reserves in an economical fashion. The average natural resource stock trades at a price in excess of breakup value. The larger this excess, the more confidence that investors have in the firm's ability to replace current production with new reserves.

The share values of these companies move in sympathy with changes in the market price of the relevant natural resource. Thus, if oil prices jump 10 percent, shares of oil companies are bound to rise.

CHAPTER 22

Financial Industry Stocks

Like natural resource companies, financial firms require a special analysis, replete with industry-specific ratios and performance measurements.

The crash of 2008 demonstrated that the information disclosure of the financial industry is inadequate for a proper security analysis. Given the political influence of the financial industry and the inertia of the U.S. regulatory structure, it is unlikely that this situation will be remedied anytime soon. As a result, the financial industry investor faces a higher degree of uncertainty than is the case within other commercial sectors.

Evaluating a financial business like a commercial bank, insurance company, or leasing firm requires analytical tools that have not been employed previously in this book. The modification in our approach stems from the singular nature of the financial company's tangible assets. Unlike a manufacturing or service business, a financial company's tangible assets are almost entirely pieces of paper, most of which are contractual in nature, such as loans, derivatives, or insurance policies. The liability side of these businesses also contributes to a specialized approach, since financial firms are highly leveraged and deal in activities that are volatile and have uncertain future obligations. Finally, the regulatory environment influences this sector more than the average industrial business, and the federal government has a policy of protecting creditors of large banks from a loss of principal in the case of failure.

The pieces of paper controlled by financial institutions often represent the savings and peace of mind of the average citizen. Reckless behavior on the part of one company can undermine confidence in the financial system and contribute to market crashes, depositor runs, policy withdrawals, and other panics. To reduce the likelihood of these events, government created a complex regulatory structure that set the industry's ground rules, and it has put into place a trillion-dollar bailout scheme that reduces the likelihood of bank failures. As noted in the first edition of this book, the past enforcement of these regulations was best characterized as benign. The system relied heavily on self-policing by the referees—the independent auditors, credit rating agencies, financial exchanges, and nongovernment regulators—that supposedly formed the first line of defense against misstatement, fraud, and abuse. Underlying the self-regulation philosophy was the industry's contention—more or less accepted by government—that an industry executive had little incentive to take undue risks, since such actions would inevitably lead to a decline in his company's stock price, and a concurrent drop in the value of his stock options. What this philosophy ignored was the sizable salaries and bonuses of many executives and their ability to cash out of stock options before bad news arrived. Thus, in 2008, the public was treated to the spectacle of Wall Street titan Lehman Brothers going bankrupt, even as its CEO, Richard Fuld, received $480 million in cash compensation over the prior eight years. Similar episodes occurred at Citicorp, Fannie Mae, Merrill Lynch, and other firms, where executives collected huge bonuses on profits that turned out to be illusory.

The other actors in the self-policing scheme were hardly innocents. The independent auditors had extreme difficulty in assigning accurate values to the complex financial instruments invented by the industry, and they generally acceded to their clients' requests to hold down auditing costs by refusing to hire third-party appraisers. The auditors also complied in certifying that the debts of the bank-sponsored structured investment vehicles (SIVs) were nonrecourse (to the bank); thus, they permitted an extravagant use of leverage that supported hundreds of billions of loans of dubious quality. In the credit rating agencies' quest to maximize profit, they cut corners on due diligence and failed to run deep recession scenarios for hundreds of billions in collateralized debt obligations (CDOs). Fixed-income investors and regulatory agencies naively relied on these ratings, and they paid the price.

Government regulators, such as the Securities and Exchange Commission, Federal Deposit Insurance Corporation (FDIC), Comptroller of the Currency, Public Company Accounting Oversight Board (PCAOB), and National Association of Insurance Commissioners, hardly distinguished themselves. As financial assets became more complex and harder to value, these regulators were assured by financial institutions and credit rating agencies that financial models and scoring systems showed the risks were small. Most of this testimony was taken at face value by the regulators, as they lacked the expertise, initiative, or desire to dig deeper. One thing there wasn't a shortage of was money, as the budgets of these multiple agencies totaled billions of dollars. The FDIC, for example, had a $1.2 billion budget in 2008, and its staff of bank examiners and supervisory staff totaled 4,800.

The regulators were hardly alone in failing to understand the risks financial companies were taking. Sophisticated private equity firms and sovereign wealth funds invested tens of billions of dollars into large U.S. banks during the second half of 2008. Despite broad management access, inside information, and consultant expertise, these investors guessed wrong and posted huge losses. Kingdom Holding Co., owned by Saudi billionaire Prince Alwaleed bin Talal, recorded an $8 billion loss in 2008's fourth quarter, after a drop in the value of large stakes in Citigroup and other financials.

The U.S. government put trillions of taxpayer dollars at risk to protect the financial system in 2008 and 2009. It allowed the socialization of many corporate losses, but the private profits of financial executives remained untouched. Few industry participants were disciplined, fined, or prosecuted, and the numerous regulators all kept their jobs and pensions. In theory, the huge cost of the government bailout and the repetitive nature of the financial panic problem should have prompted a thorough overhaul of the supervisory machinery, but progress was slow. The regulators appointed by the current administration are deeply invested in the current system, while Wall Street, which dislikes government oversight, maintains continued influence. By way of example, financial industry employees represented the largest group of donors to the Obama inauguration, and the chairman of the New York Federal Reserve Bank, Stephen Friedman, sat on the board of Goldman Sachs and had a large stockholding, even as the government provided substantial aid to Wall Street.[1]

Analysts of financial firms must remember that government actions in 2008 and 2009 were designed principally to shield the creditors of troubled banks from significant loss. Bank equity investors, in contrast, saw declines of 70 to 80 percent in many cases. Given this new environment and the past history, prospective shareholders in financial firms need to redouble their analytical efforts, yet they face huge gaps in their information base. That's one reason that Brian McQuade, CEO of money manager Columbia Financial Advisors, tends to avoid financial equity investing: "It requires substantial balance sheet analysis, it takes a lot of time, and it's hard to figure out."

This chapter examines the analytical process involved in two sectors:

- *Banks.* Cash income is derived from borrowing money at a low rate and lending it out at a higher rate (i.e., the *spread* business). The spread business is augmented by a large volume of fee-based activity and principal trading.
- *Insurance companies.* By using the law of large numbers, these firms absorb the risk of catastrophic events that are too costly for a single business or individual to incur.

Brokerage firms, hedge funds, and mutual fund companies are part of the financial industry, but the limited number of publicly held players diminishes the need for attention here.

The financial sector is mature and cyclical. The products and services offered within each subsector are fairly homogeneous, giving the industry a commodity orientation that limits profitability for most of the players. Innovation provides one way in which a company differentiates itself from others without cutting price, but few financial inventions are patented and most are copied shortly after their introduction. These factors combine to keep the P/E ratios of financial stocks below their industrial company counterparts.

PRODUCT LINES

Most of the large publicly traded companies offer multiple product lines. Goldman Sachs, for example, offers services such as lending, insurance (through derivatives), corporate advisory, retail and institutional brokerage, proprietary trading, and asset management (hedge funds, private equity funds, and mutual funds). The product lines have limited amounts of differentiation. For example:

- *Lending:* Except for interest costs and related fees, the money borrowed from one bank is identical to that from another.
- *Insurance:* Except for price and the insurer's ability to pay a claim presented to it, insurance policies and derivative contracts are similar.
- *Corporate advisory:* Reputation in this product line makes a critical leader in the M&A and securities underwriting market.

EXHIBIT 22.1 The Financial Industry

Subsector	Principal Products/Services	Nonprice Competitive Elements
Lending	Loans, transaction processing and custodial services, charge cards.	Government deposit guarantees, reputation, service efficiency, convenience, personal relationships, willingness to take risk at low price.
Insurance	Insurance against unanticipated events, various tax-deferred investment products, third-party claims processing services.	Creditworthiness, reputation, specialized expertise, service efficiency, personal relationships, willingness to take risk at low price.
Corporate Advisory	Financial advisory services for corporations.	Reputation, personal relationships.
Brokerage	Order execution and custodial services.	Distribution and trading ability for corporate accounts.
Proprietary Trading	Management of in-house funds.	Technology, market intelligence, personnel, software, risk control.
Money Management	Management of individual and corporate pension and savings accounts, in exchange for a fee.	Reputation, claims of above-average performance potential, marketing abilities, convenience.

Competition in the financial industry is dependent on nonprice factors.

- *Brokerage:* From the individual's point of view, there is little difference between the services provided by most brokerage firms. Institutional services are differentiated in a meaningful way only by the top five providers.
- *Proprietary trading:* Certain firms have better abilities than others in this regard, but the black-box nature of much of this trading makes it difficult to evaluate.
- *Money management:* Despite their claims to the contrary, the vast majority of money managers cannot beat stock, bond, or private equity market indexes on a regular basis. Their money management abilities are distressingly similar.

Success in certain of these products rests on (1) intangibles, such as marketing clout, reputation, and personal contacts, which de-commoditize the product; as well as (2) technical expertise and the operating controls and cost efficiencies that keep a firm's pricing in line with the competition. Exhibit 22.1 provides further information.

THE NATURE OF FINANCIAL ASSETS

The intangible elements of a financial business frequently represent the engine of growth, and the practitioner assesses these qualities carefully in his analysis. At the same time, he must evaluate the company's asset portfolio in the here and now, not only to appraise the accuracy of accounting estimates but also to measure management's ability to run the business.

Above all, the analyst remembers that financial assets are contractual in nature. Contracts, in the U.S. and elsewhere, are rarely 100 percent enforceable according to their terms. Thus, when a corporation stops repaying a $100 million loan or bond, the foreclosure process doesn't begin immediately. Rather, this nonpayment is the start of a negotiation. Similarly, a property and casualty insurer is circumspect in honoring a large claim. The firm defers payment until it investigates the situation, and it may contest the size and validity of the claim, depending on its interpretation of the policy. The analyst acknowledges firstly that financial assets are not governed by an absolutist legal framework.

Furthermore, the economic value of financial assets—whether they are bonds, stocks, or derivatives—is subject to systematic change. Bond prices are directly influenced by movements in interest rates, which impact common stock values also. Derivative prices exaggerate the movements of the underlying security or commodity. The historical accounting presentation may not accurately reflect such changes in economic value, and the accounting values (supplied every three months) may be out-of-date when provided for public consumption. By way of example, in the three months between September and December 2008, the value of State Street Bank's securities portfolio dropped $5 billion.

As noted earlier, the valuation of many financial assets has a high degree of subjectivity. To reduce the leeway of financial statement preparers, the federal government and the FASB developed a three-tier methodology by which securities can be categorized and valued. Even so, the valuation of thinly traded assets and privately placed securities remains highly judgmental. For example, in November 2008, private equity firms reported their interests in Harrah's Entertainment, a faltering $17 billion LBO, at anywhere between 25 and 75 percent of original cost. All of these firms had access to the same public and private information.

Independent auditors are not expert in understanding the nuances of complex securities and derivatives, and most audit clients complain about the cost of third-party appraisers so the auditors are reluctant to use them. Thus, management flexibility in defining operating results is alive and well in the financial sector. The securities analyst is alert to the possibility of inflated asset valuations, as well as the likelihood of deflated bad loan estimates or faulty insurance underwritings.

Another issue to consider is the sheer number of loans, contracts, and investments owned by a sizable institution. Outside auditors are in the spot-check business; they can't review every document. Internal risk managers, meanwhile, lack the resources to verify every trade. A simple, five-page derivative contract can fall through the cracks and cost an institution millions. Modern risk management systems rely heavily on business unit managers to self-assess potential problem areas, and that is a weakness in the framework, according to Dominiek Vangaever, risk adviser to the Inter-American Development Bank: "The system is so complex, and that makes it hard for someone on the outside to verify that no mistakes have been made."

In sum, the daisy chain of paper shuffling, the complicated nature of legal contracts, the inherent uncertainty attached to financial asset values, and the quick manner in which large sums of money change hands make the financial industry a fertile area for misstatements, promoters, and charlatans. Most publicly traded firms uphold reasonable standards of operation, but the experienced analyst guards against the disreputable managers who take advantage of the weak links in the reporting system.

TWO SETS OF SKILLS

Much of a financial institution's success relies on managerial judgment, since few loans or investments made by the institution are 100 percent guaranteed. The lending executive must select those borrowers that are creditworthy out of the many presented to him. Likewise, the asset manager tries to select those securities that provide superior returns, relative to the potential risks. The proprietary trading department selects tactics that it hopes will be profitable. Investment acumen is thus a critical quality in managing a financial business.

In certain financial sectors, success is dependent on performing simple tasks in an assembly-line fashion. A bank may process thousands of checks in a single day, an insurance company may review thousands of claims, and a brokerage firm may clear thousands of trades. In the processing field, therefore, a financial firm's operating controls and cost efficiencies should rival those of an industrial manufacturer or distributor. The lending investment culture is thus intertwined with the production environment, requiring the analyst to consider two sets of management skills.

LENDING

Lending is referred to as a *spread* business. A spread business borrows money at one rate and lends it out at a higher rate, in order to profit from the spread between the two rates. Banks and insurance firms have significant spread businesses but, as noted, their operations include other product lines that sometimes overshadow the spread component. For this reason, it is easiest to begin discussion of financial stocks with a bank that focuses mostly on lending.

In its simplest form, a spread business's income statement has only a few line items, as indicated in Exhibit 22.2

The balance sheet of the spread business is straightforward. Assets are almost 100 percent financial and leverage is high, reflecting the liquidity of the assets and the enabling regulatory environment. Additionally, the small spread on earning assets requires the business to have high leverage to produce a reasonable equity return. See Exhibits 22.3 and 22.4.

EXHIBIT 22.2   Hypothetical Spread Business
Income Statement (in millions)

Interest income from loans	$100
Interest expense from borrowing	65
Net interest income	35
Provision for loan losses	5
	30
General and administrative expenses	15
Income before income taxes	15
Income taxes	5
Net income	$ 10

EXHIBIT 22.3 Hypothetical Spread Business
Balance Sheet (in millions)

Assets	
Loans receivable	$1,000
Accrued interest receivable	10
Offices and equipment	10
	$1,020
Liabilities and Shareholders' Equity	
Deposits and borrowings	$ 930
Accruals	10
	940
Shareholders' equity	80
	$1,020

As these exhibits illustrate, the hypothetical spread business realizes a minuscule 1.0 percent after-tax return on assets (ROA), which is far lower than the return on assets achieved by the typical industrial operation. A spread business makes up for its tiny ROA by the heavy use of leverage. A federally chartered U.S. bank, for example, can have a liability-to-equity ratio of 12 to 1 or more. Compare this to the 1:1 ratio that is normal for an industrial company. High leverage transforms the low ROA into an appropriate return on equity for the banks' stockholders.

Qualitative Issues

With equity comprising 6 to 8 percent of assets, it is critical that the bank (and other spread businesses) select borrowers carefully. A write-off of only 2 percent of the portfolio, for example, decreases corporate equity by 25 percent. For this reason, the credit culture of a spread business is the key to success.

This point is well illustrated by the experience of Merrill Lynch. Merrill, along with other New York investment banks, expanded its lending business as one means of drumming up new corporate clients and new underwriting volume. The executives running Merrill's lending operations were investment bankers, who focused on closing deals rather than on putting good assets on the firm's books. As a result, credit analysis and due diligence were cursory, and the bankers piled on tens of billions of shaky LBO loans and questionable collateralized mortgage obligations (CMOs). By 2008, Merrill had run up huge loan losses after just a few years of lending expansion. Only the 2009 acquisition of the firm by Bank of America, and the accompanying $20 billion federal bailout, kept Merrill from insolvency.

EXHIBIT 22.4 Hypothetical Spread Business
Financial Ratios

After-tax return on assets	1.0%
Return on equity	12.5%
Liability-to-equity ratio	12 to 1

In part, a financial institution's credit culture can be surmised from its past record of loan losses in relation to loans booked. A high percentage of loan losses represents either an incompetent management or a risk-taking approach. Alternatively, it can indicate a loan portfolio concentrated in a sector, like residential mortgages, that has undergone tough times. In either case, the incidence of bad loans is reflective of the credit culture. If management alters tactics (as was the case with Merrill) or if the management team itself changes, the predictive ability of the past is suspect. Credit approvals are in the hands of top executives, after all, and the introduction of new managers, particularly outsiders, can mean lending choices that do not correlate well with the past. This principle was demonstrated repeatedly in the 2005–2008 period, when conservative banks allowed bank-sponsored conduits and SIVs to be run by bond traders and investment bankers. Many of these individuals instituted aggressive lending programs that soured quickly.

In addition to a solid credit culture, the principal intangible assets of a lender consist of its reputation within the community, the prominence of its brand name, and the goodwill and contacts of its managers. All of these qualities enable it (1) to attract the deposits (or the borrowings) that support the institution's asset base, and (2) to generate the leads that furnish new loans. For the analyst to measure such intangibles numerically is a difficult task. Indeed, it's far easier to cite contributing factors, such as name recognition statistics, branch locations, and federal deposit guarantees. The value of the going-concern intangibles comes through in the analyst's financial projections, which show existing loans being replaced by new loans, or in relative value comparisons, which show takeover prices exceeding tangible book value.

Financial Statement Analysis of the Spread Business

The aim of financial statement analysis is the preparation of an estimate of historical earnings power. From this estimate an analyst constructs projections. The analysis of a spread business adopts the same methodical approach covered in Chapter 8. As reviewed in Exhibit 22.5, the three financial statements are evaluated through the use of four tools, which enable the practitioner to discern trends and patterns in the subject's historical performance.

Because a lender's assets are wholly financial in nature, the ratios employed in the analysis and the vernacular used in the research report are different than what we have encountered previously. Furthermore, the sensitivity of a spread business to bad loan problems requires a thorough study of loan loss experience, existing asset quality, and reserves for future losses. Finally, the extensive use of leverage requires the practitioner to assess carefully the matching of assets and liabilities. Long-term

EXHIBIT 22.5 Financial Statement Analysis, Established Financial Business

Raw Materials	+ Primary Analytical Tools	= Results
The Income Statement	Absolute amount changes	Patterns and trends that
The Balance Sheet	Percentage changes in growth	have predictive ability
Statement of Cash Flows	Common sizes	
Notes to Financial Statements	Financial ratios	

financial assets should optimally be matched with long-lived liabilities, and vice versa for short-term items.

Case Study: Capitol Federal Financial Corporation   To illustrate the financial analysis, consider Capitol Federal's results for the three years ended September 30, 2008. Capitol Federal was a bank that derived over 80 percent of its income from its spread business. As of September 30, 2008, the company operated 42 branch offices in the state of Kansas. On total assets of $8 billion, Capitol Federal realized net income of $51 million. Summary financial data is shown as Exhibit 22.6.

EXHIBIT 22.6   Capitol Federal Financial Corporation Summary Financial Data (in millions, except per share data)

	Fiscal Year Ended September		
	2006	2007	2008
Income Statement Data			
Interest income: loans	$ 411	$ 412	$ 411
Interest expense	284	305	277
Net interest income	127	106	134
Provision for loan losses, net	—	—	2
Net interest income after provision for loan losses	127	106	132
Noninterest income:			
Fees and service charges	21	21	22
Other income	4	3	8
	25	24	30
Noninterest expense:			
Compensation	40	41	43
Occupancy	13	13	14
Other	20	23	25
	73	77	82
Income before income taxes	79	53	80
Income tax expense	31	21	29
Net income	$ 48	$ 32	$ 51
Earnings per share	$ 0.66	$ 0.44	$ 0.70
Balance Sheet Data			
Assets			
Cash and investments	$ 612	$ 685	$ 229
Mortgage-backed securities	2,083	1,414	2,234
Loans	5,222	5,290	5,321
Other	282	287	271
	$8,199	$7,676	$8,055
Liabilities and Shareholders' Equity			
Deposits	$3,900	$3,923	$3,924
Federal Home Loan Bank advances	3,269	2,732	2,447
Other liabilities	167	154	813
Total liabilities	7,336	6,808	7,184
Shareholders' equity	863	868	871
	$8,199	$7,676	$8,055

A quick glance at Exhibit 22.6 enables the reader to reach the following conclusions:

- *Profitability.* Capitol Federal was profitable through the first phase of the sub-prime crisis. Return on equity over the three-year period under consideration was 7 percent.
- *Growth.* The company's assets grew but net income was flat, with a decline in 2007.
- *One-time items.* Unlike many public firms, Capitol Federal had no one-time accounting items.
- *Asset composition.* Capitol Federal operated as a traditional bank, gathering deposits to make loans. It had a substantial exposure ($2.2 billion) to mortgage-backed securities, representing residential loans originating outside of its service area.
- *Leverage.* The equity to total assets ratio was 11 percent, which was high for a bank. The balance sheet had neither goodwill nor identifiable intangible asset accounts, lending support to the notion of a strong equity base.
- *Off-balance-sheet items and derivatives.* The firm had no significant off-balance-sheet items, such as conduits, SIVs, or nonrecourse finance arrangements. Its derivative activity was minimal.

Capitol Federal's annual SEC filing provides disclosure schedules that supplement the financial statements, including information on asset composition, asset and liability management, and loan loss experience. By the time the annual schedules reach the public, they are two months out-of-date and the quarterly filings contain less detail than the yearly reports. Despite the lack of timeliness, this supplementary data enables the analyst to gauge the impact of changing interest rates on the profitability of the portfolio, along with a sense of asset quality and management's risk-taking profile. Exhibit 22.7, for example, shows the composition of Capitol Federal's loans. Note that over 90 percent of loans were residential first mortgages, rather than commercial real estate or construction loans.

Most of the loans matured after five years, as indicated in Exhibit 22.8.

Less than one-third of the loans were adjustable-rate, so the portfolio's income was fixed in nature. See Exhibit 22.9.

The firm's deposit base was short-term in nature, but it exhibited stability over time. See Exhibit 22.10.

Asset-Liability Imbalance

It is apparent that the bulk of Capitol Federal's assets (loans and instrument securities) are long-term and fixed-rate in nature, while the majority of liabilities (deposits

EXHIBIT 22.7 Capitol Federal Financing
Corporation Loan Composition (in billions)

Residential first mortgages	$5.0	94%
Commercial real estate	0.1	2
Home equity loans	0.2	4
	$5.3	100%

EXHIBIT 22.8 Capitol Federal Financing Corporation
Loan Maturities (in billions)

Amounts Due Within:		
One year	$0.1	2%
One to five years	0.1	2
After five years	5.1	96
	$5.3	100%

EXHIBIT 22.9 Capitol Federal Financing Corporation
Fixed- and Adjustable-Rate Loans (in billions)

Fixed-rate loans	$3.7	70%
Adjustable-rate loans	1.6	30
	$5.3	100%

EXHIBIT 22.10 Capitol Federal Financing Corporation
Maturity of Deposit Base (in billions)

Demand deposits	$1.4	35%
Certificate of deposits:		
0–6 months	0.8	21
7–12 months	0.7	20
1–3 years	0.9	22
Over 3 years	0.1	2
	$3.9	100%

EXHIBIT 22.11 Capitol Federal Financing Corporation
(in billions)

	Amount	Maturity	Rate
Principal Assets			
Mortgage-backed securities	$2.2	Long-term	Fixed
Loans	5.3	Long-term	Fixed
	$7.5		
Principal Liabilities			
Deposits	$3.9	Short-term	Fixed
FHLB advances	2.4	Short-term	Variable
	$6.3		

and Federal Home Loan Bank advances) are short-term and floating rate. Capitol Federal, like most banks, has a classic asset-liability imbalance (see Exhibit 22.11). If short-term interest rates decline, the bank makes a greater spread on its asset portfolio. The opposite occurs when short-term rates rise.

Since the principal expense in a spread business is the cost of money, projecting short-term interest rates properly is important for a discounted cash flow analysis.

EXHIBIT 22.12   Capitol Federal Financial
Corporation Loss Reserves (in thousands)

	Loans Receivable
Balance, September 30, 2006	$4,433
Provision for losses	(225)
Charge-offs	27
Balance, September 30, 2007	4,181
Provision for losses	2,051
Charge-offs	(441)
Balance, September 30, 2008	$5,791

The research report should test the bank's earnings for interest rate changes and future recessions (or recoveries).

Capitol Federal's bad loan problems barely made a dent in loss reserves over the 2006 to 2008 period (see Exhibit 22.12). The favorable experience reflected a conservative credit culture and a stable Kansas economy. The $5.8 million allowance for loan losses equaled just 0.1 percent of outstanding loans.

As the reader can readily surmise, bank management may be tempted to manipulate the loss reserve account. Accruing a low loss provision (when a higher number is justified) inflates earnings; lending more money to a troubled borrower defers losses; and providing favorable seller financing promotes the sale of foreclosed real estate. All of these sins are committed on a grand scale during financial crises.

Practitioners use a dazzling array of financial ratios to interpret the historical results and management efficiency of a bank. An in-depth review of these ratios is beyond the scope of this book, but selected ratios are listed in Exhibit 22.13. They are segmented by nine categories: liquidity, deposit mix, asset mix, loan mix, asset quality, capital adequacy, profitability, interest analysis, and growth. Such ratios are calculated for a three- to five-year period, compared to similar firms' statistics, and then applied to financial projections. The problems with these historical ratios, as noted, may be evident if a new (or existing) management team installs a new credit culture to the institution. Furthermore, even a five-year look-back may fail to incorporate the impact of a previous recession on these ratios.

LARGE COMMERCIAL BANKS

Money-center commercial banks are more difficult to evaluate than Capitol Federal for several reasons:

- *Asset composition.* The asset composition of a large bank is far more diversified than Capitol Federal, which focuses on the residential loan segment. A bank's loan portfolio includes loans to consumers, small and large businesses, other financial institutions, real estate developers, import/export traders, and others. The importance of credit culture is doubly stressed.

EXHIBIT 22.13 Spread Business Financial Ratios

Liquidity Ratios
Cash and investment securities to total assets
Total borrowings to total deposits

Deposit Mix
Fixed maturity deposits to total deposits
Passbook deposits to total deposits

Asset Mix
Mortgage loans to total assets
Consumer loans to total assets

Asset Quality
Nonaccrual loans to total loans
Allowance for loan losses to total loans
Allowance for loan losses to nonaccrual loans

Loan Mix
Mortgage loans to total loans
Federally guaranteed mortgages and mortgages on one- to four-family dwellings to total loans
Fixed-rate loans to total loans
Floating-rate loans to total loans

Capital Adequacy
Shareholders' equity to total assets
Tangible equity (excluding intangible assets) to total assets

Profitability Ratios
Return on average assets
Return on average equity

$$\text{Efficiency ratio} = \frac{\text{Noninterest expense}}{\text{Net interest income plus fee income}}$$

Interest Analysis
Interest income to total assets
Interest expense to total assets
Net interest margin to total assets

Annual Growth Statistics
Earning per share
Net interest income
Deposits
Mortgage loans

Note: Many banks have diversified into conglomerates where the spread business is just one part of operations, so the significance of these ratios is diminished.

- *Fee income.* A large bank provides more services than Capitol Federal. As a result, its fee income is correspondingly higher as a percentage of revenues.
- *Complexity of business lines.* As a bank grows in size, it offers a variety of products, which sometimes overshadow the basic lending business. Most of the money-center banks are conglomerates, with separate line items for their trading, credit card, trust and wealth advisory, and investment banking businesses. A security analysis requires a review of each product line.

EXHIBIT 22.14 J.P. Morgan Chase & Company Summary Financial Data, Year Ended December 31, 2008 (in billions, except per share)

Income Statement Data		
Interest income	$ 73	
Interest expense	(34)	
Net interest income	39	
Provision for credit losses	(21)	Loan losses tripled in 2008.
Net interest income after credit loss provision	18	Gross spread income was $18 billion.
Noninterest income:		Note the diverse sources of fee income.
Investment banking	6	
Private equity	(11)	Private equity collapsed after years
Loan and deposit fees	5	of gains.
Asset management	14	
Credit card income	7	Most fee income sources were stable.
Other	7	
Total noninterest income, net	28	
Operating expenses	(43)	Compensation was half of operating expense.
Income before income taxes	3	
Income tax benefit	1	
Net income	$ 4	
Earnings per share	$ 0.65	
Balance Sheet Data		
Total assets	$2,175	
Loans	745	Loans are one-third of assets.
Loan-loss reserves	(23)	Securities and trading assets are another third of assets.
Deposits	1,010	
Shareholders' equity	167	Equity is 8 percent of assets.

The bank's return on assets (0.2 percent) and return on equity (2 percent) suffered from the financial crisis, but the balance sheet was stronger than many of its competitors'.

Exhibit 22.14 summarizes financial results for J.P. Morgan, a major New York bank with international reach. The bank organizes its business in seven segments: (1) investment bank, (2) treasury and security services, (3) commercial banking, (4) asset management, (5) retail financial services, (6) credit card services, and (7) private equity. Note the diverse sources of noninterest income as well as the substantial leverage employed.

Bank Stock Valuation Points

A bank's financial statements tell part of the story. The ability of the bank to maintain profitability is dependent not only on its financial strength but also on its management, reputation, credit culture, and transaction processing infrastructure. Banking is a cyclical service industry, and some firms provide services and recruit clients better than others. Valuation comparisons emphasize P/E and price/tangible book multiples. Analysts do not use EBITDA multiples for bank stocks. Loans, the principal assets of most banks, rarely have a market value in excess of historical cost, so the equity market price/tangible book ratio is closely watched by practitioners. Too high a price/tangible book ratio is a danger signal, and even growth-oriented bank stocks rarely break through the 2.0 barrier. Bank mergers are common and professional investors buy stocks on takeover potential.

The huge size and diversified nature of the large banks makes a proper analysis an expensive and time-consuming venture. The loan and securities portfolio values shift with capital market changes, and a September quarterly filing could be outdated by November. The principal and trading function of a large commercial bank is essentially a *black box*, from an outsider's viewpoint, meaning there is seldom enough information to evaluate earnings power and risk for this segment. Banks disclose more information than ever before in their SEC filings, but the complexity of accounting and the latitude in interpretation suggest that large bank stocks will continue to have a higher risk profile than other sectors. Anthony Lembke at hedge fund MKP Capital Management sums up the situation: "In the absence of clarity, investors are going to assume a value that will be conservative and then add a risk premium."[2]

SUMMARY

Due to the specialized nature of their assets and liabilities, spread businesses require valuation techniques using a new vocabulary and a different set of ratios. Nevertheless, the fundamental approach is identical to that for industrial stocks. The historical financial statement analysis of a bank uses the same four tools to discern business behavior and performance. This process facilitates an understanding of the company and provides certain predictive factors. Financial projections incorporate the top-down method reviewed earlier, and valuation conclusions rest on relative value and DCF techniques.

Spread lending means taking money at one rate and lending it out at a higher rate. Lending is a commodity business, and generating a reasonable profit depends on management's ability to sustain a conservative credit culture, exploit the institution's franchise, and keep transaction costs down. Reflecting the liquid nature of most financial assets, leverage is high among these businesses and asset/liability administration becomes an important concern. As a supplement to lending, most firms offer an array of ancillary services that provide fee income. For the larger banks, these service businesses overshadow the basic spread business.

Banking stocks are cyclical investments. Loan growth parallels the economy's performance, and bad loans increase with a weakening economy. In the past few years, the United States and other governments have sunk gigantic sums into protecting the financial industry from its own misdeeds, as one means of forestalling a global depression. These actions mostly benefited creditors, although shareholders gained when a bank failure was averted because their stock price stayed above zero. The revised regulatory mechanism in place is unlikely to prevent another meltdown. With creditors protected by sovereign governments, equity investors will be the industry's disciplinarians.

Insurance Companies

Insurance companies are part of the financial industry, but their main product is different from that of the spread lender. Chapter 23 examines how to evaluate insurance stocks.

In Chapter 22, our survey of financial stocks covered spread lenders—defined as commercial banks. In this chapter we continue with the financial industry by reviewing insurers.

Insurance companies seek to make a profit by providing a risk-taking service. They contract to indemnify their customers against losses arising from a specified contingency or peril that cannot be predicted at the time of the contract. Many companies supplement the risk-taking business by engaging in spread lending and money management.

GENERAL BACKGROUND

In exchange for a designated payment (i.e., a *premium*), the insurance company compensates its customer (i.e., the *policyholder*) for the cost of an expected loss. The event causing the loss, such as a fire, accident, or flood, is well-defined in the policy and its financial severity is large enough for the customer to want to avoid it. Thus, even though the chances of someone's house burning down in any given year are remote, say 1 in 1,000, the financial effects of such an event, possibly $500,000 or more, are so unthinkable for the average homeowner that the annual premium, perhaps $600, seems a small price to pay for the security of being protected against the occurrence.

Insurance companies absorb the risks that others care to avoid. They make money in the process by adhering to three basic principles:

1. *Predictable events.* Insurers try to stick to absorbing risks where the history of occurrence and severity of loss are well-known (e.g., fires, car accidents, mortality). The industry has encountered problems in untested areas such as hazardous materials and product liability.
2. *Law of large numbers.* This mathematical principle states that the greater the number of observations of an event based on chance, the more likely the actual result approximates the expected result. Thus, a company insuring 100,000 houses

against fire is able to predict its losses more accurately on an annual basis than a company insuring 100 houses. Successful insurance firms spread risk among large client bases and, failing this, they reinsure the risk with other insurers.

3. *Investment returns.* Many policies protect against risks for long periods of time. As the premiums are paid in, the insurance company invests the cash, waits for losses to occur, and then waits further to pay them out. The resultant investment income is an important element of an insurer's finances.

Part of the pricing of an insurance policy thus represents an interesting combination of the laws of chance and the time value of money. The remaining components consist of (1) *marketing*—the cost of securing the policy; (2) *underwriting and claims processing*—selecting insured risks, setting rates, and processing claims; and (3) *profit.* These categories are set forth in Exhibit 23.1.

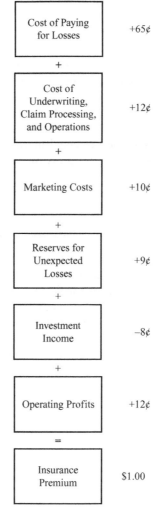

EXHIBIT 23.1   Principal Components of an Insurance Premium
Source: From *Introduction to Risk Management and Insurance* by Mark Dorfman (Upper Saddle River, NJ: Prentice Hall, 2007).

PRINCIPAL FUNCTIONS OF AN INSURANCE COMPANY

Insurance companies fall into two categories: (1) property and casualty (P&C) insurance companies, and (2) life insurance companies. The analysis of these two types is different, but the broad functions of each are reasonably similar (see Exhibit 23.2).

Rate Making

Rate making is determining the price at which an insurance company's policies are sold. Unlike the cost of producing a car, for example, where most of the expense is known prior to its sale, the bulk of an insurance policy's cost is based on educated predictions relating to loss occurrence, investment returns, and inflation. Insurers employ a specialized class of mathematician—an actuary—to (1) study the numerous statistical and financial variables involved in insurance, and (2) produce rates that cover losses, operating costs, and profit requirements.

Sales and Marketing

Insurance is sold principally through independent agents (or brokers) who represent one or more companies selling similar products. Compensation is provided on a commission basis.

Underwriting

An insurance company does not approve all customers who ask for coverage. Rather, it picks and chooses among applicants, looking for those whose *probable* loss experience fits into the actuary's rate-making framework. For example, most auto insurance companies refuse to insure convicted drunk drivers because the presumed risk of loss falls outside of the established parameters. Underwriters are asked to produce a pool of customers (i.e., *insureds*) whose actual loss experience will approximate the estimated losses of a hypothetical group, as outlined by the actuaries. Rates should thus conform to expected customer risks.

Underwriting involves a significant amount of judgment and requires gathering information about the applicant. For example, a workman's compensation policy might require an inspection of the applicant's production plant. A life insurance policy might involve a physical examination of the person to be insured. In instances

EXHIBIT 23.2 Functions of an Insurer

1. Rate making
2. Sales and marketing
3. Underwriting
4. Loss adjustment and claims paying
5. Investment management

Source: From *Essentials of Insurance* by Emmett Vaughan and Therese Vaughan (New York: John Wiley & Sons, 1995).

where the policy is renewable, the company may have the option of cancellation (or raising rates), which might happen if the customer's loss experience has been particularly unfavorable.

Loss Adjustment and Claims Paying

After a loss occurs, the insured notifies his insurance company. In life insurance, the claim is a set amount, agreed upon at the beginning of the policy. In property and casualty, the insurer's obligation is to make the customer *whole* from a financial point of view (i.e., the policyholder isn't supposed to profit from a loss). Investigating the loss, determining if the insurer is liable to pay the claim, and estimating the financial impact is the job of the *loss adjuster*.

In many claims, there is a dispute over the size of the financial loss, while with others there is a dispute over whether the policy actually covers the event. Also, numerous insurance claims are fraudulent. The adjuster tries to resolve these issues.

Investment Management of the Insurer's Own Portfolio

Insurance companies employ full-time professional investment staffs. Since premiums are paid in advance and cash outlays for claims take place years afterward, insurance companies generate cash that is invested to produce a return. The predictability of investment-grade, fixed-income securities is preferred by insurance companies. Property and casualty firms typically select short- to intermediate-term securities, reflecting the time horizon of their liabilities and the cyclical nature of their business. Life insurers are more apt to select intermediate- to long-term bonds. The life insurance companies' liabilities are easy to forecast, and they can thus take advantage of the higher yields available on long maturities.

The same staff also manages the insurer's spread and money management business, since the relevant investment portfolios are similar, in many cases, to the insurer's own positions.

When insurance companies fail, the problems tend to center in the investment portfolio as the aggressive insurer takes extra risks (compared to investment grade bonds) to secure a potentially higher return. In the case of American International Group (AIG), for example, management sought to enhance returns by writing derivative contracts that protected other firms from losses on billions in shaky mortgage portfolios. Creditors received a $140 billion government rescue, but AIG shareholders were wiped out.

INSURANCE COMPANY REGULATION

The principal regulators of insurance companies are state governments, each of which has an insurance department that attempts to regulate firms operating within the state. With the exception of New York and a few other states, the regulators are outgunned by the major insurers, and, like their federal bank regulating brethren, the state regulators function off stale information, with most insurers making detailed regulatory filings just once per year. The independent public accountants and the consulting actuaries (both required for financial statement preparation) are thus important guardians of the public interest in the absence of tough state regulators.

FINANCIAL STATEMENT ANALYSIS: PROPERTY AND CASUALTY COMPANY

Of the industries presented in this book, the property and casualty insurance industry is one of the more complex to analyze. The financial statements contain bewildering arrays of schedules and statistics. Moreover, many of the accounting reports rest on quicksand. So much of a P&C company's results are based on actuarial estimates reflecting uncertain outcomes, that one insurance executive told me, "It's one of the few industries without a true bottom line." The reader now knows, of course, that many corporate financial statements include guesstimates; it's just that the P&C industry relies especially heavily on them.

Exhibit 23.3 provides summary income statement data for the Progressive Corporation, a property and casualty company specializing in nonstandard auto insurance. *Nonstandard* means insurance for high-risk drivers such as those with DWI convictions, multiple speeding tickets, or expensive sports cars. Note how "premiums earned" substitute for revenues in the income statement. Most of Progressive's expenses reflect claims payments and loss adjustment costs.

Income Statement Data

Premiums Earned   This item *does not* equal cash premium payments received during the year. Rather, under the accrual method of accounting, a $1,000 premium paid in advance (for a one-year policy) on June 30, 2008, is only 50 percent earned in 2008. The remaining $500 is earned for accrual purposes in the first six months of 2009.

EXHIBIT 23.3   Progressive Corporation Income Statement Data at December 31, 2008 (in billions)

	2007	2008
Revenues		
Premiums earned	$13.9	$13.6
Investment income	0.7	0.6
Realized loss on securities	0.1	(1.4)
Total revenues	14.7	12.8
Expenses		
Underwriting expenses	10.0	10.0
Losses and loss adjustment expenses	1.4	1.4
Policy acquisition cost (marketing)	1.5	1.5
Other underwriting expenses	—	—
Total underwriting expenses	12.9	12.9
Other expenses	0.1	0.1
Interest expenses	0.1	0.1
Total expenses	13.1	13.1
Income (loss) before income taxes	1.6	(0.3)
Income taxes	(0.5)	(0.1)
Net income	$ 1.1	$(0.2)

Losses on subprime-related securities hurt 2008 results.

At December 31, 2008, the $500 cash asset is offset by a $500 unearned premium liability on the balance sheet.

Investment Income   This item comprises principally interest and dividends on the fixed-income portfolio.

Realized Losses on Securities   Historically, Progressive's securities losses were minimal. The 2008 crisis revealed the firm's overexposure to subprime lenders, a sector in which its losses were extensive.

Losses and Loss Adjustment Expenses   These items reflect the estimated cost of paying and handling (1) known claims plus (2) claims regarding events the company believes have occurred but have not been reported. The estimates are made by experts, but uncertainty is present. As the reader knows, even the cost of a routine traffic accident can take years to unravel, particularly if pain and suffering is alleged. The ultimate matching of loss reserves to actual cash payments becomes more accurate as time passes, and the insurers make reserve adjustments regularly. As a result, current earnings are regularly impacted by prior events.

An aggressive management may be tempted to lowball loss estimates and thereby inflate reported earnings temporarily. If the actuaries don't follow up, there is little the analyst can do in the short term. Over the long term, however, reserve deficiencies become obvious in financial statements and regulatory filings.

Combined Ratio   Insurance company analysts use standard financial ratios and several industry-specific ratios. The most popular P&C ratio is the combined ratio, which measures whether the business actually makes money in its pure insurance business, as divorced from the investment portfolio. When the combined ratio is less than 100 percent, the firm profits from underwriting. A ratio in excess of 100 percent indicates an underwriting loss. Set forth in Exhibit 23.4 is the 2008 calculation for Progressive.

In reviewing a P&C company's income statement, the reader should remember that the P&C business in the United States (where most public firms do all of their business) is mature and reasonably fragmented. Price and distribution are key

EXHIBIT 23.4   Combined Ratio Calculation for the Progressive Corporation Year Ended December 31, 2008 (dollars in billions)

		Losses and loss adjustment expenses		Policy acquisition costs and other underwriting expenses
Combined ratio	=	Premiums earned	+	Premiums earned
Combined ratio	=	$\dfrac{10.0}{13.9}$	+	$\dfrac{2.9}{13.9}$
Combined ratio	=	72%	+	21%
Combined ratio	=	93%		

Note: Progressive's 93 percent combined ratio is relatively low. Many P&C companies have combined ratios of 100 percent or more, with a corresponding higher investment income.

competitive elements. Furthermore, profitability in any given year should be evaluated in the context of the P&C business cycle, which is best described by Vaughan and Vaughan, authors of *Essentials of Risk Management and Insurance* (John Wiley & Sons, 2002):

> *The property and liability industry is highly cyclical, and goes through periods of underwriting profit, followed by periods of losses; the insurance market is characterized as "hard" or "soft," depending on the phase of the cycle. During periods when insurers are earning underwriting profits, the market is said to be "soft," as insurers engage in price cutting to increase their market share. The price cutting includes not only reduction in the absolute level of rates, but the loosening of underwriting standards. This has the natural result of generating losses, resulting in a "hard" market, during which insurers increase prices and tighten underwriting standards.*

Balance Sheet Data

Exhibit 23.5 shows balance sheet data for the Progressive Corporation. Like all P&C companies, Progressive's assets are practically 100 percent financial in nature. Liabilities consist primarily of unearned premiums and loss reserves.

EXHIBIT 23.5 Progressive Corporation Summary Balance Sheet Data at December 31, 2008 (in billions)

Assets	
Investments	
Corporate bonds	$ 9.9
Preferred stocks	1.2
Common stocks	0.7
Money-market investments	1.2
Total investments	13.0
Premiums receivable	2.4
Other assets	1.9
Property and equipment, net	1.0
	$18.3
Liabilities and Shareholders' Equity	
Unearned premiums	$ 4.2
Loss and loss adjustment expense reserves	6.2
Payables and other	1.4
Long-term debt	2.2
Total liabilities	14.0
Shareholders' equity	4.3
	$18.3

Assets are almost 100 percent financial in nature for an insurance company.

Investments Over three-quarters of Progressive's investments resided in investment-grade corporate bonds with maturities under five years. The short maturities minimize interest-rate risk. Over half of equity securities represented fixed-dividend preferred stocks. The portfolio reflects the P&C company's preference for fixed-income investments that can be sold easily if liquidity needs arise. Like a bank, the credit culture of an insurance company is important, and the analyst tests the investment portfolio for interest rate changes and future recessions. In 2008, many of the firm's previously AAA-rated subprime investments faltered, and management sold at a loss.

Unearned Premiums Since Progressive's premiums were paid in advance, inevitably a portion was not earned during the fiscal year. This 2008 item was a contra account for the cash received, but not earned in an accounting sense.

Loss and Loss Adjustment Expense Reserves Loss reserve adequacy is an important consideration in evaluating a P&C stock. Reserve estimates are based on a combination of historical experience, known facts, and interpretation of circumstances. They are thus judgmental in nature and lack the exactness of many accounting entries. It's easy for a company to skimp on reserves because the associated claims usually aren't paid for several years (much like an aggressive lender books risky loans but keeps low loss reserves). Insurers took huge hits after Hurricane Katrina (2005) because they were underreserved.

The independent accounting firm that audits a public P&C company's books, as a matter of course, reviews loss reserve estimates, but an independent actuarial consulting firm conducts the most thorough examination, providing a written opinion on the reserves' sufficiency. This annual opinion is a requirement of state regulators, who, as noted, are the primary governmental overseers of insurance companies. In addition to the actuarial opinions and financial statements, regulators examine supplemental data on P&C reserves and perform occasional field audits. As is the case in the banking industry, insurance regulators operate on stale information that inhibits their effectiveness.

Practitioners can visit the state insurance departments to obtain data not published in SEC reports, and some firms send the data to individuals upon request. Certain reserve information is located in Schedule P of these filings, and several such tables appear in SEC documents. For the beginner, these tables are hard to decipher. Exhibit 23.6 provides a portion of Progressive's consolidated Analysis of Loss and Loss Adjustment Expenses (LAE) development.

Exhibit 23.6 indicates that Progressive has overestimated its need for loss reserves in 2004 and 2005, and then underestimated in 2006 and 2007. To illustrate, in 2004 the company set aside $4.9 billion of loss reserves for policies written in that year. One year later (2005), after examining claim experience, the actuaries concluded that only $4.6 billion of reserves was needed. By 2008, four years later, most of 2004's claims had been settled and the reserve estimate (which included all paid claims) dropped to $4.5 billion, which was 9.6 percent lower than the original estimate. A similar redundancy occurred for 2005, reflecting lower than expected health care inflation, a contributing factor to the cost of automobile accidents. In 2006 and 2007, the amended reserve estimates show mild deficiencies, as losses were more

EXHIBIT 23.6 Progressive Corporation Analysis of Loss and Loss-Adjusted Expense (LAE) Development (in millions)

	For the Year Ended December 31				
	2004	2005	2006	2007	2008
Loss and LAE reserves	$4.9	$5.3	$5.4	$5.7	$5.9
Estimated reserves as of:					
One year later	4.6	5.1	5.4	5.7	
Two years later	4.5	5.1	5.5		
Three years later	4.5	5.1			
Four years later	4.5				
Cumulative redundancy	0.4	0.2	0.1	0.0	
Percentage of original estimated reserves	9.6%	4.1%	(2.0)%	(0.6)%	

This shows how the loss estimates conformed to actual losses. After four year's experience, 2004's original reserve estimate was lowered from $4.9 billion to $4.5 billion, producing a 9.6 percent redundancy. The trend for 2004 to 2008 appears mildly negative, as redundancy fell.

than anticipated. This fact might show a need for tighter underwriting standards or greater cost controls going forward.

FINANCIAL STATEMENT RATIOS

The uncertain nature of insurance liabilities and the conservative bent of state regulators serve to limit the debt incurrence ability of P&C companies. A debt to total capitalization ratio of 30 percent or more is unusual, and most firms have ratios of 20 percent or less. To measure an insurer's growth, profitability, activity, and leverage, practitioners calculate numerous ratios on prior results, evaluate trends, and compare performance to similar firms. Jack Berka and Lee Shepard, valuation experts at Houlihan Lokey Howard and Zukin, provided the key ratios featured in Exhibit 23.7.

LIFE INSURANCE COMPANIES

Unlike P&C contracts, life insurance policies have a fixed payment and mortality schedules change little. As a result, a life company's loss predictions are more accurate than those of a property and casualty company. Problems tend to occur in the investment portfolio or the policy acquisition expense area. Accordingly, a life company analyst pays more attention to investments and policy acquisition expenses than to loss reserves.

Life insurance companies traditionally combined the insurance function with a savings component. Until the 1980s, the industry was dependent on the whole-life policy, whereby a customer's premium payments built up a *cash value* over

EXHIBIT 23.7 Property and Casualty Insurance Companies' Key Financial Ratios

Growth

- Growth in earned premiums
- Growth in total revenues
- Growth in total assets

Profitability and Activity

- *Loss ratio* (including loss adjustment expenses) is loss and loss adjustment expenses divided by premiums earned. (1)
- *Underwriting expenses (including policy acquisition costs) to premiums earned* is a measure of overall operating costs. (2)
- *Combined ratio* (1) + (2) is a measure of underwriting profit before investment income.
- *Investment income to premiums earned* is an indicator of both profitability and capital adequacy.
- *Investment income to average investment* gauges both the performance of the investment portfolio and its risk.
- *Operating income (EBIT) to premiums earned* and *EBIT to total revenues* measure overall profitability on a debt-free basis.
- *Pretax income to premiums earned* and *pretax income to revenues* measure overall profitability after debt service.

Coverage and Capital Adequacy

- *Loss reserves to net worth* is a good measure of the overall level of capital adequacy.
- *Premiums earned to net worth* measures the amount of new business written to capital. If these ratios exceed 2.0, the company is considered to be capital short in terms of new business accepted

Source: Jack Berka and Lee Shepard, "Insurance Underwriting Companies," in James Zukin, ed., *Financial Valuation: Businesses and Business Interests* (Warren, Gorham, and Lamont, 1995).

the policy's duration. The income earned through the cash value buildup was tax-deferred, and made the policy's savings feature attractive relative to competing fixed-income investments. With the growth in money-market, bond, and equity mutual funds, most consumers substituted term-life policies for the whole-life product. This change forced life companies to compete for the investment dollar.

As a result, the modern life insurance company updated its investment business with two more functions: spread lending and money management. Depending on the firm, these businesses are as important as selling insurance. Due to the tax-deferred nature of its products and the oversight of state regulators, the life insurance industry is loath to refer to its spread business as such. Rather, the fixed-income product is called an *annuity* and the customer's deposit is called a *premium*. Nevertheless, annuity providers openly advertise their rates of return, like banks publicize their CD rates, and the companies disclose their respective spreads between (1) the earned rate on investment assets and (2) the promised rate on annuities. In 2008, for example, Protective Life's spread was approximately 0.7 percent, which covered operating expenses, annuity payouts, and loan losses. The money management business wraps stock-market-type products into an insurance policy, allowing the customer to realize equity gains, if any.

EXHIBIT 23.8   Protective Life Corporation Summary Income Statement Data

	Year Ended December 31	
	2007	2008
Income Statement Data		
Revenues		
Insurance premiums	$2.0	$ 2.0
Annuity fees	0.7	0.7
Reinsurance	(1.6)	(1.6)
	1.1	1.1
Net investment income	1.7	1.7
Realized investment losses	—	(0.5)
Other income	0.2	0.2
Total revenues	3.0	2.5
Benefits and expenses		
Insurance policy and annuity payments	1.9	2.0
Other benefits and expenses	0.7	0.6
Income before income taxes	0.4	(0.1)
Income taxes	(0.1)	—
Net income	$0.3	$(0.1)

Protective incurred losses from bonds tied to the subprime crisis in 2008. Other measures were stable.

Given the predictability of mortality losses and the emphasis on spread income, life insurance companies have a tendency to stretch for yield on the asset side of the balance sheet. Thus, in addition to studying the financial statements, the analyst pays attention to the investment portfolio. Most of the holdings are in corporate bonds, so knowledge of the firm's credit culture is helpful. The money management business has risks as well, particularly if stock market risks are poorly hedged. Manulife Inc., a major issuer of equity-linked annuities, increased its loss reserves in that business from $500 million in 2007 to $5 billion in 2008. Like many firms in similar straits, the board of directors took no action to penalize executives responsible for the debacle.

Exhibits 23.8 and 23.9 show financial data for Protective Life Corporation. Note that net investment income represented two-thirds of revenues. Insurance policy and annuity payments represented the bulk of expenses. Reflecting 2008 investment losses, equity was only 2 percent of total liabilities. The statistics resemble a bank more than those of a traditional life insurance company.

SUMMARY

Insurance companies have a peculiar matching problem. They receive premium revenue when a policy is sold, but are unsure of the policy's ultimate cost because the related losses occur in the future. The firm's profit capability is thus subject to more uncertainty than many industrial companies.

EXHIBIT 23.9 Protective Life Corporation Summary
Balance Sheet Data

Balance Sheet Data	At December 31, 2008
Assets	
Corporate bonds	$20.1
Mortgages	3.8
Other investments	2.7
Total investments	26.6
Reinsurance	5.3
Deferred policy acquisition costs	4.2
Other assets	3.5
	$39.6
Liabilities and Equity	
Insurance policies	$18.3
Annuities	16.6
Other liabilities	3.9
Total liabilities	38.8
Equity	0.8
	$39.6

Corporate bonds dominated the investment portfolio. Most
were rated investment grade, but the firm had been badly
burned by such securities in 2008. Derivative exposure was
minimal.

The accuracy of actuarial estimates of loss reserves depends on the type of insurance underwritten. Life insurance expenses, for example, are more easily predicted
than property and casualty claims. A firm's experience in gauging future insurance
losses is disclosed in public filings, but, as the reader knows, the past is only a partial
guide to forward results. The spread business and money-management operations
of the diversified insurers require the same analytical tools used to evaluate a bank's
lending business.

The principal assets of an insurance company are corporate securities, so asset
composition and credit culture are important components of an analysis. Many
insurance companies relied on AAA credit ratings and purchased subprime-related
bonds, which later fell sharply in value with the 2008 financial crisis. The equity
research report on an insurer should test the investment portfolio's value and its
diversification for future recessions and interest rate changes. Similar work should
be done on the firm's annuity contracts, which are closely tied to capital market
performance measures.

CHAPTER 24

Highly Speculative Stocks

Venture capitalists are the typical investors in companies with promising business ideas, but little track record of sales and profits. At times, these risky firms make it to the public market before their plans are fully tested.

Probably everyone reading this book has received a call from a broker touting a can't-miss stock, even though the issuer is an unknown company with no track record. The sales pitch stresses the "unlimited potential" of the offering, which frequently coincides with a new technology, fad, or fashion. Being human, an investor sometimes lets greed and excitement cloud his better judgment, but over the long term it's better not to base decisions on hopes and dreams. Like the other equity categories profiled in this book, the valuation of a highly speculative equity has a structure that lends method to the madness.

In this chapter, we cover the ways by which professionals value speculative stocks:

- *Discounted cash flow.* The analyst uses higher discount rates (25 to 30 percent) and fancier projections to set values for the business.
- *Relative value.* In the present, the comparable speculative firms lack consistent sales, cash flows, or earnings; thus, the application of price multiples rests on a shaky foundation. As a result, relative value techniques rely on forecasts that depict steady performance within five years, at which time the conventional PE and EV/EBITDA multiples apply.
- *Venture capital markups.* If venture capitalists paid $10 per share one year prior to the IPO, a $15 price to the public is a good starting point.
- *Portfolio approach.* Acquire 20 to 30 stocks in a speculative sector to achieve exposure at moderate risk.

BACKGROUND

For the most part, companies with little or no historical track record of sales, cash flow, and earnings are unsuitable for the public market. The expected level of operating risk and price volatility is better handled by sophisticated private investors such as venture capitalists, private equity funds, and large corporations. From time to time, certain sectors of the public marketplace are gripped by an undue optimism, and these speculative enterprises receive a warm welcome. Such was the case with alternative energy stocks, for example, in early 2008.

As the specific industry attracts more investor interest, initial public offerings of participating companies quickly enter the mainstream. No longer do regional firms and boutiques handle the underwritings. Instead, the deals go to the big-name firms such as Credit Suisse and Goldman Sachs, who invariably lend a high degree of credibility to their banking clientele. Furthermore, as valuations increase and transactions grow larger, sophisticated sponsors, such as hedge funds and Fortune 500 companies, lay off the financial risk of some of their more speculative investments by foisting a part of them onto the public—usually at a price substantially in excess of the founders' cost.

For example, in 2007, alternative energy stocks were the rage as oil prices climbed over $100 per barrel and Congress legislated special tax breaks. A small start-up company named BioFuel Energy sold $66 million in stock in its initial public offering, and it was banking on the construction of two ethanol plants. However, corn prices were rising, and ethanol's economics were faltering. At the time of the IPO, the business needed $50 million just to finish its first plant, and the second plant required costly debt financing that jeopardized future profit margins. Nevertheless, J.P. Morgan, Citigroup, and Bear Stearns, three of the Street's largest firms, acted as lead underwriters on the deal. Offering materials featured the prominent ownership positions of Cargill, the savvy billion-dollar conglomerate, and Greenlight Capital, the prominent hedge fund, both of which had bought in earlier at $5 per share. The patina of respectability provided by these two investors attracted institutional and individual interest in the stock, which nonetheless traded down sharply a few months after its IPO.

A hot market is the best time to bring a speculative issue. Inevitably, the successful introduction of numerous quality stocks provides an umbrella shielding low-quality shares from scrutiny. And, as mentioned in Chapter 3, IPOs carry commissions that are five to six times those of regular trades, so brokers have an extra incentive to push even the most dubious merchandise. They are thus reduced to selling the sizzle, not the steak, and they encourage clients to resort to wishful thinking. As the deals involve more esoteric businesses and technologies, the equity salesman is hard pressed to comprehend the issuer's business, and one becomes mindful of the salesman's old adage: "Don't tell me how it works, just give me something to sell!" See Exhibit 24.1.

Inevitably, a certain percentage of these risky investments are highly successful, and the investor makes 50 times his initial commitment. Who doesn't want to get in on the ground floor of a company like Google? But the flip side of most dicey IPOs is a short ride up followed by a long ride down when the dreams go unrealized. Referring to investors in an upcoming offering of an untested business, Wolfgang Demisch, a long-time investment banker, once cautioned: "They're pioneers, but pioneers get arrows in their backs."

Rather than discourage these investments totally, this chapter provides the reader with a rational framework for evaluating them. A businessman's risk can then be the basis for valuation, rather than a hyperbole spun by a smooth-talking salesman.

EXHIBIT 24.1 Elements of Speculative Stocks that Gain Broad Acceptance

- The company has little or no track record of generating revenue consistent with its market value.
- The company is unprofitable, with negative cash flow.
- The company participates in a hot industry receiving lots of media coverage.
- The company issues many press releases, often on minimal accomplishments.
- The company is backed by high-octane investors, such as well-known hedge funds, venture capitalists, or corporations. These investors supposedly know what they are doing, so less sophisticated players piggyback off the earlier decision process. The initial investors, however, do *not* augment their existing ownership by buying more shares at inflated prices.
- The company has research coverage from prominent brokerage firms.

DISCOUNTED CASH FLOW

The DCF valuation for a nascent enterprise starts off with the same top-down procedure employed for a seasoned business. The analyst should understand the company's place in its industry and the economic indicators affecting the industry. The first significant departure in the standard process begins with the forecast. Since the subject business has no established history, the analyst crafts projections by (1) examining management's presentations, (2) considering the early performance of similar growth firms, and (3) making logical inferences. Patrick Murphy, an analyst at Murphy Analytics, summarizes the process:

> *Evaluating early stage firms is far different from looking at IBM and examining historical results. What you really judge is the operating model (from a financial viewpoint) and the market opportunity. Just hitting revenue targets is not enough; you have to study roughly comparable businesses to see how the subject business can make money.*

From this research, a prospective investor cobbles together a future-looking financial model that makes sense, although many assumptions require a leap of faith. In the typical case, the stock provides no cash dividends for the next five years because cash flow from operations is needed to grow the business. At the end of five years, earnings are positive and the stock is presumed to sell at the same P/E multiple as an established growth vehicle, such as 20 times. The equation is as follows:

$$\text{Stock value} = \underset{2010}{\frac{0}{(1+k)^1}} + \underset{2011}{\frac{0}{(1+k)^2}} + \underset{2012}{\frac{0}{(1+k)^3}} + \underset{2013}{\frac{0}{(1+k)^4}} + \underset{2014}{\frac{0}{(1+k)^5}} + \underset{2015}{\frac{\text{P/E} \times \text{EPS}}{(1+k)^5}}$$

where P/E = Growth company P/E forecast for 2015
EPS = Subject company's earnings per share in 2015
k = Estimated discount rate

Setting up the projections is similar to the laborious procedure outlined earlier in this book, but the many guesstimates that the analyst attaches to fundamental items, such as sales, cost of goods sold, advertising, and R&D, lower the already scant threshold of forecast believability. Compensating for the greater doubt of a new business, the analyst increases the discount factor, k, far above the numbers used for seasoned growth companies. If a blue-chip firm requires a 15 percent k, the practitioner uses 30 percent for an untested operation.

To illustrate the means by which professionals place a value on such stocks, in the next section we consider a case study of a speculative investment.

CASE STUDY: BALLARD POWER SYSTEMS

In early 2009, Ballard Power Systems repositioned itself to focus on energy fuel cells, a product line that fit in well with the hot alternative energy sector. The business had modest revenues, and its massive research and development (R&D) expenses (dedicated to new and better products) contributed to sizable losses. Security analysts forecasted two years of additional losses, yet a few months earlier, the company had sold $34 million worth of common stock, placing a $400 million value on a business with significant question marks. After the 2008 crash, the price fell 80 percent, to $1.

How did a rational analyst justify a Ballard stock purchase?

Before proceeding to the DCF analysis, let's review the positive factors that prompted investors to consider Ballard shares.

Key Positive Factors

- *Hot sector.* In 2008 and 2009, Wall Street was infatuated with the alternative energy industry. Oil prices had recently hit $140 per barrel, an all-time high.
- *High technology.* Besides being an alternative energy play, Ballard was a high-tech stock. Advances in battery technology were the linchpin of its operation. Wall Street has an ongoing love affair with high-tech firms.
- *Better mousetrap.* The new battery technology offered customers, principally warehouse operators, the ability to operate forklifts with less downtime. The initial capital cost was higher, but the payback was quick, just two to three years. The customer count was growing, but breakeven was uncertain.
- *Prominent backers.* Invesco, the large mutual fund, was a 10 percent stockholder. Previously, Daimler and Ford had investments with Ballard. Was their success going to rub off on the new shareholders?
- *Prestigious customers.* Companies are known by their associations. Ballard touted Central Grocers and Exide Technologies as customers.

Ballard's stock had attractive aspects, but it involved substantial risk.

Primary Risks

- *Uncertain demand.* Ballard's short history in fuel cells did not provide a sufficient basis for extrapolating a demand curve. The product was a substitute for old-fashioned lead acid batteries, but, as noted, the fuel cell cost more. Furthermore, getting prospective customers to try anything new is a challenge.

- *Gross profit margins*. Until the business ramped up unit volume, gross margin barely covered the cost of production. At higher sales levels, management was unsure of the product pricing, and it predicted a wide range for gross margin (25 percent to 35 percent), which was then reduced by selling, general, and administrative (SG&A) expenses.
- *Research and development costs*. In trying to make a better mousetrap, Ballard spent heavily on R&D, which contributed to its net losses and cash drain. As the product line matured, these expenses were supposed to drop, but Ballard had no guarantee R&D was going to pay off.
- *Competition*. Other, more substantial firms made fuel cells, although Ballard targeted a small, niche market in forklifts and telecom backup power.

Financial Projections

Given this backdrop of positives and negatives, it is helpful to look straightaway at a composite Ballard projection, reflecting the views of sell-side analysts and management. In two reports, they followed the five steps that Chapter 11 outlined:

1. *Potential market*. Assess a demand for the new product.
2. *Subject company's market share*. Determine a likely market share for the business, once its product achieves acceptance. Express share in terms of unit volume and dollars.
3. *Revenue*. Attach revenue estimates to the predicted unit sales.
4. *Income statement*. Prepare income statements by offsetting revenue with sensible expense estimates. Working capital and financing needs are then derived from balance sheet and cash flow forecasts.
5. *EBITDA, EBIT, and earnings per share*. These calculations are part of the projected income statement.

Exhibit 24.2 shows the expected market for fuel cells. The demand for the Ballard fuel cell related directly to its cost savings for the customer. Based on the short track record, the firm had a realistic chance of capturing a portion of its addressable market (i.e., forklift batteries).

Once the market for the new product was established, the next step was fixing a Ballard market share. Unlike many new products, Ballard's fuel cell had only a few competitors in 2009, and they had a moderate emphasis on forklifts and telecom backup power. A 25 percent share of the addressable market seemed reasonable. As Exhibit 24.3 indicates, a growing market, combined with a constant share, made Ballard's revenues $167 million by the year 2012.

With revenue estimates in hand, the analysts applied expense ratios. Cost of sales was mostly variable and mainly represented by materials costs. Cost of sales thus began at 80 percent in 2008, and declined rapidly to 55 percent by 2012 as the customer count increased. R&D, the largest contributor to losses, decreased as the product line developed. SG&A, which included a heavy marketing component for the device, fell as sales rose and product acceptance widened.

As Exhibit 24.3 illustrates, profits were forecast by 2011, and deficits prior to that time were covered by the $83 million of available cash. Continued growth seemed likely after 2012, and research reports assumed that an investor could sell

EXHIBIT 24.2 Projecting Ballard's Fuel Cell Markets (in millions)

	Estimated	Projected			
	2008	2009	2010	2011	2012
Acid batteries and fuel cell market[a]					
Dollar sales ($ millions)	$2,000	$1,860	$1,950	$2,070	$2,240
Unit sales (000)	550	510	515	530	550
Unit growth (percent)	1%	(7)%	1%	3%	3%
Fuel cells as a percentage of battery units[b]	3%	4 %	6%	9%	12%
Fuel cell unit volume (thousands)	15	20	30	45	66
Fuel cell sales ($ millions)[c]	$ 135	$ 190	$ 270	$ 360	$ 470
Ballard market share (percent)	25%	25 %	25%	25%	25%
Fuel cell revenue ($ millions)	$ 34	$ 48	$ 68	$ 90	$ 118
Related service and other revenue	25	30	36	43	49
Total Ballard revenue ($ millions)	$ 59	$ 78	$ 104	$ 133	$ 167

[a]Directed principally at forklift and telecom (backup power) fuel cell market.
[b]Penetration level grows for the better mousetrap.
[c]Assumes declining price for fuel cells with greater production runs.

EXHIBIT 24.3 Ballard Power Systems, Projected Income Statement Data (in millions, except percentages and per share data)

	Actual	Projected			
	2008	2009	2010	2011	2012
Percentages					
Revenue	100%	100%	100%	100%	100%
Cost of sales	(80)	(72)	(64)	(55)	(55)
R&D	(63)	(26)	(15)	(13)	(11)
SG&A	(32)	(24)	(19)	(18)	(17)
D&A	(10)	(8)	(7)	(6)	(6)
Operating margin	(85)	(30)	(5)	8	11
Income Statement Data					
Revenue	$59	$78	$104	$133	$167
Cost of sales	(47)	(56)	(67)	(73)	(92)
Gross margin	12	22	37	60	75
Operating expenses	(63)	(55)	(42)	(48)	(57)
Operating income	(51)	(23)	(5)	11	18
Other, net	(2)	(2)	(1)	—	—
Pretax income	(53)	(25)	(6)	11	18
Income taxes	—	—	—	—	—
Net income	$(53)	$(36)	$(6)	$11	$18
Shares outstanding	85	85	85	85	85
Earnings per share	$(0.62)	$(0.29)	$(0.07)	$0.13	$0.21
EPS growth	—	—	—	—	62%

Note: Observe how sales and margins rapidly increase in the speculative business projection. The result is positive and growing EPS after several years.

his Ballard stock in early 2013 for 13 times EBITDA, or $4.80 per share, as set forth in the following calculation:

Calculating Ballard Share Price in 2013

$28 million EBITDA in 2013

×13

$364 million enterprise value in 2013

+ 46 excess cash

$400 equity value of the company

÷ 85 million shares outstanding

$4.80 price per share

In March 2009, the stock traded at $1.00 per share, so selling it four years later (at $4.80) in 2013 provided a 51 percent internal rate of return (IRR). Alternatively, an analyst could presume a 30 percent annual required rate of return for this speculative opportunity and compute a net present value, which is $1.68 per share according to the next calculation:

$$\text{Ballard share value} = \frac{D_1}{(1+k)} + \frac{D_2}{(1+k)^2} + \frac{D_3}{(1+k)^3} + \frac{D_4 + \text{Sales price}}{(1+k)^4}$$

$$\text{Ballard share value} = \frac{0}{1.30} + \frac{0}{1.69} + \frac{0}{2.20} + \frac{0 + \$4.80}{2.68}$$

$$\text{Ballard share value} = \$1.68$$

where
$$D = \text{Cash dividend}$$
$$k = \text{Ballard's discount rate of 30 percent, reflecting risk}$$
$$\text{Intrinsic value per share} = \$1.68$$
$$\text{Market price per share} = \$1.00$$

Since the $1.68 DCF valuation exceeded the $1.00 price, the stock was a buy in early 2009. To corroborate the recommendation, two analysts supplied comparative valuation multiples for similar growth firms, such as EV/EBITDA and EV/revenues, and compared them to Ballard's theoretical value multiples in 2013 (about 2 times revenues and 13 times EBITDA).

Alternative Assumptions for Ballard Stock

Experienced analysts modify the assumptions on market share, R&D expense, operating margin, terminal multiple, and discount rate to see how net present value behaves under different scenarios. As shown in Exhibit 24.4, a few negative changes produce a share value of $0.79, versus the base-case conclusion of $1.68.

The lack of attention paid to realistic market studies is a key flaw in speculative stock research, resulting in frequent overvaluations. The studies are often unavailable or expensive to obtain, so the analyst relies too much on management's optimistic pronouncements.

EXHIBIT 24.4   Modifying the Ballard DCF Analysis

Assumptions Regarding	Base Case	Downside Case Data
Market share	25%	20%
R&D as percentage of revenue	11%	15%
Terminal multiple	13×	10×
Discount rate	30%	40%
Present value calculation	$1.68	$0.79
Margin of safety	15%	15%
Actual market price	$1.00	$1.00
Recommendation	Buy	Sell

VENTURE CAPITAL MARKUPS AND IPOS

In selling a speculative IPO, brokers trumpet the presence of sophisticated investors in the ownership base. Well-known venture capital firms (and Fortune 500 companies) bring needed credibility to an untested firm. What brokers fail to highlight is what the big-name insiders paid for their shares, versus what the IPO price is. Ninety-nine times out of 100, the insider cost is less than the IPO price. Unless a substantial amount of time has elapsed between the founders' buy-in and the IPO, the analyst should consider the latest insider cost as one guide to valuation.

As Chapter 20 noted, institutions that invest in private placements have substantial advantages in the evaluation process as compared to public market investors. First, they have greater access to management and ask detailed questions. Second, they peruse corporate books and records that are unavailable to the public, including business plans and financial projections. It follows that an institution has a good handle on a firm's prospects when it commits to a private investment. If the deal occurred within 12 months of the IPO and nothing dramatic affected the firm's business in the interim, the institution's price is a jumping-off point for a public valuation.

The venture capital markup procedure covers four elements, none of which is scientifically determined: timing, rate of return, illiquidity discount, and the assumption that venture capital firms are competent. As an illustration, suppose a venture capitalist paid $20 for his Hitech common shares in June 2010 and you're analyzing the company's IPO in June 2011, a year later. Absent a huge change in the business, $43 per share is one reference point for the stock price. The valuation procedure is as follows:

Step 1: Establish Timing
> The venture capital (VC) investment was one year old. The VC firm paid $20 per common share.

Step 2: Consider VC Rate of Return
> Venture capitalists try to achieve a compound annual rate of return of 50 percent. Hitech Corporation met its business plan (otherwise it wouldn't be going public), so the public buyer can permit a 50 percent return to the VC firm. Thus, the fair value over a one-year period jumps from $20 per share to $30 per share.

Step 3: Eliminate Illiquidity Discount

There is value in the ability to sell a common stock in a liquid marketplace. A minority position in a publicly held business thus has more worth than a similar ownership stake in a privately traded firm. A reasonable private market discount is 30 percent off the public value. In the case of Hitech Corp., the $30 per share value inflates to $43 (i.e., $30 divided by 0.7, which is 1 minus the discount), thus providing one guidepost for the initial IPO.

HISTORICAL PERSPECTIVE

The stock market's infatuation with technology is nothing new, but it has mixed results for investors despite the commercial success of many scientific breakthroughs. In the late 1880s, railroad stocks were the rage and financiers furnished millions to crisscross the United States with thousands of miles of track, most of which failed to generate enough traffic to repay their backers. In the 1920s, radio stocks were hot, but the underlying technology didn't provide corporate profits for another 20 years. The early 1980s produced the personal computer craze, and the related IPOs obtained 50 to 100 P/E multiples, yet only a handful survived. Biotech stocks were fashionable in 1991 and 1992, and they raised billions with no history of sales or profits. Few of the stocks exceeded their IPO prices in later years. The Internet craze (1998–2000) created trillions of dollars of paper wealth on a temporary basis. By 2001, reality set in and the technology-laden NASDAQ index fell 75 percent.

The booms were followed by busts, and many share prices collapsed. Inevitably, a handful of the stocks left standing yielded exceptional returns, but the overall impression is that new technology investment demands careful study.

SECURITY ANALYSIS, TECHNOLOGY STOCKS, AND PORTFOLIO

Many high-tech stock promoters say that security analysis is irrelevant, but the fact remains that a substantial number of investors use discounted cash flow and relative value methods to establish pricing benchmarks. The DCF evaluation is identical to the methodology outlined in this book, with carefully constructed projections and very high discount rates, such as 35 percent, to reflect the risk of unproven enterprises. "The challenge for analytically inclined investors," says Andy Klingenstein, a venture capitalist, "is to study the underlying business plans carefully, narrow your focus, and make an educated judgment about future profitability."

Relative value adherents, faced with pricing stocks that have no accounting earnings, resort to the non-earnings-based techniques described in Chapter 17. Jim Powell, vice president of Wells Fargo Investments, voices an opinion shared by many money managers: "We use discounted cash flow and relative value to put a reasonableness factor on these stocks, but pricing is ultimately a question of supply and demand."

One path to moderating risk in a new technology is to acquire 20 to 30 stocks in a given sector. The firm-specific risk is thus diminished, and the investor hopes for a sector return above the market averages.

SUMMARY

Brokers tout the terrific future of speculative stocks, but the underlying companies have trouble generating sales and earnings in the present. These shares are better left to sophisticated investors who specialize in private placements, but from time to time the public market lays out the welcome mat to such offerings. The discounted cash flow method—with all its flaws—is the most appropriate vehicle for valuing a speculative stock. A popular double check to the DCF approach is the VC markup technique. Lacking the financial markers of sales and earnings, speculative businesses are poor candidates for the relative valuation method. Practitioners, nevertheless, gauge fair pricing by comparing current equity value to future sales, EBITDA, and EPS.

CHAPTER 25

Distressed Securities and Turnarounds

Many novice investors wonder why companies with operating losses have positive stock prices. Why do the bonds of some bankrupt companies have substantial value? In this chapter, we answer these questions by exploring turnarounds and bankrupt companies.

A distressed security doesn't always belong to a bankrupt business. For highly leveraged companies, the continuation of operating problems prompts investors to anticipate debt service troubles, causing the bonds to sell off, their prices to decline, and their yields to increase. Thus, the *nondefaulted* bonds of troubled firms can yield 5 to 10 percentage points higher than U.S. Treasury bonds having similar maturities. Depending on seniority, collateral, and other factors, *defaulted* debt may trade from pennies on the dollar to a high percentage of par value. Of course, investors in defaulted debt don't count on being repaid at maturity. They're hoping these fallen angels will be transformed into higher-value securities, once a workout or exchange offer is completed by the debtor.

As the reader can surmise, the distressed bond sector is a subset of the larger junk bond market. A *junk bond* is strictly defined as a bond that is rated lower than *investment-grade*, the category encompassing only the top four rungs of the rating agency ladder. Any bond falling into one of the lower rating levels is referred to as non-investment-grade—a junk bond, in Street jargon. (See Exhibit 25.1.) Despite the derogatory nickname, many issues falling below investment-grade belong to healthy companies, but the bonds have heightened risk when compared to their investment-grade counterparts.

Common shares falling into the distressed category belong to two kinds of firms: bankruptcies and turnaround candidates. A shareholder of a bankrupt firm derives value primarily from his ability to impede progress in the Chapter 11 proceedings. This value is primarily of the legal nuisance variety and has little to do with the firm's economics. For the purposes of this chapter, I will only discuss the shares of companies that fit the second category, namely a turnaround business. A turnaround is an established enterprise that experiences operating problems that *appear* to be temporary. After a year or two of substandard performance, investors anticipate the business will return to normal.

EXHIBIT 25.1 Bond Rating Categories

	Standard & Poor's	Moody's
Investment-grade ratings	AAA	Aaa
	AA	Aa
	A	A
	BBB	Baa
Non-investment-grade ratings ("junk")	BB, B	Ba, B
	CCC, CC, C	Caa, Ca, C
	D	D

Blue-chip money managers avoid defaulted bonds and money-losing stocks, and the business of buying and selling these instruments is relegated to a group of sophisticated hedge funds, banks, and brokerage houses. As such, the distressed securities industry falls outside of the mainstream, but it remains a niche that attracts substantial investor money. The volatility of business and the popularity of leverage guarantee an ongoing supply of problem companies, with a host of legal, operating, and financial complexities. Value discrepancies are inevitable, and the distressed securities investor is assured of an environment where detailed analysis pays off.

INVESTMENT OPPORTUNITIES

The companies falling into the distressed security investor's sights are troubled, weak, or financially crippled enterprises. Since these firms trade at substandard valuation multiples, buyers of this merchandise are sometimes referred to as the ultimate *value investors*. A more derogatory term relates to their search for bargains: *bottom fishers*. A third nickname derives from the search for weakness: *vulture capitalists*. Whatever term is used, this investor category focuses on firms fitting one of two profiles:

1. *High leverage.* The enterprise is profitable *before* interest costs, but incurs losses *after* interest expense is applied. This situation is unsustainable in the long run. Many LBOs face this problem, particularly in economic downturns. See Exhibit 25.2.

EXHIBIT 25.2 Comparing Problem Companies (in millions)

High-Leverage Company		Turnaround Candidate	
Sales	$1,000	Sales	$1,000
EBIT	50	EBIT	(10)
Interest	(75)	Interest	(15)
Pretax income	(25)	Pretax income	(25)
The high-leverage problem company loses money after interest expense.		The turnaround loses money at the operating level.	

2. *Turnaround.* The underlying business is in trouble. At the operating level, it loses money. It needs new managers, new product lines, or new funds. In some cases, the new managers are already there, and investors bet on a reversal of the downward trend. Turnarounds don't fit the distressed category until they're close to defaulting on their debts.

SCREENING TECHNIQUE

Aware of the downside exposure inherent in troubled companies, the distressed security buyer often manages risk by focusing on safe businesses and sensible valuations. Safe businesses are low-tech firms with a prior history of generating income from a stable revenue base. Sensible valuations are sizable discounts to market averages. A common screening technique employs the bottom-up approach for three ratios:

1. *Price to book.* A low price-to-book ratio, such as 1.0 or less, acts as an insurance policy. If the subject business falls apart, the salvage value of its assets should approach book value. Obviously, a P/E screen is irrelevant since *E* is small or nonexistent.
2. *Enterprise value to sales.* A marginal company with a substantial sales base does something right, because customers still buy its products. The investor pins his hopes on the management's ability to restore profitability through cost cutting. A low value-to-sales ratio leverages the chances of a positive return. Thus, Analysts International, an ailing IT services provider, traded at 4 percent of sales in February 2009. Profitable comparables traded at 30 percent of sales.
3. *Enterprise value to EBITDA.* Many firms that show accounting losses have positive cash flow, due to heavy depreciation and amortization charges. If the company's debt appears manageable, a low EV/EBITDA ratio, such as 3× to 4×, provides a safety net for the equity investor. Few public companies trade consistently at ratios below 5×.

By screening carefully, the practitioner narrows the broad field of distressed opportunities to those firms with a business that can survive. He then begins his financial analysis, and keeps his focus on the short to intermediate term. His first concern is "whether the company can generate enough cash to stay afloat, while its operations and finances are being straightened out," according to Earle Martin of NDA Partners, a turnaround investment firm. His second concern relates to time-adjusted rate of return. Will the recovery happen quickly enough to provide an acceptable profit, given the uncertainty of a turnaround? Exhibit 25.3 illustrates the investor's quandary. If he buys Problem Company's shares at $8 and the turnaround occurs in two years, his annual rate of return is a handsome 37 percent. A five-year turnaround time, in contrast, provides a mediocre 13 percent return. No turnaround, of course, means a loss.

In sum, the troubled company evaluation process emphasizes four items:

1. *Sustainable business.* The problem company has a base business that can sustain the vagaries of a turnaround situation.

EXHIBIT 25.3   Turnaround Investing: Evaluating Time-Adjusted Return

Scenario 1: Success in two years!			
	Year		
Problem Company	0	1	2
Earnings per share	$(0.50)	$0.50	$1.00
Dividends per share	—	—	—
Share price	$8	$12	$15

The investor's two-year rate of return is an impressive 37 percent on a compound annual basis. He buys at $8 and sells at $15.

Scenario 2: Mediocrity over five years.					
	Year				
Problem Company	0	1	2	3	5
Earnings per share	$(0.50)	$(0.15)	$0.10	$0.60	$1.00
Dividends per share	—	—	—	—	—
Share price	$8	$9	$10	$12	$15

The investor's five-year annual rate of return is only 13 percent because the turnaround requires more time.

2. *Likely reversal.* Management has the ability to reform the business and return it to normal profitability.
3. *Valuation.* The going-in price is relatively low. The risk of failure is well balanced against the chance for success.
4. *Timing.* The rehabilitation of the business will occur within a time frame that produces a satisfactory risk-adjusted rate of return. Target annual IRRs for the distressed security community are in the 20 to 30 percent range.

RECOGNIZE THE OPTIONS OF AN UNSUCCESSFUL TURNAROUND

Many highly leveraged companies, including LBOs, have issued bonds and stocks in the public markets. In many cases, the prices of these securities decline despite the fact that the underlying business is healthy; it's just the balance sheet that is sickly. Saddled with debts that can never be repaid, the LBO's owners have three options: (1) do nothing and pray for a miraculous recovery; (2) work out a voluntary restructuring plan with the creditors; or (3) play brinkmanship with the creditors and look toward a Chapter 11 filing. Since unpaid creditors lose their patience after a number of months, option 1 has a short duration. Options 2 and 3 extend over months or years; they are dubbed *work-outs* because the creditors and stockholders spend countless hours working out a plan to put the business back on its feet.

EXHIBIT 25.4 Work-Out Company Options

Voluntary Restructuring	Investor Tactics
Restructuring is a fancy word for paying creditors less than 100 cents on the dollar. In the rare case where the company is sold in one piece to a corporate buyer, creditors split the proceeds according to an agreed-upon formula. In most restructurings, the creditors receive a combination of new debt and equity securities in exchange for their old loans. The security package is worth less than the loans' face value. Shareholders resist debt restructurings because the new equity issuance dilutes their ownership by 90 percent or more.	An equity-type investor anticipates a restructuring and buys corporate debts at large discounts to face value. Unhappy creditors who need cash incur a loss. The new creditors form committees to negotiate a restructuring that provides the company with a solid balance sheet and provides the creditors with a controlling equity stake.

Chapter 11 Reorganization	Investor Tactics
Unable to reach a compromise with creditors, the firm files for Chapter 11, which suspends payment obligations and prevents creditors from filing lawsuits or foreclosing on assets. Unless an asset liquidation provides the highest payout on claims, the company and its creditors pursue a reorganization under the auspices of the bankruptcy court. Eventually, the business survives with a new balance sheet. Dominated by lawyers, the Chapter 11 process is time consuming and expensive; creditors and debtors alike try to avoid it.	The investor purchases corporate debts at large discounts to face value. The investor supports a reorganization that provides him with an attractive package of securities, worth more than the original commitment. The investor recognizes that most reorganized companies fail a second time.

Work-outs follow two avenues: voluntary restructuring and Chapter 11 reorganization. Both options are reviewed in Exhibit 25.4.

FINANCIAL ANALYSIS OF A COMPANY WITH LEVERAGE PROBLEMS

Out of many highly indebted opportunities, the investor narrows the field by screening for a low-tech industry and a tangible asset base. He culls the surviving candidates by concentrating on *cash flow, timing,* and *continuing operations*. The analytical emphasis takes on different elements, depending on whether the business is a restructuring candidate or a Chapter 11 bankruptcy. See Exhibit 25.5.

After his initial screen, the distressed security analyst determines *normalized* operating results for a leveraged target in an interesting fashion. Most security analysts start with a *bottom-line* analysis and look at net income and EBIT trends, but the bargain hunter does his analysis backward. He looks at *top-line* results first—that is, sales. Over the expected sales data, he superimposes the income statement template

EXHIBIT 25.5 Financial Analysis of a Troubled Leveraged Business

Critical Issues	Voluntary Restructuring	Chapter 11
Cash flow	Does the target have sufficient cash to keep creditors at bay until a restructuring is concluded? The investor carefully prepares quarter-to-quarter cash flow forecasts.	Does the target need to borrow more money from court-approved debtor-in-possession (DIP) lenders to maintain operations? DIP lenders receive priority claims at a 100 percent repayment rate, thus reducing reorganization values.
Timing	What is the investor's expected holding period? Restructuring results are uncertain. A long holding period or an unforeseen Chapter 11 filing reduces the investors' rate of return. Poststructuring, how much time is needed for the business to recover fully? The investor's experience in similar situations provides a guide.	When will the target emerge from bankruptcy? Can the investor's intervention accelerate the process? A long holding period reduces the investor's rate of return. Postreorganization, how much time is needed for the business to recover fully?
Continuing operations	What are the company's normalized operating results? Can it succeed with its new balance sheet, after losing customers, goodwill, and employees?	Same.

of a successful firm in the candidate's industry. The investor reasons as follows: If my subject company wasn't burdened with leverage problems, it might perform as well as the next company. For example, in considering the normalized results of a processed foods manufacturer in bankruptcy, the practitioner might construct the template in Exhibit 25.6 and conclude that the firm's normalized margin is in the 7 percent range.

EXHIBIT 25.6 The Analyst Normalizes the Operating Results of a Bankrupt Processed Foods Company

	Annual 2009 Sales ($ millions)	Operating Margin
Bankrupt company—actual	$ 800	3%
Other Processed Foods Companies		
B&G Foods	$ 490	9%
Flowers Foods	2,040	7
J&J Snack Foods	630	7
Lance Foods	820	5
Average		7%
Analyst Estimates		
Bankrupt company—normalized	$ 800	7%

The normalized operating margin represents a combination of healthy firm margins.

EXHIBIT 25.7 The Investor Normalizes the Operating Results of the Bankrupt Processed Foods Company (in millions)

	Year				
	Actual	Projected			
	0	1	2	3	4
Sales (from Exhibit 25.6)	$800	$880	$933	$990	$1,049
Operating income	$ 24	$ 35	$ 47	$ 59	$ 73
Operating margin	3%	4%	5%	6%	7%

Returning to industry profit margins triples operating income in four years.

With his projected margins in hand, the investor forecasts the firm's operating income going forward, using sensible sales estimates. In this example, I assume sales jump 10 percent in the first year out of bankruptcy. Sales growth then declines to a constant annual rate of 6 percent. Operating margins rebound to 4 percent in year 1, increasing to 7 percent by year 4. See Exhibit 25.7.

Note how the investment candidate's projected operating income leaps from $24 million in year 0 to $73 million in year 4. This is the ideal situation for the bottom fisher because there is a potential large value increase, with minimal perceived downside.

The bargain hunter next determines the present value of the business on a debt-free basis. The first step is estimating the enterprise value in three to five years, using the techniques described earlier in this book. This future value is discounted to the present at the estimated cost of capital, including both debt and equity cost components. In order to determine this capital cost, the analyst makes assumptions on what the reorganization plan will look like. How much will each class of creditor receive on its claims? How much debt and how much equity will be outstanding after the plan's implementation? Constructing good answers to these questions goes to the heart of the analysis.

Although every distressed situation is unique, the reorganization plan is designed to reduce existing debts to an amount that the borrower can reasonably service in the future. Once the composition of the new debt securities is determined, the remaining enterprise value is allocated to newly issued common shares. Both the debt securities and common shares are distributed to creditors on the basis of complicated formulas, which are the product of long and trying negotiations. The former shareholders end up with little in this process, as the new majority owners are the former creditors who received the most shares in the distribution.

For our hypothetical food company, a reasonable enterprise value in year 4 is $600 million (i.e., 8 times EBIT). Using a 50/50 capital structure of debt and equity, the reorganized food company's pretax capital cost is 20 percent annually (assuming debt costs 10 percent and equity costs 30 percent). Given the uncertainties associated with projections in troubled investments, this high capital cost is justifiable. Discounting the firm's $600 million future value at 20 percent over four years results in an initial *plan capitalization* value of $290 million. See Exhibit 25.8. The investor thus has a reasonable framework to assist in the investment decision.

EXHIBIT 25.8 Cost of Capital Calculation for Bankrupt Processed Foods Company

Capitalization	After Plan Implementation	Pretax Cost of Capital	Rationale
Debt	$145	10%	Equivalent to junk bond yields.
Equity	145	30	Equity investor target return.
Total	$290	20%	

As one illustration, Motor Coach Industries, a bankrupt bus maker, confirmed its reorganization plan in 2009; the company discharged $760 million of claims for $460 million of cash stock and notes, or 60 cents on the dollar. The new debt to equity ratio was 58:42, rather than 80:20.

THE INVESTMENT DECISION

Distressed security investors participate in an active secondary market for troubled company claims. Buyers and sellers trade all sorts of obligations, ranging from secured loans to trade payables to subordinated debt. The participants set prices for those instruments based on their respective views of time-adjusted returns. In February 2009, for example, the bonds of Rite Aid traded at 48 percent of face value; Freescale Semiconductor bonds traded at 22 percent of face value. The related equity securities traded for pennies.

In our example, the bankrupt Processed Foods Company has $700 million of claims outstanding. For the sake of argument, assume that each claim has the same priority in reorganization. According to our $290 million valuation model in Exhibit 25.8, the claims should trade at an average 41 percent of face value (see Exhibit 25.9), or $290 divided by $700.

This example is simplistic. In reality, bankrupt companies have a bewildering variety of claims, most of which belong to a specific creditor class. Each creditor class has a priority designation. Those with the highest priorities, such as IRS liens and secured loans, receive the higher percentage payouts in the reorganization.

In 2008, Franklin Mutual Advisors, a distressed bond fund, bought Motor Coach debt at a steep discount from par. After the 2009 reorganization, the fund received a large equity stake in exchange for a portion of its debt.

EXHIBIT 25.9 Distressed Company Financial Analysis: Simple Pricing Calculation for Bankrupt Processed Foods Company (in millions)

Claims outstanding (1)	$700
Estimated enterprise value (2)	$290
Average claim trading value (1) ÷ (2)	41%

EVALUATING TURNAROUNDS

A turnaround is not an immediate bankruptcy candidate, but it has operating problems that cause it to lose money. Leverage is a secondary factor. The operating problems stem either from economic conditions beyond the control of management or from difficulties inside the firm. Principal causes for operating losses include:

- Management ineptitude.
- Economical cyclicality.
- Failure to foresee technology, fashion, or competitive challenges.
- Poor cost controls.
- Growing sales without adequate capital.
- Unsound acquisitions.
- Lawsuits.

Companies suffering from these deficiencies survive for years. Cash shortfalls are made up through borrowings and asset sales, deferring the day of reckoning.

If the cause of the failure is external to the firm, a new approach is unlikely to reverse the situation. If the reason is found within the business, the problem is usually with the management. A new team of executives can theoretically replace old practices, find new capital, and kick-start the recovery. Assuming the underlying business is not the next buggy whip manufacturer, a firm heading for oblivion can thus be "turned around" into a successful company.

Along with new management, many turnaround stories come with a prominent brand name. If the consumers still accept the brand's goodwill, that's one item that the new management doesn't have to rehabilitate. Ten years ago, Burger King, for example, was floundering behind McDonald's, losing market share and facing lower margins. A new management team narrowed the customer focus, introduced new products, and placated franchisees. Within three years, the firm completed a successful IPO.

The next few pages cover two turnaround situations.

Case Study: Starbucks Corporation

In early 2009, Starbucks was a beleaguered business. From its high of $40 in 2006, the stock had slid to $10. An aggressive store-opening plan resulted in underperforming stores, and a menu expansion diverted the chain's coffee emphasis. Competition from McDonald's and Dunkin' Donuts turned up the heat. To stem the downturn, Starbucks rehired its former CEO, Howard Schultz, who had run the business in its glory days, from 1987 to 2000. His strategy to reform the chain included (1) cutting back on new U.S. locations while closing some stores there; (2) accelerating store openings in fast-growing overseas markets, like China; (3) lowering prices during the recession; (4) focusing on the Starbucks coffee "experience" and downplaying food items; and (5) reducing costs through employee layoffs. Summary information appears in Exhibit 25.10.

EXHIBIT 25.10 Turnaround Candidate Starbucks Corporation: Summary of Financial and Market Data (in millions except per share data and ratios)

	Year Ended September 30				
Income Statement	2006	2007	2008	2009(E)	2010(P)
Revenues ($ billions)	$7.8	$9.4	$10.4	$9.8	$10.1
EBIT ($ millions)	893	945	504	830	1,030
Net income ($ millions)	580	672	316	500	620
EPS	0.76	0.90	0.43	0.68	0.84
Trend	Up	Up	Down	Up	Up

Comments: Starbuck's upward results reversed in 2008.

Balance Sheet ($ billions)	At December 31, 2008	
Total assets	$5.5	*Comments:* Leverage
Total debt	0.9	was low, so the business
Stockholders' equity	2.6	had flexibility to make changes.

Stock Market Data	At February 13, 2009	
Share price	$10	*Comments:* By pricing
Trailing 12 months EPS (Dec. 2007 to Dec. 2008)	0.26	the stock on forward earnings (2009), an
P/E multiple (trailing 12 months EPS)	38.5×	investor could justify the
P/E multiple (2009 EPS)	12.5×	high P/E (38.5×) on
Price/book value	3.0×	trailing 12 months'
Enterprise value/revenues	0.7×	earnings.
Enterprise value/EBITDA	7.1×	
Dividend yield	None	

Case Study: Analysts International Corporation

Analysts International Corporation provides information technology (IT) consulting services, with prominent Fortune 500 firms, such as IBM, as clients. For a number of years, the company faced modest margins and uneven sales. In 2006 new executives arrived and started to clean house, reducing staff, selling off noncore divisions, and ending certain prestigious (but unprofitable) customer relationships. The downsizing required two years and sales fell 20 percent. By early 2009, investors saw light at the end of the tunnel, as profitable operations seemed likely. See Exhibit 25.11.

LIQUIDATIONS

In the rare case, a publicly held company is a liquidation candidate. It has poor prospects as an operating business and shows a loss history. Investors appraise the business not as a going concern, but rather as a collection of assets better off in the hands of others.

EXHIBIT 25.11 Turnaround Candidate Analysts International Corporation: Summary of Financial and Market Data (in millions, except per share data and ratios)

Income Statement	2006	2007	2008	2009	2010
Revenues	$347	$360	$284	$260	$270
EBIT	—	(1)	9	10	12
One-time charges	—	(13)	(10)	—	—
Net income	(1)	(16)	—	7	8
EPS	(0.04)	(0.65)	(0.03)	0.26	0.31
Trend	Down	Down	Mixed	Up	Up

Comments: After a string of increasing losses and declining sales, the firm projected a reversal in 2009. Analysts anticipated near-normal margins by 2010, providing a $2 share price.

Balance Sheet	At December 31, 2008	
Cash	$2.3	*Comments*: Analysts
Total assets	54.3	International had little
Total debt	—	debt, enabling
Stockholders' equity	30.4	management to make
		necessary changes.

Market Data	At March 16, 2009	
Share price	$0.43	*Comments*: At $0.43,
P/E multiple	N.M.	the stock traded at just
Price/book value	0.4	3 percent of revenues
EV/EBITDA (2008)	4.6	and 40 percent of
Dividend yield	None	book value. Downside
		risk appeared minimal.

In performing a liquidation analysis, the practitioner examines the worth of each asset category in a quick sell-off, aggregates these values, and subtracts from this sum the cost of closing the business and paying off its liabilities. If this calculation provides a positive number, such as $10 per share, the would-be investor has established his ceiling price. From this $10, he then subtracts his time-adjusted rate of return.

Few struggling businesses have substantial intangible assets such as respected brand names, exclusive patents, or quasi-monopoly rights. As a result, the analyst's back-of-the-envelope evaluation focuses on balance sheet data. For each item, the analyst determines a range of *liquidated value* percentages, which are based on experiences from similar businesses. Consider the hypothetical case of Siegel Corporation, a troubled manufacturer of construction materials, as presented in Exhibit 25.12.

The reader will note that Siegel's $50 million liquidation value is a fraction of the $170 million stockholders' equity. This significant discount to book value is characteristic of most liquidation analyses and it emphasizes an important point: Firms realize a better stock price when they are viewed as going concerns, whereby their values are based on future earnings power rather than on tangible asset compositions. To prove this assertion, one need only look at the March 2009 pricing for the Dow Jones Industrials, which were then trading at 2 times historical book value.

EXHIBIT 25.12 Siegel Corporation Summary Liquidation Analysis (in millions, except per share data)

Assets	Historical Book Value	Estimated Liquidation Percentages	Estimated Liquidation Values
Cash	$10	100%	$10
Accounts receivable	40	70	28
Inventory	40	50	20
	90		58
Plant and equipment	100	40	40
Goodwill	20	0	0
	$210		$98

Liabilities and Stockholders' Equity			
Short-term debt	$15	100	$(15)
Other current liabilities	25	100	(25)
	40		(40)
Stockholders' equity	170	Costs of shutdown	(8)
	$210	Net outflows	$(48)
		Net liquidation value (98 − 48 = 50)	$50
		Shares outstanding	÷5
		Value per share	$10

Unless the practitioner works for a firm that can take over Siegel Corp., there is no way for him to unlock the liquidation value. Thus, his rate of return requirement must reflect not only the uncertainty of his estimates but also (1) Siegel's burn rate, and (2) the likelihood of its acquisition by someone interested in unlocking those values. Assuming a 40 percent IRR requirement and a two-year holding period, the $10 liquidation value translates into a $5 investment price (i.e., $[\$10/1.40]^2$ equals $5.10).

SUMMARY

A large number of practitioners research the securities of troubled companies, believing such investments don't attract the interest of the broad market. Their investment rationale suggests that problem situations provide above-average returns, assuming the relevant opportunity is thoroughly investigated.

Analyzing the troubled business is more rigorous than the conventional evaluation. Typically, the subject firm has severe operating, financial, and legal problems that prove difficult to interpret properly. The uncertainty surrounding a turnaround is therefore balanced by a high expected return.

The risk of a turnaround and the intensity of the research combine to make troubled company investment an area best left to full-time professionals.

CHAPTER 26

International Stocks

In an attempt to reduce risk and boost returns, U.S. portfolio managers buy more foreign stocks. This trend corresponds to the increasing globalization of the economy and the growing internationalization of security analysis. American companies and private equity firms are also investing more resources abroad, and they devote more resources to international business analysis. This chapter reviews the evaluation of foreign companies and foreign stocks.

Investing in international stocks is popular, and foreign securities are accessible to American buyers. This situation mirrors the increasing globalization of the economy and reflects U.S. portfolio managers' desire to diversify a portion of their holdings out of the domestic market and out of the U.S. dollar. Besides the obvious diversification benefits, there is the perception that many foreign securities are not as efficiently priced as their U.S. counterparts. Business traditions (such as Japanese funds being passive stockholders, even in the face of managerial incompetence), regulatory barriers (such as Mexico forbidding insurers to invest in equities), and infrastructure conditions (such as few local personnel with CFA-style financial training) contribute to this view. The presumed inefficiencies leave opportunities for U.S.-schooled analysts who are willing to perform the extra work required of an international evaluation. Lastly, many foreign economies, particularly in poor developing countries known as *emerging markets*, expand faster than the United States. The implication is that rising GDP *top lines* translate into larger corporate *bottom lines*. Since earnings growth is the main engine behind higher stock prices, U.S. investors look overseas.

THE ROLE OF SECURITY ANALYSIS

As U.S. investors go abroad, the demand for international security analysis increases, and institutions employ professionals to focus full-time on foreign stocks. These individuals apply the techniques of top-down review, discounted cash flow, and relative value to the international marketplace. Unfortunately, U.S.-style business valuation, like fine wine, does not always travel well, and the results of this technology transfer are mixed.

Problems with the Standard Approach

As the reader knows, the security analysis process is heavily reliant on informed decisions. Not only must the data for a top-down study be available and reliable, but the prices of comparable securities must be based on open and honest trading. Such standards are usually met in the United States, assuming the analyst makes a determined effort, but achieving the desired result in most foreign markets is problematic. Only the UK and Canadian stock markets approach domestic levels of full disclosure and transparent trading. The remainder have various degrees of shortcomings, including the following:

- *Less information.* Foreign regulators require less corporate disclosure than their U.S. counterparts. The information that is submitted by issuers faces little official scrutiny. Depending on the country, the availability and accuracy of macroeconomic, capital market, and industry data are also suspect. Moreover, much of the source material is not translated into English. For the security analyst, less information means more guesswork.
- *Lack of fair and honest trading.* Insider trading remains a problem on the fringes of the U.S. market, but it is widespread on foreign exchanges. In most countries, insider trading is not illegal. Even those nations that have prohibitions rarely enforce them. Front-running and poor execution by brokerages is an ongoing concern for institutions.
- *Inconsistent accounting standards.* Relative value analysis requires consistent accounting methods, yet foreign firms enjoy more liberal rule interpretations than U.S. public companies. Indeed, the International Financial Reporting Standards (IFRS) are principle-based, versus the U.S. rule-based generally accepted accounting principles (GAAP), leaving foreign managers with more flexibility. The inconsistent application within a country (and across countries) diminishes the worth of financial statement analysis.
- *Fewer comparables.* The U.S. market is so large that almost every public company has a few comparables. As one proceeds to smaller economies, the number of comparables decreases rapidly. Practitioners compensate for this shortage by comparing similar companies across national boundaries. Given the differing country environments and accounting systems, the weakness of this approach is readily apparent.
- *Reduced emphasis on share price enhancement.* Outside of the United States, Canada, and England, corporate managements are under minimal pressure to boost their share prices. Proxy fights are rare and corporate shareholdings are dominated by founding families or associated banks, which hold the long view on value creation. It is not uncommon for U.S. investors to become frustrated with management's lack of interest in promoting the share price.
- *Liquidity concerns.* Outside of the United States and a few other rich countries, most listed stocks have small floats. Even if the analyst sees a bargain, his employer/client will have difficulty profiting from his recommendation, because anything more than a token buying effort sharply boosts the stock price (or lowers it in a short sale).

EXHIBIT 26.1   FX Movements Turn a French-Based Euro Gain into a US$ Breakeven

Date	Action
January 1, 2010	1. Exchange US$20 million into 15 million euros (1:0.75).
	2. Buy 1 million French shares at 15 euros per share.
January 1, 2011	3. French shares rise to 16.50 euros per share, a 10 percent gain.
	4. Sell 1 million French shares, realizing 16.5 million euros.
	5. Exchange 16.5 million euros into US$20 million at new 1:0.83 exchange rate.
	6. Bottom line: Invest US$20 million on January 1, 2010 and receive US$20 million on January 1, 2011. No US$ income on 10 percent French price gain.

Currency Movements

Overriding all these stock picking concerns is the possibility of an adverse currency movement. U.S. investors determine their ultimate returns in U.S. dollars, though the earnings propping up a given foreign stock price are denominated, for most issuers, in a different currency. If the U.S. dollar gains in value relative to the currency—perhaps independently of the foreign company's situation—the U.S. investor can lose money even if his stock selection advances in local terms.

For example, suppose a U.S. investor bought one million shares of a French company for 15 million euros (i.e., 15 euros per share), or a total of US$20 million. One year later, the stock price rises to 16.50 euros per share, a 10 percent gain. Before converting this result into U.S. dollars, the investor is proud of his stock-picking abilities. Unfortunately, over the same period, the US$/euro exchange rate shifts from 1:0.75 to 1:0.83. On a US$ basis, the investor's profit is nil, as the declining euro wipes out the share price increase. Exhibit 26.1 illustrates the investor's dilemma.

On the flip side, if the euro *appreciates* against the U.S. dollar as the stock price increases, the U.S. investor achieves a *double dip*. Not only are his stock-picking skills rewarded, but his net returns (in US$) are boosted due to the favorable foreign exchange (FX) movement.

In a few foreign markets, U.S. investors eliminate the impact of unforeseen currency movements by buying insurance, which is available in the form of foreign exchange futures contracts. Such insurance is not cheap and its practical use is limited to a handful of the most developed economies.

AMERICAN DEPOSITARY RECEIPTS

To facilitate the foreign investment process, U.S. stock exchanges promote the use of American Depositary Receipts (ADRs). An ADR is nothing more than a legal certificate establishing the investor's ownership in a stated number of foreign shares, which are held *on deposit* in the vault of a respectable bank. Because they are denominated in dollars and trade within U.S. borders, the unfamiliar currency, legal, tax, and regulatory complications of trading *in country* are avoided with ADRs.

DEVELOPED COUNTRY MARKETS

Foreign stock markets fall into two categories: developed country and emerging market. The rest of this chapter considers developed country stocks; Chapter 27 covers emerging markets.

Developed countries are those nations that approach the United States in terms of wealth and economic development. Prominent examples include Japan, Germany, England, France, and Italy. Smaller developed nations include Denmark, Switzerland, and Sweden. These countries have stable economies with favorable prospects. Their capital markets are sophisticated and trading is reasonably aboveboard. A strong currency and moderate inflationary outlook allow the issuance of long-term, fixed-rate corporate bonds, which serve as a reference for equity market returns. In such markets, the analytical tools of discounted cash flow and relative value are highly relevant to the stock pricing function.

Hundreds of developed country stocks trade in the United States as ADRs. Well-known examples include:

- Accor (France), an international hotel chain.
- BHP (Australia), a global mining company.
- British Airways (UK), a top international airline.
- Ericsson (Sweden), a large telecom equipment manufacturer.
- NTT (Japan), a Japanese telephone company.
- Nestlé (Switzerland), an international consumer products company.

Security Analysis Approach—Developed Country

The evaluation of a developed country ADR is similar to the methodology employed for a U.S. equity. Financial reports are in English, corporate executives speak English, and the company responds to investor inquiries. A U.S.-based analyst can thus obtain the framework for a DCF projection. To assist the relative value estimation, databases provide comparable publicly traded firms and acquisitions, which, due to the small size of the home market, usually cross national borders. As a result, the DCF and relative value approaches quickly gain substance. The main problem for the U.S.-based ADR investor is gaining local knowledge on the economy, capital market, and industry. This information is tough to interpret off a computer screen. For this reason, large institutions employ analysts around the world, rather than just in the United States.

In terms of operations, the ADR multinationals resemble giant U.S. firms. They ship products and services to dozens of countries, and they have a majority of revenue in stable currencies such as the dollar, euro, or yen. Assuming that accounting differences are normalized, practitioners are comfortable in applying U.S.-type discount rates and valuation multiples across sovereign boundaries. Thus, Roche Holdings, the Swiss drug giant, is frequently compared to U.S. pharmaceuticals, such as Merck and Eli Lilly. As the issuers get smaller and more localized in operation, practitioners take a country-specific approach to relative value. Thus, a media analyst is likely to contrast Associated Newspapers (UK) to United Newspapers (UK), rather than including a U.S. firm like A. H. Belo in the comparison.

EXHIBIT 26.2 Rate of Return Calculation, Honda Motor ADRs, April 2009

Step 1: Determine US$ Cash Flows

| | For Year Ending March 31 | | | | |
| | Actual | Projected | | | |
Honda Results	2008	2009	2010	2011	2012
Earnings per share (yen)	Y330	Y102	Y47	Y170	Y260
Dividends per share (yen)	70	25	10	40	65
Yen/US$ exchange rate	—	98:1	97:1	96:1	95:1
US$ Cash Flows					
Dividends	—	$0.26	$0.10	$0.42	$ 0.68
Sale price	—	—	—	—	43.80
US$ cash flows	—	$0.26	$0.10	$0.42	$44.48
Discounted at 13 percent[a]	—	$0.23	$0.08	$0.29	$27.28

Terminal value calculation[b]
Sale price = (EPS × 2012 P/E multiple) ÷ exchange rate
Sale price = (Y260 × 16) ÷ 95
Sale price = US$43.80

Step 2: Compare Present Value to Current Market Price

A. Present value of ADR = $0.23 + $0.08 + $0.29 + $27.28
       = US$27.88

B. Market price of ADR = US$25.90

Conclusion
The present value of Honda Motor ADRs is 8 percent higher than the market price. The difference falls within the 15 percent margin of safety, so no action is taken.

One ADR represents one Honda share.
[a]The discount rate reflects Honda's beta (versus the Tokyo stock index) and U.S. indexes.
[b]The terminal P/E corresponds to a long-term average.

For large and small stocks, the U.S. institution completes projections in the issuer's local currency. It then translates the dividend flow and terminal value into U.S. dollars at the forecast exchange rate. The resulting net present value (NPV) shows the institution's estimated return in U.S. dollars, which remains its base performance metric. An example for Honda Motor appears as Exhibit 26.2.

Discount Rates—Developed Country

As Chapter 14 described, one way for determining the discount rate for the present value of a U.S. stock is the capital asset pricing model (CAPM), whereby:

$$k_{U.S.} = R_F + \beta(R_M - R_F)$$

where $k_{U.S.}$ = Expected rate of return on U.S. stock
R_F = U.S. Treasury 10-year bond rate
β = Beta of the stock
R_M = U.S. government bond rate plus a 6 to 8 percent equity market return premium

Applying the formula to a foreign stock creates some problems. First, many foreign stocks lack a meaningful β against U.S. indexes because they have a short or illiquid trading history. Second, data services sometimes calculate a β for a foreign stock's behavior in its local market, but this number has limited utility for U.S. investors. Third, practitioners are unsure on whether (1) to use the local government bond rate and the local market return in the equation, or (2) to continue with the U.S.-derived variables and then add a foreign risk premium. Fourth, if the analyst wishes to work with a foreign risk premium, how large should the premium be?

One view is to calculate the foreign stock's k entirely with local variables. R_F is the local government bond rate, R_M is the expected return on the local market, and β is measured against the local index. The resultant present value of the stock's predicted cash flow is denominated in a foreign currency, which is then translated into U.S. dollars at the current exchange rate. This technique has some theoretical strengths, but it doesn't have wide application. A more popular approach is an equity buildup return (see Chapter 14) that incorporates a foreign risk premium.

Given two similar firms separated by national boundaries—a U.S. and a German company, for example—the discount rate on the German stock is higher for the U.S. investor. The reduced information access, the less transparent trading environment, and the potential adverse currency movement combine to make the foreign security a riskier choice. Quantifying this extra risk into a single number is a subjective exercise, and people do it differently. A starting point for most practitioners is the difference between the 10-year U.S. Treasury yield and Germany's sovereign US$ denominated bond rate. Thus, if this spread is 0.5 percent between the United States and Germany, the foreign risk premium (FRP) has a floor of 0.5 percent. Exhibit 26.3 shows an example for In Bev, a Belgium brewer that bought Budweiser for $52 billion in 2008.

EXHIBIT 26.3 Belgium Brewing Company: US$ Discount Rate for US$ Cash Flow Projection, April 2009

Risk-free rate (10-year U.S. Treasury bond yield)	4.00%
U.S. equity risk premium (premium for investing in broad based index)	7.10
Belgium country risk premium (sovereign US$ yield minus U.S. Treasury bond yield)	0.90
Industry premium (Brewing industry is recession-resistant.)	(1.50)
Size premium (In Bev is a large-cap firm.)	0.00
Individual company premium (In Bev has substantial U.S. presence through Budweiser, but substantial acquisition debt.)	0.75
	11.25%

The industry, size, and individual company premium reflect analyst's estimates, based in part on historical data from U.S. and European capital markets.

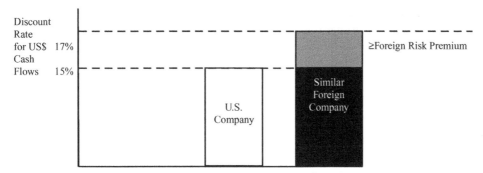

EXHIBIT 26.4 Higher US$ Discount Rates for Foreign Companies Based in Wealthy Developed Countries

The analyst's assessment of the information, trading, and family control issues may add additional premiums to the discount rate. For most developed country stocks, the FRP has a 1 to 3 percent range. See Exhibit 26.4.

RELATIVE VALUE MULTIPLES

As noted earlier, the preponderance of business valuation relies on the relative value approach. It is reasonable to compare foreign-based multinationals with their U.S. counterparts. Indeed, many prominent U.S. companies have large overseas exposure. Coca-Cola, for example, derives three-quarters of its revenue from outside the United States. Exhibit 26.5 compares the key multiples for top international brewing companies.

As noted in Chapter 15, the objective of preparing charts such as Exhibit 26.5 is to identify discrepancies in relative value. If Asahi, Fosters, and In Bev have similar businesses, historical results, and future prospects, then their respective shares should have similar valuation multiples. A lower-than-average multiple indicates a bargain, whereas a high multiple means an overpriced stock. Brokerage firm reports on multinationals are chock-full of these comparisons.

EXHIBIT 26.5 Relative Value Crossing Boundaries: Developed Country Stock Comparisons of Major Brewers, April 2009

Multinational	Home Country	P/E Ratio	Enterprise Value/EBITDA
Asahi	Japan	14×	8×
Fosters	Australia	12	7
Heineken	Holland	16	9
In Bev	Belgium	10	6
Kirin	Japan	13	8
Molson Coors	United States	17	9
SAB Millers	United Kingdom	15	9

The sovereign differences between the comparables signify that the analysts compare apples to oranges in many ways. No matter. Since the discounted cash flow technique is out of favor on Wall Street, practitioners need a rational basis for investment recommendations. Relative value fills the void.

SUMMARY

Practitioners transfer U.S. valuation techniques to international securities. Developed country equities approach the U.S. model in many ways, but significant differences exist. The risk of adverse currency movement is difficult to quantify, but it suggests a premium rate-of-return requirement for the dollar-based investor.

CHAPTER 27

The Emerging Markets

In their search for profits, equity investors travel far and wide. They appear regularly in Third World countries, with undeveloped stock markets and uncertain ground rules. In this chapter, we apply rational analysis to these markets.

When I began work at the World Bank's private sector affiliate, the International Finance Corporation (IFC), in 1991, emerging market equity investment was an obscure backwater; now it is an established asset class on Wall Street. From a base of almost zero only 20 years ago, hundreds of billions have flowed into these stocks, and a host of money managers specialize in the category. Despite this growth, the investment industry has yet to develop a research function that capably appraises these dynamic, but risky, opportunities.

Before proceeding, it is helpful to define what is meant by *emerging market*. The World Bank coined the term 30 years ago as a positive-sounding synonym for *developing country*. A developing country has an economy that is quite poor relative to the highly developed, rich economies represented by the United States, Canada, Western Europe, Japan, Australia, and a few other countries. According to the World Bank, developing nations include all countries with an annual per capita income of less than $11,000. Pakistan, for example, has a per capita income of $1,100. (By comparison, per capita income in the United States is $42,000.) This designation covers countries encompassing 85 percent of the world's population and includes those whose GDP is growing (e.g., Indonesia) as well as those whose economies are moving backward (e.g., Zimbabwe).

For people who haven't traveled extensively, it is difficult to visualize the grinding poverty afflicting most developing countries. Things that we take for granted in the United States—a telephone, a decent home, and a family car—are not within the means of the average Third World breadwinner. Well-paying jobs are scarce and economic advancement opportunities are limited, as wealth is concentrated in the hands of a small elite who promote a rigid class structure. Most such countries have low standards of democracy, industrialization, and social welfare.

For decades, the majority of these nations clung to statist or socialistic policies, which tended to retard economic growth, rather than foster it. The failure of these policies and, later, the fall of communism brought economic liberalization to many of them. Demonstrated successes in selected nations such as China, Chile, and Thailand

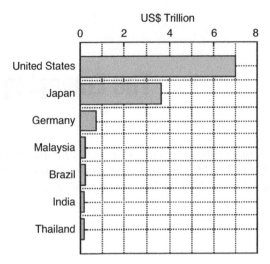

EXHIBIT 27.1   Comparative Sizes of
Market Capitalization

(and corresponding increases in local share prices) convinced foreign investors of the
potential for gains in equity values as certain countries "emerged" from a period of
stagnation to one of rapid growth.

Today, more than 70 developing countries have stock markets and the number of domestic companies listed on their exchanges approximates 25,000 (which
is a healthy fraction of the developed country total). Of this number, fewer than
10 percent trade actively, and an even smaller number represent the bulk of market
capitalization. In India, the situation is typical: Twenty stocks account for 30 percent of the market's value. As a result, institutional investors usually focus on just
30 to 40 stocks in a given market. Exhibit 27.1 graphically depicts the differences in
market capitalization among a sampling of countries. Exhibit 27.2 shows the typical
balance of companies contributing to an emerging market.

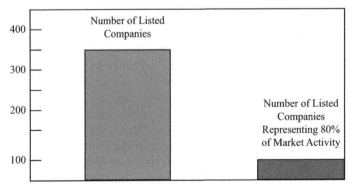

EXHIBIT 27.2   Typical Emerging Market

The stock markets are tiny compared to those of major industrial countries. The largest, China (including Hong Kong), is about 10 percent as large as the U.S. market, but most others are less than 1 percent. Of the $40 trillion in global equity market value in early 2009, emerging markets represented about 14 percent. Most of the local stocks are thinly traded, as prominent families maintain majority control. Considering the illiquidity of most stocks, the base of investment opportunities for U.S. and European investors is minuscule relative to their home economies. For this reason, Western institutions allocate small amounts, such as 5 percent of assets, to emerging markets.

EMERGING MARKETS AND SECURITY ANALYSIS

Practitioners try to apply conventional security analysis to these markets. They write research reports incorporating top-down reviews, financial projections, and relative values. Despite such attempts at rational research, the approach is valid only in a handful of the more advanced countries, and perhaps with just a few of the dominant stocks in the lesser markets. A gambling mentality prevails, and the serious investor who isn't willing to dedicate a full-time effort is better off participating in a country fund that more or less indexes a given market. Even savvy investors emphasize the country first, and the individual stock second. Tim Drinkall, manager of Morgan Stanley's frontier markets fund, says, "We believe 60 percent of our premium return is due to country selection and 40 percent to the company choice."

The six factors that inhibit effective security analysis in international developed markets (as mentioned in Chapter 26) come up in spades in the emerging markets. To review, these factors are:

1. Less information.
2. Questionable trading practices.
3. Unclear accounting standards.
4. Few comparables.
5. Reduced emphasis on share price enhancement.
6. Liquidity concerns.

A discussion of these factors in the emerging market context follows, along with a review of emerging market-specific risks.

Less Information

Emerging markets have fewer disclosure requirements than developed countries. Furthermore, many Third World firms are lax in reporting events affecting their businesses, and they release financial results in an untimely fashion. Unlike many U.S. and European companies, the firms do not generate reams of statistics, thus frustrating outside analysts. Many corporations are family-controlled, and the managers (who usually are family members) are reluctant to provide information and meet with analysts, citing competitive reasons. Exceptions to this behavior are the developing nation companies that have ADRs listed in the United States and Europe; they must adhere to the relevant stock exchange standards.

Questionable Trading Practices

Insider trading, front-running, poor execution, and other unsavory practices are common on emerging market exchanges. The situation is reminiscent of the U.S. market's lack of regulation in the early 1900s. Eduardo Vidal, an attorney at Hughes Hubbard, summarized the problem: "One of the biggest complaints of the Latin American financial markets has been not that there's a lack of laws on the books, but rather there's a lack of enforcement." Foreign investors in these markets consider such practices a cost of doing business.

Unclear Accounting Standards

The emerging markets are evolving to International Financial Reporting Standards (IFRS), but the manner of application of IFRS and the variety of accounting regimes in the developing world present the analyst with challenges in interpreting financial results and estimating earnings power. The difficulties increase as one goes down the corporate status chain.

The large emerging market firms that list their ADRs in the United States adhere to the strictest accounting certification and presentation. Furthermore, they show their results in US$ equivalent and provide U.S. GAAP translations. The remaining blue-chip firms, numbering from 30 to 40 companies in an emerging market, release financial statements that are a fair representation of the economic results of their respective businesses. Nevertheless, in my experience, the practitioner needs to examine these statements with a great deal of care, and he must ask management pointed questions if he expects to uncover well-hidden deficiencies. For example, one Mexican company I visited papered over operating losses by buying small businesses at prices below book value. Management then wrote up the assets and realized a gain. All of this was permitted by the firm's independent auditor. Furthermore, a Big Four accounting firm does not mean guaranteed protection. India's Satyam, a global IT business with a multibillion-dollar market cap, suffered through a major accounting scandal even though its auditor was Price Waterhouse.

As the investor proceeds to the second-tier firms that make up 40 to 50 percent of an emerging market's capitalization, the accounting shenanigans increase. At many such firms, a key objective is minimizing asset, value-added, and income taxes. As a result, perhaps 10 to 20 percent of sales go unreported and the tax burden is commensurately reduced. Furthermore, the majority of second-tier firms are family affairs, so there is little hesitation in placing personal charges on the company's books, obviously at the expense of outside shareholders. Also, transfer pricing between the family businesses is frequently an undisclosed issue. If the publicly traded pulp firm purchases its lumber from the family's privately owned timber operation, the price of that timber should be a matter of public record. Finally, local regulations require that listed companies have their books audited by an independent accounting firm (or designated auditor), but local auditors often turn a blind eye to these practices or simply fail to perform the necessary investigations.

EXHIBIT 27.3   Emerging Market Companies Quality of Accounting Disclosure

Companies with ADRs listed in the United States and Europe	High standard of disclosure. Accurate audits with supplementary presentation in U.S. GAAP.
Other first-tier emerging market companies	Financial statements provide a reasonably fair presentation of economic results. The analyst must still conduct a thorough study to estimate current earnings power.
Second-tier firms	Publicly disclosed accounting results are suspect. Income tax avoidance and family enrichment are normal practices. Foreign investors should seek an extra margin of safety.

The majority of equity research reports on emerging markets fail to highlight these accounting problems. See Exhibit 27.3. This deficiency highlights the need for intense study of these investments, before the average institution takes the plunge.

Few Comparables

Relative value adherents, which include most professional investors, find the shortage of comparables for any given stock to be a real problem. The usual solution is to compare a telephone company in Thailand with a similar firm in another poor Asian country, such as Indonesia or India. Since sovereign factors dominate the pricing of securities in these nations, this approach has a critical weakness, yet professionals continue the practice.

Reduced Emphasis on Share Price Enhancement

The preponderance of emerging market companies are controlled by their respective founding families. Therein lies the fundamental conflict between listed firms and their outside shareholders. In my experience, families are not driven to maximize value for the benefit of outside shareholders. Rather, the emphasis is on keeping the family executives in power, so they can preserve their status and influence within the community. This represents an important philosophical difference with U.S.-style investors, who want to see an issuer pursue aggressive tactics that boost its share price.

The "family first" attitude is manifested in several ways. First, the business may pass on promising growth opportunities if the resultant financing requirement means ownership dilution. Second, the company may display a marked preference for family executives, as opposed to hiring skilled outside managers. And third, the firm may permit the family's enrichment (through personal expenses or insider deals) at the expense of the passive outside shareholder. Exhibit 27.4 provides a summary of these issues.

As institutional shareholders play a larger role in the emerging markets, the family-first preoccupation will diminish. In the meantime, investors who want to

EXHIBIT 27.4   Family Influence in Emerging Market Stocks

The family-controlled firm often:
- Is not driven to maximize shareholder value.
- Is reluctant to meet with analysts and provide information.
- Prefers family executives rather than professional managers.
- Sacrifices growth opportunities to avoid shareholder dilution.
- Permits improper insider arrangements.
- Stresses income tax avoidance instead of complete financial reporting.

minimize the problem should focus on public privatizations and new technology businesses. Public privatizations are businesses that were formerly owned by the government. As a result, there is no founding family and ownership is dispersed. Prominent shareholders of these privatizations often include multinationals that believe in creating value quickly. New technology businesses, like cellular phones or cable TV (i.e., these technologies are new in the emerging markets), are frequently run by a combination of local investors and international companies. The latter share the American portfolio manager's penchant for near-term gains.

Liquidity Concerns

The stock markets of most developing nations are far less liquid than the stock markets of large wealthy countries. Investors wanting to obtain more than a token position in a stock may require several weeks of patient buying. Similarly, getting out of an equity investment—without causing a price drop in the security—means careful selling.

Three risks that have a high profile in the emerging markets are currency risk, country risk, and political risk.

Currency Risk   Emerging market stocks present the U.S. investor with considerable currency risks. Unexpected devaluations against the U.S. dollar are common occurrences and they contribute to stock price declines in both local and US$ terms. Over the past 10 years, sudden devaluations exceeding 50 percent against the U.S. dollar have occurred in multiple countries, including Argentina, Turkey, Romania, and Zambia.

Unlike developed markets such as Japan and Germany, emerging markets don't have currency hedging mechanisms. Plenty of investors want to protect against devaluations in poor countries, but no financial service provider wants to stand up and insure against the possibility. The risk of devaluation is simply too great.

Country Risk   Unlike the United States, most developing nations lack an independent central bank. Economic stability is compromised by capricious government policies, and legislators fail to appreciate the benefits of a strong financial market. In contrast, foreign investors seek a stable country in both a political and economic sense, although they make exceptions for companies that deal primarily in export industries, such as gold mining or oil exploration, where revenues are generated in a hard currency like the U.S. dollar.

Political Risk   Besides macroeconomic matters, foreign investors assess the likelihood of government interference with their equity investment. Defined as political risk, these actions include foreign exchange blockage, legal discrimination, and expropriation. For example, prior to this book's release, Russia squeezed out foreign oil companies, Venezuela nationalized Western subsidiaries, and Bolivia stiffed foreign creditors.

STOCK PRICING GUIDELINES

In the typical Third World country, the quasi-scientific investors who rely on the discounted cash flow and relative value techniques are greatly outnumbered by the speculators, country rotators, and momentum investors. As a result, the pricing of a stock often has little relation to its perceived economic value, as calculated using this book's methodology. These discrepancies present interesting investment opportunities (both on the long and short side), but the time it takes for the market to correct itself is sometimes prolonged, relative to the time needed for pricing inefficiencies in the United States to resolve themselves. Veteran emerging market professionals acknowledge the situation and urge investors to consider the long-term perspective.

Mark Mobius, director of the Templeton Funds' emerging market effort, summarizes the long-term philosophy: "... taking a long view of emerging markets will yield excellent results for the investor prepared to be patient and willing to apply sound and tested principles in a diligent and consistent manner. The approach we take in our reports is not to focus on the short term since we invest the funds entrusted to us not for a three-month, six-month, or even one-year period, but for at least a five-year period."[1] Nonetheless, there is little evidence to suggest that emerging markets provide premium returns relative to developed markets when adjusted for risk. Andrew Gunther, an executive of the International Finance Corporation, offers an explanation: "The problem with investing in the emerging markets, relative to developed countries, is that you have to get everything right—*country*, *politics*, and *currency*, in addition to the usual concerns of company finances and management."

Third World stock markets tend to be more volatile than those of the United States and Western Europe; they lurch quickly from one extreme to another, unlike the U.S. market, for example, which has longer time frames between peaks and valleys. An investor can buy a Venezuelan stock at 5,000 bolivars per share, believing its intrinsic value is 7,000 bolivars. If market sentiment becomes negative, the stock price can easily drop 30 percent (to 3,500 bolivars) in a few weeks. Even though the margin of safety has widened to 50 percent, it takes an investor with a strong stomach to double up at the lower price. He's never quite sure when the crash will bottom out.

A thorough review of stock selection in the emerging markets is beyond the scope of this book (interested investors can consult *The Emerging Markets: A Practical Guide for Corporations, Lenders, and Investors* by Jeffrey C. Hooke, John Wiley & Sons, 2001), but a few principles can be applied to the individual segments of the top-down format. These are summarized in Exhibit 27.5.

EXHIBIT 27.5   Emerging Markets Stock Selection Guidelines

A few things to look for in buying an emerging market stock include:

Country
- Reasonably stable economic indicators.
- Moderate political risk.

Capital Markets
- Semblance of fair trading and honest disclosure.
- Degree of liquidity for investor ease in getting in and out of positions.

Industry
- Good growth prospects.
- Internationally competitive.
- Profits not reliant upon:
  - Tariffs
  - Quotas
  - Other trade barriers
- Oligopoly ensures profit margins.

Company
- Modern management techniques.
- Widely held ownership or influential multinational shareholder that promotes share price enhancement.
- Strong government connections through family or management.
- Good track record and solid balance sheet.
- Favorable growth prospects.
- A portion of revenues are exports and denominated in U.S. dollars and euros.
- Share price meets margin-of-safety rule.

Capital Markets

Since few stocks move against the general trend, the investor needs to be confident of the market's upward direction (or downward move, in the case of a short sale). Additionally, a minimal standard of fair trading and honest disclosure is a strong plus for the foreign participant. With many countries suffering from high inflation and currency risk, interest rates can be high by U.S. standards. Russia, one of the largest emerging markets, consistently has local interest rates in the mid-teens.

Industry

The primary focus of the foreign investor is finding local industries with growth prospects. Surprisingly, many sectors considered stodgy in the United States are considered hot in the emerging markets. One illustration is the electric utility industry. In the United States, this industry is mature; unit sales growth is only 2 to 3 percent annually. In contrast, electricity demand growth can be double this rate in a market such as the Philippines or Brazil, because advancing prosperity means more electric appliances and devices. In 2010, Vietnam had one car for every 100 people, a tiny fraction of the ratio in a wealthy country. Vietnam's auto sales are forecast to grow at 10 to 12 percent annually for many years.

To ensure long-term shareholder returns, the local industry must be cost competitive, or substitute providers enter the market. Determining the economic efficiency of a local industry and the magnitude of this threat is a challenge. In many emerging markets, local industries are strongly protected against foreign competition by high tariffs, import quotas, or obtrusive government regulations. Because of an artificial pricing environment, a local industry that is inefficient by international cost standards can generate consistent profits. The auto industry in Vietnam, for example, survives imports through a government-imposed excise tax.

Alternatively, the artificial environment enables the local industry to charge oligopolistic prices, thus providing excess profits and the image of premium economic returns. In Mexico, for example, Telmex controls 90 percent of the local phone market despite repeated attempts by well-heeled prospective local and foreign competitors to participate. The political influence of Telmex and its billionaire CEO, Carlos Slim, stymie attempts at competition and price reduction. The result: Telmex is a very profitable monopoly.

Depending on the nature of the protections, the analyst determines whether they represent a sustainable competitive advantage. Does the industry have enough influence with the government (and with future governments) to maintain the status quo? If the answer is no, the analyst assesses the likelihood and timing of a rollback of the protections. The Mexican cement industry, for example, enjoyed import protection through numerous administrations. The packaged food industry, however, never had this benefit.

The practitioner also considers the funding required by local participants to fight off international competitors. More investment means fewer dividends and more share issuances, translating into a lower share price.

If the industry's international advantage is readily apparent—such as inexpensive labor, cheap currency, lax environmental regulation, or natural resources—you need to be sure of the duration of that advantage. High wages in Singapore sent low-tech assembly industries to lower-wage Malaysia. As Malaysian salaries increased, the jobs went to Indonesia. Paul Ziegler, Asian CEO for Asea Brown Boveri, the Swedish power equipment manufacturer, said in a Bloomberg interview, "It's just common sense. You make these things where they are cheapest to make." Lax environmental regulation in China made it an attractive location for polluting industries. As the country took stock of the damage caused by the chemical, mining, and energy sections, it looked to regulate some of the worst offenders, thus increasing their operating costs. Mexico's oil reserves are declining at a rapid rate, and without the discovery of new reserves, its economy is threatened.

Company

The company selection process incorporates appraisal techniques that are similar to those discussed earlier in this book. Good growth prospects, a solid balance sheet, Western-style management, and enlightened owners are notable for emerging market equities. Furthermore, because of the heavy government influence and arbitrary regulation that characterize these economies, a firm with close ties to the ruling party is a good bet. Since governments come and go in these countries, political influence can wane, so it is important that the firm selected for investment have intrinsic competitive qualities. Helmut Paul, a senior advisor to Darby Overseas

EXHIBIT 27.6 Projecting Local Currency Results into U.S. Dollars: Natura-Brazilian Company (in billions)

	Estimated	Projected				
	2008	2009	2010	2011	2012	2013
Average FX rate (R$ to US$)	1.78	2.00	2.05	2.12	2.17	2.22
Sales in Brazilian reals (R$)	3.6	4.0	4.7	5.3	5.6	6.2
Sales in US$	2.0	2.0	2.3	2.5	2.6	2.8

Funds, explains, "In today's global arena, it's not enough for an emerging market company to be excellent by country or by regional standards; it must be competitive by world standards. And a good distribution system or local brand name is not sufficient; these can be duplicated by international competition."

FINANCIAL PROJECTIONS

As in foreign developed markets, practitioners complete projections in the local currency, which are then converted into U.S. dollars. This action involves assumptions about future exchange rates, which have less certainty than similar foreign exchange (FX) assumptions in wealthier, developed nations. For example, in November 2008, investment banks published cash flow forecasts for Natura, a Brazilian personal care company. Above the local currency projection for each year was a presumed FX rate for the Brazilian real and U.S. dollar; the report then incorporated this rate to local results in U.S. dollars. See Exhibit 27.6. The reasoning for this presentation is that the analyst's audience was U.S. and Western European investors.

As Exhibit 27.6 shows, the analyst forecast a modest devaluation of the Brazilian real (versus the US$), from 1.78 in 2008 to 2.22 in 2013. That forecast was optimistic. By March 2009, a scant five months later, the real traded down to 2.40, as investors sought safety in major currencies during the financial crisis.

Balance Sheet Caution

Because of the high risk of currency devaluation in the Third World, many countries exhibit high interest rates, as local currency investors need to be compensated for the risk. In Brazil, for example, short-term rates for prime corporate credits are typically in the 15 to 20 percent range, even when inflation is low. Like most emerging markets, Brazil has no fixed-rate, long-term debt in its local currency. The prospect of holding on to such an instrument is too scary for institutions and individuals alike.

To match long-term assets against long-term liabilities, developing country firms sometimes borrow at fixed rates in a foreign currency, usually U.S. dollars or euros. A top Brazilian firm in 2008, for example, might borrow at 8 percent in U.S. dollars versus 18 percent in the home market, thus providing an immediate savings.

EXHIBIT 27.7 Brazilian Borrower and Local Currency Devaluation (in R$ millions)

Capital Structure	Before Devaluation	After 50 Percent Devaluation
Debt:		
R$–denominated	1,000	1,000
US$–denominated	1,000	2,000
Equity	4,000	3,000
	6,000	6,000
Debt/(debt + equity)	33%	50%

However, in the case of a severe devaluation, such as 50 percent, the borrower needs to generate twice as much local cash flow to pay off the foreign debt. Without some U.S. dollar–denominated export revenue, timely repayment is a challenge. The confluence of devaluation and foreign debt has caused many Third World borrowers to become insolvent in the past, and for this reason, an analyst pays special attention to foreign-denominated debt on a Third World company's balance sheet. Exhibit 27.7 shows how a currency devaluation boosts leverage.

In the 2005 to 2007 time frame, numerous developing nation currencies *appreciated* against the U.S. dollar, reversing a long-term trend of *depreciation*. With the arrival of the 2008 financial crisis, investors flocked to the safety of the U.S. dollar, and the trend returned to normal. In Poland, millions of Poles bought homes with loans denominated in low-interest Swiss francs. When the zloty, the Polish currency, collapsed in 2009, losing half its value against the Swiss franc, Polish mortgage holders found their payment doubling in zlotys, the currency in which they received salaries.

EMERGING MARKET EQUITY DISCOUNT RATE

Despite the heightened profile of emerging market stocks in institutional portfolios, academics and practitioners have yet to agree on a definitive mechanism by which to determine a discount rate on any given stock.

CAPM

Attempts to apply the U.S. capital asset pricing model run into problems with (1) the question of a beta-driven regression formula being applied to the local market and the U.S. market; (2) the credibility of beta when the local market is dominated by a handful of stocks rather than a broad portfolio; (3) the sovereign and currency risk implicit in the calculation of the beta in any given Third World stock; and (4) the quickly changing environment of emerging markets, whereby historically driven formulas are of questionable use. Nonetheless, practitioners utilize CAPM by (1) averaging the nonleveraged betas of comparable companies in wealthy countries;

(2) releveraging this number with the emerging market firm's own debt to equity ratio; and (3) inserting this makeshift beta into the discount rate formula, as follows:

$$k_{\text{Emerging Markets}} = R_F + \beta\ (R_M - R_F) + \text{Country risk premium}$$

where $k_{\text{Emerging Markets}}$ = Expected rate of return on a foreign stock in U.S. dollars

R_F = 10-year U.S. government bond yield

β = Implied beta of the stock (i.e., the unlevered average beta of comparable U.S., European, and Japanese firms, releveraged for the emerging market company's debt/equity ratio)

R_M = U.S. government bond rate (R_F) plus 7 percent

Country risk premium = Sovereign bond yield minus U.S. government bond yield

Equity Buildup

The equity buildup method is preferred by the practitioner community, even though it rests on less-than-scientific assumptions. As noted for U.S. firms in Chapter 7, the process begins with the foundation of the risk-free rate plus the U.S. equity risk premium. To this sum is added (1) a premium for *country risk* (defined as the spread of the sovereign's US$ denominated bonds over the U.S. Treasury Bond); and (2) rough estimates of the local industry risk and company-specific risk (both of which are based on similar industry and company risks in the wealthy stock markets). The equity buildup method prescribes a 16.20 percent US$ rate of return for Natura at October 2008. See Exhibit 27.8.

Once a discount rate is established, the analyst (1) takes his Natura cash flow projection; (2) estimates a terminal value for the business (typically using the EV/EBITDA ratio); and (3) applies the discount rate to the annual cash flow and terminal value. Like most such DCF analyses, the terminal value represents most of the NPV. The calculation suggested an intrinsic value of US$10.26 per Natura share. The stock was trading at R$17.00, or US$8.50 at the time. Using a 15 percent margin of safety, Natura was a buy. See Exhibit 27.9.

EXHIBIT 27.8 Brazilian Company Natura, Estimating US$ Discount Rate for US$ Cash Flow Projection, October 2008

Risk-free rate (10-year U.S. Treasury bond yield)	6.00%
U.S. equity risk premium (premium for investing in broad based index)	7.10
Brazilian country risk premium (sovereign US$ yield minus U.S. Treasury bond yield)	4.80
Industry premium (consumer care industry for Natura)	(1.20)
Size premium (Natura is a large-cap firm)	0.00
Individual company premium (Natura is low debt and diversified)	(0.50)
	16.20%

EXHIBIT 27.9 Natura—Net Present Value Calculation at October 2008 (in millions)

	2009	2010	2011	2012	2013
FX rate forecast	2.00	2.05	2.12	2.17	2.22
Net cash flow (US$)	$ (56)	$112	$214	$308	$ 367
Terminal value (US$)	—	—	—	—	8,000
	$ (56)	$112	$214	$308	$8,367
Discount factor	1.16	1.35	1.57	1.82	2.12
Enterprise NPV	$4,315				
– Debt in 2008	(260)				
+ Cash in 2008	336				
Equity NPV	$4,391				
Number of shares	÷428				
DCF value per share at October 2008	$10.26				

The calculation presumes a modest decline in the value of the Brazilian real and a 16.20 percent discount rate in US$ terms.

The discount rate of an emerging market stock is several percentage points above the discount rate of a comparable U.S. security. The minimum difference should be the sovereign bond yield spread. (Exhibit 27.10 shows several spreads.) As the degree of risk grows, so does the premium. Because country and currency risks dominate firm-specific factors in emerging markets, practitioners group risk premiums by countries. A low-risk country such as Chile stands in contrast to a high-risk country such as Russia. Exhibit 27.11 provides a brief listing alongside target rates of return.

Given the high targeted returns, many newcomers to the emerging markets expect the stocks to trade at low P/E and EV/EBITDA ratios relative to their developed

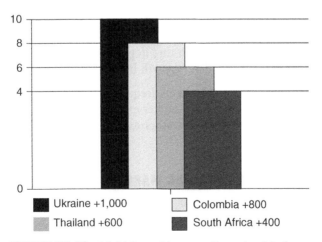

EXHIBIT 27.10 Yield Spread between Emerging Market Sovereigns and U.S. Treasury in October 2008

EXHIBIT 27.11   Emerging Markets Target
Equity Returns by Country

Low Risk	Target Rate of Return
Chile	
Malaysia	15% to 20%
Thailand	
Medium Risk	
Brazil	
China	20% to 25%
India	
Mexico	
Turkey	
High Risk	
Bangladesh	
Nigeria	25% to 30%
Russia	

country counterparts. After all, the larger one makes k in the dividend discount models, the smaller P becomes, as illustrated in the following equations:

Steady-State or Constant Growth Model

$$P = \frac{D_1}{k - g}$$

Two-Step Growth Model

$$P = \frac{D^1}{1 + k} + \frac{D^2}{(1 + k)^2} + \frac{\frac{D_{n+1}}{(k - g)}}{(1 + k)^n}$$

where $P = $ Price of stock
   $D = $ Annual cash dividend
   $k = $ Investor's annual required rate of return in percentage terms
      (k_n may be lower than k in the two-step model)
   $g = $ Annual dividend growth rate in percentage terms
   $n = $ Year in which dividend growth becomes constant

Despite this view, emerging markets frequently trade at premium P/Es. Counterbalancing the higher desired k is a higher expected growth rate. Furthermore, as the countries' economies mature, investors expect k to decline, which supports a higher P/E.

RELATIVE VALUE IN THE EMERGING MARKETS

Despite the logical foundations of the dividend discount models, research analysts give them short shrift. As the reader knows, k and g calculations are not exact. In addition to DCF-based intrinsic value, investors desire relative value analysis,

EXHIBIT 27.12 Wireless Telecom Comparables—Emerging
Markets Typical Relative Value Table, October 2008

Company	Country	Enterprise Value/EBITDA
MTS	Russia	2.8
Mobinil	Egypt	4.1
MTN	South Africa	4.8
Turkcell	Turkey	4.3
Vimpelcom	Russia	3.2
Zain	Middle East, sub-Saharan Africa	6.6

A shortage of comparables forces the emerging market telecom
analyst to make comparisons across borders. Zain has the most
risky macro environment, but the sub-Saharan African countries'
cell phone use was rapidly rising.

where researchers assess the positive and negative aspects of a stock against those
characteristics of similar securities. The stocks' valuation multiples are then compared and contrasted.

For emerging market stocks, dividend discounting poses difficulties identical
to those confronted in the developed markets, but relative value is problematic as
well. In most emerging markets, the analyst has a small or nonexistent pool of
comparable stocks from which to derive EV/EBITDA, P/E, and other ratios. He
is forced to evaluate the relative merits of industry that are located in different
countries. Thus, Telmex (Mexico) is compared to Telebras (Brazil), Telefonica de
Argentina (Argentina), and CTC (Chile). There is an obvious problem here. The
macroeconomic *top* of the top-down chain of projections for each of these firms is
dramatically different, since they are based in separate countries. See Exhibit 27.12
for a wireless industry table.

The EV/EBITDA and P/E statistics used in the comparisons should be adjusted
by the analyst to reflect sovereign concerns, but typically they are not, at least not
in quantifiable terms. Country and currency factors for these stocks are mixed into
these valuation ratios, with little discussion of trade-offs. For this reason, Andrea
Teixeira of J.P. Morgan Equity Research says, "Because of the maturing stages
of these emerging market firms, we tend to weight discounted cash flow more heavily
than comparables. It is also hard to find similar high-growth businesses, so we
estimate cash flows at varying growth phases. Still, there is a lot of resistance to
accept discounted cash flow as a valuation metric from equity investors who have
been cautious about the earnings visibility and the risk of growth in periods of
economic turbulence." Should we reduce a Brazilian stock's multiple by 4.0 relative
to a Chilean company, which is arguably based in a less risky country? No one wants
to define these numbers.

The end result is that emerging market practitioners sometimes blend DCF and
relative value results in the same manner that we covered in Chapter 19. A typical
weighting at March 2009 was 60 percent DCF and 40 percent relative value.

SUMMARY

Most U.S. and European institutions allocate a portion of their equity portfolios to the emerging markets. Good investment opportunities are apparent, but the bottom line is that U.S.-style research doesn't travel well. The lack of consensus on discount rates, the small comparable company sample, the poor information disclosure, the suspect regulatory environment, and the market illiquidity conspire to frustrate investors using the techniques set forth in this book. To some degree, added research moderates the negative impact of these factors, but this kind of effort is uneconomical unless the investor takes a large position.

The pattern of actual trading suggests that traditional stock picking takes a back seat to sovereign concerns. Investors ignore the important distinctions among individual stocks, focusing instead on countries as a whole. This behavior makes for inefficient pricing, but the practitioner relying on fundamental analysis to earn a premium return must be prepared to ride out the speculative waves. As a result, only investors with a strong stomach should pursue these markets.

CHAPTER 28

Asset Booms and Busts

The 2008 stock market crash exposed serious flaws in the security analysis profession, the investment business, and the broader financial industry. Attempts to reform Wall Street will fall short, exposing economies to the prospect of another financial panic. Security analysts, and those individuals in business valuation, should try and learn from the lessons of this latest boom and bust.

Over the past 10 years, there have been two bear markets in which stocks fell by at least 40 percent. The severity and the swiftness of the declines caught most analysts unaware, and laid waste to the claim that equities, by any account, are superior investments relative to corporate bonds or cash. Over long periods of time, a diversified stock portfolio outperforms bonds and cash, but in the intermediate term, investors are subject to downturns that wipe them out, at least temporarily. This problem was compounded in 2008 because global indexes—the U.S., Western Europe, and emerging markets—plunged in concert, so there was no place for the equity investor to hide. The interrelationships inherent in linked economies mean that the performance of national stock markets correlate well, and U.S. investors are frustrated in finding securities that move opposite to the domestic market. Besides an illustration of the ebb and flow of capitalist economies, the 2008 crash brought the sense that government overseers failed the public.

The manner in which the financial industry and the regulatory apparatus deal with these issues in the future affects the investment evaluation process. The stakes are high—the savings and peace of mind of millions of ordinary citizens.

THE 2008 CRASH: CONTRIBUTING CAUSES

The 2008 crash was fundamentally a credit bubble, housing bubble, and consumption bubble, all rolled into one. Lax lending standards promoted a period of exuberance in real estate prices, and investors believed that housing prices would never decline (even though they had dropped in the 1990–1991 recession). The paper profits in real estate drove sizable increases in consumer spending, which contributed to economic growth, corporate profits, and higher stock prices. The enhanced corporate performance promoted record numbers of leverage buyouts, risky bank loans, and shaky junk bonds, few of which went through a recession stress test. "There was enough of a feeding frenzy that you didn't want to lose your place in line," explained Julian Mann, a portfolio manager for First Pacific Advisors who passed on many deals. "A lot of people knew this was bogus, but the money was too good."[1]

For those objecting to the short-term obsession with trading commissions and transaction fees, unemployment seemed likely. To illustrate, consider whistleblower Paul Moore, the head of the risk division at British megabank HBOS. In official testimony, Mr. Moore stated that he had warned the Financial Services Authority (FSA), the UK bank regulator, that "HBOS was growing too rapidly, that the sales culture was out of control, and that anyone who spoke out was labeled a 'troublemaker' or a 'spoilsport.'"[2] The bank fired Mr. Moore, and the FSA ignored his warnings. HBOS later received a gigantic government bailout after billions in losses.

COLLAPSE OF THE U.S. HOUSING BUBBLE

The 2008 market collapse began after a nonstop climb in U.S. housing prices. Lenders grew increasingly optimistic about housing values and disregarded their previous reservations—born of decades of experience—about making loans to risky borrowers with minimal down payments, such as 5 percent (or less) of the purchase price. The originating lender's detachment from possible default was accentuated by *securitization*—the new practice of selling pools of individual home mortgages to investment banks, which then resold them in bulk to institutions that were far from the local real estate market. As a result, the crisis saw the curious occurrence of a major German bank going broke because of California mortgage defaults.

When housing prices moderated in 2008, millions of borrowers found their loans to be underwater (i.e., the home value was less than the mortgage principal). Rather than continue to invest in a wasting asset, many chose to walk away from their mortgage, and lenders, according to most state laws, could seize only the underlying collateral, rather than attach the borrower's personal assets for repayment. Another sizable chunk of bad loans stemmed from the 2008–2009 recession, as large numbers of borrowers lost their jobs and couldn't afford to make mortgage payments.

The complexity of securitized loan pools made pinpointing bank portfolio losses difficult, and the prospective size of the losses made capital markets nervous. Those financial institutions with substantial exposure to U.S. home mortgages spanned the globe, so the crisis crossed many borders. Interbank lending, commercial paper, and other money markets froze up; and, thus, the problems of the mortgage sector cascaded into alternative industries, all of which rely, to one degree or another, on access to credit. Equity investors sought safe haven and billions poured out of hedge funds, equities, and real estate. The resultant stock market decline—54 percent at one point—ensnared high-profile investors such as the legendary Warren Buffett (down 51 percent) and Legg Mason's famous Bill Miller (down 56 percent).

As it had in the past with Internet stocks, emerging markets, and biotech firms, the great Wall Street marketing machine got hold of residential real estate and pushed it hard. Unlike earlier asset bubbles, "Wall Street and Washington (i.e., the federal government) acted in concert to provide an artificial sense of a safety net," indicated Brian Yerger of Arda Advisors, referring to the 2008 panic. The federal government, through Fannie Mae, Freddie Mac, and certain legislation, encouraged the expansion of subprime lending, and its light regulation of such loans allowing the sector to mushroom into a prominence that brought down others when it fell.

The undue optimism of participants was supported, in part, by the lack of understanding of many with regard to the valuation of subprime mortgages, the related securitizations, and the intertwined derivative contracts. These products were purchased by institutions, such as banks, insurance companies, and pension funds, most of which did little independent research on the underlying collateral and its susceptibility to home price declines. Instead, they relied on the credit rating agencies, which assigned high ratings to many securitizations in the mistaken belief that real estate price declines were remote. The rating agencies, however, never claimed infallibility, and their ratings were limited to the amount of due diligence an agency can perform within the bounds of a modest rating fee, such as $120,000, which was applied even to large securitizations, such as $1 billion.

In hindsight, the institutions should have performed their own credit analysis, but they wanted to avoid the expense, which, in the short term, hurt the bottom line. For example, suppose an institution wants to buy $200 million of a $1 billion home mortgage securitization. The securitization contains 5,000 subprime loans with an average principal amount of $200,000. To verify the underlying loan quality, the institution selects 10 percent of loan files (500) at random. The individual review of each file, the software-driven analysis of the loans, the stress-testing of the portfolio, and the write-up of the conclusion costs $175,000. Upon the completion of such tasks, the institution has an objective report to compare against the rating agency's evaluation. At a $175,000 price point (about 0.09 percent of the $200 million under consideration), the institution fulfills the goal, set forth in Chapters 12 and 19, of generating a double check before making an investment decision.

This action is no guarantee against losses, but it reduces the margin for error. From 2005 to 2008, however, short-term profit goals dominated long-term considerations for many institutions. "They choose not to spend large amounts on evaluations," noted Nicholas Haffenreffer, president of Resolute Capital.

FAILURE OF THE REFEREES

The U.S. capital markets have a number of referees that try to instill a sense of order and fairness. All of them dropped the ball prior to the 2008 panic, leaving investors and citizens worse off. The three main referees are:

- Government regulatory agencies.
- Independent public accounting firms.
- Credit rating agencies.

Secondary referees provide a further check on stock prices and issuer abuses. These groups include:

- Security analysts.
- Stock exchange and industry regulators.
- Whistleblowers.
- Business media.

Government Regulatory Agencies

The patchwork of federal regulators was well funded, but they failed miserably. Indeed, the *New York Times* editorialized, "There are no officials or regulators, past or present, who have distinguished themselves by giving early warning of the impending catastrophe or by taking strong action against the excesses that were fueling it."[3] The prominent federal agencies such as the SEC, Federal Reserve, FDIC, and PCAOB were reactive, rather than proactive. They continued their habit of answering the mail and taking financial filings at face value. Their inaction cost the government and investors trillions more than might have been the case with strong initiative and solid enforcement.

Despite large budgets, the alphabet soup of federal regulators is woefully behind on financial technology and overly staffed with attorneys, who know little about how slick operators and dodgy issuers game the rules. My 2009 survey of the top eight federal regulators uncovered just 45 employees (out of more than 10,000) with the CFA designation, a minimal yardstick for financial acumen. The ambitious employees who are competent often quit to take industry jobs that pay more than government.

The inability to critically analyze led to the SEC adopting consolidated supervision capital rules in 2004 for the largest broker-dealer holding companies, such as Lehman Brothers, Bear Stearns, Merrill Lynch, and Citigroup, all of which ran into serious trouble. The new ruling relaxed capital requirements and accepted the firms' own models for calculating risk.

Contributing to the oversight problem is the phenomenon of "regulatory capture," which has been noticed by observers of government at all levels. Whether it is the local zoning board falling under the sway of local developers, the state public service commission taking orders from regional utilities, or the federal watchdog being unduly influenced by the industry it oversees, the regulator begins to see the powerful regulated companies as its "partner," rather than the numerous, and less visible, citizens it is authorized to protect. The phenomenon is particularly costly in the financial sector because of the large amounts of money involved.

Independent Public Accounting Firms

The massive Enron accounting scandal caused the bankruptcy of that company in 2001 and the demise of Arthur Andersen, one of the nation's top public accounting firms. The Enron mess exemplified the sloppy reporting endemic to public companies during the Internet go-go years. The resulting investor outcry paved the way for the Sarbanes-Oxley legislation, which created new regulations that burdened public companies with additional accounting requirements and extra auditing expenses. Ironically, the legislation proved to be a revenue boom for CPAs, who benefited greatly from the problems they helped create.

The new regulations generated a lot of paper shuffling, but they had little lasting impact. Case in point: off-balance-sheet accounting. Loopholes in the earlier rules allowed Enron to avoid consolidating huge debts and to keep them off the balance sheet. The rules were tightened after Sarbanes-Oxley, but that didn't stop Citicorp and other financial behemoths from guaranteeing mammoth liabilities for in-house conduits, and then keeping those obligations off the books. The result: Citicorp had a debt-to-capital ratio that, in reality, was far higher than the numbers filed with regulators. The public accounting firms were enablers in this shameful process, which contributed significantly to the financial panic.

The accounting firms also took on the job of opining on the values of the subprime mortgage securities and derivatives residing on the financial institutions' books, despite a lack of expertise in these complex and untested investments. This policy saved the firms' clients from the expense of hiring third-party appraisers to validate book entries, but it served lenders and investors poorly. In multiple cases, an accounting firm certified the balance sheet of a client one day, and two months later the numbers turned out to be fiction as the client incurred a huge write-down. In one instance, a Justice Department report noted, "KPMG allowed subprime lender New Century Financial to change its accounting to show strong profits during the housing boom, when a conservative treatment would have shown losses. The company lowered its reserves for bad loans even as bad loans increased."[4]

Accountants bending the rules for clients contributed to the federal government and investors losing trillions of dollars, yet, as of this writing, no Big Four accounting firms have been penalized for such actions. No Big Four employees have been indicted, or even sanctioned, for their roles in the $300 billion scandal regarding bank conduit accounting. Irrespective of the losses, the accountant-being-paid-by-the-client relationship remains unchanged; thus, the accountant feels pressure to cave in to demands for aggressive application of the rules, or risk losing the client. Robert Vesco, a king of white collar crime in the 1970s, described the dynamic well: "All the big accountants were the same. They'd put up a fight and raise their bills but ultimately they'd play the tune they were supposed to play. They'd blow the whistle only on absolute fraud."[5]

Credit Rating Agencies

Many individuals reading this book may not know that the credit rating business is a government-sanctioned oligopoly. This coveted status originated in the 1980s, when savings and loan and insurance company blow-ups cost federal and state governments hundreds of billions. The regulator takeaway from this disaster was that government-insured financial institutions could not be trusted to make investment decisions without the help of a third-party arbiter. Since governments had minimal expertise in this area, the authorities outsourced the function to the credit rating agencies. From that time on, virtually every sizable bond issue and syndicated loan required a credit rating, or institutions refused to buy it, lest the regulators force them to post extra-high loss reserves on an unrated instrument. The arrangement proved highly profitable for the two main credit rating agencies, Moody's and Standard & Poor's (who bill the issuers rather than the government), but it fostered a trend among institutions of relying on the ratings at the expense of doing their own in-house research.

Until the explosion in securitized mortgages, the system worked reasonably well. For example, the agencies had little involvement in the investor-driven plunge into emerging market bonds 15 years ago because the agencies assigned low ratings to the countries that later had economic problems. The agencies were also relatively unscathed by the 1999–2001 Internet boom, since few high-tech firms had operating histories that justified large bond issues. The 2005–2008 real estate bubble, however, was credit driven, and the agencies stood front and center, ladling out investment-grade designations to huge volumes of securitization deals. The unexpected defaults spread havoc through a daisy chain of commercial banks, insurance companies, and investment funds that relied on ratings.

Like the public accounting firms, the rating agencies escaped penalties for their negligence in the mortgage sector. Indeed, regulators still use ratings in determining capital requirements for lenders, and the agency oligopoly retains the profitable conflict of interest inherent in issuers paying for their own ratings. The system is thus open to another era of *grade inflation*, when one agency seeks to boost market share at the expense of another.

Government regulators, independent public accounting firms, and credit rating agencies represent the A team of referees in the capital markets. The B team consists of security analysts, industry regulators, whistleblowers, and media reporters.

Security Analysts

Brokerage firm analysts are a part of the Wall Street marketing machine and, as a result, they are reluctant to issue sell recommendations on firms they cover, for fear of endangering their employers' banking relationships, cutting off information access from the firms, or losing their jobs. Such was the case for financial industry analysts in 2008: Their sell recommendations arrived long after the stocks had fallen by 60 percent or 70 percent.

Buy-side analyst advisories are unavailable to the public and reserved for in-house portfolio managers. For the most part, the buy-side analyst is graded on relative performance; if his financial industry picks fall 50 percent when the sector index is down 60 percent, he declares victory. He is thus reluctant to recommend that a portfolio manager pull out of a sector entirely. The portfolio managers of mutual funds and investment funds function along the same lines—if the large-cap index drops 50 percent, and the manager's large-cap fund declines 45 percent, then the manager beat the market. Partly as a result of this measurement system, neither analysts nor portfolio managers were active in sounding the alarm. Short-sellers are a check on this behavior, but they are vastly outnumbered by the buy-side, and hampered by regulators and industry.

Stock Exchange and Industry Regulators

Equity markets, like the New York Stock Exchange, have in-house regulators who are supposed to deter abuses. Their history in exposing wrongdoing is abysmal.

Whistleblowers

Whistleblowers see misconduct and expose it to a regulator or newspaper; they receive little personal benefit for the actions and face reprisal from their employers. Although they initiated Wall Street scandals in the past, whistleblowers did not play a large part in forestalling the 2008 panic. Legislation that rewards whistleblowers would create more of them, but such efforts are derailed time and time again by industry.

Business Media

As noted earlier in this book, the business media is not a formidable fact checker, despite the importance of finance and industry to the average American. Only a few newspapers, such as the *Wall Street Journal, New York Times,* and *Financial Times,* dedicate substantial resources to the topic. Many magazines specialize in business reporting but, with the exception of *Barron's* and *Forbes,* most fail to bring a skeptical eye to their stories. Prior to the 2000 and 2009 crashes, the print media ran an assortment of stories questioning the international real estate run-ups, but without consistent repetition, the stories were overshadowed by the Wall Street marketing machine. Business TV, meanwhile, tended to collude, perhaps inadvertently, with Wall Street in promoting the bubbles. CNBC, for example, "hosted a parade of corporate executives, fund managers and investment analysts with an interest in talking up stocks," according to the *Washington Post.*[6] To provide balance, several network shows now feature bearish commentators from time to time, but the tone of business TV remains relentlessly bullish, even after its shameful performance prior to the 2008 crash.

THE CERTAINTY OF ANOTHER CRASH

The exuberance, sloppiness, and corner-cutting that are the precursors of a market crash are doomed to be repeated. For starters, the U.S. economy seems to be in a 7- to 10-year cycle of booms and busts, whereby the object of investors' affections shifts from one asset class to another, leaving the referees paying attention to the last war instead of the new threat. "The cycle is human nature," comments Christian Picot, a family office manager for Paris-based Rosario Partners. "It's always been there. The equity markets are a capitalistic way of funding a business; you can't change human greed."

Wall Street's avarice is fueled by transaction commissions, short-term trading profits, and asset management fees, rather than providing investor-clients with steady, absolute returns. The largest financial scandals of the past 10 years (see Exhibit 28.1) all had such motivations as a starting point, but neither the clients nor the regulators did much to reform the industry's compensation structure. Furthermore, the vast majority of offenders get off scot-free. Few individuals involved in the scandals were convicted of a crime, or even run out of the business. Instead, regulatory authorities punished selected employers (and their outside stockholders) by imposing fines that were modest in relation to the ill-gotten gains, making unethical behavior a profitable venture. Often, the minimal financial penalties were levied in concert with window-dressing legal settlements, whereby the wrongdoers neither admit nor deny a wrongdoing—but promise never to do it again! This surreal enforcement encouraged Wall Street in all its incarnations—investment bank, commercial bank, S&L, insurance company, hedge fund, mutual fund, and so on—to push the legal boundaries over and over again.

With such systematic failure in regulation, it would be beneficial for the federal government to junk large parts of the current apparatus and start fresh, like Roosevelt did in creating the SEC in the 1930s. Treasury Secretary and former Federal Reserve Bank of New York Chairman Timothy Geithner said as much when talking about

EXHIBIT 28.1 Financial Industry Scandals, 1999–2009

Financial Industries Scandal Focus	Description
Mortgage-based credit ratings	Credit rating agencies place unduly high ratings on hundreds of billions in mortgage securitizations.
Commercial bank conduit (or structured investment vehicle) scheme	Independent auditors allow hundreds of billions of bank-supported conduit liabilities to be placed off-balance-sheet.
Fannie Mae, AIG, and Enron accounting scandals	Various overstatements escape auditor diligence and cost investors and governments hundreds of billions.
Swiss Bank secret accounts	UBS lawsuit exposes thousands of U.S. residents parking money in Swiss banks, which refuse to cooperate with U.S. authorities.
Madoff Ponzi scheme	Bernie Madoff's fictitious $50 billion hedge fund escapes SEC notice for 10 years, despite multiple warnings.
Auction rate preferred stock	The $500 billion market for these securities collapses as investors discover that brokerage firms rigged auctions and misrepresented assets.
Front-running	Major brokerage firms are caught front-running client orders in order to make billions in profits at the client's expense.
Mutual fund cheating	Mutual funds allow selected hedge funds to trade in their shares after hours at the expense of other mutual fund holders.
Mutual fund kickbacks	Major brokerage firms place tens of billions of client money in certain mutual funds, without telling clients that the firm received referral payments from those same funds.
Stock options backdating	Hundreds of publicly traded companies provide executives with lowball prices on stock options, at the expense of outside stockholders.
Internet equity research	Major investment banks settle case for $1.4 billion, accusing them of manipulating Internet equity research to boost IPOs and trading commissions.

The size, cost, and frequency of scandals indicates the need for stronger regulation, but industry participants and the regulators themselves avoid accountability.

this 2008 crisis: "I wish I had worked to change the framework, rather than to work within that framework."[7] The 2008 panic's multitrillion-dollar loss to the U.S. economy (and massive amounts elsewhere) justified a radical overhaul, but true reform is unlikely. At this writing, Congress is considering options for more effective regulation, but chances are the existing players will simply gain larger portfolios, as the SEC, Federal Reserve, and other regulators jockey for position. The passive, technology-deficient cultures of these agencies will dominate, exposing investors to another crash after complacency sets in again. Jamie Court, president of the nonprofit group Consumer Watchdog, said it best: "When you deal with the same dogs, you're going to end up with the same fleas."[8]

Similarly, a few of the industry's prominent clients, such as the California state pension fund, are demanding changes in the way Wall Street is paid, but the majority of customers are too fragmented and too disorganized to seek reform. A better compensation scheme and a strong regulatory structure won't reverse the behavior that produces bubbles, but they could smooth out the peaks and valleys. Until that happens, security analysts, business valuators, and equity investors have to anticipate another crash.

Moreover, nothing is to be done about downsizing the giant firms like Bank of America, Fannie Mae, and Goldman Sachs that are considered "too big to fail." These firms, with their economic power and political muscle, outmaneuver government regulators. Thus, the stage is set for future moral hazards, whereby these megafirms take undue risks and investors keep lending to them, safe in the expectation of a government bailout.

Similarly, postcrisis, it appears that accounting firms and credit rating agencies will operate with the same conflicts of interest; that is, the referees are paid by the clients they oversee. The simple solution is for both the accountants and the rating agencies to be rotated on a random basis among public companies every few years. In that way, neither the accountant nor the agency has an incentive to bend the rules to keep the client, since the client disengages on a regular basis. Other observers have suggested the same idea, but it never makes inroads in Congress.

HOW MIGHT SECURITY ANALYSIS AND BUSINESS VALUATION CHANGE?

Dan Trosch, a director at Fortigent LLC, says, "Investors must be resigned to a sizable bear market every seven to eight years," and he probably isn't far off. The question is, how do security analysts and business valuation consultants change their basic approach in light of this prognosis?

To begin, some have stated that investors should use a higher equity risk premium (for the U.S. market) than historical statistics indicate. Instead of the conventional 6 to 7 percent, a premium of 9 to 10 percent might be applicable. Also, analysts should run more recession scenarios in their earnings forecasts, making straight-line projections a thing of the past. They might also expand the use of 3-, 5-, and 10-year average value ratios (EV/EBITDA and P/E) in their reports. The impact of the latest year's results (particularly in a boom year) is therefore diminished. And finally, with the federal government running massive deficits far into the foreseeable future, and showing an inclination to interfere more in business, a U.S. equity research report should spend time on a country risk, a discussion that Wall Street generally ignores for domestic equities. The prospects of high inflation, dollar devaluation, or a sovereign rating downgrade (from AAA to AA) are heightened in the United States. The practitioner should discuss country risk in connection with firm-specific valuations.

From a job perspective, some public equity analysts may find themselves graded over a longer period of time, such as two to three years, versus the quarterly/annual approach favored by most employers. At certain institutions, there may be a shift to absolute return measurement for analysts, as opposed to relative performance, pushed, in part, by investors who have been paying fees (of 0.5 percent to

EXHIBIT 28.2   Security Analysis and Business Valuation, Postcrash

The Process

- The use of higher equity risk premiums than historical statistics indicate.
- The use of recession scenarios in corporate earnings forecasts, rather than the typical straight-line projections.
- The use of average (or weighted average) value multiples, spread over 3, 5, and 10 years, to diminish the impact of trailing 12 months' results and to incorporate the business cycle.
- The use of a country risk section for U.S. equity research reports, reflecting the perception of higher sovereign hazards due to U.S. fiscal, monetary, and regulatory policy.

The Job

- The use of longer periods of time, such as two to three years, to grade analysts (versus 3 to 12 months), and the consideration of absolute returns versus relative performance.
- The use of the "sell short" recommendation on an increased basis, in addition to buy, sell, and hold.
- The use of reality checks on existing value ratios, by comparing to similar statistics in prior booms and busts.

1.5 percent annually) to managers who lose money. In line with the notion of absolute return, there may be a push for analysts (both buy and sell side) to select more "sell short" recommendations, to complement the traditional calls to buy, sell, or hold. See Exhibit 28.2.

Lastly, sophisticated equity research consumers may want more sanity checks in their research reports, whereby value ratios in an industry are compared (and contrasted) with similar statistics spread over prior boom and bust cycles. This last change might be trying for analysts, who may be asked to forecast a top or bottom for their industry, even when the market consensus moves the other way.

SUMMARY

The U.S. government is good at applying resources to financial firm bailouts, but it is ineffective in preventing the price run-ups and abuses that lead to busts. This situation is expected to continue in the indefinite future, as efforts to strengthen financial referees fall short of what is needed. The analyst must exercise due diligence in interpreting corporate filings, audited statements, and credit ratings.

To deal with the prospect of recurring market downdrafts, the consumers of equity research and business valuation reports should encourage security analysts and business appraisers to consider high discount rates, recession scenarios, and U.S. sovereign risks in their work. The effect will be to place a cap on EV/EBITDA and P/E ratios for U.S. equities and those around the world.

CHAPTER 29

Closing Thoughts

Since the release of the first edition, tumultuous forces have buffeted the financial industry and the security analysis profession. Two global stock market crashes prompted massive government interventions in the capital markets, and abuses within the financial system led to new rules and regulations, some of which directly affected equity and business valuation. These events necessitated modifications to the traditional approach—all of which this book has described—even as the foundations of business valuation remain unchanged.

This book presented a comprehensive guide to security analysis and business valuation. It described the process of evaluating a company in a step-by-step fashion and noted the pitfalls one is likely to encounter along the way. The careful reader now has the tools to appraise every kind of business—just like the pros do!

Individual share prices go down as well as up, and I ask the reader to venture into the appraisal process with a skeptical eye. *Caveat emptor* reigns supreme on Wall Street, and the emphasis is on clients buying stocks, rather than selling. Both issuers and brokers are prone to exaggerations and half-truths, and the system's overseers are unwilling, or unable, to thwart most transgressors. Individual analysts in the pursuit of the most accurate valuation are often compromised by career concerns, corporate compensation schemes, or conflicts of interest. These factors may be subtle, and they may affect a practitioner's effort unintentionally.

Security analysis is not a hard science, and each valuation method incorporates imprecision related to the assumptions and judgments embedded in the process. Nevertheless, a set of past experiences, shared expectations, similar practitioner training, academic logic, and common sense combine to establish a rational price for most businesses.

Past experiences
Shared expectations
Similar practitioner training } Tendency for rational equity values
Academic logic
Common sense

On a 7- to 10-year cycle, emotional forces and financial panics overwhelm the conventional approach, and it is incumbent on the practitioner to try to anticipate these events. The goal of security analysis is to generate investment ideas that provide superior *absolute* and *relative* returns. Why do I stress absolute returns? Because an investor shouldn't be satisfied when his portfolio value drops 10 percent, even as the market declines by a greater number, like 20 percent. Losing 10 percent is still *losing*. Only the large money managers declare victory when their portfolios *lose* less than the market, because their base fee income alone provides them with sizeable incomes. On a *relative* basis, the time and expense dedicated to researching equities properly suggests that this effort should provide more profit than a passively managed index fund.

To balance the risks of public equity investment against the potential rewards, the key to success is the disciplined approach outlined in this book. A critical part of this approach is the preparation of a written research report, which includes a thorough top-down review along with detailed financial projections and comparative studies. This same approach is followed by business valuation, M&A, and private equity professionals.

Model Research Report

1. Introduction
2. Macroeconomic Review
3. Relevant Stock Market Prospects
4. Review of the Company and Its Business
5. Financial Analysis
6. Financial Projections
7. Application of Valuation Methodologies
8. Recommendation

It's important to mention that a research report doesn't rely entirely on the Internet, published information, and management interviews. The practitioner supplements this data with hands-on field work that includes discussions with the company's customers, suppliers, competitors, line employees, and government agencies. The report and its recommendation are the culmination of an investigation. Instead of accepting management's rosy forecasts, the experienced analyst uses independent sources to determine if corporate expectations are realistic.

Security analysis, business valuation, M&A, and private equity rely on several valuation techniques:

- *Intrinsic value (discounted cash flow).* A business is worth the net present value of its dividends.
- *Relative value (comparable companies).* Determine a company's value by comparing it to similar companies' values.
- *Acquisition value.* Calculate a company's share price by determining its worth to a third-party acquirer, such as another operating business or a leveraged buyout firm. Then apply a 25 percent discount for a passive minority investment.
- *Sum-of-the-parts value.* One values a multiline business by segmenting its components and valuing each separately. The whole is thus the sum of its parts.

In pricing a security, the practitioner tries to apply multiple techniques to a business, because each approach is a useful check on the others. For example, if the DCF calculation provides an intrinsic value for a firm that is much higher than the comparable company method, the analyst double-checks his numbers to see if his projection was overly optimistic or if his discount rate was too pessimistic. Finding fault with neither, he might conclude the market values the firm's industry too cheaply.

Most of the time, the public equity investor applying these four techniques is frustrated. The resulting estimates usually fall within the ±15 percent of the stock's trading price, indicating no buy or sell decision. In other words, the analyst just spent a lot of time and money and has nothing to show for his efforts, except further demonstration of the market's efficiency. He shouldn't be discouraged. In perhaps 1 out of 10 company-specific reviews, he'll find a meaningful price discrepancy, which may reverse itself and provide an above-average profit. Even in this small universe of opportunities, however, the analyst doesn't have to be 100 percent right; being correct 60 to 70 percent of the time makes you a Wall Street superstar.

Furthermore, to make a difference, a practitioner needn't beat the market by leaps and bounds. Just exceeding the popular indexes by 3 percent per year places you in the top rung of money managers. Consider the math. If an S&P 500 index fund returns 10 percent for 10 years, a $1,000 investment becomes $2,600. If the use of security analysis increases the annual return to 13 percent from 10 percent, the $1,000 grows instead to $3,400, an $800 difference.

By necessity, the professional adhering to the principles of security analysis sometimes takes a contrarian approach—he may be selling a stock when the market is buying, for example. This requires the courage to maintain a view at odds with conventional wisdom. It also suggests a long-term horizon since the market may take time to accept the requisite rationale. During this period, the investor following such advice may underperform the market on a quarterly basis, and the analyst faces career setbacks if he is graded on short-term thinking.

Business valuation plays a major role in today's business world. Fortunes can be made or lost by the manner in which a company's future is interpreted by public stock investors, private equity funds, M&A players, and government regulators. At the same time, crucial corporate decisions hinge on whether lending institutions will provide financial backing that is premised on forecasts. On the investment side, millions of individuals and organizations commit a substantial portion of their savings to equities, with the hope of achieving satisfactory returns within a sensible risk framework. With so much at stake, it is essential that individuals active in business, finance, and government develop an understanding of business valuation, particularly as it's practiced on Wall Street, where the actual money changes hands.

Since the first edition, the security analysis profession has become increasingly global, and the subject matter is utilized and taught in many countries. More firms go public and M&A transactions continue their secular rise, boosting the need for business valuation expertise. The number of private equity funds, hedge funds, and sovereign wealth funds has increased dramatically. Recent public accounting and government regulations promote the corporate valuation business as well as the number of individuals needing knowledge of the subject.

In closing, the reader is now armed with the requisite tools to evaluate individual equities, entire companies, and the broader markets in a rational way. He knows that business valuation represents a jumble of academic theories, practical applications, economic expectations, cyclical factors, and emotional influences. Underlying this morass of conflicting forces is a series of time-tested techniques that instill a fundamental order to the pricing process. Notwithstanding the wide acceptance of current approaches, the key elements comprising a specific corporate appraisal are subject to frequent change; and financial projections, which play an important role in valuation, are inherently uncertain. This dynamic environment—along with the big money involved—contributes to making security analysis an interesting and vibrant occupation.

Notes

This book is based, in part, on dozens of interviews. I have not cited these interviews in these notes. All interviewees whom I quote in the text are identified by their real names. Where I relied on quotes published by others, sources are noted herein.

CHAPTER 1 Why Analyze a Security?

1. Benjamin Graham and David Dodd, *Security Analysis: The Classic 1940 Edition* (New York: McGraw-Hill, 2002), 33.

CHAPTER 2 Who's Practicing Security Analysis and Business Valuation?

1. Standard & Poor's Indices Versus Active Scorecard, Year End 2008, http://www2 .standardandpoors.com/spf/pdf/index/SPIVA_Report_Year-End_2008.pdf.

CHAPTER 6 Industry Analysis

1. Asher Hawkins, "Drug Shock," *Forbes*, December 24, 2007, 110.

CHAPTER 7 Company-Specific Analysis

1. Michael Porter, *Competitive Advantage* (New York: Free Press, 1998), 16.
2. Randall Stross, *The Microsoft Way* (New York: Basic Books, 1997), 27.
3. Thomas H. Lee & Co. legal filing, quoted in Paul Davies, "Refco Officers Are Sued," *Wall Street Journal*, C3.

CHAPTER 9 The Limitations of Accounting Data

1. The precepts have been set forth in a number of financial statement analysis texts, such as *The Analysis and Use of Financial Statements* by Gerald White, A.C. Sandi, and D. Fried (Hoboken, NJ: John Wiley & Sons, 2002) and *Analysis for Financial Management* by Robert Higgins (New York: McGraw-Hill, 2005).
2. Quoted in "Stocks Overvalued? Not in the New Economy," *Wall Street Journal*, November 3, 1997, A1.
3. Erik Lie, "On the Timing of CEO Stock Option Awards," *Management Science* 51 (May 2005): 802–812.
4. Quoted in Terrence O'Hara, "The Fannie Mae Report," *Washington Post*, February 24, 2006, D1.
5. Professors Ludovic Phalippou and Oliver Gottschlag noted this value inflation phenomenon in their academic paper, "Performance of Private Equity Funds: Another Puzzle," 2007.

CHAPTER 11 Financial Projection Pointers

1. A. Anandarajan, L. Becchetti, I. Hasan and M. Santoro, "Analyst Forecast Bias: Rational Judgment or Herd Behavior?" *Journal of Theoretical Accounting*, 2007.
2. Quoted in Yahoo! Inc., press release dated April 22, 2008.
3. Patrick Cusatis and Randall Woolridge, "The Accuracy of Analysts' Long-Term Earnings Per Share Growth Rate Forecasts," Pennsylvania State University, January 24, 2008.

CHAPTER 20 Private Equity

1. The following academic studies cover private equity funds' inability to beat market averages: Kaplan and Schoar, "Private Equity Performance: Returns, Persistence and Capital Flows," University of Chicago and MIT, 2005; Gottschlag and Phalippou, "Performance of Private Equity Funds: Another Puzzle," INSEAD (France), 2007; Fung, Hsieh, Naik, and Ramadorai, "Hedge Funds: Performance Risk and Capital Formation," London Business School, Duke and Oxford, 2006; Gottschlag, Phalippou, and Lopez-de-Silanes, "Caveats When Venturing into the Buyout World," University of Amsterdam, 2007.

CHAPTER 21 Natural Resource Companies

1. "Bre-X Scandal Takes Toll on Investors," *Washington Post*, July 17, 1997.

CHAPTER 22 Financial Industry Stocks

1. Chris Cooper and Brody Mullins, "Wall Street Is Big Donor to Inauguration," *Wall Street Journal*, January 2009, A4.
2. Quoted in Vikas Bajaj and Stephen LaBaton, "Risks Are Vast in Revaluation of Bad Assets," *New York Times*, February 2009, A13.

CHAPTER 27 The Emerging Markets

1. Mark Mobius, *The Investor's Guide to Emerging Markets* (Trans Atlantic Publications, 1994).

CHAPTER 28 Asset Booms and Busts

1. Quoted in Zachary Goldfarb, "What Went Wrong," *Washington Post*, December 16, 2008, A6.
2. Quoted in Mary Jordan, "UK Bank Regulator Resigns Amid Furor," *Washington Post*, February 12, 2009, A13.
3. *New York Times* editorial, January 7, 2009, A30.
4. Justice Department report on New Century Financial, covered by *Trusted Professional* (newspaper of NYSSCPA) II, no. 7 (April 15, 2008); Melissa Hoffman Lajara, "Bankruptcy Report Alleges Auditor Missteps," *Trusted Professional* II, no. 7 (April 15, 2008).
5. Quoted in Arthur Herzog, *Vesco: From Wall Street to Castro's Cuba* (Author's Choice Press, 1987, 2003), 70.
6. Zach Goldberg, "Jon Stewart Indicts the Business Press," *Washington Post*, March 13, 2009, A1.
7. Quoted in Robert O'Harrow, Jr., and Jeff Gerth, "As Crisis Loomed, Geithner Pressed and Fell Short," *Washington Post*, April 3, 2009, A14.
8. Quoted in Daniel Wagner and Matt Apuzzo, "No Pink Slips for Bailed-Out Bank Execs," Associated Press article, January 27, 2009, taken from Yahoo! News.

Jeffrey C. Hooke is managing director of Hooke Associates, LLC, a business valuation firm, and a managing director at FOCUS, LLC, an investment bank where he heads the valuation practice. He has broad experience in the valuation of companies in the United States, Europe, and the emerging markets. Formerly, he was a director of Emerging Markets Partnership, a $5 billion private equity fund focused on developing countries. Earlier, he was an investment executive covering Latin America for the International Finance Corporation, the $20 billion private sector arm of the World Bank. Previously, he spent 10 years in New York as an investment banker with Lehman Brothers and Schroder Wertheim, working on corporate finance transactions involving U.S. and European companies. The author of four books on finance, he has taught at several universities, spoken before multiple CFA forums, and conducted numerous executive education courses.

Index

Printed and bound by CPI Group (UK) Ltd, Croydon, CR0 4YY

23/04/2025

14660929-0005